The Cold War and
American Science

The Cold War and American Science

The Military-Industrial-Academic Complex at MIT and Stanford

Stuart W. Leslie

Columbia University Press
New York

Publication of this book is made possible in part by a grant from David Bendel Hertz, Distinguished Professor Emeritus, University of Miami.

Columbia University Press
New York   Chichester, West Sussex

Copyright © 1993 Columbia University Press
All rights reserved

Library of Congress Cataloging-in-Publication Data

Leslie, Stuart W.
    The Cold War and American science : the military-industrial-
academic complex at MIT and Stanford / Stuart W. Leslie.
        p.   cm.
    Includes bibliographical references and index.
    ISBN 0-231-07958-3 (alk. paper)
    ISBN 0-231-07959-1 (pbk.)
    1. Military research—United States.   2. Education, Higher—
Political aspects—United States.   I. Title.
    UA393.L47   1993
    355'.07'0973—dc20   92-28295
                                                            CIP

Printed in the United States of America
c 10 9 8 7 6 5 4 3 2 1
p 10 9 8 7 6 5 4 3 2 1

TO MY FATHER

In the apprehension of the group in whose life and esteem it lives and takes effect, this esoteric knowledge is taken to embody a systematization of fundamental and eternal truth; although it is evident to any outsider that it will take its character and its scope and method from the habits of life of the group, from the institutions with which it is bound in a web of give and take. . . . A passably dispassionate inquiry into the place which modern learning holds in modern civilization will show that such is also the case of this latest, and in the mind of its keepers the most mature, system of knowledge. It should by no means be an insuperably difficult matter to show that this "higher learning" of the modern world, the current body of science and scholarship, also holds its place on such a tenure of use and wont, that it has grown and shifted in point of content, aims and methods in response to the changes in habits of life that have passed over the Western peoples during the period of its growth and ascendancy.

—Thorstein Veblen, *The Higher Learning in America* (1918)

Contents

Contents

Acknowledgments

Any historian who has waded into the ocean of documents surviving from the Cold War era will attest that only the assistance of skilled archivists can keep one from drowning. At Stanford University, where I first began this study, Roxanne Nilan, Linda Long, and their staffs in special collections gave me invaluable advice on where to look and what to look for, and Henry Lowood took time from his own research to share his encyclopedic knowledge of Silicon Valley and its history. At MIT, Helen Samuels and Kathy Marquis and their staff likewise made me feel as much like a friend as a visiting scholar, leading me through the maze of interlocking collections and introducing me to some of the living legends at the Institute. At the American Philosophical Society, Elizabeth Carroll-Harrocks showed me the ins and outs of the John Slater Papers, and Edward Carter gave me a chance to try out some of my early ideas in a symposium he organized there around Slater's life and work. Carrie Browse dug up important materials on Stark Draper for me at the Draper Laboratories, and Michael Yeats did the same at the MIT Museum. Darwin Stapleton took time to help me locate some significant documents on Arthur von Hippel at the Rockefeller Foundation Archives, and treated me to a delightful lunch besides. Richard Bingham at the U.S. Army Communications-Electronics Command kindly sent me some key sources on the early history of the Sylvania Electronic Defense Laboratory.

An NEH Fellowship at the Hagley Museum and Library gave me the time off from teaching I needed to write this book as well as a congenial place to work on it. I am grateful to Glenn Porter and Patrick Nolan for making my stay on the Brandywine both enjoyable and productive. I learned much from conversations with Robert Friedel and Patricia Cooper, my fellow fellows during that year, and from senior scholar Edward Lurie, who reawakened my interest in Thorstein Veblen and Randolph Bourne. Michael Nash showed me some important manuscript sources on the Sperry Gyroscope Company that would have otherwise escaped my attention. And as always, the entire staff made me feel like Hagley was my personal library.

My colleagues and students at Johns Hopkins, past and present, have listened to my ideas with patience and insight for more years than they, or I, care to remember. I would like to single out a few for special thanks. Robert Kargon and Erica Schoenberger, whose joint research project with me has touched some of the same themes as this book, will recognize, I trust, how much they have contributed to my thinking and writing. Harry Marks and Robert Smith kindly read sections of the manuscript and gave me more good suggestions than I could work into the text. Louis Galambos convinced me to come to Johns Hopkins in the first place and has provided constant guidance and encouragement ever since. Bruce Hevly, now at the University of Washington, helped me work out many of these ideas in an article we wrote together while he was still in graduate school. Michael Dennis's comparative study on the MIT Instrumentation Laboratory and the Johns Hopkins Applied Physics Laboratory will redefine the problem of knowledge and authority in a way I can only envy.

Along the way, many historians of science have shared with me their knowledge of different aspects of postwar science and government. A group of Smithsonian Institution scholars deserves special mention, including Allan Needell and David DeVorkin at the National Air and Space Museum and Nathan Reingold and Paul Forman at the National Museum of American History. Forman's pioneering studies of science and the military served as a constant reminder of the moral obligations of the historian in the largest sense.

Eugene Ferguson has probably given me as much sound advice on this project as he did with my dissertation and has always been my model of all that a historian can be.

Walter Vincenti and William Rambo, former Stanford professors who appear frequently in these pages, kindly consented to read and comment on selected chapters. I did not always agree with their criticisms, but I always took them seriously. I sincerely appreciate their efforts to educate me on important points, political as well as technical. Vincenti seems to know everyone worth knowing at Stanford and opened many doors for me there. I realize that we differ on some of my conclusions, but I respect his willingness to help me reach them independently.

John Heilbron, editor of *Historical Studies in the Physical and Biological Sciences*, made important suggestions for improving the articles on the university and the military that I originally published there, and he has generously given me permission to use sections of them here. Kate Wittenberg, my editor at Columbia University Press, waited long and patiently for me to deliver this manuscript, and offered me advice and reassurance along the way whenever I needed it most.

Nearly a decade of studying science and its patrons has made me particularly sensitive to the importance of funding. The National Science Foundation (SES 8520152) provided financial assistance at a crucial juncture.

Finally, my greatest debt is to my father, the original Stuart W. Leslie, who lived and worked through much of this history, who carefully read my account of it, and who, while he may have disagreed with much of what I had to say, gave me the gift of independence to go my own way.

The Cold War and
American Science

Introduction

For better and for worse, the Cold War redefined American science. In the decade following the Second World War, the Department of Defense (DOD) became the biggest single patron of American science, predominantly in the physical sciences and engineering but important in many of the natural and social sciences as well. Driven by the politics of national security and by the Pentagon's belief in the competitive advantages of high technology, spending for defense research and development surpassed its wartime peak (already fifty times higher than prewar levels) by the end of the Korean War, then climbed to dizzying heights after Sputnik, reaching $5.5 billion a year by 1960. On average, the DOD accounted for about 80 percent of the federal R&D budget throughout the 1950s.[1]

While DOD's share of federal R&D spending steadily decreased over the next two decades, reaching a postwar low of about 20 percent in the late 1970s, that decline merely reflected the growth of the National Science Foundation, the National Aeronautics and Space Administration, and (most of all) the National Institutes of Health, not a diminished military presence in American science. The defense buildup of the 1980s actually pushed military R&D spending (in constant dollars) past the record levels of the mid-1960s.[2]

In the political economy of the Cold War, science was anything but academic, with the blueprint for significant aspects of the nation's industrial policy being drafted by the military.[3] Defense contractors, led by giants such as Lockheed, General Electric, General Dynamics, and AT&T, won the lion's share of military R&D appropriations. Overall, the DOD accounted for about a third of all industrial R&D spending in those years, but in defense-dependent sectors such as electronics and aerospace it was closer to three-quarters.[4] Similarly, defense contractors employed (and continue to employ) something like a quarter of the nation's electrical engineers and a third of the physicists and mathematicians.[5]

While university research may have represented a relatively minor item on the DOD ledger, the university remained an indispensable partner in what Senator J. William Fulbright later called the military-industrial-academic complex.[6] For only the universities could both create and replicate knowledge, and in the process train the next generation of scientists and engineers. The universities provided most of the basic research and all the manpower for the defense industry.

The "golden triangle" of military agencies, the high technology industry, and research universities created a new kind of postwar science, one that blurred traditional distinctions between theory and practice, science and engineering, civilian and military, and classified and unclassified, one that owed its character as well as its contracts to the national security state.[7] The short-term benefits of this partnership—bigger budgets, better facilities, more political clout in Washington, ever more sophisticated military hardware, and even a few Nobel prizes—were obvious to everyone. But the long-term costs only gradually became apparent in academic programs and corporate products so skewed toward the cutting-edge performance of military technology that they had nothing to give to the civilian economy.[8]

President Dwight Eisenhower, despite his better instincts, presided over much of the Cold War buildup and so better than most of his contemporaries appreciated "its grave implications." His famous farewell address pointedly identified the "military-industrial complex" as a threat to both political and intellectual freedom. Specifically, he warned that in such a climate the "government contract becomes virtually a substitute for intellectual curiosity" and that the "prospect of domination of the nation's scholars by Federal employment, project allocations, and the power of money is ever present."[9]

What mattered, however, was not only where all that money was going, but where it was coming from. The danger was not so much that federal funding would somehow dampen the intellectual spirit, but that military funding would corrupt it.

Without question, the university showed what it could do in the name of national defense, but at what cost to itself and, ultimately, to the nation? That question troubled radical essayist Randolph Bourne back in the First World War and has continued to trouble some critics ever since. With a growing sense of alarm and outrage, Bourne watched the universities mobilize for the war effort and saw professors fired for their opposition to the war. But beyond the immediate threat to academic freedom he glimpsed larger questions, and far-reaching implications, about the relationship between a nation's political economy and its intellectual life.

"War is the health of the State," Bourne insisted. What he meant was that war gave full range and expression to the political and coercive power of the state, whatever the cost to the nation's moral and economic well-being. He saw how militarism and the state defined one another, how each required the other for its strength and legitimacy, and how together they threatened at home the very democratic values the nation claimed to be fighting for abroad. The state, Bourne observed, "is eternally at war," either in actual combat or, more often and just as dangerously, in "a continual state of latent war."[10] A later generation would call it the Cold War.

Bourne correctly judged the First World War a potential watershed for the American political economy and for American science, as the state conscripted both industry and the universities.[11] Under the War Industries Board, leading industrialists and financiers—"dollar-a-year" men, most of them—mobilized the American economy, and so forged the first links in what would become the military-industrial complex.[12] The board, seeking a middle way between the British model of a civilian-controlled ministry of defense and the German model of a virtual military directorate, generally left procurement decisions to the armed forces, and industrial control and coordination to big business. For board chairman Bernard Baruch and the other moguls of mobilization, the lesson of the Great War was that future preparedness would demand full coordination of the nation's industrial resources, which in turn would demand extensive peacetime planning. And so at least some industrial and military leaders spent the interwar years preparing for the next war, culminating in the War Production Board of World War II, dominated, like its predecessor, by an alliance of military officers and corporate executives. [13]

Just as industrialists mobilized industry for the Great War, so scientists mobilized science. Under the National Research Council (NRC), leading members of the scientific establishment such as Robert Millikan and George Ellery Hale reorganized science in the conviction, as Hale put it, that "war should mean research."[14] They convinced President Woodrow Wilson to recognize the NRC as the government's official adviser on scientific preparedness, and convinced an often skeptical military bureaucracy to pay attention to its advice. Because the NRC's leaders shared with their business counterparts a commitment to private initiative and a distrust of federal intervention, they, like the members of the War Industries Board, relied on cooperation and compromise rather than administrative fiat.[15] Instead of taking charge themselves, they worked with military agencies and corporate laboratories as expert advisers. Their subsequent wartime successes in submarine detection, radio signaling, artillary range finding, and chemical weapons confirmed the confidence both scientists and industrialists had in the new alliance of science, government, and big business.

The university, however, was conspicuously absent in the wartime coalition. The NRC mobilized scientists, but not science (or at least not academic science). Academic scientists ran most of the NRC subcommittees and contributed impressively to major weapons projects, but not as representatives of their home institutions. American universities did their part to further military science, notably by hosting the Reserve Officers' Training Corps (ROTC) and the Students' Army Training Corps, but did little to advance science for the military.[16]

As Bourne so prophetically sensed, the wartime experience prefigured new patterns for mobilizing science in the national interest, but not ones that would be realized in his own generation. Bourne did not survive the Armistice, and neither did the coalition of the military, industry, and academia he had railed against. The military agencies, under congressional mandate, cut back their postwar research budgets severely and spent what money they did have in their own laboratories, where they could keep tighter control over the results.[17] Big business, freed from wartime restrictions, turned its research energies in civilian directions. General Electric, AT&T, Du Pont, and other so-called war profiteers dramatically expanded their corporate laboratories in the postwar years in an effort to anticipate, plan for, and control their commercial destinies, either by finding ways to protect existing markets or by creating new ones.[18]

Academic scientists, rebuffed in their efforts to secure funding and policy positions at the national level,[19] turned instead to cultivating local alliances with business and philanthropic foundations. Hale and Millikan parlayed business and philanthropic support into a fund-raising effort that rebuilt the California Institute of Technology (Caltech) from an obscure regional engineering school into one of the top scientific universities in the world.[20] President Karl Compton rescued MIT from its limited horizons and quarterly budget mentality and remade it on the Caltech model as a modern research university.[21] With the sole exception of aeronautics, however, the military played only a marginal role in an interwar political economy of science presided over within the universities by the Rockefeller Foundation and other private philanthropies, and in the corporate sector by the burgeoning laboratories of General Electric, AT&T, and Du Pont, and their many smaller imitators.[22]

For university scientists and engineers, business proved at best a fickle and demanding partner. MIT, working with selected corporations, built up sizable cooperative education and sponsored research programs in chemical and electrical engineering in the 1920s, only to see them founder in the Depression.[23] Stanford physicists, looking for a way out of the economic hardships of the 1930s, likewise turned to industry for research support, only to discover corporate agendas at odds with academic mores and values.[24] Such tentative alliances between business and academic science foreshadowed later institutional structures and tensions that would characterize the postwar university.[25] In a few cases, industrial sponsorship even altered the content of specific disciplines, putting problems of long-distance power transmission at the center of electrical engineering, for instance, and the problems of petroleum cracking at the center of chemical engineering.[26] But these were the exceptions in what remained a department-oriented and pluralistically funded university. Nothing in the prewar experience fully prepared academic scientists and their institutions for the scale and scope of a wartime mobilization that would transform the university, industry, and the federal government and their mutual interrelationships.

For science, World War II marked a more decisive turning point than had World War I.[27] As many scientists later came to realize, it may also have marked a point of no return. What made the difference was not only the scale of mobilization (billions instead of millions of dollars for research, development, and production) but where and how that money was spent. As before, big business, committed to preserving the status quo, controlled procurement policy through the War Production Board and so again appropriated the bulk of the military production contracts. Half the contracts went to the thirty largest industrial corporations and two-thirds to the largest one hundred.[28]

But this time around the universities also won a substantial share of the funds, with research and development (though not production) contracts that actually dwarfed those of the largest industrial contractors. At the top of the list, MIT alone was awarded $117 million in R&D contracts, Caltech $83 million, and Harvard and Columbia about $30 million each, compared with just $17 million for Western Electric (AT&T), $8 million for GE, and less than $6 million each for RCA, Du Pont, and Westinghouse, the top industrial R&D contractors.[29]

Vannevar Bush, the chief architect of wartime science policy and a strong advocate of university research, was the man behind the change. A generation younger than his World War I counterparts, Bush had come of age at MIT during the 1920s and 1930s, rising to dean of engineering and vice president before moving on to Washington in 1938 to head the Carnegie Institution and chair the National Advisory Committee on Aeronautics (NACA).[30] Bush's experiences in Washington, especially with the NACA, convinced him that the nation was not prepared for the scientific challenges of any coming war and that even the military's own laboratories were not up to the job of getting the country ready. So Bush, along with some influential friends within the scientific community, convinced President Roosevelt to appoint the National Defense Research Committee (NDRC) in June 1940, with Bush himself as chairman. Its purpose, essentially, was to circumvent what Bush and company considered an overly cautious military bureaucracy, by using the committees' civilian power to contract for research with scientific or educational institutions, public or private. A year later, in response to complaints that the NDRC did not have sufficient control over the development phase of weapons R&D, the President put Bush in charge of a new and more powerful agency, the Office of Scientific Research and Development (OSRD). The OSRD ultimately spent $450 million on weapons research and development and played a key role in most of the technical breakthroughs of the war.[31]

Bush, a staunch conservative, had no more interest in upsetting the established order than had his colleagues on the War Production Board.[32] Like them, he thought the war could best be won by working through existing channels and so skewed OSRD contracts toward a few prominent institutions. To further minimize the OSRD's impact on the postwar world, Bush kept his relationships with universities and industry contractual, restricted in time and in scope, and kept OSRD out of production altogether. He always considered OSRD a strictly emergency operation and dismantled it promptly at the end of the war, despite considerable opposition from the Pentagon and the White House.

But the military, shaken out of its traditional complacency by the wonder weapons of the war—radar, the proximity fuse, solid fuel rockets, and of course the atomic bomb—and by the power of the contract to deliver them, was willing and able to prolong the wartime pattern of cooperative research. General Dwight Eisenhower drew up detailed plans for extending the partnership of science, industry, and the military into the postwar world.[33] Admiral Harold Bowen, having reached the same conclusion about the importance of science for future preparedness, laid similar plans for the Office of Naval Research as a kind of in-house OSRD, complete with university and industrial contracts.[34]

Instead of demobilizing the wartime academic laboratories, the military establishment either picked them up under new contractual agreements (the Navy with the Johns Hopkins' Applied Physics Laboratory, the Army with Caltech's Jet Propulsion Laboratory, the Atomic Energy Commission with Berkeley's Los Alamos Weapons Laboratory) or kept them in business with short-term funding until more permanent arrangements could be made.[35] Even under Truman's fiscal ax, military R&D budgets fell off only slightly from their wartime peak despite deep cuts in overall military spending, and then began to climb in response to mounting Cold War tensions underscored by the Berlin crisis, the first Soviet atomic bomb test, and the "loss" of China.[36] By 1950 defense R&D budgets were right back at wartime levels.

The Korean War completed the mobilization of American science and made the university, for the first time, a full partner in the military-industrial complex.[37] Virtually overnight, defense R&D appropriations doubled, to $1.3 billion. Military money flooded into industrial and academic laboratories. The armed forces supplemented existing university contracts with massive appropriations for applied and classified research, and established entire new laboratories under university management: MIT's Lincoln Laboratory (air defense); Berkeley's Lawrence Livermore Laboratory (nuclear weapons); and Stanford's Applied Electronics Laboratory (electronic communications and countermeasures).[38]

Everyone recognized that the postwar university had changed dramatically, and not necessarily for the better. Sociologist Robert Nisbet, along with many other conservatives, blamed the federal government for creating what he called the "higher capitalism," the system of contracts and project grants that seemed to have undermined the traditional structure and values of the university.[39] What Nisbet and others did not fully recognize was how the increasing predominance of one patron, the military, was indelibly imprinting academic (and industrial) science with a distinct set of priorities, and how those new priorities would in turn set the future direction for much of American science.

As economist and social critic Thorstein Veblen so trenchantly observed back in 1918, knowledge inevitably embodies the particular circumstances of its creation. Even science, "the latest, and in the mind of its keepers the most mature, system of knowledge," he emphasized, "will take its character and its scope and method from the habits of life of the group, from the institutions with which it is bound in a web of give and take."[40] Just as Veblen could have predicted, as American science became increasingly bound up in a web of military institutions, so did its character, scope, and methods take on new, and often disturbing, forms.

Consequently, the full impact of weapons research on American higher education cannot be measured simply by federal and university budgets, or by the numbers of laboratories and scientists and engineers devoted to military projects. Rather, the long-term costs must be reckoned both in dollars and in sense, in terms of our scientific community's diminished capacity to comprehend and manipulate the world for other than military ends. As philosopher Ian Hacking has persuasively argued, weapons research poses as much of a danger to the world of mind as to the world of affairs by limiting our focus to particular forms of scientific knowledge. "It is not just the weapons . . . that are being funded," Hacking explains, "but the world of mind and technique in which those weapons are devised."[41] Indeed, that new world of mind makes seeing and understanding the world that it replaced (and the worlds it foreclosed) all the more difficult, and all the more urgent.

In many disciplines, the military set the paradigm for postwar American science. Just as the technologies of empire (specifically submarine telegraphy and steam power) once defined the relevant research programs for Victorian scientists and engineers,[42] so the military-driven technologies of the Cold War defined the critical problems for the postwar generation of American scientists and engineers. Indeed, those technologies virtually redefined what it meant to be a scientist or an engineer—a knowledge of microwave electronics and radar systems rather than alternating current theory and electric power networks; of ballistic missiles and inertial guidance rather than commercial aircraft and instrument landing systems; of nuclear reactors, microwave acoustic-delay lines, and high-powered traveling-wave tubes rather Van de Graaff generators, dielectrics, and X-ray tubes. These new challenges defined what scientists and engineers studied, what they designed and built, where they went to work, and what they did when they got there.

As Eisenhower understood all too well, the missile was as much a symbol of postwar science as of postwar politics, evidence of what he called "almost an insidious penetration of our own minds that the only thing this country is engaged in is weaponry and missiles."[43] Only by coming to terms with how military interests and intentions became fixed in the very fabric of postwar American science, in its disciplinary structures and rewards, in its research priorities, in its graduate and undergraduate teaching, and even in its textbooks can we understand something of this new world of mind and technique. And only then can we begin to appreciate what was at risk in letting the military play such a crucial role in setting the academic agenda.

Sensitive readings of selected scientific artifacts of the Cold War era have already begun to reveal some of the ways in which broader patterns of political intention became embedded in contemporary technological knowledge.[44] Donald MacKenzie, in his study of nuclear missile guidance, rightly insists "that the more deeply one looks inside the black box, the more one realizes that 'the technical' is no clear-cut and simple world of facts insulated from politics."[45] By locating the hardware history of inertial guidance within an intense interservice struggle over control of strategic weapons, and ultimately within the wider Cold War contest for international supremacy, MacKenzie demonstrates how "mere technicalities" were not mere details at all but rather tangible examples of how politics got built into hardware, and with what consequences. Similarly, David Noble's history of industrial automation shows how Cold War politics became fixed in machines themselves. Numerical control won out over rival approaches to machine tool automation not because numerical control was somehow technically or even economically superior, Noble argues, but because it decisively shifted control over machine programming from the shop floor to the engineering office, and so supported the obsession of military planners and their corporate clients with reducing their dependence on skilled, and strike-prone, labor.[46] Like inertial guidance systems, numerically controlled machine tools incorporated political assumptions at the most fundamental level.

Yet the knowledge behind (and within) such artifacts embodied the prevailing political culture as fully as the artifacts themselves. As Charles Rosenberg has pointed out, academic disciplines and departments offer strategic sites for understanding how larger social expectations "intrude even upon the internal texture of academic discourse."[47] Disciplines (which might be considered the software of science), like artifacts (the hardware), reflect and reinforce the larger political agendas that create and sustain them. Just as disciplinary histories of physical chemistry[48] and biochemistry for an earlier era reveal the critical "connection between institutional contexts and disciplinary styles,"[49] so the history of postwar scientific disciplines highlights the connections between the changing context and content of American science.

At the same time, scientific disciplines, like artifacts, fix as well as order knowledge so that present politics, once embedded in disciplinary form, endure beyond the social structures that gave rise to them in the first place. Just as Robert Moses' bridges, by restricting public transportation to Long Island beaches, continued to reinforce prevailing patterns of social segregation in New York City long after the political consensus that had built the bridges had collapsed,[50] so scientific disciplines reshaped by Cold War politics will continue to align American science along a military axis long after the end of the Cold War.

"Big Science" was one of the hallmarks of the scientific enterprise in the postwar period, and one whose genesis and destiny was closely tied to the fortunes of the national security state.[51] But it was not only at Los Alamos, Oak Ridge, and Lawrence Livermore or at Lockheed, General Electric, and MITRE that American science was being transformed, but also in the individual classrooms and laboratories where the people who would one day work in those institutions were being trained. Only at the local level, in particular universities and in particular departments, can we really observe the intimate dialectic of context and content and so begin to understand the full implications of what historian Hunter Dupree has called "the Great Instauration" and its aftermath.[52] Only in the day-to-day practices of scientists and engineers can we watch the links being forged between organizational forms of power and organizational forms of knowledge.[53]

MIT and Stanford offer some especially revealing insights into the postwar coalition of the military, the high technology industry, and the university and how this combination has so fundamentally trans-

formed the meaning and mission of postwar American science. MIT
emerged from the war as the country's largest university defense contractor, consolidated its lead in the postwar years, and has never been
seriously challenged since.[54] Stanford, a benchwarmer in World War
II, learned from MIT's experiences and used postwar defense contracts to propel itself from a respected regional university into a science and engineering all-star. By 1967 Stanford had climbed to third
on the defense contracting list[55] and to the top of the national rankings in electrical engineering, aeronautics, materials science, physics, and other hot fields. MIT and Stanford prospered greatly from
the Pentagon connection, both financially (which everyone seems to
remember) and intellectually (which many critics seem to have forgotten).

Similar stories could be told for other universities, for Berkeley or
Michigan or Caltech or, in more recent times, for Georgia Tech and
Carnegie Mellon.[56] But in some of the most strategic disciplines of
postwar science and engineering—electronics, aeronautics, materials science, and physics (especially those aspects most closely related
to microwave and solid-state electronics and to nuclear engineering)
—MIT and Stanford set the pace. They had the biggest contracts and
the best rankings.[57] They supplied the Pentagon with advisers and the
defense industry with consultants. They trained the graduate students
who went off to industry and to teach at other leading universities.
Their faculty members literally wrote the books for particular specialties and through those texts reshaped their disciplines across the
country. Their faculty and students started the companies, most of
them defense-oriented, around which Silicon Valley and Route 128
(themselves largely a by-product of defense spending) crystallized.
They were the yardsticks against which other academic programs
measured themselves, and the models others sought to emulate. And
when, at the height of the Vietnam War, there was a widespread and
occasionally violent backlash against the military presence on campus, they bore the brunt of the criticism.

Whether or not recent efforts to reforge an older alliance between
big business and academic science will confirm Bourne's old fears
that the university would be "degraded from its old, noble idea of a
community of scholarship to a private commercial corporation,"[58]

the greatest challenge to the autonomy and integrity of the American university over the last half century has come from the state, and more specifically from its military agencies. As Senator Fulbright so forcefully reminded us a generation ago: "When the university turns away from its central purpose and makes itself an appendage to the Government, concerning itself with techniques rather than purposes, with expedients rather than ideas, dispensing conventional orthodoxy rather than new ideas, it is not only failing to meet its responsibilities to its students; it is betraying a public trust."[59]

1 | A University Polarized Around the Military

Sizing up MIT in 1962 from his perspective as the director of the Oak Ridge National Laboratory, physicist Alvin Weinberg, who coined the term "big science," quipped that it was becoming increasingly hard "to tell whether the Massachusetts Institute of Technology is a university with many government research laboratories appended to it or a cluster of government research laboratories with a very good educational institution attached to it."[1] With nearly a hundred million dollars in annual government-sponsored research contracts by the early 1960s (a figure that would almost double by the end of the decade), science and engineering at MIT had become big business.

A closer look at where that money was coming from suggests that this was big business of a very specialized nature. The military had a significant, even predominant, influence in setting the agenda for big science at MIT. At the end of World War II, MIT was the nation's largest nonindustrial defense contractor, with seventy-five separate contracts worth $117 million, far ahead of second-place Caltech ($83 million) and third-place Harvard ($31 million).[2] It held that lead throughout the Cold War years, often with three times the contracts of the second-ranked school and still ahead of some large defense-oriented corporations. In the early 1960s its contracts with the Department of Defense totaled $47 million, plus additional obligations of some $80 million to its federal-contract research centers, the Lincoln and Instrumentation laboratories.[3] In 1968 MIT ranked fifty-fourth among all defense contractors, sandwiched between missile giants TRW and Thiokol Chemical.[4] Its prime military contracts for 1969 topped $100 million.[5]

Where and how that money was spent was perhaps as important as the sheer magnitude of the total amount. Most of it went into MIT's interdepartmental laboratories, the Research Laboratory of Electronics (RLE), the Laboratory for Nuclear Science and Engineering, Lincoln Laboratory, and their many spinoffs. These became the centerpieces of postwar MIT, the places where the important research was done, graduate students trained, widely adopted textbooks written, and future Institute leaders groomed. These laboratories also provided the benchmarks, the models, and the faculty for MIT's many competitors and imitators.

The Research Laboratory of Electronics was MIT's first interdepartmental laboratory and the template for those that followed. In its organization, funding, and choice of subjects, it was a striking example of the emerging military/industry/university partnership that would do so much to shape the postwar political economy of knowledge. The RLE quickly attracted national attention through its support of extremely successful scientific and engineering programs, ranging from microwave electronics to communications theory. By the early 1960s, three hundred doctoral, six hundred master's, and six hundred bachelor's degree students had trained there.[6] Many of the Institute's future leaders—including two of its presidents, three directors of Lincoln Laboratory, several departmental chairs, and dozens of distinguished faculty members—came up through RLE. It also spawned other important laboratories in military electronics, artificial intelligence, solid-state and plasma physics, and gave rise to dozens of private companies.

On the occasion of RLE's twentieth anniversary, one of the alumni, Julius Stratton, who had climbed the ranks from laboratory director to provost to Institute president, inventoried its contributions to MIT:

The founding of the new electronics laboratory in 1946 represented a major new departure in the organization of academic research at M.I.T. and was destined to influence the development of interdepartmental centers at the Institute over the next two decades. These centers have been designed to supplement rather than to replace the traditional departmental structure. They take account of the fact that newly emerging fields of science commonly cut across the conventional disciplinary boundaries. And they afford a common meeting ground for science and engineering, for the pure and applied aspects of basic research, to the advantage of both. Perhaps more than any other development in recent years they have contributed to the special intellectual character and environment of M.I.T.[7]

Stratton and his colleagues recognized that the academic environment was increasingly being dominated by the military and its corporate contractors, where before it had been companies and philanthropic foundations. What they did not realize was how this change was in turn transforming not only the traditional structure and power relationships of the university but the very character of the knowledge created and replicated within it.

Round Hill

Although the Research Laboratory of Electronics developed primarily out of the wartime experiences and expectations of MIT's physicists and electrical engineers, it had roots also in an older tradition of cooperative research dating back to the 1930s. Many of the laboratory's founders, including Stratton, got their start in the Institute's pioneering communications program at Round Hill.[8] Beyond its considerable technical contributions to microwave theory and practice, Round Hill was significant in foreshadowing the shape of things to come. It was interdisciplinary, mission-oriented, independently funded, and off-campus. Like the Institute itself, it moved from a pattern of philanthropic support and commercial orientation toward new alliances with the military and industry. And Institute leaders noticed the change. Commenting in 1939 on the microwave research program initiated at Round Hill, the chairman of the electrical engineering department told his president, "This project has, in fact, shown the benefit derivable from cooperation between departments with the Institute, and between the Institute and industry, and the Army."[9]

When Stratton came to study electrical engineering at MIT as an undergraduate in 1920, he found himself in a department infused with chairman Dugald Jackson's belief that the dollar sign was the most significant variable in any engineering equation. Coming from Wisconsin in 1907, Jackson had made MIT the biggest and best department in the country largely by strengthening its ties with industry. He initiated cooperative education programs, strongly encouraged faculty consulting (his rule of thumb was that half a professor's income should be earned on the outside), and reshaped both the undergraduate and graduate curricula around the technical and managerial challenges of long-distance power networks.[10]

For Stratton, who was looking for fresh challenges in radio and other newer specialties, the electric power courses seemed like "deadly stereotypes."[11] Bored with the standard curriculum, he took advanced courses with the younger professors—brilliant mathematician Norbert Wiener and computer pioneer Vannevar Bush.[12] Stratton kept up his interest in radio, earning a commercial operating license and taking what courses he could, while serving as secretary of the MIT Radio Society. He wrote his undergraduate thesis on a radio topic—calibrating wave meters—under Edward Bowles, another radio enthusiast who had just completed his master's degree under Bush, with a study of vacuum tube design.[13]

Bowles, given charge of communications, updated the program with new courses, laboratories, and cooperative education in radio engineering.[14] In those days AT&T, GE, and RCA (actually a holding company controlled by the other two) dominated the radio business as GE and Westinghouse dominated power engineering, with research and development activities way ahead of anything in the universities.[15] To keep pace with commercial developments, Bowles followed Jackson's lead and introduced a cooperative education program with AT&T. "Three or four years of such procedure have given us an apparent preeminence in the electric power transmission field as far as the colleges go, which I believe we can likewise establish in a relatively brief time in the communication field," Jackson told Frank

Jewett, president of the newly formed Bell Laboratories.[16] Bell Labs sent engineers to teach advanced courses to the communications students, and the department in turn sent coop students to Bell Labs and AT&T's operating and manufacturing divisions.[17] "Here was a vicarious means of invigorating our program and making up for the Institute's past waywardness," Bowles recalled.[18] Before the end of the decade, Bowles had built his "communications option" into the department's best-funded and best-attended division.[19] One of its early graduates was Stratton, who, at Bowles's invitation, returned from a year abroad to work as a research assistant in the communications laboratory and earn his own master's degree.[20] Having then exhausted MIT's offerings, Stratton left in 1926 to study electromagnetic theory with the distinguished physicist Peter Debye in Zurich, and returned two years later with his doctorate.

Round Hill gave Bowles a unique opportunity to consolidate MIT's position at the academic forefront of radio engineering. When MIT's president learned of financier Edward H. C. Green's interest in radio, he wrote Green saying that he had "asked our radio experts to get in touch with you in regard to cooperation in investigational work."[21] Green accepted the offer and put MIT's experts to work installing a broadcasting station on his Round Hill estate on the coast south of Boston.[22] Still looking to bigger things, the department drew up a blueprint for a radio research institute with a $1.5 million endowment and a governing board headed by Green himself.[23] It was to concentrate on increasing the range and effectiveness of radio broadcasting.[24] Green was not thinking that big, but he did offer MIT $5,000 for shortwave equipment and research support, plus the use of his station and cottages on the estate.[25] Though somewhat smaller than they had hoped for, Green's donation was roughly a third of MIT's total research budget at the time.[26]

Over the next few years Bowles built up a sizable operation at Round Hill, with several faculty members, a dozen graduate students, and a $40,000 annual budget. In keeping with Green's original interests, the research focused primarily on commercial broadcasting —frequency standards, atmospheric interference, and antenna design and operation. Stratton's return in the fall of 1928 to study radio transmission through fog culminated in a classic paper on microwave scattering, published in 1930.[27] Even after switching to the physics department that same year, Stratton continued to collect a third of his budget from Round Hill, which also got about a third of his time. Wilmer Barrow, another Bowles student who had gone on to complete his doctorate in physics in Germany, rejoined the team in 1931, concentrating on microwave wave guides and horn antennas.[28] Their research established MIT as an academic center of microwave theory and practice and led, in 1933, to a revised electrical engineering curriculum with electronics and electromagnetic theory at the core.[29]

Hard hit by the Depression, Green finally ran out of money for the Round Hill experiment in 1934. He died two years later. Bowles and his staff struggled along for a time with small grants from the American Philosophical Society and the Smithsonian Institution. They held a somewhat larger Navy contract for vaporizing fog with hygroscopic salts[30] but, having made little progress by 1937, the Navy canceled the fog dissipation study.[31] With nowhere else to turn, Bowles closed down Round Hill that fall.

Back on campus, a deteriorating international situation gave fresh importance and direction to MIT's microwave research program. Everyone recognized the obvious military implications of the idea that sufficiently powerful and narrow radio beams could be used to detect or guide airplanes. "The records of the work of the department clearly show the anticipated use of ultra-high frequency radio beams for airplane detection, navigation, altitude measurement, etc.," Bowles explained to Institute president Karl Compton.[32]

Sperry Gyroscope, one of the top defense contractors of the day, kept especially close tabs on that project. Alert to the rapidly changing market for naval and aircraft technologies, Sperry's aggressive new research director, Hugh Willis, in 1937 arranged a joint contract with the Bureau of Air Commerce for research at MIT on blind landing systems. The bureau may have been thinking about civilian applications, but Sperry already had an eye on the military market. "Sperry is interested in this primarily for use in aircraft detection and is anxious to have the program kept secret or, rather, to have any mention of use for aircraft detection avoided," Compton noted.[33] Sperry put $6,000 into Barrow's antenna research and $3,500 into related microwave beam studies. The company also provided Stanford physicist William Hansen, then working for Sperry on an improved microwave generator called the klystron, with a $2,500 fellowship so he could come East and compare notes with Bowles's group.[34] Sperry won a substantial contract from the Army Air Corps for a blind landing system and, more important, positioned itself for the enormous defense contracts ahead.

MIT's revitalized microwave program also attracted attention from International Telephone & Telegraph and tycoon Alfred Loomis. Like Sperry, ITT was looking toward new markets in high-power microwave tubes and systems, and had contracted with MIT electrical engineer Arthur von Hippel for studies of the ultrahigh-frequency dielectrics so crucial for improved magnetron design.[35] Loomis knew about the microwave work through his high-level contacts in MIT and in Washington. Eager "to aid in the development of this art for the practical detection of war hazards," Loomis personally funded research on microwave propagation and detection, including studies by Stratton and Barrow, at the Institute and in his lavish private laboratory on Long Island.[36]

Sensing the increasing urgency of the microwave research, Compton asked his executive committee in May 1940 for temporary funding to keep the group together until further support could be found. "A substantial appropriation is justified as an emergency measure and it will likely lead to additional outside support as other organizations come to realize its importance," he argued.[37]

The Radiation Laboratory

Not even Compton imagined the eventual scale of that outside support or its implications for MIT. On June 27, 1940, President Roosevelt established the National Defense Research Committee (NDRC) to mobilize American science and technology. The idea for such a step had come from Vannevar Bush, who, after moving up at MIT to dean of engineering and vice president, had left for greater opportunities in Washington as president of the Carnegie Institution and chairman of the National Advisory Committee on Aeronautics (NACA). Convinced that the military was too conservative to be

trusted with its own research and development program, Bush proposed an alternative, a civilian agency that would contract defense
research through industrial corporations and universities, as had the
NACA. Bush drew up a plan for NDRC, won presidential approval
for it, and became its first chairman. Other original members included Karl Compton and Frank Jewett, president of Bell Labs. [38]

The NDRC's first pressing assignment was to investigate microwave
radar. Compton appointed a Microwave Committee, with Loomis as
chairman, Bowles as secretary, and representatives from Bell Labs, GE,
Westinghouse, RCA, and Sperry to evaluate recent developments. [39]
The committee spent the summer surveying American efforts and the
fall learning about recent British breakthroughs with high-power cavity
magnetrons. In October it agreed to create a major American laboratory for advanced microwave radar. [40] Jewett wanted the facility attached to an industrial laboratory (preferably his own), but the MIT
contingent prevailed. [41] The Radiation Laboratory (a deliberate mis-
nomer) and the half-million-dollar budget went to the Institute under
an NDRC contract.

"Rad Lab" members liked to say that radar won the war, the atomic
bomb only ended it. [42] Indeed, the laboratory rivaled the Manhattan
Project in size and importance, with a staff of four thousand, an annual
budget of $13 million, and industrial contracts worth $1.5 billion. Its
responsibilities ranged from managing theoretical research to acting as
liaison between the industrial contractors that built the equipment and
the military officers who used it. The projects ranged from microwave
aircraft detectors to long-range, low-frequency ship navigation systems.

Compton acknowledged the Rad Lab's debt to Round Hill, telling
Bowles privately that MIT "owed the existence here of this great defense research structure, its staff and its building, to Colonel Green
under whose sponsorship our ultrahigh-frequency radio research
program had its beginnings." [43] Yet, while the Rad Lab, as the center
for wartime radar research, represented the institutional and intellectual culmination of prewar trends at MIT, it took surprisingly little
advantage of the Institute's early preeminence in microwave physics
and engineering. MIT had administrative responsibility for the laboratory but turned its day-to-day management over to outsiders, most
of them physicists—Lee DuBridge from Rochester, Wheeler Loomis

(Alfred's brother) from Illinois, and I. I. Rabi from Columbia. Electrical engineering department chairman Harold Hazen recalled with some bitterness: "Engineering over the country as a whole did not have the intellectual standing that science had, so, paradoxically, the Department's pioneering work and those in the Department who had done it had much less influence on the Radiation Laboratory than what often seemed to us the headstrong scientists from elsewhere. It was often ironic for our group to watch the scientists repeating the mistakes that our people had made in the earlier years, disdaining to take advantage of the work that had been done in the Department."[44] Barrow left after a short time to teach in MIT's Radar School, and later joined Sperry's fire control division. Bowles too found himself an odd man out among the physicists, "in the desperate situation where I had little open to me excepting a last resort position," and left in 1942 for Washington and a job as expert consultant on radar to Secretary of War Henry Stimson.[45]

MIT's own physicists were not prominent at the laboratory either. Department chairman John Slater recalled that "The Physics Department was not consulted or even informed by the administration about the plans for the Radiation Laboratory, and did not take part in its organization."[46] Slater worked there on magnetron theory for a time, but grew increasingly unhappy with the laboratory's management and eventually left for a similar magnetron project at Bell Labs. "Rabi is . . . such a confirmed sceptic," he confided to a friend, "that I think he has a depressing effect on research, his attitude toward anything is that he doesn't believe it, and even if it is so, he doesn't see that it is good for anything."[47] Stratton studied radio propagation at the Rad Lab and worked on long-range radio navigation there before joining Bowles as an expert consultant to Stimpson.

Along with many of his colleagues, Slater concluded that the same kind of military/industry/university partnership that was taking shape at the Rad Lab and Bell Labs could fundamentally reshape their post-war world. As he put it, "A number of us at MIT were becoming conscious of the close interplay between science and technology in the field of microwaves, and we began to lay plans to try to prolong this interplay in our post-war planning."[48]

In the summer of 1944 Slater, Hazen, Stratton, and Compton,

though scattered among various defense projects, began talking about ways to exploit the unique opportunities offered to MIT by the Rad Lab. "Our first and most immediate problem toward the end of the war was how to consolidate our position in the field of microwaves," Slater recalled. [49] He sketched out for Compton an interdepartmental research program: "The field [is that] which one might call microwave electronics. The central problem of the field would be the behavior of electronic and gaseous discharges at microwave frequencies—triodes, velocity modulation tubes, magnetrons, etc. I have recently developed fundamental points of view toward these problems which are applicable to all such types of tubes. The object of the study would be two-fold: To understand more thoroughly how existing types of tubes work, and to apply this knowledge to the improvement of existing tubes, the development of new types, and the extension to shorter and shorter wavelengths."[50] Slater foresaw a host of applications. He imagined that the new laboratory would follow the pattern set by the Rad Lab but on a smaller scale, with a staff of perhaps only seventy. The electrical engineers shared Slater's enthusiasm. Hazen agreed that "microwaves and their applications are probably the outstanding scientific outgrowth of this war," and suggested a number of specific applications of his own. [51]

In Slater's view, Stratton's experiences and connections, both within the Institute and outside, made him the obvious choice to head the proposed laboratory. "His very high standing with the industry and the armed services would be most valuable in outside contacts which would be very necessary if such a project were to succeed."[52] Slater convinced Stratton to turn down a tempting management offer from Bell Labs in order to head the new laboratory, recruited several senior researchers from the Rad Lab (including Jerome Wiener, Albert Hill, and Jerrold Zacharias) to help staff it, and persuaded MIT to appropriate $50,000 to get it off the ground until other support could be found. "Each reading of your proposed program fills me with a longing to be in Cambridge," Stratton told him. [53]

Having the Rad Lab on campus certainly gave MIT a recruiting advantage. To lure the most promising young scientists and engineers, Slater and Stratton offered research associateships at salaries competitive with industry. Slater thought the associates' hands-on experience would add a "practical touch that the senior members in their more executive and theoretical capacities had not gained," and would also make them effective teachers for the enormous undergraduate classes in physics and electrical engineering MIT expected in the postwar years. "Our planning had been sufficiently early so that we were ready with a definite plan at the crucial moment, which no other universities were," Slater boasted.[54]

Exactly where the laboratory's future financial support would come from was still unclear. Even Stratton, who was closer to the wartime centers of government power and planning than anyone else, told Slater as late as the spring of 1945 that "It is apparent from a number of conversations that I have had since I last saw you that no one has any fixed ideas as yet on the future relations of educational institutions to federal laboratories."[55] With the probable dismantling of wartime laboratories looming on the horizon, MIT looked to industry as the most promising sponsor and sent out letters to a number of the Rad Lab's most important contractors, including Raytheon, ITT, and RCA, asking for support. All expressed polite interest, but offered nothing more than graduate fellowships.[56]

Stratton sensed that the political winds were already beginning to shift, however: "Twenty-five years ago everyone talked about the end of war; today we talk about World War III, and the Navy and Air Forces, at least, are making serious plans to prepare for it. Inevitably, this national spirit will react upon the policies of our educational and research institutions. It always has, and we might just as well face it. . . . We shall have to deal with the Army and Navy and make certain concessions in order to meet their needs."[57]

What the military had in mind, Stratton knew, was something his wartime boss, Edward Bowles, had recently called a "continuing working partnership" of America's universities, industries, and armed services.[58] In a memorandum that Bowles passed along to Stratton and Compton, General Dwight Eisenhower laid out the strategy: "The lessons of the last war are clear. The armed forces could not have won the war alone. Scientists and business men contributed techniques and weapons which enabled us to outwit and overwhelm the enemy. Their understanding of the Army's needs made possible the highest degree of cooperation. This pattern of integration must be translated into a peacetime counterpart which will not merely familiarize the Army with the progress made in science and industry, but draw into our planning for national security all the civilian resources which can contribute to the defense of the country."[59] Not surprisingly, his counterparts in the Navy and the Army Air Force were reaching the same conclusions.[60]

With Congress and the administration deadlocked over the configuration and control of a national science foundation, the military, led by the newly created Office of Naval Research (ONR), took the initiative in funding university science and engineering. Bolstered by millions of dollars from recently canceled procurement contracts, ONR became the predominant patron of academic research, and set the precedent for the postwar relationships between the military and the university.[61] Many academics, having enjoyed the prosperity of the booming war years, welcomed the new funding. A few, like astronomer Harlow Shapley, feared the consequences, predicting gloomily, "Those who were worried about domination of freedom in American science by the great industries, can now worry about domination by the military."[62]

The Research Laboratory of Electronics

The military quickly took steps to consolidate and extend its wartime partnership with the universities, acting first to transform the Rad Lab's basic research division into the Research Laboratory of Electronics. Fearing that this unique resource might be lost in the postwar demobilization, the armed services agreed to continue funding the research division for six months after the official termination of the Rad Lab itself at the end of 1945, and to transfer to it a million dollars worth of surplus equipment. In March 1946 they set up the Joint Services Electronics Program (JSEP) to take over financial support of RLE and similar laboratories at Harvard and Columbia.[63] RLE opened for business with seventeen faculty members from MIT's physics and electrical engineering departments, twenty-seven staff members, plus a number of graduate students formerly employed by the Rad Lab, and a $600,000 budget from JSEP.[64]

Stratton took special pride in the degree of freedom the laboratory's

JSEP contract allowed. As he told his staff, it not only "insures the continuation of our Laboratory on approximately its present scale for at least another two years, but also . . . sets a pattern for the proper sort of relation between an academic institution and a sponsoring agency."[65] RLE's administrators interpreted the JSEP task order as calling for basic, unclassified electronics research, with no restrictions on publishing or exchanging ideas with outsiders and with education as a top priority: "The laboratory adheres strictly to the point of view that graduate students are here to obtain the best possible education in their fields, and their assignment to duties is governed accordingly. They are not in the Laboratory primarily to help us fulfill a contract; or rather the terms of the contract will best be met if each student derives a maximum personal profit in terms of training from his research. It is our understanding that this policy coincides entirely with the views of our sponsors."[66]

Stratton and his colleagues could not have foreseen how radically basic research and graduate education would be redefined in the postwar world. It was true that in the first few years the overwhelming majority of the laboratory's research was not classified, including some sixty theses done on a highly classified guided missile project. But much of its work was directly tied to military interests in microwave electronics, secure communications, missile telemetry, and other specific fields, and overseen by a technical advisory committee of military scientists.[67] Predictably, its stated basic research agenda included developing certain types of microwave tubes and wave guides at specific frequencies. Even more esoteric subjects often had rather narrow technical objectives. For example, Stratton reported that the laboratory's studies of superconductivity might well lead to microwave cavities of exceptionally high gain.[68]

RLE organized or actively participated in many of MIT's technical conferences and the so-called summer studies—essentially intensive faculty seminars, funded by the military, which focused on themes of particular relevance, including air defense (Project Lincoln), nuclear aircraft propulsion (Project Lexington), and defending maritime shipping (Project Hartwell). Slater had anticipated as much: "Although it is intended that the activities of the Laboratory shall cover broadly the field of electronics, the heritage of the War makes it inevitable that emphasis will fall heavily on special areas."[69]

Very soon, and despite its best official intentions, RLE found itself immersed in classified military research through Project Meteor, a multimillion dollar contract with the Navy for an air-to-air missile. Stratton, named chairman of the Guided Missile Committee in January 1946, sent the guidance and telemetry portion of Project Meteor to RLE. Though classified, this research was expected to have close ties to the basic electronics program at RLE. Stratton told his Navy sponsors, "Work carried out in the Electronics Laboratory on electronics fundamentals, although not included in the attached program, will greatly strengthen the ability of the Electronics Laboratory to solve the particular problems which guided missiles present."[70] Graduate students were welcomed on the project. Henry Zimmerman, who had taught at the Radar School during the war, took charge of the guidance group in January 1947 and supervised some thirty theses in RLE related to Meteor's radar homing systems. William Radford, a Round Hill alumnus who had spent the war as a consultant to the missiles division of NDRC, supervised another thirty degree theses on telemetry.[71] RLE also set up a graduate course on missile guidance for Navy officers.

RLE researchers frequently discovered that the intellectual challenges of peace had been substantially reshaped by the experiences and tools of war. For instance, RLE's microwave tube laboratory, under Louis Smullin, took wartime radar research and extended it into high frequencies and power. Smullin, after taking his master's degree at MIT, completed his education on the job at the Rad Lab and at ITT. At RLE, his group dramatically increased the range and power of magnetrons (for radar transmitters) and made significant contributions to klystron and traveling-wave tube design as well. It also organized the first of the annual microwave tube conferences, which brought together interested researchers from the armed services, industry (chiefly defense contractors such as GE, Bell, RCA, Sperry, and Raytheon), and other universities. Reflecting on the boost the war and the Rad Lab had given to tube research, Smullin joked, "We were the real war profiteers; there's just no question about it."[72]

MIT's plasma physics program got its start with the collaboration of Sanborn Brown and William Allis, Rad Lab alumni and charter members of RLE. Allis had joined the physics department back in the 1920s, left to study electron scattering with Arnold Sommerfeld in Munich, and returned to the Institute to continue his investigations of slow electrons with Brown. The war dramatically shifted their attention. Allis, who worked briefly on magnetrons with Slater at the Rad Lab and then became a liaison officer to the Lab for the Army, recalled: "World War II interrupted our work, but then supplied a vital element: we fell heir to the microwave equipment and techniques of the Radiation Laboratory, and this directed our efforts in microwave discharges."[73] The magnetron offered an ideal way of investigating the behavior of ionized gases in cavities, and so opened up the whole field of microwave discharges. With about $60,000 a year from RLE, Allis and Brown formed one of the country's first "plasma" schools, with a dozen researchers and twenty graduate students.

They purposefully kept their program small and basic. Allis was later quite critical of the AEC's large-scale fusion project because, as he said, the money was "for research with colossal machines in laboratories off-campus which, therefore, had little educational value."[74] Still, the RLE program did have a practical side, including important applications for radar switching and improved microwave tube performance. Most of the graduates went to work at GE, RCA, and Bell, and the faculty frequently consulted on projects in those laboratories. The plasma group also organized a series of Gaseous Electronics Conferences, with many of the same industrial participants as the microwave tube conferences.

Although the DOD remained its predominant sponsor, accounting for all but about 3 percent of the budget throughout the 1950s, RLE did not neglect the industrial side of the ledger. It organized a series of conferences to keep selected corporate engineers up to date on the RLE research program, with laboratory tours and lectures by leading scientists.[75] It also ran a parallel conference series for the military establishment featuring demonstrations of the latest developments in microwave communications, telemetering, guidance, and so on. Zacharias gave the keynote address, entitled "Basic Research—A Military Asset," at the inaugural symposium.[76]

Through its research programs and its graduates, RLE helped significantly boost the local electronics industry. Established companies like Raytheon and Sylvania looked to MIT to give them the edge in the defense electronics business. They hired scores of recent graduates, put dozens of faculty members on the payroll as consultants, and occasionally convinced top people to jump ship for the corporate world. Like RLE, their research and development efforts and their product lines mirrored the military predominance in postwar electronics. Raytheon's military business, for instance, climbed from a relatively small percentage in the 1940s to a third by 1951 to four-fifths by 1956, where it stayed for a decade. Most of its competitors followed a similar pattern. So pervasive was the military presence in Massachusetts electronics that a 1961 Boston bank study suggested replacing the textile spindle with the Hawk missile as the symbol of the local economy.[77]

A surprising number of RLE faculty members and research associates went into business for themselves. The laboratory gave rise to fourteen companies in its first two decades[78]—most of them specializing in microwave electronics and devices—including Metcom and Bomac, an $8 million-a-year tube manufacturing firm acquired by Varian Associates (a Stanford spinoff) in 1959. A few, like Adcom (sold to Control Data Corporation in 1964), entered the computer field. Nearly all did a substantial percentage (if not all) of their business with DOD and specialized in components and systems for pulse array radar, missile electronics, and related fields where technical expertise and the right Pentagon contacts counted more than production experience or marketing and financial savvy. Looking back, one military administrator suggested that what would later be called Route 128 followed a straightforward pattern of development: "A clearly visible impact of JSEP activity at university centers has been the evolution of industrial activity, usually not far from those centers, entrepreneured, manned, and carried forward by students who have gone into those industries."[79]

The defense orientation of RLE's early years left its mark on the undergraduate and graduate curriculum as well as the industrial landscape, and not only at MIT. Scores of future professors received their graduate degrees there, and later taught their own students with textbooks written by their former professors. As Carl Barus, who did his graduate work at MIT and worked in the Rad Lab. before leaving for a career teaching electrical engineering at Swarthmore College, perceptively pointed out, "Professors teach what they know. They write textbooks about what they teach. What they know that's new comes mainly from their own research. It is hardly surprising, then, that military research in the university leads to military-centered undergraduate curricula."[80] Among the influential examples which Barus cites are a number of texts that got their start at RLE, including Zimmerman and Mason's *Circuits, Signals, and Systems* and *Electronic Circuit Theory*, Guillemin's *Introductory Circuit Theory*, and Fano, Chu, and Adler's *Electromagnetic Fields, Energy, and Forces* and *Electromagnetic Energy Transmission and Radiation*. Similarly, Slater's *Microwave Electronics*, Yuk Lee's *Statistical Theory of Communication*, Davenport and Roots's *Introduction to the Theory of Random Signals*, and Fano's *Transmission of Information* all reflected the military character of the early RLE research program.

RLE members also played leading roles in updating MIT's electrical engineering curriculum. Under chairman Gordon Brown, the department committed itself to revamping the classic "bluebook" series written by MIT faculty back in the 1930s. "Other institutions are looking to us for leadership in this area," Brown declared.[81] He discussed his plans with top electrical engineering educators at Caltech, Berkeley, and Stanford and with practicing engineers and found a surprising consensus, at least among those "who had had the wartime experience of radar and electronics."[82] Brown then appointed a blue-ribbon Committee on Educational Policy to introduce a new set of undergraduate courses, laboratories, and textbooks. The result was a coordinated curriculum strongly oriented toward electronics, communications, and electromagnetic and circuit theory.

Acknowledging that it had been "heavily influenced" by MIT faculty research, Brown debuted his curriculum at a nationally attended MIT workshop.[83] Neither the texts nor the courses considered military problems directly, just as their predecessors had not considered commercial problems directly. But the new curriculum did reflect a series of choices about what electrical engineering should be on a conceptual and thematic level, choices significantly influenced by the kinds of military-oriented problems their authors were considering at the time. Brown literally scrapped the old electrical machinery laboratory, the tangible expression of MIT's earlier commitment to electric power engineering and the place where generations of undergraduates had learned their trade. He envisioned a curriculum rooted in engineering science and defined by the general problem of energy conversion. [84] What he got instead was a curriculum structured by the more pressing demands of the applied electronics at the heart of postwar military systems. A 1956 faculty committee on engineering education concluded that a decade of dependence on defense funding had, in selected areas at least, seriously undermined MIT's educational mission. "Too great a proportion of our research funds in engineering involves the purchase-order type of commitment which has characterized so much of postwar research," the committee agreed. "Often the result is poor research, or something which is not research at all. Moreover, the very spirit of such an arrangement can easily pervert the educational role of research at a university."[85] Only by gaining more financial independence, broadening the scope of the research centers, and securing funding that was "thematic and programmatic, rather than narrow, prescribed, and directed," the members insisted, could MIT free itself from the "bondage" of sponsored research. That idealistic vision would turn out to be an endlessly receding mirage.

The Korean War mobilization of 1950 revealed just how blurred the lines between fundamental and applied research in many of RLE's programs had become. As early as 1948 there had been complaints "that the sponsors were pressing for more and more applied work and that the importance of basic research was not sufficiently recognized."[86] Large-scale, classified research had become a regular feature of the laboratory's work. Harold Zahl, who had negotiated the original JSEP contract for the Army and who sat on RLE's technical advisory committee, later recalled a meeting with new MIT president James Killian, Stratton, present RLE director Albert Hill, and future director (and Institute president) Jerome Wiesner at which he offered them a classified contract that would effectively double the size of the laboratory's budget. As Zahl remembered it, Killian asked Hill to think over the proposal for a month and come back with a decision.

" 'I don't need 30 days,' Al replied. 'Jim, I can answer that question in 30 seconds, and the answer is yes!' "[87] That general posture established, RLE quickly took on three big new classified projects—electronics air defense for the Air Force, improved radar and sonar presentation for the Navy, and combat communications systems for the Army.

Wiesner's and Robert Fano's research in spread-spectrum communications exemplified the new look at RLE. Wiesner got the basic concept from discussions at Project Hartwell, an MIT-sponsored summer study in 1950 devoted to protecting overseas transportation. Among other things, the participants discussed ways of protecting fleet radio communications by thinning out the signals so that they could not be distinguished from ordinary noise until they had been reconstructed with special reference and correlating equipment. Intrigued by this idea for secure communications, Wiesner talked it over with RLE colleague Fano, who then brought aboard Wilbur Davenport, one of his former graduate students. Fano and Davenport then initiated a classified study of spread-spectrum applications for radar and communications at RLE and reported their results in secret quarterly laboratory reports.[88]

Lincoln Laboratory

In December 1950 the Air Force asked MIT to extend its commitment to classified research even further, through the creation of a new laboratory for air defense. The recommendation came from a special Air Force Science Advisory Board (SAB) committee chaired by George Valley. A Rad Lab veteran and an editor of its technical publications series, Valley had joined the MIT physics department in 1947 with great expectations of applying his wartime electronics experience to cosmic rays research. But like so many of his colleagues, he found himself increasingly drawn into military advising, starting with the SAB's electronics panel. After the first Soviet atomic test in 1949, he became alarmed by America's vulnerability to air attack. At his urging, the SAB appointed an ad hoc Air Defense Systems Engineering Committee (ADSEC) in December 1949, with Valley as chairman and four other MIT faculty (and SAB representatives), along with two outsiders, to study the air defense situation. Over the next months the so-called Valley Committee consulted with Air Force laboratories and industrial contractors, organized an informal weekly roundtable—often featuring talks by RLE representatives—and brainstormed ideas. Out of these discussions came the idea of an integrated air defense network of ground-based radar and antiaircraft weapons tied together through digital computers. [89]

The Korean War gave a renewed sense of urgency to the committee's work and led to discussions at the highest levels of the Air Force about a new Rad Lab devoted to air defense. In December 1950, during a luncheon meeting at the Pentagon, the chief scientist for the Air Force "coaxed" Valley into drafting a letter for Air Force chief of staff Hoyt Vandenberg asking MIT to consider such an enterprise. "The Air Force feels it is now time to implement the work of the part-time ADSEC group by setting up a laboratory which will devote itself intensively to air defense problems."[90] Because of its existing expertise in microwave electronics and digital computing, MIT was, in the opinion of the Air Force chief of staff, "almost uniquely qualified to serve as a contractor to the Air Force for the establishment of the proposed laboratory."[91]

Initially, many of MIT's top administrators resisted committing the Institute to something the size of the Rad Lab. In a confidential memorandum to president Killian, Stratton pointed out that "every university in the country is watching M.I.T. for the first signs of a new Radiation Laboratory," and warned that "we might as well hang a dead albatross around our necks as to engage at this time on a large-scale project whose avowed primary purpose is the air defense of the United States."[92] Some of his colleagues, notably Wiesner and Zacharias, opposed the venture out of fear that it might dilute their own RLE programs.[93] Gordon Brown complained that shifting projects and research groups to the air defense project "will impose considerable hurt upon RLE. Already the work of RLE has begun to atrophy as a result of the transfer of the emphasis of personnel to Lincoln and away from RLE." RLE's Army and Navy sponsors similarly "were fearful that their influence with MIT was about to be eroded" by the proposed Air Force laboratory.[94]

To assuage such concerns, the Air Force commissioned a "summer study" of air defense code-named Project Charles. Like MIT's other famous summer studies, it brought together some of the Institute's best faculty with selected experts from industry, government laboratories, and academe. Beginning in February 1951, under the leadership of Wheeler Loomis, chairman of the physics department at the University of Illinois and second in command at the Rad Lab during the war, the Project Charles team reconsidered, and largely confirmed, the Valley Committee report. "For a while it was interesting to convince all those earnest members of Project Charles that the views of ADSEC were also theirs," Valley later told Killian. "But on looking back at Project Charles, I remember chiefly the luncheons, which were fattening."[95] Its recommendation led to a tri-service contract (with the Air Force carrying the major share of the budget) for Lincoln Laboratory in 1951.

Reflecting on the decision to go ahead with Lincoln, Stratton gave Killian his impression of the reasons for this change of heart: "Among educators our relations were and are almost unique in the opportunities afforded us to know the true state of our national defenses and to evaluate the threat from abroad. Conceivably the three of us [Stratton, Killian, and Compton]—and several of our faculty to a lesser extent—were infected by Washington war fever; certainly such a suggestion has been made from time to time. Be that as it may we came to the conclusion that the threat of war had now become real and serious and the Institute owed a major duty to the country."[96]

Lincoln was an intellectual as well as contractual extension of RLE. Its steering committee included Wiesner, Zacharias, and several other top scientists. Valley served as assistant (and later associate) director. Most of its early researchers, including Hill (the second director), Wiesner, Fano, and thirteen of the original twenty-two group leaders came directly from MIT.[97] RLE's long-range radio communications, radar, and solid-state physics groups simply moved into new quarters on campus. Radford brought over his communications group to become Division 3 (Communications and Components), responsible for radar and long-range communications techniques. Smullin joined to head Division 4 (Weapons), in charge of airborne early warning, radar, systems components, and ordnance.[98]

Lincoln soon dwarfed its own parent, as it grew rapidly into an enterprise with a staff of two thousand (including seven hundred scientific and engineering professionals, a third of them from MIT) and an annual budget of nearly $20 million.[99] In 1954 it moved twelve miles off campus to quarters adjoining Hanscom Air Force Base, near the newly completed Route 128. For the most part, the laboratory enlarged and, with the close collaboration of MIT faculty and students, accelerated projects already well under way on campus. Lincoln even found a use for Round Hill, which Green's descendants donated to MIT after the war. Wiesner and Radford did research there on "scatter communications," and Charles Townes, who later joined MIT as provost, did some of his pioneering laser studies in the wine cellar.[100]

Lincoln's first big project, the SAGE (Semi-Automatic Ground Environment) system—a nationwide network of radar and antiaircraft weapons linked with digital computers—represented the natural culmination of MIT's "basic" electronics research program. It drew together studies on long-range radar, communications theory, microwave electronics, and digital computing into the largest military R&D enterprise since the Manhattan Project. SAGE occupied most of Lincoln's budget and energy over its first decade and ended up costing the government $8 billion.[101]

SAGE's brain was the Whirlwind computer.[102] Tracking thousands of aircraft with dozens of overlapping radar, with virtually no downtime for maintenance or repair, demanded computers of unprecedented speed and reliability. From the start, Valley realized that a sophisticated computer would be a prerequisite for any effective air defense system. By chance, what he was looking for was right next door, in Jay Forrester's Project Whirlwind laboratory. Valley heard about Forrester's work from a "What's new?" chat with Wiesner in January 1950.[103] He did some checking, and then went to have a look for himself.

Forrester's team had been working on advanced computers for the Navy since the middle of the war. Initially they concentrated on developing a programmable flight simulator using an analog computer. In 1946, looking for improved accuracy, speed, and reliability, they switched their attention to a digital design and began phasing out the simulator in favor of a "general purpose computer" with broad-ranging military applications, including aircraft and missile tracking. [104] Along the way, Project Whirlwind chalked up an impressive list of technical firsts, including magnetic-core storage and marginal checking (for determining which of the thousands of computer vacuum tubes would blow next). At the same time, the project earned a reputation for being consistently behind schedule and over budget, with costs running an order of magnitude more than competing computer programs. To ONR, Forrester and his men seemed more interested in building the world's best, or at least most expensive, digital computer than in doing anything specific with it. [105] Stratton zeroed in on this serious shortcoming when he advised Killian: "Many other institutions can compete with us in the design and construction of large digital computers or simulators; none, not even Harvard or Princeton, can muster the resources of M.I.T. for exploring the possibilities of utilization. This should be our forte." [106]

Lincoln saved Project Whirlwind. Impressed by the computer's potential, if not its performance to that point, Valley invited Forrester to brief the ADSEC on digital computers in February 1950. A month later he put Forrester's group on an Air Force budget, at $500,000 for openers. [107] With secure financial backing, the engineers turned their full attention to tracking and mapping the position of enemy bombers from radar data. In 1951 Project Whirlwind became Division 6 (Digital Computer) of Lincoln Laboratory, first on campus and later in the new facility in Lexington, Massachusetts.

Corporate subcontractors then spread Lincoln's innovations to industry. IBM won the production contract for a second-generation Whirlwind computer (the AN/FSQ-7), sixty machines at $30 million apiece. It was IBM's largest single contract at the time, involving nearly eight thousand people and accounting for more than half the corporate R&D budget. [108] Besides providing substantial revenue— perhaps half the corporation's profits in the 1950s—the project introduced IBM to many of the key technologies of the future, from magnetic memory and time sharing to the light pen and circuit packaging. [109] Corporate managers knew the stakes: "I.B.M. will be recognized as the undisputed leader in the large-scale, high speed, general purpose digital computer field. If a competitor were performing on this contract, that competitor might gain enough advantage to force I.B.M. into a relatively secondary position." [110] IBM's immensely profitable Semiautomatic Business-Research Environment airline reservations system of the 1960s owed, as its name suggests, a substantial debt to SAGE. The telephone link contract gave AT&T a similar edge in digital data communications. System Development Corporation, created specifically to write the system software, trained thousands of programmers and systems analysts who later spread what they had learned throughout the emerging data-processing industry.[111]

Despite its obvious concentration on applied and classified research programs, Lincoln, along with its administrators, sponsors, and parent institution, continued to view itself as a significant, even essential, part of MIT's educational mission. "What . . . can Lincoln Laboratory do for engineering education?" one of its directors asked. "It can provide entirely new opportunities to advanced students who wish to work in the complex fields at today's technological frontier. . . . It is now becoming apparent that graduate education in many of today's crucial problems requires the resources of research centers larger than M.I.T.'s laboratories in Cambridge. In radar and in space surveillance, in radio physics and astronomy, in information processing and in communications, major physical facilities are available at Lincoln Laboratory. There is a growing recognition among educators that these facilities are not regrettable manifestations of mid-century complexity, but are the environment in which tomorrow's scientists and engineers must learn to live and work."[112]

Lincoln clearly exploited its academic image for recruiting. One staff member admitted, "The publication of scientific papers may seem somewhat irrelevant in comparison with the Air-Defense job; however, these play an extremely important role in establishing the professional reputation of the laboratory."[113] Many top Institute administrators did have a genuine commitment to making Lincoln an important part of MIT's educational program. Stratton commented: "The Institute has always accepted sponsored research projects as an integral part of its educational system. Such work, whether on the campus or in the defense laboratories, provides unusual opportunities for both graduate students and faculty to participate in research at the frontiers of their respective fields."[114]

Lincoln's impact on the campus was substantial. During its first decade it supported dozens of graduate students (Whirlwind alone had twenty-seven electrical engineering research assistants in the spring of 1954, most of them working on master's degrees), while its staff members cosponsored twenty-one MIT doctoral theses.[115] In the same years, fifty-five Lincoln researchers earned MIT degrees, including sixteen doctorates. Lincoln staffers often continued to hold their previous departmental appointments, and shuttled back and forth to campus to teach classes (in twenty-one different subjects) and meet with graduate students. A surprising number of those students did their theses on classified Lincoln projects. Under Davenport, a half dozen graduate students (including military officers detailed to the laboratory) studied various aspects of spread-spectrum communications techniques or NOMAC (NOise Modulation And Correlation), as it was called at MIT. Virtually all of their work, including the acronym, was secret.[116] Some of those graduates stayed on at Lincoln to develop prototype stored-reference NOMAC systems for the Army, and to help Sylvania put them into production as RAKE, an antijamming high-frequency radio-teletype link.[117]

The famous DEW (Distant Early Warning) Line also borrowed heavily from the "basic" concepts pioneered by RLE. A summer study at Lincoln in 1952 recommended constructing a network of surveillance radar stretching across the polar gateway to the United States. In designing it, as a subcontractor to Western Electric, Lincoln built directly upon RLE's expertise in "scatter" broadcasting (essentially techniques for bypassing ground interference by bouncing radar off the troposphere) and high-performance radar.[118] Among other firsts, the DEW Line included a Lincoln-designed automatic alarm radar. The Line went into service in 1957. Beginning in 1955, Lincoln increasingly turned its attention toward detecting and tracking missiles and satellites, culminating in BMEWS (Ballistic Missile Early Warning System), put into service in 1961.[119]

MIT's creation in 1952 of a special division of Defense Laboratories for Lincoln acknowledged, though by no means resolved, the special challenge of integrating an enterprise the size (a professional staff of 720 and an annual budget of $22.5 million by 1958) and character of Lincoln with the rest of the Institute. That challenge only intensified over the years. As SAGE evolved from a prototype into a working air defense system, its director conceded that "the character of the Laboratory gradually changed from that of a research organization to that of a technical support contractor."[120] To prevent Lincoln from becoming just another industrial support contractor, MIT spun off MITRE (MIT REsearch) in 1958 as a nonprofit corporation with "systems engineering" responsibility for SAGE, essentially coordinating the various technical subsystems and industrial contractors. About a third of Lincoln's professional staff transferred to the new enterprise.

That left Lincoln without a clear-cut mission. Valley, back in the physics department after the better part of a decade at Lincoln, saw the MITRE divestment as an ideal opportunity for the laboratory to strengthen ties with the campus: "Just as the departure of the SAGE effort poses new problems to Lincoln, it gives MIT a new freedom in administering Lincoln. For previously it was a justifiable MIT policy to hold Lincoln at arm's length so that, for instance, a SAGE catastrophe, if it came, would injure MIT the least. But now SAGE is almost over with, and the bear need no longer be held by the tail. I suggest you embrace it."[121] Lincoln Laboratory director Carl Overhage too urged a closer relationship between his laboratory and its parent in the conviction that Lincoln would reinvigorate academic engineering with a hefty dose of real-world experience. But could that be done, he asked, without risking Lincoln's future? "We may believe at M.I.T. and at Lincoln Laboratory that what the nation needs first and foremost is more research; if the Department of Defense does not wish to fund such research at M.I.T. and Lincoln Laboratory, our belief is not pertinent," he said. "The old analogy of the doctor (who gives the patient not what he wants but what he needs) does not apply here: The Department of Defense has not asked to be cured."[122] Overhage wondered if Lincoln could survive another SAGE and still preserve its academic integrity, or whether renewed Air Force demands for large-scale programs in strategic communications and ballistic missile defense might simply overwhelm the laboratory's fragile balance of basic and applied research. He offered a pessimistic assessment:

> We shall soon rediscover that these large responsibilities call for a kind of discipline related to schedules and costs that is quite different from

the demands of diligent study, rigorous analysis, and imaginative research. . . . Our concern for interaction with the educational and intellectual activities on the Campus will have to be relegated to a subordinate position on the agenda. Our primary motivation will no longer be the advancement of electronics, but the accomplishment of a specific task for the Department of Defense. How will Lincoln Laboratory differ from the non-profit technical support corporations, from Aerospace, from MITRE, from the System Development Corporation?"[123]

But instead of becoming another MITRE, Lincoln remained pretty much what it had always been, a vital, though separate and distinctive, part of the Institute. Faculty and staff members continued to move back and forth between the laboratory and the campus. A. L. McWhorter transferred from the electrical engineering department to Lincoln's solid-state division. Harry Gatos went the other way. Fano spent a year with the Lincoln communications group. Other MIT electrical engineering faculty and graduate students worked on Lincoln projects in masers and lasers, communications engineering, radio astronomy, antenna design, computer science, and solid-state devices. Lincoln researchers taught special courses in radar astronomy, high-power radar design, and microwaves and ferrites on campus. Lincoln also loaned some of its unique technical equipment to MIT researchers. Smullin, for example, borrowed Lincoln infrared masers and telescopes for his "Luna-See" experiments, in which he bounced radio signals off the moon. Bruno Rossi used Lincoln-designed circuitry on his interplanetary plasma probes.[124] By 1962 the laboratory's annual subcontracts with MIT departments reached $400,000. By the end of the decade Lincoln had forty MIT faculty consultants on the payroll, thirty-one staff members teaching on campus, twenty-four staff members supervising MIT theses, and thirty research assistants enrolled in MIT degree programs.[125]

After MITRE, Lincoln found its primary mission in high-performance radar and antiballistic missile systems. It designed and built radar and optical (laser) equipment to detect missile reentry, along with the computer systems to analyze the data, and deployed them for test purposes on the Pacific missile-testing range. It developed extremely powerful radar, like the 120-foot-diameter Haystack, for satellite communications and space surveillance, specialized

MTI (moving-target indicator) radar for detecting enemy soldiers in the jungles of Vietnam as well as underwater communications systems for the nuclear fleet, and at the same time extended its basic radar and antenna studies. [126]

Lincoln had even more impact on the local electronics industry than RLE. SAGE alone cost billions to deploy. The ballistic missile defense project, which never actually led to a working system, nonetheless generated a billion dollars worth of production contracts. [127] That kind of money naturally attracted intense industrial interest. Lincoln spun off dozens of companies over the years—from one-man consulting outfits to computer giant Digital Equipment Corporation (DEC). Most of them stayed clustered around Lincoln, where their founders kept up contacts with former colleagues, and around Lincoln's areas of expertise in digital computers, systems analysis, simulation, tropospheric radio systems, and airborne radar. [128]

The companies that did the best stayed closest to those specialties. Even those that deliberately diversified into commercial electronics, as did Digital Equipment, borrowed heavily from Lincoln's technical inventory. Digital Equipment made its early reputation with a minicomputer modeled on the TX-O, a high-speed, transistorized computer that corporate founders Kenneth Olsen and Harlan Anderson had been perfecting at Lincoln. [129] According to one MIT economist, DEC's minicomputer was a "clear-cut example of an absolutely direct technology transfer from a defense sponsored research project into the industrial market."[130] Most of Lincoln's spinoffs got their start with defense contracts, often under subcontract to Lincoln itself, and continued to do most of their business with the DOD. By 1986, Lincoln's forty-eight spinoff companies accounted for $8.6 billion in annual sales and employed more than 100,000 people. [131] Weighing the crucial role of the military market in creating and sustaining these enterprises, one policy analyst wondered if perhaps "MIT's unusual success in 'parenting' new firms at this time was tied in part to its willingness to accept military contracts at a time when many other academic institutions were turning them down."[132]

By 1958, RLE had already grown so big (68 faculty members, 44 research associates, 124 graduate students, and 107 support staff) that Gordon Brown half-jokingly predicted, "If this continues, pretty soon all the research at MIT is going to be done at RLE."[133] RLE's real importance, however, was not so much its sheer size as its role, in Brown's words, as a "model of excellence" for the rest of MIT.[134] That May, Brown, as chairman of electrical engineering, sketched out his vision of MIT for his department's visiting committee.[135] At the center of his drawing was the undergraduate school, surrounded by a series of concentric rings representing first the graduate school, then the various departments of science and engineering, and finally, swirling in from the circumference, the interdepartmental centers, all superimposed on a line drawing of the great MIT dome. Brown titled it "A University Polarized Around Science" and intended it to illustrate how research generated in these centers would reinvigorate the Institute's teaching core. Just a year later, Brown got the chance to activate his master plan when the Ford Foundation gave MIT $9.2 million for a comprehensive revision of the engineering education program, and he was appointed dean of engineering.[136]

Brown's diagram represented what MIT might become, not what it was. It included centers for regional planning, energy utilization, international studies, and transportation mobility, among others. Surprisingly, RLE, which MIT's proposal to the Ford Foundation had cited as an exemplary research center, was not included. Also missing from Brown's map of the new MIT was any context, any sense of where the Institute stood in relation to the world outside. Beyond Brown's spheres lay one of far greater size and influence, dominated by the military and its industrial clients, that, like the prime mover of Aristotelian cosmology, ultimately translated its motion and meaning to that seemingly self-contained inner world. A truer portrait of MIT might have been titled "A University Polarized Around the Military."

At least a few of the founding fathers appreciated the irony, and resisted its implications. Smullin, disillusioned because his great technical successes at RLE and Lincoln had had such little impact on national security (especially after the laboratory's work turned from air to missile defense), suggested a new set of priorities. In 1959 he proposed a Project Charles-type study of "the major non-military engineering problems of the modern world."[137] MIT had already shown what big R&D laboratories could do to solve the most challenging of military problems. Now it was time, he said, to turn those talents toward investigating civilian air traffic control, alternative energy sources, soil conservation, fusion energy, desalination of sea water, and other pressing engineering challenges confronting both developed and developing nations. Smullin envisioned an internationally oriented Lincoln Laboratory, with technical representatives from around the globe. "The ultimate political importance of such an enterprise, if it goes well, hardly needs emphasis," Smullin wrote. "If there is an initial success, one can imagine the creation of similar centers at various major university centers around the world."

Smullin's Lincoln Laboratory for civilian technology received no support whatsoever, although student protesters would later adopt the conversion theme, using it as a rallying cry on campus. Twenty years later Smullin was still complaining that "we are about at the limit of where it is practicable to make anything fancier in the way of weapons. . . . We don't really know what to do with our fancy, sophisticated engineers and scientists, in terms of the ordinary daily needs of people."[138] And a decade after that he tried yet again to resurrect the idea of a laboratory for civilian technology, this time in the name of economic competitiveness. What America needed, he said, was a civilian counterpart to the Defense Advanced Research Projects Agency.

No one denied that MIT had profited enormously in those first decades after the war from its military connections and from the unprecedented funding sources they provided. With those resources the Institute put together an impressive number of highly regarded engineering programs, successful both financially and intellectually. There was at the same time, however, a growing awareness, even among those who had benefited most, that the price of that success might be higher than anyone had imagined—a pattern for engineering education set, organizationally and conceptually, by the requirements of the national security state.

2 | Steeple Building in Electronics

Pondering the choices facing postwar Stanford, electrical engineering professor (and future dean of engineering and provost) Frederick Terman mused, "The years after the war are going to be very important and also *very critical* ones for Stanford. I believe that we will either consolidate our potential strength, and create a foundation for a position in the west somewhat analogous to that of Harvard in the East, or we will drop to a level somewhat similar to that of Dartmouth, a well thought of institution having about 2 per cent as much influence on national life as Harvard. Stanford can be a dominating factor in the West, but it will take many years of planning to achieve this."[1]

Terman's dream may have been to emulate Harvard, but in the postwar years MIT became his first target. Certainly Stanford could not try to match MIT in every science and engineering field, at least not right away. Catching such a formidable competitor would, Terman knew, require a long-range agenda, picking spots where Stanford had an edge, working niches its powerful rival had overlooked. Terman respected MIT's strength, especially in electrical engineering: "I shudder to think of the corner MIT could get on all the electrical engineering brains of the country if they really went out to dominate the situation with some carefully laid and well executed plans."[2]

Terman, however, had some carefully thought out plans of his own. Two decades of climbing the academic ladder at Stanford and five years running a major defense electronics laboratory at Harvard had taught him a few things about building top-notch academic programs, lessons he later set down for his protégé and successor as engineering dean.[3] Do not waste time with the undergraduate programs, Terman advised, for they never pay big dividends no matter what kind of resources are devoted to them. Instead, he said, put the effort into the graduate departments, where national reputations are forged. Do not deviate from the guiding principles of the "mainstream theory" and the "steeple concept." There was no point in creating excellent programs in fields no one cared about, Terman believed. Stay in the mainstream and make the programs count. Far better to build superb programs in a few crucial fields than to try for comprehensive coverage and end up doing lots of things well but none with distinction. Or, as Terman liked to say, better one seven-foot high jumper on the team than lots of six-footers.[4]

Following that strategy, Terman built Stanford from a respected regional institution into one of the world's preeminent centers for the study of science and engineering, most notably in his own specialty of electronics. By nearly any measure—research dollars, academic ranking, graduate student enrollment, faculty publications and honors, and perhaps most significant of all, imitation—Terman's planning paid off. From almost nowhere Stanford rose to challenge MIT for leadership in electrical engineering, and in most other science and engineering fields as well. It became, as Terman had predicted, not only a "dominating factor" in the West, but in some respects supplanted even Harvard as a contemporary model for higher education.

Yet Stanford's achievement came, as had MIT's, at the cost of realigning its research and teaching programs toward the military priorities that had made such rapid growth possible in the first place. Stanford got a late start in the race with MIT, but caught up quickly. In 1946 its total government (including defense) contracts came to only $127,599. Ten years later, thanks largely to Terman's aggressive campaign, its DOD obligations totaled some $4.5 million, and then tripled to some $13 million over the following decade. By the mid-1960s, Stanford had jumped from the back of the pack to third on the list of top university defense contractors, not counting the more than

$50 million in AEC money for the Stanford Linear Accelerator Center.[5]

Predictably, given where the money was coming from, Terman's "steeples of excellence," as he called them, graphically revealed the military blueprint for postwar science and engineering. Electronics at Stanford, as at MIT, predominantly meant military electronics, from the actual hardware prototypes produced in classified laboratories to the most "basic" theoretical research which made them possible, and from the academic laboratories and classrooms that trained future electronics engineers to the local defense contractors that hired most of them. Terman's Stanford Electronics Laboratories (SEL) set the pattern for postwar steeple building—create a first-rate academic program with defense contracts, use the money to bring in faculty members with industrial experience, and attract ongoing corporate support through continuing education, industrial affiliates programs, and extensive faculty consulting. Like MIT's RLE, SEL gave rise to dozens of companies whose character, like the knowledge that built and sustained them, bore the imprint of the military agenda for electronics.

A Communications Option

If anyone deserves to be called "the father of Silicon Valley," it is Terman, who first envisioned its mutually reinforcing climate of academic, military, and industrial science and engineering, and who trained the first generation of students who made it happen.[6] As the son of the celebrated Stanford psychologist Lewis Terman (and one of the subjects of his famous study of gifted children), Terman had literally grown up on campus. Through his studies there in electrical and chemical engineering he came to appreciate the industrial relations of academic engineering. Terman's mentor was Harris J. Ryan, chairman of the electrical engineering department. Coming West from Cornell in 1905, Ryan had rapidly earned a reputation for responding to the commercial challenges of the day in high voltage transmission and insulation. Like his one-time business partner Dugald Jackson, Ryan built up his department by working closely with industry. He directed his own research toward long-distance, high voltage transmission. He consulted with Pacific Gas and Electric on several important projects, including the transmission line from Big Creek to Los Angeles that was to carry power nearly four hundred miles at 100,000 volts. Urging "Research Cooperation Between Universities and Utilities," he took on a variety of commercial projects in his own Stanford laboratory. And to fund a state-of-the-art high-tension laboratory at the university, he organized a consortium of West Coast utilities and electrical equipment manufacturing firms.[7] The laboratory (later named for Ryan) opened in 1926 and gave Stanford, in Terman's words, "unchallenged leadership in the field of high voltage insulation and phenomena associated with the long distance transmission of power."[8]

With Ryan's counsel that "MIT is by far the best," Terman joined a generation of promising electrical engineering graduate students who eagerly made their way to Cambridge to complete their studies.[9] The department he joined in 1922 was still very much dominated by chairman Jackson's conviction that the proper business of engineering was business. Terman was impressed by the young, dynamic Vannevar Bush and extended his undergraduate Stanford studies in high voltage with a dissertation on the "Characteristics and Stability of Transmission Systems," which he completed in 1924. Given slightly different circumstances, Terman might well have made a career at MIT. He was offered a teaching position there, but declined in order to spend a year back at Stanford recuperating from a bout with tuberculosis. He taught electrical engineering part-time for a year while regaining his strength, and then accepted a full-time appointment in 1926 at a salary of $2,500.[10]

Compared to the intense atmosphere of what many considered the world's best electrical engineering department, Terman found Stanford's program (with the exception of Ryan) to be second or even third rate. Mediocre appointments, heavy teaching loads, and meager rewards for publishing had relegated Stanford to the minor leagues. Terman's MIT experiences convinced him that Stanford could only compete by encouraging more and better faculty research. What seemed to set MIT apart was not its curriculum ("If it did we could all copy it, and there would be hundreds of schools made as great as Tech overnight"), nor the quality and work habits of its students, or even its facilities. Its "secret," Terman realized, was a faculty on the frontiers of research. "A large portion of the Tech staff know what is going on in their own field with a thoroughness comparable to that with which Prof. Ryan knows the high voltage field," Terman told the dean.[11] At Stanford, no one had published anything outside the high voltage field for fifteen years.

Terman went public with the theory, provoking controversy with his suggestion in an article in *Science* that electrical engineering research in universities was far inferior to its corporate counterpart. According to Terman's count of articles in the *Transactions of the I.E.E.E.*, university researchers were contributing little better than 10 percent overall, and even less in glamour fields such as radio: "There are very few colleges that can give as good an answer to a 'red-hot' question in electrical engineering, as the engineer in the laboratories of the General Electric Company, Bell System Laboratories, etc."[12] Terman's scorecard had MIT far ahead of everyone else at the university level, with Johns Hopkins and Stanford its only real but still distant rivals. Terman drew two important conclusions from his statistics—that connections with industry kept an electrical engineering program on the leading edge of research, and that even small investments in research could repay big dividends to academic departments. "So little electrical engineering research is now being carried on in the universities that even a modest program of investigation covering the entire industry will bring much prestige," he told Ryan. "With its past reputation as a center of high voltage research, and with the establishment of the Ryan Laboratory, Stanford is in an excellent strategic position to initiate a pioneer movement that will make this the national research center of electrical engineering."[13]

Even as an assistant professor, Terman's ambitious goal was to remake Stanford's electrical engineering department in MIT's image. With high voltage research at Stanford already well positioned, Terman turned his attention toward the emerging field of radio and communications. Terman had taken a course in communications at MIT but realized passing up the opportunity to study with Bowles had been a mistake. Terman talked the department into letting him set up a new graduate program in communications. Radio, he pointed out, was already a big business that universities could not afford to ignore.

"Opportunities for university work in radio wave propagation are almost without limit," he said. "This is a new field just now being opened up, and one that will not be worked out for many years."[14]

From his attic laboratory over the engineering shop, Terman launched an aggressive, commercially oriented program in communications.[15] Following MIT's lead, he convinced Bell, Pacific Telephone and Telegraph, Raytheon, and other companies to donate the equipment. He drew research problems from industry, investigating in the first few years high-efficiency vacuum tube amplifiers and ways of increasing the number of radio stations able to broadcast on a single frequency. He published a dozen articles in the *Proceedings of the Institute for Radio Engineers* (mostly on vacuum tube design), filed some thirty patents, and earned a reputation as one of the country's most productive academic radio researchers. Even Terman's textbook, *Radio Engineering*, reflected this strong commercial bent. It became an immediate bestseller because, like his courses, it placed real-world problems at the center with an elegance and simplicity that especially appealed to working engineers. Put on the market in 1932, it was used in courses at Caltech, Illinois, Michigan, Cornell, Harvard, Johns Hopkins, and even MIT.[16] Interestingly, Terman never took a sabbatical to write this or any of his later influential texts. Instead, he set himself the deceptively easy goal of one page a day and actually managed to turn out a shelf full of books that way.[17]

Outstanding students always counted more with Terman than well-equipped laboratories. "The primary function of the university should be to turn out leaders rather than to amass a pile of stone," he said.[18] When Ryan retired in 1932, Terman began attracting more electrical engineering graduate students than any other Stanford professor. During his first six years of teaching, Terman supervised thirty-three advanced degrees (out of sixty-four in the department and 172 in the engineering school).[19] He kept close tabs on competitors, especially MIT: where their graduate students came from, how much fellowship money they got, and where they were hired after graduation. After carefully studying the matter, he decided that what brought graduate students to a university was not reputation but money. MIT offered its graduate students $91,000 a year in fellowships, another $40,000 in assistantships, and $25,000 in loans—in other words, about $600 a year per student. Consequently, it could attract the very best of the graduate student pool. Three-quarters of MIT's students were recruited from other institutions. Stanford, on the other hand, normally offered only $150 to $300 a year per student. The result, Terman noted, was that most of its graduate students (forty-four out of sixty in a typical year) came from its own undergraduate ranks. [20] Stanford had to compete financially for the best students, and Terman began looking for money from local electronics firms for this purpose. Whatever it took, he did it. In an effort to wheedle a fellowship out of S. W. Gilfillan, Terman wrote up an illustrated article on Gilfillan's radio company for a university publication, sent background material and a personality profile to the alumni office ("I have been told . . . that he is rather susceptible to flattery"), visited his company to give him a pep talk on Stanford radio engineering, and even included some illustrations of Gilfillan's radios in one of his forthcoming textbooks. [21]

To help place his students, Terman kept in touch with the employment offices of major radio corporations. He told Stanford's president, "I have learned by experience on the Pacific Coast that personal acquaintance is invaluable in placing graduate students to advantage in industry."[22] By the mid-1930s he had former students at GE, Bell, RCA, Zenith, Pacific Telephone, and a half dozen other electronics firms, and only two in academic positions.

By the late 1930s, Terman had built an outstanding graduate program in radio electronics. His attempts at building a complementary local electronics industry were somewhat less successful. [23] Most of his best students still left for jobs with the East Coast giants. [24] The few who stayed were out of the mainstream in highly specialized technical niches that could compete in an industry dominated by eastern laboratories and patents. A tireless promoter of western companies, Terman arranged field trips to local electronics companies (some, like Heintz and Kaufman, founded by Stanford graduates) and invited their engineers to give seminars about their research on campus. David Packard, then a graduate student in the radio laboratory, recalled the tours as the highlights of the courses. "Here, for the first time, I saw young entrepreneurs working on new devices in firms which they themselves had established. One day Professor Terman remarked to me that many of the firms we had visited, and many other firms throughout the country, had been founded by men who had little formal education. He suggested that perhaps someone with a formal engineering education and with a little business training might be even more successful."[25]

Terman was right, of course, although he helped things along, backing Packard's venture into business with another communications graduate student, William Hewlett. "I hired him half-time for $55 a month, and he paid his tuition out of the $55. Now today you can't find people with the potential of David Packard who will work half-time for $55 a month!" Terman joked long afterward.[26] In 1939 Hewlett and Packard, with an idea they had heard about from Terman, started their own company to manufacture a resistance-tuned oscillator. This was the first step in Hewlett-Packard's climb from Packard's Palo Alto garage to a $10 billion-a-year company. And Terman, naturally, was one of their first investors. Terman also gave Charles Litton his start as a research associate. His company too would one day become an industry giant. None of these companies became very large before the war, but they did develop a range of innovative products that distinguished them from the East Coast's industry and laid the institutional groundwork for the postwar defense boom.[27]

Terman took special pride in his growing entrepreneurial skills. He told the dean of Cornell's engineering school, "Along with other things I find myself becoming something of a promoter and much to my surprise find that I really enjoy this phase of things very much. If someone had said a few years ago that at this time I would be laying out and running a program for obtaining financial aid for the engineering school, I would have thought the person to be of unsound mind. However, I have been learning the techniques involved and have already built up my own philosophy as the proper way of handling the promotional side of the university, at least insofar as it applies to engineering."[28]

The Radio Research Laboratory

Those organizational skills were put to the test when Vannevar Bush, as chairman of the NDRC, arranged Terman's appointment as director of the Radio Research Laboratory (RRL), a spinoff of MIT's Radiation Laboratory housed up river at Harvard and devoted to radar countermeasures. [29] In choosing his distinguished former student for the important wartime post, Bush told Terman's dean that "the Radiation Laboratory was too greatly staffed with Physicists and that a few engineers would be good for that lab."[30] Bush also knew that Terman's many connections within the engineering community would help recruit top talent for the laboratory. Terman's recent election as president of the Institute of Radio Engineering (IRE), at the age of only forty, testified to his stature within the engineering community. Karl Compton made the appointment official, reminding Terman of "the ultra-secret character of this project," so secret that few people at the Rad Lab even knew, or would know, about it. Terman came East in February 1942 to begin organizing the laboratory. [31]

Off to a relatively late start compared with other defense laboratories, Terman found recruiting more difficult than he expected. Many good researchers had already been lured elsewhere. Terman complained in his notes that the best physicists had gone to the Rad Lab itself. [32] Still, he made good use of the professional connections Bush had counted on. By the end of the year, he had assembled 250 staff members, including a hundred scientists and engineers. At its peak in late 1944 the RRL would have some eight hundred employees, including about two hundred professional researchers. [33] Terman did especially well at bringing in promising younger scholars, and some not so young, who were soon to make their marks in the field. Among his prominent catches were two future Nobel laureates in physics (Stanford colleague Felix Bloch and Harvard's John Van Vleck), four future members of the National Academy of Sciences, and a future president of the IRE.

Terman selected his RRL research associates from industry (sixty-nine), especially from the CBS color television staff, from teaching ranks (fifty-seven), and from graduate students (twenty-two). About a third of them had physics training, the rest backgrounds in electrical engineering. Understandably, he leaned heavily on his Stanford ties, admitting early on that RRL was "going to have a pretty strong Stanford flavor."[34] Thanks to what he called his "ivory hunts," it did. [35] He told Hugh Skilling, acting department head back at Stanford, that "In the event that any of the boys are getting restless and are contemplating leaving the University, be sure that they are not allowed to slip through my fingers without having given this project considera-tion."[36] Not many of the good ones got away, and at different times some thirty Stanford faculty and graduate students served tours of duty at RRL. Many of these would later return with Terman to Stan-ford to launch its postwar electronics program.

Under Terman's leadership the RRL developed a number of im-portant radar jamming and countermeasures devices. His scientists and engineers worked out ways to "hear" and pinpoint radar with di-rection finders, to jam it with high-frequency transmitters, and to fool it with false targets. Much of the initial countermeasures re-search, like the early work on radar, had been done by the British. During a six-week tour in April and May of 1942, Terman scrutinized the results, but his laboratory was soon making significant contri-butions of its own. For instance, the British first hit upon the notion of confusing radar with reflecting foil strips which, when dropped from an airplane, would create spurious targets and misdirect radar-controlled antiaircraft fire. RRL researchers did theoretical studies of scattering, developed special machines for turning out mass quanti-ties of the foil, and worked out techniques for dispersing it properly—in short, made it practical to use. "Window," as they called it, proved so effective that it was sent along with every Allied bomber mission after late 1944. Other RRL breakthroughs included "Carpet," an air-borne, high-frequency jammer which, like window, put antiaircraft batteries out of business; "Tuba," a very high-powered jamming sta-tion, which cleared a flight path for returning bomber squadrons; radar direction finders; and methods for protecting friendly radar from enemy countermeasures. Altogether, the armed services or-dered $300 million worth of RRL-designed equipment.[37]

Terman, it seems, spent much of his time at RRL shuffling papers. "At desk for 9 and a half hours but got a lot of things done (all rou-tine)," he recorded at one point in his daybook.[38] But as Terman rec-ognized, without good administration, RRL was unlikely to fulfill its mission. Terman set the research agenda, kept on top of work being done at other centers of research at home and abroad, managed a large staff, and perhaps most importantly, coordinated his labora-tory's work with the production engineering of outside contractors, who would manufacture the equipment RRL invented. Despite the inevitable bureaucratic headaches, Terman enjoyed a few compensations. One colleague joked to a Stanford colleague after spending some time at RRL that Terman "enjoys being a Big Shot and hobnobbing with Admirals, millionaires, and what not."[39]

Social pleasures aside, Terman learned important lessons at RRL about managing large-scale research. As director, Terman had responsibility not only for creating new countermeasures devices but for teaching Bell Laboratories, GE, RCA, and Westinghouse how to manufacture them, and military officers how to use them. For a few crash programs the RRL engineers hand-built the devices. Generally, they would prepare fifteen or twenty prototypes and then turn them over to the industrial contractors. "I have learned a tremendous amount," Terman told a colleague back at Stanford, "for I had never before realized the amount of work required to make a device ready for manufacture after one had a good working model, such as the number of drawings, the amount of detailed design that is involved to turn out a good job, the problems of how to get stuff made to meet specifications, testing and standardization problems, etc."[40] To smooth the always bumpy road from the laboratory to the field, Terman invited corporate engineers to work with his design teams at RRL, and sent some of his people back to the production plants. He also held monthly meetings with contractor and service representatives to keep up to date with tactical requirements. At first, these were formal meetings in Cambridge, but later, as everyone got to know one another, they would meet informally at "smoke-filled sessions" in Washington hotel rooms.[41]

Terman's RRL experiences convinced him that the emerging partnership of universities, industry, and government that was helping to win the war would continue on in the postwar world with equally profound results. And to fit in, future engineers would need far more sophisticated educations. "It was quite clear that the war showed that the training of engineers was inadequate, that they didn't measure up to the needs of the war," he said. "Most of the major advances in electronics were made by physicists and people of that type of training rather than the engineers."[42] Engineers would be able to move to the leading edge of electronics, Terman believed, only by working closely with physicists and matching their rigorous scientific training.

Winning the West

Terman returned to Stanford as dean of engineering in 1946 with a core of RRL electronics veterans and a new vision of the university and its industrial partners. "The west has long dreamed of an indigenous industry of sufficient magnitude to balance its agricultural resources," he wrote. "The war advanced these hopes and brought to the west the beginning of a great new era of industrialization. A strong and independent industry must, however, develop its own intellectual resources of science and technology, for industrial activity that depends upon imported brains and second-hand ideas cannot hope to be more than a vassal that pays tribute to its overlords, and is permanently condemned to an inferior competitive position."[43]

Terman did not expect the fledgling western electronics industry, despite its rapid wartime growth, to carry Stanford financially, at least not right away. Rather, he believed that, initially at least, the university should carry industry, by strengthening selected academic programs with military contracts. Stanford had not received any major wartime contracts, putting its energies instead into education and military training programs. Terman, having seen for himself what government contracts could do for the universities fortunate enough to have received them, had no intention of letting Stanford's fair share of the scientific spoils of war slip through his fingers. To one administrator who tried to keep electronics colleague Karl Spangenberg back at Stanford with the argument that a leave of absence would deplete the university's teaching ranks and thus lower its academic reputation, Terman telegrammed a sharp rebuke: "Your attention [is] called to [the] fact that war research which [is] now secret will be basis [for] post war industrial expansion in electronics. Without opportunities such as presented in war laboratory like this Spangenberg['s] future work will be definitely handicapped."[44]

Terman thought that Stanford's most promising niche would likely be in microwave electronics, which he anticipated would play the same kind of role in postwar industry that broadcasting had played after World War I.[45] Getting the jump on the competition seemed especially important because Terman guessed, correctly as it turned out, that MIT was busy planning its own program in microwave electronics. MIT's close ties with the Rad Lab, and its long tradition of interdepartmental research in the microwave field would, he feared, give it a significant edge.

Looking ahead, Terman told Stanford's president, "Government-sponsored research presents Stanford, and our School of Engineering, with a wonderful opportunity if we are prepared to exploit it. . . . We failed to take advantage of a similar opportunity presented by the research activities of the war. We are fortunate to have a second chance to retrieve our position. It is doubtful if there will ever be a third opportunity."[46]

Terman and the core of electronics veterans he brought back with him from RRL and other wartime laboratories were well positioned by their wartime contacts and contracts to take advantage of those new opportunities. Terman himself was close to the group of Naval officers then organizing the ONR. He had no illusions then or later about ONR's primary mission. "Even though much of the basic research work that these agencies support is carried on in universities, the *primary motive is not to aid education* but rather to accomplish their mission of meeting the national need represented by their mission," he wrote.[47] But he believed that with proper safeguards he could use ONR contracts to advance academic education and at the same time fully satisfy the Navy.

Stanford's traveling-wave tube (TWT) program exemplified the new style of postwar electronics.[48] Perfected at Bell Laboratories during the war by a team that included recent Stanford graduate Lester Field, the TWT offered significant improvements in bandwidth over other microwave tubes, making it capable of scanning a range of frequencies and therefore particularly useful for countermeasures applications.[49] Terman kept informed about Field's work and, recognizing its implications, lured him back to Stanford in 1947. The ONR shared Terman's enthusiasm and immediately arranged funding for Field's group at $76,000 a year.[50] Although it was a shoestring budget compared with the money backing industrial efforts at Bell Labs and

RCA, Field rapidly established himself as one of the best men in one of the most competitive specialties of postwar electronics. The group very quickly succeeded at developing new kinds of TWTs, increasing their power and reducing their noise levels. Field's patents alone brought in some $30,000 in his first three years, while his research contract grew into one of the largest within the university. After Field turned down a number of very tempting offers from Harvard, Illinois, GE, Hughes, and the Naval Research Laboratory, Terman crowed that this "ensures that Stanford will have the most outstanding research activity in electronics of any university in the country, not even excepting M.I.T. or Harvard."[51] As, in the words of his chairman, "the best teacher in the department on either undergraduate or advance levels," Field was able to attract some of the best and brightest of Stanford's graduate students, including Hubert Heffner, Dean Watkins, and Stanley Kaisel.[52] Advancing the department's work, they concentrated on some aspect of low noise or higher-powered TWTs, projects with obvious implications for improved countermeasures devices.

Karl Spangenberg's postwar career similarly illustrated the new directions and opportunities of postwar electronics. He had joined the department back in the 1930s as Terman's first faculty appointment in communications, and then spent time in Washington as a technical consultant during the war. Back on campus, he too turned toward microwave electronics and won Stanford's first ONR contract, $141,000 a year for studies of microwave electron devices, specifically reflex klystrons as local oscillators for radar applications.[53] Spangenberg's work so impressed his sponsors that they appointed him the first head of ONR's electronics division, with responsibility for overseeing research programs in industry and at a dozen universities, including Stanford.[54] He took a sabbatical to accept his new position, setting a new pattern at Stanford of top electronics people moving back and forth between university research and the government advisory panels that planned and paid for it. Spangenberg's 1948 text on vacuum tubes, published as part of a McGraw-Hill series on electrical and electronics engineering edited by Terman, included entire chapters on klystrons, magnetrons, and microwave technology.[55]

For Oswald G. Villard, Jr., the war literally expanded horizons in radio propagation and ionospheric research. He had come up through Terman's recruiting system, earned his engineer's degree during the war for the design of an ionosphere sounder (under an NDRC contract), and then joined Terman at RRL. Returning to Stanford to complete his doctorate, Villard turned to the study of a strange interference pattern—whistles—he had observed at RRL while listening to shortwave broadcasts. His research confirmed that these whistles were radio echoes from ionized meteor trails and won him a $34,000 contract from the ONR. Villard's radio-sounding techniques subsequently revealed how meteor trails and other ionospheric conditions limited long-range radar and communications, and suggested important military applications for extending radio range in the presence of jamming. His work led also to the discovery of new layers of ionization at low latitudes, while it earned him his doctoral degree and a faculty appointment. [56]

The career trajectories of men like Spangenberg, Field, and Villard contrasted sharply with those of the department's more traditional power engineers. Those who went after contract money themselves, like J. S. Carroll, director of the Ryan Laboratory, whose $59,000 a year Signal Corps contract for insulation research ranked among the highest in the engineering school at the time, kept pace. [57] Those who did not often fell behind and were passed over at promotion time. The chairman of the electrical engineering department conceded that one faculty member, while "a good research man and a good teacher," nonetheless could not be "advanced as fast as those men who worked in fields of more immediate military applications." [58]

In 1947 Terman consolidated Spangenberg's klystron project, Field's TWT program, Villard's ionospheric research, and a scanning spectrum analyzer study led by Joseph Pettit (yet another Stanford radio laboratory doctorate and RRL veteran) into a single JSEP contract called Task 7, the intellectual and financial foundation of the future Stanford Electronics Laboratories. [59] For administrative purposes, the department created the Electronics Research Laboratories (ERL), which, though officially part of the electrical engineering department, reported directly to the dean. The sponsors may have been military, but as at MIT, the laboratory was strictly academic, at least in the eyes of its researchers. Field perhaps best captured the idealistic founding spirit of the enterprise: "Many of us are in a university atmosphere for the purpose of doing scientific work, invention, analysis, and experiment in a cool, unhurried and scientifically provocative atmosphere."[60] The projects were on campus, unclassified, supervised by faculty and done by graduate students.

Even in its early years, ERL made substantial contributions to Stanford's electrical engineering budget and educational program. With an annual budget of $225,000, it represented the lion's share of a sponsored research budget that had soared from virtually nothing at the end of the war to $502,000 a year by 1949 (representing $116,000 in university overhead).[61] It paid the salaries for nontenured research faculty members like Villard. It supported three-quarters of the department's forty doctoral students and a substantial number of its master's candidates. And, through a careful reinvestment strategy, it assured departmental strength for the future. "Such an allocation of funds is essential if Stanford is to compete with the aggressive schools that realize government funds will be a major factor in research from now on, and play the game accordingly," Terman argued. Not doing so, he cautioned, "will result in our being squeezed back into the minor leagues where we were during the war."[62] Terman was so effective at making the contracts support the engineering school that undergraduate tuition fees more than covered instructional costs, leaving Stanford in the enviable (if somewhat embarrassing) situation of spending half as much per student as a state school like UCLA but charging eight times as much tuition![63]

By 1950 Terman's steeple-building campaign had made Stanford, if not yet the Harvard, then at least the MIT of the West. In electronics, Stanford's far smaller faculty had pulled even with MIT in the number of doctorates awarded each year, and its microwave tube design and radio propagation programs were arguably the best in the country. Stanford was attracting more prestigious NSF graduate fellows in engineering than any institution except MIT.[64] In his annual report for 1949, Terman boasted, with some justification, "In electronics, Stanford completely overshadows all other schools west of the Mississippi. According to ratings by the military services in connection with government sponsored research, Stanford definitely ranks among the top three schools in the country. This is particularly important because electronics is where the attention is now centered, where the most productive work is being done, and where the greatest student interest lies. Thus, to be at the top in electronics is to be at the top of electrical engineering."[65]

The Korean Mobilization

It took the Korean War to transform this academic empire into big business. In light of the national emergency, JSEP reviewed its contract with Stanford, which it already considered "from the point of view of value to defense . . . 'about first in usefulness,' " with an eye toward augmenting it with an applied research contract. As Terman explained it to the university administration, what the Navy had in mind was a program that would translate Stanford's basic electronics research into practical military hardware, something "intermediate between fundamental research and industrial development, and [which] in many ways would resemble the work carried on at the Radio Research Laboratory, and the Radiation Laboratory during World War II."[66] Terman also warned that unless Stanford acted quickly, the Navy would take its business elsewhere. "If there is a delay of even one month we are likely to be passed over for the present and may then never regain our present position."[67] With surprisingly little debate, the university's board of trustees approved the contract, which called for $300,000 in applied electronics research the first year, and $450,000 the next.[68]

For Terman the applied contract was a natural extension of the basic research program, in his words "the payoff that has come from the program of government sponsored basic research in electronics that we have carefully built up since 1946."[69] Rather than disrupting the existing educational program, Terman believed that the new contract would contribute to it. He told Stanford's president that the applied contract offered Stanford a unique opportunity to "consolidate our already strong position as one of the great university centers for research and graduate work in electronics" and at the same time afforded "the best possible insurance that we will continue to receive the government support required to conduct a large program of faculty research and graduate training at high levels at a minimum expense to the university." Certainly Terman did not hope for an all-out war, but he pointed out that if one should happen, Stanford electronics might well grow in size to rival the old Rad Lab.

Virtually overnight, Stanford doubled the size of its electronics program without any significant change in content or direction. The applied research simply enlarged, accelerated, and extended technical projects already well under way. As Terman explained, "although this work is classified, it has a high academic value as virtually all of it represents the exploitation and further development of electronic devices that have originated in our basic program."[70]

For security reasons, Terman kept the new Applied Electronics Laboratory (AEL) administratively distinct from ERL, with "applied" and classified research in one and "basic" and unclassified research in the other. In practice, however, the movement of faculty and graduate students back and forth eroded any meaningful distinctions between the two.[71] Faculty and graduate students (if they held clearances, as many did) worked both sides of the fence, doing classified studies (and even theses) and at the same time publishing in the open literature. Sometimes classified projects yielded only unclassified material, including one that led to an encyclopedia article and even an appearance on the national television game show "I've Got a Secret"![72]

Everyone considered classified research a normal, if occasionally troublesome, part of engineering education in the postwar world. It was also becoming an essential ingredient of academic programs, a way, one staff member put it, of broadening the research "into very important areas in electronics otherwise inaccessible to universities."[73] As Terman saw it, not doing classified research would have restricted Stanford's financial resources, impaired its ability to compete on the cutting edge of technology, and infringed on the academic freedom of faculty and staff, by preventing them from pursuing certain kinds of electronics problems. Even Spangenberg, who had charge of the unclassified portion of the electronics research, saw the benefits of the classified work: "There is a real advantage to doing a limited amount of classified research in that it gives us access to much important information, and gives us a head start in directions which are often only subject to temporary classification. . . . In addition, we have as graduate students an appreciable number of officers from the Military departments who come here with near mandates to do work in classified areas of research."[74] Acknowledging rather quickly that the division between the two kinds of programs was fairly arbitrary—after all one of the purposes of the basic contract was "to provide ideas which can be exploited in the development of new devices and systems in the applied electronics program"—Terman merged them by forming SEL in 1955.[75] That year, with an increase in the tube contracts, Stanford moved into sixth place among university defense contractors and was bringing in more *overhead* on those contracts ($465,086) than the entire original JSEP contract.[76]

Though the applied program did not as a rule develop devices beyond the prototype stage, part of its understanding with its military sponsors was that it would work closely with industrial firms that did.[77] Program administrators encouraged faculty consulting, brought corporate engineers to campus, and participated in an annual, JSEP-sponsored technical review for the contractors building the reconnaissance, countermeasures, and radar tubes based on Stanford designs.

A decade later, after student protests had forced Stanford's administration to reassess the place of classified research on campus more critically, Terman could still not understand what all the fuss was about. As he told the president in a confidential memorandum on classified research, the whole controversy seemed to him almost, well, academic:

> As an inheritance from this Korean War period work, we are still doing classified work relating to electronic warfare, and to the propagation of radio waves. Both of these activities are closely related to the research interests of faculty members and to our unclassified research. They represent work that, if unclassified, would be continued without change, because it deals with fundamental concepts and contributes to our position as a leader in the field of electronics.[78]

Where the money came from seemed to Terman almost beside the point. As a kind of footnote, he added, "It just happens that some of this work is also of importance in the defense of this nation."

Business as Usual

By the mid-1950s Stanford, as the intellectual center for microwave electronics, actually began shifting the location of the whole industry. Just as the Korean mobilization transformed the university's research programs, so too it transformed the electronics companies increasingly dependent upon those programs and their graduates. The sudden demand for microwave tubes for radar, electronic countermeasures and communications gave local electronics enterprises an inside track in securing defense contracts, especially research and development contracts. California's share of prime military contracts doubled during the course of the war, from 13.2 to 26 percent (representing some $13 billion in total contracts), as it overtook New York State, the previous longtime defense contract leader. [79]

Much of that money went to southern California aerospace contractors, but Santa Clara County companies won their share. Varian Associates, a Stanford spinoff specializing in microwave tubes for defense applications, grew from $200,000 in sales in 1949 to $1.5 million two years later. Litton Industries, a small vacuum tube fabricator founded by Charles Litton back in the 1930s, sold out to an aggressive group of former Hughes Aircraft employees in 1953. They dramatically expanded the operation to meet the demand for pulse magnetrons and tunable klystrons for jamming and missile guidance systems, and promptly tripled sales (to $6.2 million) and backlog (to $36 million) and quadrupuled employment (to 2,115). [80] Eitel-McCullough, another established local tube maker, similarly rode the wave of defense appropriations. It supplied high-power microwave tubes for virtually every major air defense project and, on the strength of those contracts, grew to 2,600 employees and $29 million in sales by the end of the decade. [81]

Stanford's laboratories continued to spawn innovative start-up companies looking for opportunities to commercialize the latest microwave technologies being developed there. Huggins Laboratories got its start in 1948 when R. A. Huggins, a former research associate, put the first traveling-wave tube on the market. He rapidly diversified into a variety of specialized tubes, all based on research done at Stanford, and became an early leader in TWT technology.[82] Ray Stewart, one of Lester Field's technicians, started his own company in 1952, producing the first commercial backward wave oscillators.[83]

Under the original JSEP contract, Field had trained a brilliant cadre of graduate students who dramatically improved the range and performance of TWTs and, in the process, compiled an impressive list of technical firsts. Most of them subsequently took industrial positions—Kaisel at RCA, Watkins at Hughes Aircraft, Heffner at Bell Labs—and then returned to Stanford as the classified program took off. They too came to recognize the commercial importance of some of their research. Kaisel left for Litton; then, convinced that he could make longer-lived and more reliable TWTs than anything currently on the market, cofounded Microwave Electronics Corporation. Specializing in low-power, low-noise TWTs for electronic countermeasures, MEC built up a $5 million-a-year business before selling out to defense giant Teledyne.[84]

Undoubtedly the most financially successful of the new Stanford spinoffs was Watkins-Johnson. In 1953 Dean Watkins essentially swapped places with Lester Field, taking over the Stanford TWT program after Field left for Hughes. Over the next few years Watkins cemented his reputation as one of the top academics in TWTs, especially for his research on low-noise tubes. In 1957 he and former Hughes engineer Richard Johnson cofounded Watkins-Johnson to design and manufacture microwave tubes for surveillance, reconnaissance, countermeasures, and telemetry, all directly based on the technologies Watkins had been perfecting at Stanford. The company turned a profit its first year and never looked back. Sales rose from $500,000 in 1958 to $4.6 million in 1961 to $9.5 million in 1964.[85]

That kind of success naturally attracted the attention of established East Coast companies ready to cash in on the burgeoning military electronics market. By East Coast standards, the West Coast start-ups were still puny. Industry leaders GE and RCA posted 1956 sales of $725 million each. Admiral, Sylvania, Philco, Zenith, Westinghouse, and a dozen other companies had sales of over $100 million. By contrast, Varian Associates, the biggest of the new West Coast firms, had only $25 million in sales for 1956. But with half of all electronics sales going to the military that year—$3 billion in all—and an increasing share of that going for high technology equipment for missiles and avionics, even the most myopic component manufacturer could read the writing on the wall.[86] As *Fortune* pointed out, military electronics represented a "whale of a good business," both because the defense market was generally steadier than its commercial counterpart and because military R&D contracts offered an inexpensive entry into new fields and enticing prospects for commercial spinoff.

Sylvania, primarily a manufacturer of television and radio tubes, got its chance to break into the military market when the Army Signal Corps offered it a contract to construct a new laboratory for missile countermeasures research. The Signal Corps had been considering some kind of facility for "quick reaction capability" (QRC) in electronic warfare since 1949.[87] Forced into action by the Korean emergency, the Signal Corps offered Stanford a $5 million contract in 1952 to develop "engineering test models" of guided missile countermeasures. (Missiles in those days used radio guidance systems and so were susceptible to jamming.) Stanford, concerned that any new contracts might overwhelm its already taxed resources, begged off.[88] So the next year, following a formal competition, the Signal Corps awarded Sylvania a $3 million initial contract for studying and designing prototype electronic countermeasures against surface-to-target missiles, two-thirds of the money for R&D and the rest for QRC. The Army equipped the facility and funded the research, while Sylvania provided the land and recruited the staff. For the company the contract represented a quick and inexpensive entry into the military electronics business. For the Army the laboratory represented an important step toward parity with the Air Force and the Navy in the missile race.

Although Stanford would not manage the laboratory directly, it nonetheless played a key role in determining the laboratory's eventual location and research priorities. Sylvania's central research laboratory was then in Bayside, Long Island. The Army, however, insisted on putting the new laboratory somewhere that would be a less obvious target. Sylvania already knew about Stanford's expertise in countermeasures and already had a small tube factory in nearby Mountain View. So it built the new Electronics Defense Laboratory (EDL) there, close to prospective Stanford consultants and graduating engineers. The Signal Corps likewise recognized the advantages of putting EDL within Stanford's orbit, so that subcontracts on the search receivers, converters, and other electronic warfare equipment being developed by university researchers could be more easily arranged. [89]

Over its first decade EDL grew into one of the largest local electronics enterprises, with 1,300 employees and $18 million in annual contracts. [90] From a "captive" Signal Corps laboratory it branched out into electronic intelligence (intercepting and interpreting missile telemetry and guidance signals) for all the defense agencies. EDL also built, on a month's notice, the spread-spectrum communications systems designed at Lincoln Laboratory and deployed in the Berlin crisis. [91]

As anticipated, EDL drew extensively on its Stanford connections. It recruited heavily among both research associates and recent graduates. It hired several top faculty consultants, including Terman himself. And it became the first participant in the honors cooperative program, Stanford's pioneering effort to encourage more formal collaboration between high technology enterprises and the university. Local companies, starting with EDL and Hewlett-Packard, sent their best young engineers back to school part-time for advanced degrees. Stanford got first-rate students with practical experience and, through a special arrangement worked out by Terman, double tuition. Industry got better-trained people and a direct pipeline to Stanford's ideas. In its first three years the program's enrollment soared from sixteen to 243, representing more than a third of Stanford's entire graduate engineering enrollment. By 1959, honors cooperative students accounted for 324 of the engineering school's 750 students. [92] By the early 1960s, EDL alone was sending ninety-two people a year to the program.

Along the way, EDL spun off several other laboratories devoted to specific technologies. In 1956 Sylvania set up an independent Microwave Physics Laboratory for advanced research in ferrites and plasmas, two emerging Stanford specialties. The next year it established the Reconnaissance Systems Laboratories for research on satellite detection. And in 1964, EDL director William Perry and a half dozen of his top lieutenants broke away to found Electronic Systems Laboratories as a direct competitor in electronic intelligence.

General Electric came West in 1954 looking for ways of enlarging its already considerable share of the defense electronics business by tapping into Stanford's expertise. GE's Electronics Division had recently established an advanced radar laboratory at Cornell to assist its heavy military electronics group in Syracuse. At Stanford, GE saw a similar opportunity to cash in on academic research in microwave tubes.[93] In 1954 it opened what it called the General Electric Microwave Laboratory at Stanford. Like Sylvania, GE hired a number of recent Stanford faculty members, graduate students, and research associates outright, and signed up others as consultants. It also joined the honors cooperative program. At one point sixteen of its top forty scientists and engineers had been either former Stanford faculty members or graduate students.[94]

At first GE's new laboratory concentrated almost entirely on elaborating concepts originally developed in Stanford laboratories, but gradually it established an independent reputation for research on high-power TWTs for radar and on low-noise TWTs for electronic countermeasures. It supplied the TWTs for GE's Rainbow (the first frequency diversity radar), the klystrons for the Nike-Hercules radar, the mammoth klystrons for Westinghouse's missile defense systems, and the low-noise TWTs for Sylvania's countermeasures systems. The division doubled in size after two years, doubled again in three more, and then doubled once again to 336 employees and a $5 million annual budget by 1958.[95]

Following Sylvania and GE's lead, other East Coast companies established outposts around Stanford. Chicago-based television and radio giant Admiral, sensing the shift in the electronics market, opened a Palo Alto laboratory in 1955 for research on radar, guided missiles, and communications systems.[96] The next year Zenith set up a research laboratory there under the direction of one of Terman's former group leaders at RRL.[97]

By 1960 a third of the nation's multimillion-dollar-a-year TWT business (nearly all of it for defense) was located just off campus. "Obviously, this is not a coincidence," noted Terman, "there was real technical fall-out from the Stanford activity."[98]

To encourage further collaboration between Stanford laboratories and these high technology companies, Terman enthusiastically supported the Stanford Industrial Park, the earliest and perhaps most successful effort to foster academic-industrial cooperation by developing a high technology park on university land.[99] Varian Associates was the first tenant, in 1951, followed by GE's microwave tube division, Microwave Electronics Corporation, Watkins-Johnson, and a number of other electronics firms.[100]

The emerging microwave electronics industry and the university reinforced one another. The Stanford faculty, in consulting for local companies, launching their own businesses, or talking with former students at places like Stanford Research Institute (SRI), constantly discovered new technical challenges to explore back at the laboratory bench. A few, like Watkins, kept up their faculty appointments while running their new companies, blurring the line between corporation and university as they had previously blurred the line between basic and applied research.[101] As one SEL staff member explained, research "works in both directions, military needs influence the direction of the research; the results of the research are translated more quickly into terms which are of interest to the people facilitating the practical problems."[102] Demands for low-noise tubes, for instance, led Watkins to theoretical studies of circuit/electron beam interaction, which led in turn to his breakthrough "velocity jump" techniques and to significant noise reductions in working tubes. Military interest in backward wave oscillators (BWOs), tunable versions of the TWT, suggested other new directions for SEL researchers.

The Stanford style had educational implications far beyond the Santa Clara Valley. Charles Susskind, then a research associate at SEL and soon to be a faculty member at Berkeley, certainly appreciated the dimensions of the issue. "Virtually every member of the teaching faculty is simultaneously a member of the research staff—a situation which has had profound influence on the electronics curriculum and teaching methods," he wrote.[103] By 1954 twenty SEL graduates had found teaching positions and begun research programs of their own, usually, Terman reported, "based on work which they started as students at Stanford." The same year, a national survey by Susskind revealed that the number of courses in microwave electronics had risen from a mere handful after the war to a sizable proportion of all electrical engineering courses at the ten leading universities in the field.[104]

SEL's Radioscience Laboratory, under Villard, showed similar evidence of this military/industrial/educational "fallout." Its ionospheric research led not only to a more precise understanding of how atmospheric conditions hindered long-distance radio communications but of how to turn those conditions to military advantage. Operating under what grew into a million dollar classified contract, Villard's laboratory made important contributions to jam-resistant communications systems and to new surveillance techniques for detecting rocket launches and nuclear tests. Its expertise in ionospheric measurement also played a central role in the early development of over-the-horizon radar. Only when the story broke in 1964 could Villard fully reveal to Stanford's president the full extent of the laboratory's involvement in the project, including the participation of nearly one hundred students at all levels. "According to an opinion currently held in the Defense Department, U.S. universities are not contributing as much as they should to defense technology, because professors tend to confine their efforts to publishing papers on fascinating but inconsequential aspects of important problems," Villard told him. "In view of the record of SEL in many areas, it is doubtful that this charge can be levelled against Stanford."[105]

Like the microwave tube studies, ionospheric research spun off its share of commercial enterprises. One of Villard's graduate students and collaborators, William Ayer, cofounded Granger Associates (with John Granger) in 1956. The firm leased a facility in the industrial park and produced ionospheric sounders and military communications equipment based on their academic research. By 1962 it was doing $5 million dollars a year in sales.[106] Two other Villard students founded Technology for Communications, International, a manufacturer of high-frequency antenna systems. Villard himself worked closely with the companies that developed commercial meteor-burst communications systems.[107]

SEL's Systems Techniques Laboratory (STL), the most applied of its five divisions, was something of a business all by itself. Created in 1951 under the applied contract, its mission was, as Terman put it, to "fill the natural gap between the results of basic research and the specific needs imposed by new military problems—in our case, problems in countermeasures and counter-countermeasures."[108] Under William Rambo, yet another Terman protégé from RRL days, STL turned out "packaged breadboards" of rapid-scan receivers and other reconnaissance and countermeasures hardware, using tubes and techniques perfected in other SEL laboratories.

Despite its largely classified character, STL remained an integral part of Stanford's educational and research mission. Its work drew from and fed into less mission-oriented studies. Rambo provided an illuminating example of how STL brought together "basic" and "applied" research in useful and not altogether fortuitous ways:

> As part of our basic research program a number of years ago, one of our faculty became interested in the question of tuning rates for electronically-tuned backward-wave oscillators. His research led to such a device having the quite phenomenal characteristic of a tuning rate in excess of 70,000 megacycles per microsecond—70,000 megacycles per microsecond. A few years later, a graduate student earned a Ph.D. in the networks area by studying the properties of dispersive microwave filters exhibiting time-compressive properties. Still later, a third student earned a Ph.D. through the study of some of the basic aspects and properties of spectrum analysis involving sweeping filters and incorporating signal compression. Now you can begin to see the connection and the interesting relationship of initially unrelated pieces of basic research. One of the profits of this coordination of effort is evident in . . . a microwave intercept receiver. Through the combination of a very fast tuning plus an interesting form of pulse compression, it has been possible to devise a receiver which exhibits a very interesting combination of properties—high intercept probability plus a resolution that is quite substantial and a very satisfactory over-all noise figure. You can imagine that this result is of particular interest to certain of our military sponsors. [109]

STL's million-dollar-a-year budget provided financial support and thesis material for thirty to forty graduate students a year, and for an equal number of research associates working part-time to support their educations. [110]

Understandably, given its strong applications orientation, STL turned out entrepreneurs as well as researchers. And like the laboratory where they had been trained, the companies they founded specialized primarily in military electronics. STL's most successful spin-off, Applied Technology, manufactured reconnaissance receivers and long-range detecting and monitoring equipment based on designs developed at Stanford. [111]

Revolution in Miniature

It was microwave electronics, not solid state, that set the pattern for what was to become Silicon Valley. Until the mid-1950s, when transistor inventor William Shockley left Bell Labs to set up Shockley Semiconductor in Palo Alto, microwave tube technology dominated the electronics industry around Stanford. Few of the original firms successfully made the transition to solid state, but their experiences served as a prototype for the integration of academic, corporate, and military R&D behind Silicon Valley's later takeoff. As before, the West Coast took ideas and men nurtured in East Coast laboratories and, in reshaping them, created a technical revolution, albeit in "miniature." [112]

Always alert to new opportunities to strengthen Stanford's electronics, Terman had been watching the solid-state field closely since the announcement of the transistor in 1947. To keep SEL's research program up to date he sent Pettit and a few of the graduate students (then working on wideband TWTs) back to school at the University of Illinois in the summer of 1953 to learn transistor physics. [113] Looking for stronger corporate ties as well, he kept in touch with William Shockley and, hearing rumors of Shockley's possible interest in setting up his own company, gave him a strong sales pitch for relocating near Stanford. "It is an exciting business to observe the University and the technical community grow cooperatively to the benefit of both," Terman told him. "We hope you will see your way clear to participate in it." [114] Shockley did and established Shockley Semiconductor in the industrial park as a subsidiary of Beckman Instruments in 1955.

Shockley proved less successful at managing technical talent than in recognizing it, but although the company foundered, its impact on the industrial future of the region was considerable. In 1957 eight of its best engineers quit to found Fairchild Semiconductor, beginning a period of corporate spinoffs that would characterize Silicon Valley for years to come.

Stanford's solid-state electronics followed the same path to the top as the earlier microwave venture: create a first-rate academic program with military contracts, bring in faculty with complementary industrial experience, and attract corporate interest and support through industrial liaison efforts and an honors cooperative program. It really got going with the appointment of John Linvill in 1954, with funding from Gilfillan, whom Terman had kept after all those years.[115] A graduate of the honors cooperative program at MIT, Linvill had taught there a few years before moving on to Bell Labs to learn about transistors. Dissatisfied with the corporate world, particularly with its publication and patent policies, he jumped at Terman's offer to head his own solid-state electronics laboratory at SEL.

Linvill promptly began building his own steeple of excellence. Drawing on his MIT experiences, he initiated an industrial liaison program aimed at attracting corporate support for microelectronics.[116] In return for pledging $5,000 a year for five years, the program offered member companies a sneak peek at Stanford's research and its graduate students during an annual two-day technical review, copies of all technical and quarterly progress reports, and a faculty guest lecture at the company. Linvill lined up nineteen affiliates, including local firms like Varian, companies with local electronics divisions like Sylvania, and national concerns looking for access to Stanford, like Texas Instruments. Linvill also set up informal consulting arrangements with local companies, including Shockley's.

Recognizing that much of the best research in solid-state electronics was being done in corporate laboratories, Linvill looked to industry for faculty as well as financing.[117] He talked Bell Labs into loaning Gerald Pearson (coinventor of the junction transistor) as a visiting professor and then talked Pearson into taking early retirement to stay on at SEL. Other key faculty members in solid state came from places like Bell Labs and Philco.

Within a couple of years Linvill's group was a major factor in SEL, with seven faculty and twenty-five doctoral students.[118] The transistor electronics course alone drew more than one hundred graduate students, making it one of the most popular offerings at the university. Linvill introduced a variety of specialized courses in semiconductor theory and devices, solid-state circuits, and related fields, and turned his own course notes into another text on Terman's McGraw-Hill list.

Like microwave electronics before it, SEL's solid-state program reflected changing military priorities, which at this time were aimed at developing compact, reliable, and durable microelectronics for guided missiles, communications, and the first generation of so-called "smart" weapons. The JSEP contract increasingly emphasized solid state, as did the bigger and more specific contracts with individual services. A $250,000 Air Force contract for studies of adaptive systems (for improving the reliability of military electronics systems) supported about half of SEL's total solid-state electronics effort.[119] A Signal Corps contract for research on silicon breakdown (critical in preparing for the harsh environment of missile nosecones, for example) paid for a sizable portion of the rest. Although "basic" in the same sense as the early tube studies, all of this research had significant implications for military hardware and systems. As Rambo, who had risen to SEL director, pointed out, "We must necessarily keep our program consistent with (and hopefully in the forefront) of the trends in electronics research. And since our sponsorship is largely through military organizations, we must be responsive to the basic needs of those sponsors with respect to future military capabilities."[120]

SEL's budgets told the story. In 1960 it had received $330,000 from the JSEP contract, about $2.3 million from individual contracts with the Army, Navy, and Air Force, and only $200,000 from everyone else, including just $32,000 from the NSF.[121] NASA's contribution increased dramatically from virtually nothing to roughly a third of the laboratory's budget over the following decade, but DOD money and interests continued to predominate.

Occasionally someone protested that the research program (and by implication the military interests behind it) was setting the agenda for the entire electrical engineering department. Back in 1957 Karl

Spangenberg warned that with a contract budget so much larger than the departmental budget, "We obviously need to operate carefully lest the research tail wag the academic dog in the electronics activity. . . . In particular, I feel we should avoid operating in such a way that we effectively have a group of Research Institutes which overshadow the EE department."[122] A decade later the research institutes *were* the EE department, and dog and tail were essentially indistinguishable, which in large measure was intentional.

Stanford's administrators always claimed that they handled defense contracts quite differently from their competitors. As the dean of the graduate school emphasized, "Stanford does not operate a Livermore, nor a Radiation Laboratory, nor a Project Lincoln. *By policy our programs are directed by faculty and must be directly related to basic research and graduate training.*"[123] What gave the dean's boast its measure of truth was that SEL so fully integrated sponsored projects with academic programs that they had become inseparable. Speaking for the classified program, Rambo put the matter more bluntly: "We chose at Stanford the more dangerous route of 'being different' and have insisted that *all* of our programs must provide an outlet for the research inclinations of our faculty and must blend with our graduate programs. As a consequence, our research laboratories are intermingled with instructional laboratories [and] classrooms."[124] Only later did it become clear that this "dangerous route" led not to a sponsored research program constrained by academic priorities but instead to an academic program directed by the demands of its sponsors.

Looking back on his more than four decades as Stanford professor, dean, and finally (from 1965 to 1970) provost, and on the university's extraordinary climb from the minor into the major leagues, Terman reflected, "This game of improving an educational operation is great fun to play because it is so easy to win. Most of the competition just doesn't realize that education is a competitive business, like football, only with no conference rules."[125] What won the game for Stanford? Partly it was being hungrier and willing to take more risks than its rivals, Terman said, though he hastened to add that Stanford "wasn't prepared to go nearly as far as M.I.T. was obviously quite willing to go." In some respects, though, it was Terman who had been willing to go further, for it was at Stanford that the boundaries between sponsored research and education, between basic and applied research, became blurred to where there was little meaningful distinction.

Terman had correctly predicted that the booming postwar period would be an intensely competitive one for universities, like "football . . . with no conference rules." He and his colleagues in electronics learned how to win, but their very success raised troubling, and enduring, questions about the extent to which the military establishment set the rules and determined how the game would be played. In this new academic environment, it was no longer clear how the score would be kept, and what winning and losing would really mean.

3 | Military Guidance and Control

In the fall of 1958, Charles Stark Draper, head of Aeronautical Engineering at MIT, decided that his department needed a new name, something to herald its entry into the space age. Trying to be helpful, the dean of humanities and social studies put one of his best young classicists on the job. He came back with a half dozen highly original suggestions, including the Department of Euthyphoric (the science of flying a true course) Technology and the Department of Phoromorphics (the study of the structure and appearance of inanimate flying objects). The dean liked the Department of Archophorology (the science of initiating and controlling flight) and passed it along to Draper "not with the idea that you are going to do anything with it but simply for a moment of passing amusement and to demonstrate to you that we here in the Humanities always have the best interests of the School of Engineering at heart."[1]

Although Draper went with the more conventional Department of Aeronautics and Astronautics, the classicist's grandiose title did capture, however awkwardly, something of the department's distinctive character under Draper. Starting back in the early 1930s with a single course, a handful of discarded aircraft instruments, and a couple of graduate students, Draper made his Instrumentation Laboratory into the world's leading academic center for inertial guidance research and development, and built in the process an academic empire rivaling MIT itself. By the time he retired in 1969, the laboratory's $54 million annual budget equalled the rest of the Institute's laboratory budgets (excluding Lincoln's) combined.[2]

Draper candidly admitted the source of his department's great strength. "Aeronautics and Astronautics at M.I.T. as it now exists has been very strongly influenced by sponsored research carried out under government sponsorship," he acknowledged in his annual report for 1959. Not only had the contracts given the department unique resources and facilities, he explained, they had created a new kind of academic discipline. "Sponsored research has been one of the main sources of knowledge and experience for the Aeronautics Faculty in the generation of new curricula and courses that have consistently fulfilled current requirements and anticipated trends in aeronautical and astronautical engineering."[3]

What Draper did not further elaborate was that nearly all of that sponsored research was being done for the military. In 1958, for instance, Draper's own laboratory had a $12.9 million budget—$9.8 million from the Navy (the lion's share for the Polaris missile guidance system) and $3.1 million from the Air Force (the lion's share for the Titan II missile guidance system).[4] The Naval Supersonic Laboratory, with a $1.5 million budget, got its money from the Army and Navy for studies on the aerodynamic heating of infrared guidance systems. The Aeroelastic and Structures Research Laboratory, with a $608,000 budget, specialized in research on the effect of nuclear blasts on aircraft and missiles. Indeed, except for small contracts with jet engine manufacturers (themselves major defense contractors) in the Gas Turbine Laboratory, virtually the entire $14.6 million department research budget came from DOD.[5] So did most of the graduate students. Of 104 students enrolled in the department for 1958–59, fifty-nine were military officers detailed to MIT for special (sometimes classified) courses in weapons systems, instrumentation, propulsion, or aerodynamics.[6]

A sponsored research program dominated by military money and expectations led inevitably to an academic curriculum dominated by the same money and expectations. The implications of this extended far beyond MIT. With a bigger faculty, more graduate students, closer ties to industry, and better representation on government ad-

visory panels than any other institution, MIT set the pattern for postwar aeronautics. Its graduates went on to become executives and
chief engineers at leading aerospace contractors from Long Island to
Los Angeles, highly placed officers in the Army, Navy, and Air Force
(including two Secretaries of the Air Force), and top academics at
MIT and other universities. They took with them not only technical
skills but a distinctive worldview that placed national security issues
very close to the center.

Looking to Industry

Thanks to the Navy, MIT boasted one of the country's earliest programs in aeronautical engineering.[7] Its founder was Jerome Hunsaker, Assistant Naval Constructor at the Boston Navy Yard, who was
sent to the Institute in 1913 to teach a special series of courses in aerodynamics for Navy officers. "As the establishing of a school of aero-
plane design, etc., will be of great advantage to the Navy Department," he explained to his superior, "it may be proper for an officer to
be detailed to assist in its development."[8] Hunsaker spent the summer
catching up with the latest advances in Britain, France, and Ger-
many, then designed and built a wind tunnel for MIT modeled after
one he had studied at Britain's National Physical Laboratory. His student assistant on the project was David Douglas, later founder of
the aircraft company bearing his name. Hunsaker's first course was
"Aeronautics for Naval Constructors," and his first students were
all military officers sent to MIT for advanced training in aeronautics.

Under Hunsaker and his successor, Edward P. Warner, a wartime
graduate of the program, the military continued to play a central role
in MIT aeronautics into the 1920s. The Army kept MIT's wind tunnels busy with contracts, as it had during the war.[9] And it kept sending students (about half the total graduate enrollment in those years),
including Jimmy Doolittle, who took his master's degree in 1924.
Warner left for Washington in 1926 to become the first Assistant Secretary of the Navy for Aeronautics, setting a pattern of MIT faculty
members shuttling back and forth between academic appointments
and top military posts and advisory positions. Though officially on

leave, he kept close tabs on the program and was reported "to determine the policies followed."[10]

With the postwar cutbacks in defense appropriations, MIT looked to private philanthropy and industry to make up the difference. In 1926 it applied for a $230,000 grant from the Daniel Guggenheim Fund for the Promotion of Aeronautics, a trust created by mining heir Daniel Guggenheim and administered by his son Harry for the purpose of reviving commercial aviation. [11] MIT got the money, with promises of research programs aimed at reliability and service rather than at the kinds of all-out performance required by military aircraft. "We feel that it is the role of the Institute to serve the designer and the industry, and especially the designer and builder of commercial aircraft," MIT president Samuel Stratton assured the Guggenheims. [12]

At a stroke, the Guggenheim grant tripled the aeronautical engineering program's annual budget, to more than $100,000, [13] and encouraged other private initiatives. In 1928, General Motors president (and MIT alumnus) Alfred Sloan, looking after GM's growing aviation investments, gave $85,000 for an Internal Combustion Engine Laboratory connected to the Guggenheim Laboratory. [14] C. F. Taylor, who had recently joined the staff from the Wright Aeronautical Company, became its first director.

MIT again turned to industry to update its aging wind tunnels. Incoming president Karl Compton brought Hunsaker back as chairman of mechanical engineering and head of the aeronautics course in 1933. Under orders to match Caltech's recent initiatives, including its highly successful cooperative research programs, [15] Hunsaker raised $230,000 for a new wind tunnel, much of it from aviation companies and industry executives. [16] Completed in 1938, the Wright Brothers Wind Tunnel paid for itself with industrial testing contracts, just as Hunsaker predicted, with $59,000 coming in the first two years alone. [17]

MIT repaid much of its corporate debt with well-trained graduates. By 1939 the department had a total enrollment of 233, including thirty-six graduate students. "The effect of our graduates on the airplane industry cannot be estimated. But it is of interest to note that M.I.T. graduates include the chief engineers or engineering directors of Curtiss Wright, Glenn L. Martin, Pratt & Whitney, Vought,

Hamiliton-Standard, Lockheed, Stearman, and Douglas, as well as the engineer officers of the Naval Aircraft Factory and of Wright Field. Our younger graduates are prominent as project engineers, research men and key men everywhere," Hunsaker boasted. [18]

Along with his colleagues, Draper earned a reputation in the 1930s for taking care of business. [19] Draper got his start as a research associate in Taylor's aeronautical engine laboratory measuring detonation, or knock, in internal combustion engines. Working with Taylor's younger brother Edward, their studies culminated in the successful development of the MIT Knockmeter. [20] In 1934 Draper founded the Instrumentation Laboratory, where he and a small team of graduate students and assistants, always with a rigorous and distinctive mathematical style, extended their research to altimeters, airspeed meters, magnetic compasses, and other aircraft instruments. [21]

Draper's work attracted the attention of the Sperry Gyroscope Company, a major supplier of gyrocompasses, gyrostabilizers, fire-control systems, and automatic airplane controls for the Navy. [22] By the mid-1930s, Sperry was looking for new markets in naval aviation and toward new partnerships with academic engineers at MIT and elsewhere. It put $5,000 a year into Draper's detonation indicator project, a sizable sum at a time when, as Draper recalled, "all of the stuff I made I got out of the automobile junkyard." [23] Sperry also arranged a contract on an in-flight vibration monitor Draper was concurrently developing for the Navy, with an annual fee and a 5 percent royalty to MIT in return for an exclusive license. [24] Sperry's investment paid off immediately. In just six months it sold $20,000 worth of "M.I.T.-Sperry Vibration Apparatus" to the Navy. [25]

Draper's Sperry contacts and contracts increasingly drew him toward new applications of gyroscopic technology, a traditional Sperry specialty. With $1,500 a year in corporate funding, he designed and built an improved bank-and-turn indicator, with spring supports in place of ball bearings and with liquid damping. [26] When Sperry decided, for commercial reasons, not to pursue the idea, Draper put it into the blind landing system being developed by Sperry, along with the Bureau of Air Commerce and the Army Air Corps, at Round Hill. He rigged up a bank-and-turn gyroscope to indicate to the pilot, as a point of light on a cathode-ray oscillograph, the changing attitude of the airplane as it came in for a landing. [27]

Sperry further strengthened its ties to Draper's laboratory by providing financial support for the students and by hiring its graduates. By the end of the 1930s, Draper had built up a free-standing division within the aeronautics program with three professors, two instructors, an assortment of technicians, instrument makers, and mechanics, and twenty-five graduate students, most of them working on one Sperry contract or another.[28] Since Draper made up his classes as he went along ("I never taught any course out of a book. I made them up out of the experience I was having in the laboratory at the time"),[29] as his commercial research interests expanded, so did his course offerings. In 1938, for instance, he added a new course on "Vibration Measurements," which drew directly on the research he and George Bentley were doing for Sperry and the Navy.[30] Bentley wrote his doctoral thesis on the in-flight vibration monitor and took a job with Sperry to perfect the instrument for commercial use. Walter McKay wrote his thesis on a new kind of compass analyzer and joined Sperry's gyrocompass department. Walter Wrigley tied his thesis so closely to Sperry's proprietary interests that he could not divulge all the details.[31] He too joined Sperry right after graduation.

Despite these pressing commitments to research, teaching, and consulting, Draper somehow found time to earn his own doctorate—in physics in 1938—and his pilot's wings. He bought a small private airplane for testing instruments and for fun and left a memorable impression on his colleagues with his daredevil flying.[32] Students from those days remembered him arriving for class in his usual green visor and dirty lab smock, trailing an entourage of eager assistants. Typically, he spent the hour animatedly outlining ideas he had come up with the night before.[33] Colleagues recalled him as creative and hard-driving, and occasionally hard drinking, with a penchant for strong shots of whiskey after 5:00 P.M., which (thanks to a cleverly designed circuit rigged to his desk clock), he arranged to appear at the touch of a button.

The War

The war, and especially the alarming strength of Japanese air power, gave a new urgency and direction to Draper's work. Sperry backed his idea for transforming the bank-and-turn indicator into a lead computing gunsight (for automatically leading a target by the appropriate distance) and then sold it to the British admiralty—at that time taking heavy losses in the Pacific—as an antiaircraft gunsight. [34] The American Navy learned about it from a group of young officers detailed to MIT to study the latest advances in servomechanism theory and practice with electrical engineer Gordon Brown, who held a separate Sperry contract for fire-control research. The officers also took courses from Draper, and two of them wrote a classified thesis on applying gyroscopic control to antiaircraft guns. [35] Impressed by Draper's progress, they helped arrange official trials with the Navy's Bureau of Ordnance. Those trials, in turn, led to a production contract with Sperry for 2,500 of the so-designated Mark 14 sights. [36] At the same time, the Navy gave Draper a contract for a Confidential Instruments Development Laboratory (CIDL) at MIT to further advance gyroscopic gunsight technology.

Having perfected the basic concept, the CIDL extended it to bigger guns and longer ranges, adding telescopic sights, fuse-setting computers, and radar ranging for blind firing. [37] "We did everything," Draper recalled. "We conceived the stuff; we did the mathematics; we did the design; we did the making of the parts; we did the assembly of the parts; and we did the testing. So we were a small design, engineering, and test outfit. We did everything until we came out with a piece of working hardware, in which case we then transferred information to whatever company was going to manufacture the material." [38] Draper's engineers taught Sperry's engineers—at one point the company had fifty technical people assigned to the laboratory—how to build the sights and taught military officers how to deploy them. Sperry eventually manufactured some 85,000 Mark 14s, earning MIT (as patent holder) $400,000 in royalties, and Draper (as coinventor) $10,500. [39] By the end of the war, CIDL had a staff of one hundred, a six-figure annual budget, and contracts with the Army Air Corps, the Navy, Sperry, and AC Sparkplug.

War research drew in MIT's other aeronautical engineering laboratories as well. John Markam ran the Wright Brothers Wind Tunnel two shifts a day, seven days a week, testing models of new aircraft designs for Martin, Grumman, Lockheed, and other aircraft manufacturers. The Taylor brothers put the Sloan Laboratory to work on aviation fuel studies. Manfred Rauscher, with funding from the Army Air Corps and the Navy, designed and built a special "flutter tunnel" for studies of wing, aileron, and tail vibrations at high speed, and supervised thousands of trials with it, including model tests of the new Vought SB$_2$U and Grumman Hellcat.[40]

The Gas Turbine Laboratory

Looking for ways of turning these new patterns of cooperative research to MIT's advantage, a faculty committee under Hunsaker convinced the administration to establish a Gas Turbine Laboratory, with $24,000 up front until other support could be found.[41] The gas turbine engine, little more than a promising concept before the war, emerged from massive wartime research and development programs in Germany, Great Britain, and the United States as a revolutionary technology no top-notch academic program could afford to ignore.[42]

In the spring of 1944 Karl Compton started talking with prospective corporate contributors, including Alfred Sloan, whose own company (through its Allison division) was already a major supplier of military aircraft engines and who was anxious to keep pace with new developments. Sloan contributed $40,000 so that MIT could purchase from the Navy a wartime fuel laboratory adjoining the Sloan Laboratory to house the Gas Turbine Laboratory (GTL).[43] Sloan wanted an exclusive research contract with GM. Compton, perhaps with some bad memories of overly restrictive commercial contracts from the late 1920s, talked him out of it, explaining that he "had some doubt as to whether M.I.T. ought to follow any policy which would close the doors of a laboratory to its students or which would tie to one company interest a group of professors, many of whom had varied consulting arrangements with other companies."[44] Instead, the department's visiting committee raised the rest of the money needed to fund the laboratory from a consortium of aircraft engine makers. Hunsaker made the pitch that: "The American airplane engine builders face a threat to their business. They can't lead by copying what the British turn out or what G. E. and Westinghouse [the two major wartime turbojet contractors] do here. They can, in my opinion, use their great design skill to create advanced power plants based on fundamentals of the new art. To use such fundamentals they must acquire young engineers skilled in special techniques and also acquire, through research, critical information as to their own applications. The proposed M.I.T. Gas Turbine Laboratory can provide such men and such information."[45] Curtiss Wright, GE, Westinghouse, and United Aircraft (Pratt & Whitney), tossed in $125,000 each, and General Machinery Corporation $25,000.[46]

The Gas Turbine Laboratory opened for business in 1947, with Edward Taylor as director. GE, Westinghouse, Curtiss Wright, and, later, Allison provided continued funding, with annual contributions of $10,000 each, in return for laboratory reports, consulting, and a "gentleman's agreement . . . to delay publication of results for one year after results have been reported to the sponsors."[47] It rapidly grew into a top academic center, second in size and reputation only to Cornell's Aeronautical Laboratory, an off-campus facility in Buffalo with no educational commitments. Over its first decade the staff of the GTL published 249 articles and technical reports and trained 134 students, including ninety-three master's and seventeen doctoral candidates.[48]

Even with the best of intentions, Taylor found military contracts too available and too lucrative to refuse. From the start, it took on substantial defense projects, including studies of supersonic diffusers and compressors. With the Korean War, defense obligations rapidly increased to about 40 percent of the GTL's annual budget.[49] In any case, the military's intense interest in gas turbine technology completely overshadowed the laboratory's civilian research. Although Taylor originally envisioned strong commercial support from automotive, locomotive, shipbuilding, and passenger airline firms, the companies that actually contributed were making turbojets exclusively for military applications. "The Army and Navy, as well as industry, are usually interested in projects leading to some immediate goal rather than projects intended to improve our understanding of some particular field," Taylor acknowledged.[50] In the postwar years the immediate goal for the Army, the Navy, and their industrial contractors, was delivering high-performance turbines for military aircraft.

The Naval Supersonic Laboratory

Just months after the end of World War II, the Navy's Bureau of Ordnance awarded MIT a mammoth contract for a "comprehensive research and development program embracing all scientific and technical activities necessary for the development of one or more types of jet propelled, radar homing, supersonic, antiaircraft missile suitable for shipboard use."[51] Code-named Project Meteor, it drew upon five academic departments, six laboratories, fifty faculty members, and included subcontracts with Bell Aircraft for the missile, United Aircraft for the ram jet, and Bendix for the control system.

To evaluate missile stability, control, and maneuverability at supersonic speeds, MIT's aeronautical engineers needed test data from a supersonic wind tunnel. Unfortunately, the only one was the NACA's new tunnel at the Ames Research Center, a continent away and fully booked with its own top-secret missile and aircraft studies. Determined to move the $10 million program ahead as quickly as possible, the Navy, with some prompting from MIT administrators, agreed to build MIT a comparable supersonic tunnel.[52]

By the time the Naval Supersonic Wind Tunnel was completed in December 1949, at a total cost of $2.6 million, Project Meteor's budget had been cut by a third in favor of other guided missiles projects, leaving MIT with a state-of-the-art tunnel, a sixty-member staff, and nothing to do.[53] John Markam, recognizing the implications of "the enormous effort now underway to develop supersonic fighters, bombers, and missiles,"[54] renamed his facility the Naval Supersonic Laboratory, and opened it to all takers. The Air Force and its industrial contractors were a new and ready market for the wind tunnel. In 1953 alone NSL brought in $223,185 in research and testing contracts from the Wright Air Development Center, and another $243,250 from Boeing, Hughes, Pratt & Whitney, and McDonnell, substantially more than the Project Meteor contract at its peak.[55] In 1955 NSL turned a $20,000 "profit," which by the following year grew to $350,000.[56] Air Force interests increasingly turned NSL's attention toward classified studies of aerodynamic heating of missiles, nose cone configurations, and the aerodynamic problems of carrying and dropping missiles and bombs at supersonic speeds. NSL also ran related wind tunnel tests on advanced aircraft (e.g., the B-58) and missiles (e.g., BOMARC) for Boeing, Convair, Hughes, McDonnell, North American, and other aerospace contractors.[57] Its biggest single research program, supported by an annual budget of $90,000 from the Air Force and the Navy, was an evaluation of the effects of aerodynamic heating on infrared guidance systems.[58] NSL did both theoretical and applied work aimed at improving infrared guidance performance at extremely high speeds and temperatures, and performed the first wind tunnel tests on operating Sidewinder and Sparrow missiles.[59] In 1956 it organized a national conference on infrared guidance systems and cosponsored a summer course on aerodynamic heating of aircraft structures that attracted one hundred corporate and government representatives.[60]

At its dedication, MIT president James Killian predicted that NSL would provide not only research "of vital importance to national security," but also "an exciting research opportunity for graduate students in this new field."[61] The laboratory actively recruited graduate and undergraduate students, even for its classified research programs. "INTERESTED IN PART-TIME WORK OR EXCELLENT THESIS OPPORTUNITIES?" asked a recruiting poster. "Don't overlook M.I.T.'s NAVAL SUPERSONIC LABORATORY." It outlined current laboratory interests in "aerodynamic and thermodynamic problems of missile guidance systems," "predictions of trajectories, heating and performance of high altitude rockets and missiles," "aerodynamic design, testing, and evaluation of unusual supersonic configurations," and "numerous other problems or phases of those above which cannot be described because of security restrictions."[62]

Markham recognized that NSL's most important contribution to the defense effort would most likely be graduate students and former staff members his laboratory trained and sent on to the aerospace industry, with their specialized knowledge of supersonic aerodynamics, infrared guidance, and other key technologies.[63] At any one time, NSL had twelve or fifteen graduate students, and perhaps twice that many undergraduates, along with staff engineers studying part-time for advanced degrees. Their work, though generally unclassified, contributed significantly to the sponsored research program. For instance, the laboratory's unclassified studies of diffusion cooling,

Markham explained, had "enormous implications for use in long-range high-speed missiles."[64] Judson Baron's doctoral thesis ("The Binary-Mixture Boundary Layer Associated with Mass Transfer Cooling at High Speeds") grew directly out of the laboratory's work on aerodynamic heating of missiles at hypersonic speeds and led to a large Air Force contract to find ways of countering the intense heating of missiles at hypersonic speeds.[65] Baron later joined the department as an assistant professor.

The Aeroelastic and Structures Laboratory

At the Aeroelastic and Structures Laboratory (ASL), the winning weapons—the atomic bomb and the strategic bomber—pointed toward the future they had so irrevocably remade. With funding from the Air Force and the Navy's Bureau of Aeronautics (where he had worked before joining MIT in 1946), Raymond Bisplinghoff made ASL a world center for simulating and measuring the aerodynamic effects of atomic weapons. To study how close strategic bombers could fly to atomic explosions without falling apart, Bisplinghoff and his colleagues designed and built a 98-foot-long "shock tube," which was essentially an extremely powerful wind tunnel. Atomic bomb–sized blasts (up to twenty tons of force) could be unleashed against scale models, and the impact measured with interferometers, balances, and high-speed photographic equipment.[66] The shock tube became the laboratory's biggest single research program, with a staff of ten and an annual budget of $685,700.[67] Staff members wrote dozens of classified technical reports on "Atomic Bomb Effects on Aircraft Structures" for the Air Force and the Navy's Bureau of Aeronautics, and even supervised actual atomic blast tests at Los Alamos and Eniwetok Island in 1951.[68] They later extended these studies to ballistic missiles.

The increasing speed and performance of military aircraft redefined traditional problems in aeroelasticity and structures research as well. To evaluate flutter at supersonic speeds, the laboratory built a variable Mach number supersonic test section for the Wright Brothers Wind Tunnel. Even as assistant professors, Holt Ashley and Robert Halfman held research contracts with the Air Force and the

Navy's Bureau of Aeronautics worth $240,737. Bisplinghoff super-
vised three additional structures contracts worth $374,500 ("Shock
and Impact on Structures," "Airplane Design Criteria," and "Gust
Studies"). Even conventional problems like fatigue got a second look,
as the low-cycle/high-stress fatigue of military aircraft suddenly became more interesting than the low-stress/high-cycle fatigue of their
commercial counterparts.[69] By 1958 the laboratory had six faculty
members, twenty graduate students, forty-two support staff, and a
steady budget of $600,000, every penny from the DOD or its indus-
trial contractors.[70]

The laboratory took special pride in making its contracts serve its
teaching. Bisplinghoff claimed that "the excellent course content in
aeroeleasticity and structures reflects the fact that these courses are
taught by the active Project Supervisors in the sponsored research
program."[71] Indeed, the laboratory virtually created the modern specialty of aeroelasticity. It turned out at least ten graduate students a
year, all of them supported by sponsored research contracts. Its faculty members introduced a series of unique courses in aeroelasticity,
including laboratory work at both the undergraduate and graduate
levels. Bisplinghoff and Ashley, lacking a suitable text, wrote their
own—*Aeroelasticity* (1955), which they characterized "as a combination text and basic reference for the aircraft industry";[72] it became a widely adopted standard teaching text.

The teaching, like the research, closely followed the advances of
military aeronautics. Convinced by 1952 that "personnel in government laboratories, in industries developing high-speed airplanes and
missiles, and in some of our own laboratories" would all need more
advanced training in aerodynamics, Ashley and his colleagues developed a new curriculum with courses in thermal effects, waves and
shocks (including a section on shock tubes), unsteady flows, and hypersonics and superaerodynamics.[73] Ashley introduced an experimental course, "Aerodynamics and Dynamics of Guided Missiles,"
in 1957 and discovered such strong interest that he continued it as a
regular class the next year.[74] The department designed a special
shock and vibration course for Air Force officers,[75] and later declassified "Rockets, Guided Missiles, and Projectiles," a restricted
class for Air Force and Navy officers. Then, "to match the increasing

interest in rockets and missiles," it reworked the "undergraduate courses such as Aeromechanics, Aerodynamics, Airplane Stability and Control [to] introduce consideration of the respective problems from the missile as well as the airplane point of view."[76] Seniors taking the missile option course in 1957 found themselves designing a ground-to-air interceptor missile, complete with airframe, engine, aerodynamics, and controls.[77] Bisplinghoff, giving the department's visiting committee his perspective on the contributions of the sponsored research to teaching, pointed out that it provided not only financial support for the students and millions of dollars worth of equipment that the Institute could not possibly afford on its own, but also, and perhaps more importantly, challenging research problems and "a contact with the aircraft industry and the government services which is valuable to the student upon graduation."[78]

The laboratory's active support of an industrial liaison program helped keep the doors to the aerospace industry open. Each spring a two-day symposium on aeroelasticity and aircraft structures showcased the laboratory's work, with faculty lectures, student presentations, and tours of the shock tube and other facilities.[79] ASL also organized summer courses for the industry on missile aerodynamics and satellites. The courses attracted more than one hundred participants each time,[80] and the lecture notes were reprinted and distributed to reach an even wider audience.[81] Faculty members continued to provide consulting services for leading aerospace firms. Ashley spent seven weeks with Convair's structural dynamics group in the summer of 1956.[82] Paul Sandorff, who had come to the MIT aeronautics department from Lockheed in 1952, returned to the company during a sabbatical ten years later. "His experience in industry brings a most welcome flavor of real-life practice into the engineering courses given by the Department," the chairman reported.[83]

The laboratory's research engineers, many of them recent MIT graduates looking for some experience before entering the job market, frequently went on to introduce the laboratory's latest techniques directly to Martin, Douglas, North American, Boeing, Convair, and other aerospace giants.[84] Providing what amounted to postgraduate training was, Bisplinghoff felt, a vital part of the laboratory's mission.[85] "Although technicians and other service employees make permanent careers . . . staff members are encouraged to regard it as a period of post-graduate education at M.I.T.," he wrote. "This is an intangible educational process not involving courses and degrees, but it has nevertheless turned out to be one of the most important educational functions that we are performing."[86] A few staff members went into business for themselves. One founded Allied Research in 1952 to undertake atomic blast studies. Two others left to start Calidyne, a manufacturer of electronic "shakers" and other aerodynamic test equipment.[87]

As the Vietnam War intensified and military fascination with combat helicopters heightened, the laboratory turned its experience and expertise to new challenges. Once again, the laboratory had close ties both to the military advisory panels that promoted these weapons (one top researcher chaired the Scientific Advisory Panel for Army Aviation) and to the contractors that manufactured them. As might be expected, the laboratory's publications and theses continued to reflect the predominant military interests of the day.

The Instrumentation Laboratory

Draper's former students kept the Instrumentation Laboratory on the leading edge as the Air Force and the Navy turned their attention in the postwar years to strategic bombers and ballistic missiles. Reaching targets deep inside Soviet territory demanded something better than conventional radar or visual navigation and guidance systems could provide. Draper had been considering, as an alternative, an inertial guidance system. Using sophisticated gyroscopes and accelerometers, such a system could, at least in theory, measure all changes in orientation, acceleration, and gravity between the launch point and the target, and so guide a weapon without external commands or corrections of any kind. Draper liked to call it just an advanced type of dead reckoning.[88] Its big advantage would be its invulnerability to jamming, but the most obvious pitfall was that gyroscopes and accelerometers precise enough to hit something halfway around the world were not likely to be small enough to fit into a bomber or a missile. Most experts, including George Gamow, a leading member of the Air

Force Science Advisory Board's Guidance and Control Panel, considered inertial guidance hopelessly impractical.[89]

Leighton Davis, head of the Army Air Force's Armament Laboratory at Wright Field, wanted to take a closer look. He had taken Draper's fire-control courses as a young officer, remained in close touch, and helped Draper win a $100,000 contract from the Armament Laboratory for a gyroscopic fire-control system for fighter bombers in the last years of World War II. The A-1 gunsight was not completed in time to see action until Korea, but Davis grew to have great confidence in Draper and his laboratory.[90] Just weeks after the formal Japanese surrender, Davis awarded the Instrumentation Laboratory a study contract for a "stellar bombing system" based on the inertial guidance principles he and Draper had been talking about during the waning days of the war. "Lee and I got it out of a bottle of whiskey," Draper would later joke. Even then they had something bigger in mind than just building a better bombsight: "The Stellar Bombing System is to be designed primarily for operation in jet propelled aircraft as a bombsight, but the possibility of eventually robotizing the system for use with guided missiles should not be neglected."[91]

The Air Force followed up the initial study contract with a series of design contracts for inertial navigation systems. FEBE (for Pheobus, the sun), though cumbersome and crude by later standards (4,000 pounds with a ten-mile error in four hours of flight), demonstrated that an airplane could be successfully navigated by inertial guidance alone, expert predictions notwithstanding.[92] SPIRE (SPace Inertial Reference Equipment) eliminated the backup celestial tracker, cut the weight to 2,800 pounds, and increased the accuracy to a ten-mile error in twelve hours. Confounding the skeptics, Draper flew a SPIRE-equipped B-29 from Hanscom Field in Lexington, Massachusetts to Los Angeles on February 8, 1953, to attend a top-secret conference on military navigation systems, missing his "target" by less than nine miles after a twelve-hour flight.[93] SPIRE Jr., weighing half as much, flew the same course in 1957 with an error of less than two miles. It made news the following year by carrying reporter Eric Sevareid, Draper, and a half dozen laboratory engineers on a nationally televised cross-country flight to a classified destination.

The Killian Panel put the Instrumentation Laboratory in the ballistic missile business. Appointed by President Eisenhower in 1954 to assess American vulnerability to growing Soviet strategic strength and chaired by MIT president James Killian, the panel gave top national priority to developing and deploying both intermediate range and intercontinental ballistic missiles.[94] With a green light at the highest policy level, the Air Force, under General Bernard Schriever's Western Development Division, moved aggressively to consolidate its lead in the missile race.[95]

Though still considered too experimental and too heavy by many experts, inertial guidance had at least one perservering champion in B. Paul Blasingame, resident guidance specialist at the Western Development Division and one of Draper's officer graduates. Blasingame convinced his superiors to award the Instrumentation Laboratory a contract for a backup (to radio) guidance system on the Atlas, and for the primary system on the new Thor intermediate-range ballistic missile.[96] General Motors' AC Spark Plug division, builder of the A-1 bombsight, received industrial subcontracts for both. In 1959, largely on the strength of its Thor performance, the Instrumentation Laboratory won the guidance contract for the Titan II, the first all-inertial Air Force ICBM, with AC Spark Plug as the subcontractor for the inertial platforms and IBM for the guidance computers.[97] In the post-Sputnik missile buildup (1957–63) the Air Force pumped $9 million a year into the Instrumentation Laboratory for ballistic missile guidance research and development.[98]

The Killian Panel gave an equal boost to Navy ambitions by endorsing a sea leg of the nuclear triad. Fearing that conventional surface weapons might soon be obsolete, the Navy had already begun winding down its postwar fire-control contracts at the Instrumentation Laboratory in favor of new concepts like the submarine inertial navigation system (SINS).[99] Although intended, like SPIRE, as a self-contained navigation system, emphasizing long-term stability and reliability over short-term accuracy, SINS anticipated the special demands of strategic submarines for precise locational information. Its very name was classified as late as 1959.[100]

Polaris, calling as it did for "an all-weather capability to deliver from ships to strategic targets at intermediate ranges, with minimum susceptibility to countermeasures," seemed a challenge tailor-made for the Instrumentation Laboratory.[101] Having the right man (Instrumentation Laboratory graduate Samuel Forter) in the right place (the Navy's Special Projects Office) clinched the deal.[102] The laboratory won the Polaris guidance contract in late 1956. First deployed aboard the nuclear submarine fleet in 1960, the MIT-designed and General Electric–built Mark 1 guidance system weighed just 225 pounds, an order of magnitude less than the early airplane systems. Its successor, the Mark 2 for the intercontinental Polaris A3, gave even better accuracy, at one-third the size and weight.[103] Polaris firmly established the laboratory's reputation for "womb-to-tomb" systems engineering and brought in about $8 million a year at its peak in the early 1960s.

The Polaris and Titan contracts, along with smaller, and generally more basic, programs on advanced inertial systems and related components, increased the laboratory's annual budget to $20.8 million and its total staff to 1,275, including some two hundred visiting engineers on corporate liaison assignments.[104] Though formally just another division of the aeronautical engineering department, the Instrumentation Laboratory was already twenty times bigger than the rest of the department's laboratories combined, as big as Lincoln, and growing.

In 1961 the laboratory won the contract for the Apollo navigation and guidance system. Again, some old connections—NASA head James Webb and his deputy Robert Seamans—paid off. Webb had been a top executive with Sperry during the war, while Seamans had completed his doctoral thesis ("Comparison of Automatic Tracking Systems for Interceptor Aircraft") in the Instrumentation Laboratory and worked there on the A-1 bombsight before joining RCA's missile electronics division. The NASA contract was worth $4.4 million the first year, $12.8 million the next, and $25.9 million at its peak in 1969.[105] Always ready for new challenges, Draper went so far as to volunteer for the moon mission. "I fully realize my limitations as a test pilot," he told Seamans, "but I feel that my qualifications in scientific and engineering fields should be considered as a worthy background for a crew member."[106] If he never made it to the moon, his guidance system ensured that others did.

The sheer size of the Apollo contract dramatically shifted the laboratory's balance of military and civilian commitments, from virtually all military in 1961 to about half and half by 1965, but without reducing the size or influence of the military programs. With ballistic missile and satellite guidance research for the Air Force, and Poseidon and advanced inertial navigation contracts for the Navy, the military side of the ledger grew to $29.5 million by 1968.[107]

The financial weight of the Instrumentation Laboratory alone gave Draper considerable leverage within the department and the Institute. As both laboratory and department head, he juggled the books to suit his purposes. "I never fought with them [the Institute administration] about the budget," he recalled, "because I could let them give me what they wanted and then I had enough money in the laboratory, with the stroke of my own pen, to fix things the way I wanted anyway."[108]

What Draper primarily wanted was a teaching laboratory. As one colleague described that commitment: "To Draper there has never existed a dichotomy between teaching and research; the two are of one and the same fabric. Nor has he bothered often to distinguish between the formal and informal processes of education. With Stark, teaching is something that goes on through all the waking hours, consciously or instinctively, in his office, at lunch, in the laboratory, at the colloquium, or in the lecture hall; discoursing with technicians, with his colleagues, with undergraduates, with naval officers assigned to his laboratory, with all and sundry who gather about to debate and learn. . . . The Laboratory is indeed part and parcel of Stark Draper's approach to engineering education. Through it he is able to impart tangible reality to theory and to vest it with importance."[109] Sponsored projects, Draper said, offered his students the real-world experience and responsibility he believed essential for a proper engineering education. The students were "not just doing an exercise to please me when they hand in a paper or to pass before a committee, their equipment is riding the bird, and if it doesn't work, why, you know it as well as everybody else, and they know it, too."[110]

The Instrumentation Laboratory got its students, like its money, primarily from the military. For a time the officers outnumbered the civilians seven or eight to one, which actually limited the openings for nonmilitary students.[111] Into the late 1950s military officers—

typically thirty to forty a year, mostly in guidance and control—
made up about half the department's graduates.[112] To accommodate
the increasing numbers of military students, the department inaugurated a separate Weapons Systems Engineering course in 1952, under
Draper protégé Walter Wrigley.[113] Beyond the usual departmental
requirements, the curriculum included classified classes and laboratories in fire control, radar systems, weapons structures, and special
problems in the design of rockets, guided missiles, and projectiles.[114]
In any one year up to half the department's students took the Weapons Systems Engineering course.

Draper and his colleagues met regularly with the military officers
responsible for inertial guidance research and development, to com-
pare notes and discuss thesis topics. After giving a lecture on fire control at the Navy's postgraduate school in Monterey, California, Draper reported back to the Navy's administrative officer at MIT that he
had "spent several hours discussing the Weapons Systems course with
Captain Lee, Commander Smith and various members of the Post
Graduate School faculty. A number of suggestions were discussed in
working out the best method for coordinating our Graduate School
teaching here at M.I.T. with the requirements for navy officers' education."[115] The Air Force's commanding general considered the
course uniquely advantageous: "The Weapons Systems Engineering
course at the Massachusetts Institute of Technology, conducted by
Dr. C. S. Draper, is especially valuable to us because of the close
association of the students and staff with current Air Force research
and development projects, such as Spire and Lincoln. There is no
other institution in the United States that can provide the environment that the Massachusetts Institute of Technology does for our officer educational programs."[116] By 1958 the course had graduated
118 Air Force officers, more than all other academic programs in
aeronautical engineering combined. Ninety percent of the graduates
remained on active duty in military research and development.[117]

The laboratory always considered classified research, and classified theses, part of the cost of doing business with the military. One
aeronautics professor remarked, "It is somewhat paradoxical to realize that both classified and unclassified projects contribute to the educational aspects of the Instrumentation Laboratory."[118] Some stu-

dents wrote unclassified theses on classified projects, while others wrote unclassified theses that ended up being classified. Philip Lapp completed his master's degree in 1951 with an unclassified thesis on the theory of ballistic missile guidance theory, supported by the inertial guidance contracts with the Wright Field Armament Laboratory. By the time he completed his doctorate in 1955, all research on ballistic missile guidance, including his own thesis, was classified.[119] To make sure that secrets were kept and that students could still complete their degree requirements, Draper appointed Wrigley "thesis declassification officer" in 1956, a post he held until the end of the 1960s.[120]

No one had to tell Draper and his staff what sponsored research meant for the aeronautical engineering curriculum. Wrigley explained: "The output of the various projects in the Laboratory represent new technical information that will not appear in textbooks for a few years. Such material first appears in academic circles in graduate courses as lecture notes by the professor. The notes become formalized, books appear and in a very short time the once-new material becomes a part of the undergraduate curriculum. This pattern has been an outstanding achievement of the Instrumentation Laboratory."[121]

Ironically, one of the laboratory's most important texts almost never got published. Draper had been hoping for some time to produce a synthetic account of recent advances in inertial guidance theory and practice, research "largely unknown and unavailable to professionals in the field since so little of an unclassified nature has been written about it."[122] He thought he had an understanding with the Air Force about subsidizing a three-volume text, but learned otherwise after he had already published the first volume and set up the other two. He had to dip into a special overhead account for $86,000 to pay the printer, raising a few eyebrows even among the generally forgiving (where it concerned the I-Lab) MIT administration. "He realizes that he has spent a considerable sum without authorization and is penitent," commented the dean of engineering.[123] In the end, Draper got his money, and aeronautics got the classic *Instrument Engineering*.[124] Even on the undergraduate level, instrument engineering became, as Draper put it, "an integral part of undergraduate teaching in aeronautical engineering . . . on the same level of importance as aerodynamics, structures, and power plants."[125]

The growing number of students who studied in the Instrumentation Laboratory give some measure of its educational impact. From 1946 to 1952, an average of twenty students a year wrote theses there. From 1953 to 1964 the average was up to fifty students.[126] Hundreds of others worked in the laboratory, part time during the academic year or full time during the summer.[127] By 1969 the laboratory boasted nearly eight hundred alumni. Laboratory staff taught dozens of courses for the department, with combined enrollments of hundreds of students a year.[128]

Draper ran his laboratory more like a corporation than a university department. It even looked like the old factory it once had been. "To this day I swear I can walk through the corridors and still smell shoe polish," Seamans later joked.[129] Draper never cared much for glistening laboratories and plush offices anyway. "I've lived in broom closets all my life," he liked to say. He preferred stalking the laboratory in his green visor, surprising everyone from experienced engineers to newly hired lathe operators with probing questions and sage advice. Underneath the affected informality, Draper meant business. Ralph Ragan, one of the program managers in those days, recalled: "As for the Athenian Democracy, few group leaders would accuse Doc of having a light management touch. Rather, micromanagement was the order of the day. The key technology was managed on a daily basis—sometimes seven days a week and at night."[130]

The laboratory introduced the latest advances in fire control and inertial guidance to industry as well as the military. In the summer of 1951 it organized a twelve-week seminar for sixteen IBM engineers and three engineers assigned by the Air Force Armament Laboratory: "The object of the course was to attempt to train this group for undertaking development work for the U.S. Air Force in the field of airborne armament equipment."[131] In 1953 Seamans coordinated a similar summer course on automatic control for eighty-six representatives from aerospace companies and federal laboratories, while Draper ran a fall symposium on airborne fire control and aircraft flight control for two hundred industry and government scientists and engineers.[132]

Continuing a pattern begun with Sperry during the war, the laboratory put hundreds of corporate engineers on the payroll, giving them the hands-on experience essential to the successful transfer of complex technology from laboratory to production. At the height of the Polaris, Titan, and Apollo programs, the laboratory had 286 resident engineers from AC Spark Plug (seventy), Raytheon (fifty-one), Bendix (seventy-two), Kollsman Instrument (twenty), Honeywell (ten), and other companies.[133] From 1954 to 1971, AC Spark Plug engineers logged 91,662 man-days at the Instrumentation Laboratory; Bendix, 42,908; General Electric, 16,255; Honeywell, 14,628; IBM, 16,728; and Kollsman, 16,792.[134] Draper admitted he kept salaries low to encourage turnover to industry. For whatever reason, from 1946 to 1970 the laboratory sent 931 people on to industry, many of them to Raytheon, Honeywell, GE, Bendix, and other direct contractors.[135]

Seeking closer ties to the laboratory and better access to its graduates, industrial contractors set up divisional laboratories nearby and hired Draper graduates to staff them. AC Spark Plug established a branch R&D facility in Wakefield, Massachusetts, in 1959 and brought in two of Draper's former inertial guidance experts to run it.[136] In 1955 RCA's Airborne Systems Laboratory (later the Missile Electronics and Controls division) in Burlington, Massachusetts, hired away Seamans, who in turn brought aboard several other Instrumentation Laboratory veterans.[137] Northrop's Nortronics division, collaborating with the laboratory on a miniaturized inertial ship navigation system for the Polaris program, set up a branch facility in Norwood, Massachusetts, in 1959 and hired a former laboratory engineer as director. All but Nortronics were clustered along what would become Route 128.

Recent graduates of the Instrumentation Laboratory and experienced staff members alike were aggressively recruited by industry. General Motors took out full-page advertisements in Boston newspapers announcing the opening of its new AC Spark Plug division, urging engineers to "step into the space age with the greatest name in industry. . . General Motors."[138] Sperry countered with ads in *Technology Review*, MIT's glossy alumni magazine, touting its recent

work on SINS: "To provide exact navigation data, Sperry is developing for the Navy advanced electronic and gyroscopic systems that will
stabilize the sub, continuously establish its precise position and true
speed, and feed target data automatically into the missile's guidance
system. *That's* the kind of assignment you will get at Sperry. . . .
Check Sperry—now!"[139]

Draper's entrepreneurial spirit proved contagious. By 1965 the Instrumentation Laboratory had spun off twenty-seven companies,
with nine hundred employees and total sales of $14 million.[140] Near-
ly all of them specialized in some aspect of inertial guidance analysis,
testing, and manufacture (nine), circuit and systems design (eight), or
computer and logic design (four). Three commercialized the modu-
lar electronics packages developed for Polaris. Most of the spin-off
companies started by consulting and then went into manufacturing.
Like their parent, they did almost all their business with the DOD or
its industrial contractors. To keep pace with the latest developments,
they stayed close to home, either in old warehouses in Cambridge,
near the Instrumentation Laboratory and the Air Force Cambridge
Research Center, or out in Lexington and Concord, near Lincoln
Laboratory and Hanscom Field. Dynamics Research, one of the
most financially successful, followed the typical pattern. Founded in
1955 by two engineers who had worked on an Air Force guidance program, it initially specialized in analyzing inertial guidance and navigation systems and later expanded into designing and manufacturing
components and subassemblies for these systems. Along the way it
grew from a couple of consulting engineers to a corporation headquartered in Lexington with three hundred employees and $4.3 mil-
lion in annual sales. By 1971 its engineering staff included seventeen
former Instrumentation Laboratory members, who had logged 1,789
cumulative man-days visiting their former associates.[141]

Draper himself even considered going the profit-making route at
one time. In 1963 he talked seriously with Edward Bowles and Ralph
Ragan (a former student and manager of Raytheon's guidance and
reentry systems division) about joining Raytheon, either by becoming head of an independent corporate laboratory or by bringing some
part of the Instrumentation Laboratory along with him.[142] But in the

end he chose the relative autonomy of an academic laboratory over the lure of big money.

Draper and his colleagues never denied how much their academic specialty had come to mirror military interests and money. By the late 1960s, however, some of them began questioning the department's overwhelming dependence on defense contracts, and the implications for their research and teaching. The visiting committee acknowledged that virtually all the graduate students owed their educations to federal (military) contracts, meaning that "there are areas of graduate research which do not get support—they lack 'sex appeal.'"[143] Leon Trilling, who had come up through the ranks in the department, openly deplored the inflexibility and short-sightedness of defense contracts, with their unsettling patterns of boom and bust and their external research agendas. He urged his colleagues "to consider more than we have the economy, reliability, producibility, and safety aspects of air vehicles as contrasted to performance," and to build themselves a financial "flywheel" from the overhead on the defense contracts for pursuing civilian technology.[144]

Draper too felt more of a need to emphasize his laboratory's contributions to civilian technology. Defense projects predominated, he explained, only "because long-range consistent funding for military work effectively using Laboratory capabilities could be obtained while support for civilian tasks could not be found."[145] Aside from the Apollo navigation system, itself a spinoff from military technology, support for civilian efforts just never materialized.

Jerome Hunsaker had anticipated as much. For thirty years—as MIT's first instructor in aeronautics, its first doctoral candidate, and as founding (and longtime) head of its department—he had watched the rising tide of military interest and had increasingly worried about its consequences. In 1948 he prepared for the development office a historical sketch of his department's research and teaching, a history that might have opened his colleagues' eyes to the pervasive military presence in MIT aeronautics. Recounting his own assignment in 1914 as a Navy officer to teach the inaugural courses, his successor's appointment as Assistant Secretary of Navy Aeronautics in 1926, the numbers of Army and Navy and Air Force officers detailed to the program for specialized training, the amount of testing and research done for the armed forces, and the percentage of graduates who had gone to work for the military establishment all led him to speculate at the end: "Perhaps there should be envisioned an aeronautical industry without a military object. The past says no; the immediate future, again, no; but work towards such an industry in the distant future is an object deserving of utmost financial effort."[146] Hunsaker stepped down as department chairman three years later and did not live to see that future. His successors envisioned a far different future, and Hunsaker's dream was more distant still.

4 | Sonic Boom

When Nicholas Hoff came West from Brooklyn Polytechnic to head Stanford's aeronautical engineering program in 1957, he inherited a struggling division of mechanical engineering with two aging faculty members, a handful of students, and an annual research budget of $4,500. In just six years, he turned it into one of the top departments in the country, with a faculty of twelve, 179 graduate students, and a research budget of $657,546.[1] Even more remarkably, he did it all at no financial cost to the university. With contract overhead, industrial affiliates' support, and tuition, the department more than paid its own way. No wonder Terman singled it out in a letter to the university president as "An Example of a Successful Graduate Department" for others to emulate.[2]

Of course, where that money came from told quite a story of the nature of that success. Nearly all of it came from military contracts or from military contractors. Lockheed's ties to the program were especially close. It relocated its missiles and space division from southern California to nearby Sunnyvale and set up a complementary research laboratory in the Stanford Industrial Park. Hundreds of Lockheed employees participated in the honors cooperative program. The company also sent some of its researchers to teach at Stanford and hired hundreds of new employees directly out of graduate school. While the industrial and academic worlds were each transformed by their common dependence on defense funding, they were transforming each other through the intermingling of people and money between the two. Even more than electronics, postwar aeronautics owed its distinctive intellectual character and direction to the specific objectives of its military patrons.

Getting off the Ground

Stanford first became a recognized center of aeronautical research between the wars, under the direction of William Durand. Durand, along with his friend and colleague Harris Ryan, had been a protégé of the great engineering educator Robert Thurston at Cornell. As head of Cornell's graduate program in naval architecture and marine engineering, Durand had earned his reputation for classic studies of propeller design. Passed over for a well-deserved promotion, he left for Stanford in 1904, bringing Ryan and Everett P. Lesley, one of his former graduate students and research collaborators, with him. Following Thurston's example, Durand considered commercial projects a natural extension of, and complement to, his academic duties, and consulted for a number of large western hydroelectric and water supply projects. [3]

On the eve of World War I, Durand unexpectedly found himself at the center of the American aeronautical engineering community. Though he had never worked directly in aerodynamics (nor even flown in an airplane), Durand's research in fluid mechanics and marine propeller design made him an expert at a time when only Europeans considered the subject a serious academic specialty. As a member of a special presidential committee, Durand played an important role in establishing the National Advisory Committee for Aeronautics (NACA) in 1915, then served as one of its initial members and later as its second chairman. [4]

Eager to turn opportunity to advantage, Durand persuaded the NACA to fund a study of propellers at Stanford aimed at providing the same kind of practical design data for airplanes that his earlier towing basin tests had provided for ships. Durand's $4,000 contract for building a wind tunnel and related measuring instruments represented 40 percent of the NACA's entire research budget and was larger than all its other university contracts (with MIT, Columbia, and Cornell) combined. The NACA contract, renewed annually for a decade, put Stanford on the map as a center of academic aeronautical engineering research. Following Durand's detailed instructions, Lesley undertook a series of trials on a family of two-blade models. Although this research offered no new theoretical insights, it gave practicing designers for the first time precise specifications for choosing the proper propeller for any particular airframe and application.[5]

The NACA contracts had surprisingly little impact on Stanford's educational program, however. "It is significant that these studies of propellers were conducted with little or no involvement of graduate students," Terman later pointed out. "Neither were they used as a vehicle to recruit and develop young faculty members of outstanding promise. In spite of his diverse accomplishments and leadership qualities of high order, Durand was not notable as an organizer of academic programs or as a developer of faculty talent."[6]

If Durand missed the opportunity to build an academic empire, he certainly raised enough money to have done it. As a liaison officer during the war he had gotten acquainted with Harry Guggenheim, a young Navy officer with a passion for aviation and a personal fortune to match. Convinced that the war had distorted the proper development of the airplane by placing undue emphasis on "speed, maneuverability, and other military characteristics, while aerodynamic safety which is of a secondary consideration in war has been neglected," Guggenheim determined to do what he could to redress the balance.[7] He convinced his father, heir to the famous mining fortune, to establish a private foundation for the support of civilian aviation. In January 1926 they founded the Daniel Guggenheim Fund for the Promotion of Aeronautics, with Harry Guggenheim as president and a $2.5 million endowment. Modest enough compared with the Rockefeller Foundation and other scientific philanthropies of the day, the Fund nonetheless represented a sizable investment in an infant industry.[8]

The Guggenheims believed that they could get the most for their money in influencing the future direction of the industry by funding higher education. Through sizable grants for research and teaching, they planned to help train a new generation of aeronautical engineers more oriented toward civilian industry.

As one of the Fund's trustees, Durand had no trouble getting money. Learning that Caltech's Robert Millikan was negotiating with the Fund for a half-million-dollar endowment for aeronautical research, Durand promptly prepared his own proposal (over Stanford president Ray Wilbur's signature) and personally delivered it to Harry Guggenheim on May 14, 1926, just days ahead of Millikan. Durand asked for a $330,000 endowment for hiring two professors and a junior instructor, and funds for upgrading Stanford's aging wind tunnel. That August, Harry Guggenheim publicly announced the award of "a fund amounting in all to the income from a sum of approximately three hundred thousand dollars to Leland Stanford University for the conduct of study and experimentation in the art and science of aeronautics and aviation," enough, he estimated, for ten years of research and teaching.[9]

With Guggenheim support the aeronautical engineering program added Alfred Niles, a young structural engineer at the Army's flight research center at McCook Field in Ohio, and Elliott Reid, a rising star in aerodynamics at NACA's Langley Laboratory in Virginia. Niles, thirty-three and an MIT graduate, headed the structures section at McCook Field and had recently published an important monograph on airplane design for the Army.[10] Reid had joined NACA straight out of Michigan's aeronautics program, helped design the famous NACA low-drag cowling, and advanced to head of one of the laboratory's wind tunnel sections. At twenty-seven, he became Stanford's youngest full professor.[11]

Using the Guggenheim grant, Stanford also replaced its aging Aerodynamics Laboratory, a facility so decrepit that even the dean admitted "that the good of the University as a whole justifies demolishing this structure at once."[12] The new center included classrooms, library, shop, offices, and—the centerpiece—a 90-mph wind tunnel.

Thus well equipped and funded, Lesley, Reid, and Niles (Durand formally retired in 1924) fashioned an aggressive and commercially oriented research and teaching program.[13] They launched important new research, introduced innovative courses, wrote new texts, and trained some two hundred students, who went on to leave their marks on the industry. Lesley extended his earlier propeller studies into new configurations, including variable pitch propellers and three- and four-blade contrarotating tandem propellers. Reid focused on the boundary layer (the crucial film of air in contact with an airfoil), with an eye toward predicting its behavior theoretically and controlling it experimentally. Niles studied a range of structural problems, from classic stress analysis to such detailed studies as landing gears and the behavior of airplane structures with cutouts. [14]

Although the Guggenheim money provided financial security, the aeronautics program continued to attract NACA and other smaller contracts as well. In a good year these generated several thousand dollars in "profit," an invaluable insurance policy at a time when the Depression necessitated a 5 percent budget cut across the board at the university. [15]

Niles and Reid reinvigorated the teaching program too, most notably at the graduate level. Niles prepared a range of new courses in structural theory, for both undergraduate civil engineers and advanced students of structural design. Hard of hearing and, consequently, somewhat distant and reserved in the lecture hall, he nonetheless became a highly respected and popular instructor. Reid, on the other hand, was remembered for his tough questions and tougher grades. "In the classroom he insisted on a precision of understanding and expression beyond that required by most teachers," one former student recalled. "His caustic remarks when his high standards were not met made his class meetings at first a formidable experience. Later his students came to regard his methods with exasperated affection."[16] Reid taught graduate courses in aerodynamics, fluid mechanics, and related areas.

Their textbooks became classics. Niles's *Airplane Design* (1929), written in collaboration with his former McCook Field assistant Joseph Newell, remained "the bible of aircraft structural design into the 1950s." Reid's *Applied Wing Theory* (1932) was as rigorous and precise as his lectures. "If a point was plotted on a graph by Elliott Reid," said one student, "you knew that that point was as close to the right place as human care and labor could possibly make it."[17] In 1934 Stanford was recognized by the American Council on Education as one of three American universities (MIT and Caltech were the other two) fully accredited to offer the doctorate in aeronautical engineering, though in practice it awarded only the two-year "engineer's" degree.[18]

The Guggenheim Laboratory left an enduring legacy through the careers of the many students who trained there. Over the ten years of the original grant, 201 students attended classes offered by the laboratory's staff. Seventy-one completed a one-year course of study in either aerodynamics or structures. Thirty-four earned engineer's degrees in aeronautical engineering.[19] A number worked their way through school as research assistants in the wind tunnel, making $75 to $150 a month.[20] Thanks to Reid, some of the best went on to Langley and eventually found their way back to the West Coast after the NACA opened its new aerodynamics laboratory in 1939 in Sunnyvale, seven miles from Stanford. H. Julian Allen, for instance, earned his reputation at Langley for his new theory of subsonic airfoils, then transferred to the NACA's new research center as a specialist in high-speed aerodynamics and head of the theoretical group. John Parsons served his apprenticeship in Langley's full-scale wind tunnel, led the design team on its first high-speed wind tunnel, and later joined Allen at Ames. John Wheatley did pioneering studies of rotating wing aircraft (helicopters) at Langley before taking a job with Douglas. Altogether, nine Stanford graduates put in some time at Langley in the 1930s.[21]

Other Stanford graduates went directly into industry. At Douglas, John Buckwalter became project engineer for the DC-4 and Leo Devlin project engineer for the DC-5. Edward Wells rose to chief engineer at Boeing, Philip Coleman to chief aerodynamics engineer at Lockheed, and Kenneth Ridley to chief engineer at Hughes. By the late 1930s, Stanford had placed some forty aeronautical engineering graduates throughout the industry, most of them on the West Coast, and one at Mitsubishi Aircraft's wind tunnel.[22]

Missed Opportunities

The Guggenheim money ran out in 1939, however, and the remaining NACA contracts barely covered expenses. Guggenheim himself had no more money to give.[23] The NACA's new laboratory offered bright promise for the future but, despite Niles's best promotional efforts, had nothing to offer Stanford at the moment beyond jobs for the graduates.[24]

To keep the program going, Reid reversed his long-standing prohibition against commercial testing contracts and opened the wind tunnel to industry. The laboratory would pay its own way. Contracts with North American (for the B-29 prototype), Hughes (for wing designs), and S. Morgan Company (for a wind turbine) earned the laboratory some $10,000 in 1940.[25] But the effort took its toll. Reid confessed that to fulfill the contracts he had "given up outdoor exercise, vacations, the majority of his Saturdays, Sundays and evenings, all vestiges of normal social life, and . . . become a stranger to his wife and daughter."[26] His students, who put in 6,726 collective hours on the tests, started falling asleep in their classes. His chairman even began questioning the impact on Reid's own teaching. "These tests merely confirm my previous observations that commercial testing and student instruction can not be successfully carried on simultaneously by the same staff," he told Stanford's president. "Frankly, I believe these tests will lead us into temptation—good teaching may be sacrificed for expected profits."[27] Reid denied the charge, claiming that since "such work provides the only known means of keeping the faculty—and, therefore the graduate students—abreast of current developments in this field of ultra-rapid progress, it is an obvious prerequisite to the maintenance of a high academic reputation."[28] In any case, the contracts were scarcely enough to keep the program aloft, much less assure its future.

Ultimately, the kind of large-scale wartime contract that might have positioned Stanford for leadership in postwar aeronautics proved elusive. In late 1943, a year before the Army officially established the Jet Propulsion Laboratory (JPL) at Caltech, Army Ordnance officers approached Stanford about managing a secret rocket research program.[29] Specifically, they wanted a laboratory to develop small rockets for infantry and aircraft applications, with strong participation by Stanford faculty, including Niles and Reid. Disappointed that Stanford had so far played such a limited role in the war effort, the dean of engineering pushed hard for the contract. "Personally, I should like very much to see Stanford undertake such a major war research project," he told the university's president. "There are such at the

University of California and at the California Institute of Technology. I believe it would give members of the faculty and the Stanford family a feeling that Stanford was assuming leadership in the war effort. And above all else I would hope that we could succeed in making such major contribution in spite of the war manpower shortages."[30] He approached Terman at RRL about how to go about organizing and running such an enterprise, but in the end Stanford lost the $3 million contract to Caltech's JPL, which grew into a wartime giant.[31]

Thwarted in their efforts to bring a major aeronautics laboratory to Stanford, Niles and Reid set out to rebuild Stanford aeronautics by raising a second endowment from the companies that had benefited most from Stanford's graduates. Impressed by the example of Caltech, which had collected more than a million dollars for a high-speed wind tunnel from a consortium of southern California airframe companies, they prepared a detailed prospectus, "Post-War Aeronautical Engineering Training and Research Program for Stanford University," in the spring of 1944 and sent it around to selected industry executives for comment.[32]

In making their pitch, Niles and Reid positioned Stanford at the center of the western aeronautical engineering industry, both geographically (midway between Boeing on the north and Lockheed, Douglas, North American, and Consolidated Vultee on the south, and close to the NACA's facility in Sunnyvale) and intellectually ("in that broad intermediate field which lies between the extremely urgent ones of current-model development and the basic one so comprehensive that it can be undertaken only by federal agencies—which, unfortunately grind slow as well as fine"). They offered industry a broad research program and promised contributors access not only to a new wind tunnel but "to the nation's most promising engineers—men so unusually able and so thoroughly trained as to represent gilt-edge investments to potential employers." Nor did they ignore bottom-line considerations, pointing out that new tax laws allowed corporations to write off virtually all of their gifts to higher education. Under those rules, a $140,000 contribution to Stanford would cost only about $14,000 in real money. "Doesn't our plan appeal more than the thought of just tossing the money into the general government pot?" they asked.[33]

Anticipating a postwar slump, the aircraft industry gave Niles and Reid a surprisingly cool reception. "The proposal which you have outlined comes about a year too late," Clarence "Kelly" Johnson, famed designer of the P-38 Lightning and Lockheed's chief research engineer, told them.[34] Like most of its competitors, Lockheed had already made its postwar plans and was not looking for any long-term academic investments. Douglas's chief engineer explained that from his company's point of view, the tax angle had been worn "threadbare," and that in any case Douglas had always gotten all the Stanford men it wanted without paying for their educations: "We have not in the past found it necessary to underwrite fellowships and this does not seem to be the time to start."[35]

By the fall of 1947 Reid and Niles had completed the last of their commercial contracts, fired the secretary, and closed the books on twenty years of the Guggenheim Laboratory. Reid penned a poignant epitaph: "Thus, after twelve years of endowed existence and eight in the status of quasi-orphan—during which period many of the present leaders of aeronautical research and design were trained here—the Stanford establishment for instruction and research in Aeronautical Engineering, once renowned for pioneering accomplishment, now consists of two middle-aged professors, some student assistants, a pitifully obsolete wind tunnel, a library and miscellaneous laboratory equipment of considerable value—and a hoard of invaluable teaching and research experience."[36]

The Missile Gap

As expected, the American aircraft industry retrenched sharply after the war. The government canceled $9 billion worth of aircraft contracts on V-J day, and $12 billion more by the end of 1945. By 1947 industry sales had fallen from a wartime high of $16 billion (in 1944) to $1.2 billion, with employment and profits dropping commensurately. Established firms took huge losses and closed most of their new war plants, while the "war babies" and other marginal firms went out of business altogether.[37]

The Cold War quickly brought the industry out of its tailspin, though. The National Security Act of 1947 created (along with the

Department of Defense) a separate Air Force, and with it a zealous new constituency for aircraft procurement. The same year, an important presidential commission, named for its chairman, Thomas Finletter, concluded that air power would be the keystone of the country's future defense and strongly endorsed rebuilding the industry with massive defense contracts. Finletter got an unparalleled opportunity to put his own recommendations into practice when he was appointed Secretary of the Air Force in 1949. With the Korean War came an additional $8 billion allocation for the purchase of aircraft, which brought the industry close to its wartime budget high.

The Cold War also introduced a new variable into the strategic equation—the ballistic missile. Convinced that rockets could not be made accurate or reliable enough to replace manned bombers for some time, the military establishment limited its program to anti-aircraft missiles, long-distance cruise missiles, and tests with captured German V-2s in the immediate postwar years. The first ballistic missile study contract went to Consolidated (Convair) in 1946 and was canceled a year later as an economy measure. Then came the hydrogen bomb in 1952 (with an explosive power that made accuracy far less critical) and secret intelligence about Soviet nuclear weapon and ICBM developments. In response, the Air Force established a special Strategic Missiles Evaluation Committee in 1953, which gave top priority to ballistic missile research and development under "missile czar" General Bernard A. Schriever.[38]

Lockheed was one company that quickly read the writing on the wall. It had earned more headlines than money in the 1920s with record-setting flights by Wiley Post and other famous test pilots, gone bankrupt in 1932, and recovered with its acclaimed all-metal Electra passenger series just in time to cash in on the mobilization bonanza. The war transformed Lockheed into an industry giant and a major defense contractor. It sold 10,000 copies of Kelly Johnson's P-38 Lightnings, 20,000 aircraft altogether, and earned $2 billion. Along with its competitors, however, Lockheed found postwar commercial aviation a losing proposition. "There's money in the commercial airline market," one company president quipped. "We know because we put it there."[39] Lockheed kept aloft by converting its C-69 transport into the commercial L-049 Constellation, and with military sales of its C-130 Hercules troop transporter and F-104 Starfighter, the work-horse of the Korean War.[40]

Lockheed, like other traditional aircraft companies entering the missile age, found itself poorly prepared for the unprecedented challenges of hypersonic speeds, exotic materials, and sophisticated guidance systems. Ballistic missiles and satellites changed the rules of the game as much for the defense contractors as the defense analysts.[41] Just as the turbojet revolution had dramatically shifted the balance of power in the aircraft power plant industry from conventional piston-engine manufacturers to companies with experience in high-speed turbines like GE and Westinghouse, so the missile revolution gave the edge to new companies like Ramo-Wooldridge, with experience in electronics, guidance, or systems engineering. With 80 percent of their sales to the DOD, and with missiles beginning to look like a significant share of that market, airframe manufacturers had no real alternative but to learn to compete in these new high-tech fields.

For Lockheed, the challenge was especially daunting. As late as 1956 it had no missiles sales at all. To compete for its share of the missiles and space business, Lockheed had to learn new technologies and learn them fast, or risk being closed out of the new growth market.

Lockheed saw one important opening in space-based reconnaissance. The same 1954 Killian Report that had given top priority to developing the ICBM and the DEW Line had given equal emphasis to developing high technology intelligence capability. Lockheed won the subsequent contract for an ultrahigh-altitude photo-reconnaissance aircraft with the U-2, designed by Kelly Johnson and assembled by his famous Skunk Works team in less than three months. Under CIA sponsorship, the U-2 began overflights of the Soviet Union in the summer of 1956.[42]

A spy plane, even one as good as the U-2, offered at best a temporary, and vulnerable, window. Soviet antiaircraft missiles finally caught up with the U-2 (as American experts expected they would) on May 1, 1960, when the Soviets shot down and captured U-2 pilot Gary Powers.[43] Only spy satellites promised a long-term edge in espionage. The Air Force had been considering such an option since the end of the Second World War. In 1946 the RAND Corporation (at that point still a division of Douglas Aircraft, with funding from the Air Force) issued the first in a series of secret reports on building and deploying reconnaissance satellites.

Lockheed followed this work closely and hired several of the principal authors of the RAND reports. With that kind of insider knowledge and connections, Lockheed beat out RCA and Martin in the initial Air Force reconnaissance satellite design competition in 1956.[44] Lockheed's entry called for the spy camera to be carried aboard a second stage, dubbed the Agena, of an Atlas rocket. The satellite would then transmit its data back to earth either by television scanning or by ejecting the film capsule itself.[45]

Simultaneously, Lockheed set its sights on the emerging market for fleet ballistic missiles. The Killian Report had also endorsed a sea-launched, intermediate-range ballistic missile system to complement the ICBM program. The Navy's Special Projects Office, initially in partnership with the Army and later on its own, moved aggressively to develop a solid-fueled version of the Jupiter rocket for submarines.[46] Lockheed won the study contract for the design of the missile itself (renamed Polaris in late 1956) while Draper's Instrumentation Laboratory won the contract for the inertial guidance system.

To demonstrate to its military clients its commitment to the missiles and space business, Lockheed established a new Missiles Systems Division in 1954 at its Burbank, California, headquarters.[47] The military preferred a separate division because that offered tighter control over individual projects. Lockheed's management likewise favored an independent organizational structure as a way of insulating the new programs from a corporate culture still dominated by airplane enthusiasts.

Convinced that the fledgling division required an infusion of outside scientific talent (and with an eye toward future contracts as well), top management brought in a new team headed by retired Air Force General E. P. Quesada in 1954. Quesada believed that the best way to remake Lockheed in a high technology image would be to foster closer collaboration with universities, where new knowledge was being created and where the best young scientists and engineers were being trained. He promised to run his division "more like a university than a hardheaded business," to hire the best research talents he could find, pay them top salaries, and then turn them loose to follow their own instincts. "Scientists function best when they know they can work without dictation and develop theories irrespective of military contracts," he said. "We hope that through our ability to be original we will be able to translate a military requirement into a military weapon." Quesada recruited men like Ernest Krause, former head of nucleonics at the Naval Research Laboratory, who shared his conviction that modern military and industrial laboratories should be modeled on universities. Krause had been a vocal supporter of NRL as a "university of applied research." Quesada called his new research facility a "campus" and told his staff that he would "encourage them to soak up academic atmosphere by letting them teach part-time at three nearby universities: Cal Tech, U.C.L.A., and U.S.C."[48]

Quesada's university-in-exile almost immediately found itself at odds with the rest of Lockheed's more traditional corporate culture. Quesada quit, under pressure, in November 1955, followed a month later by Krause and fifteen other top Lockheed missile scientists, leaving Lockheed with a $31 million missile backlog.[49] Krause and some of his colleagues formed their own company, Systems Research Group, which eventually became part of Ford's aerospace division.

Having failed to create its own in-house "university," Lockheed settled on an alternative strategy—going into partnership with one. Lockheed had supported academic research on a modest scale for some time, funding the high-speed wind tunnel at Caltech and offering graduate fellowships in selected fields. But the company recognized that competing in the missile business would demand updating the company's conventional expertise in aircraft manufacturing with the key technologies of the missile age—electronics, guidance and control, and ultrahigh-temperature structures and materials. It would take an all-out effort to attract top scientific and engineering talent. And it would require closer ties with an increasingly active NACA missile research program.

After a careful study of possible sites, including ones near MIT and Princeton, Lockheed concluded that the Santa Clara Valley offered the best combination of academic resources, land value, potential industrial suppliers, and government and military connections. Such a location was near Stanford, the NACA's Ames Research Center (and its ongoing studies of reentry and hypersonic aerodynamics), im-

portant electronic components makers, and possible missile test sites
in the Santa Cruz mountains. In February 1956, Lockheed president
Robert Gross announced that the company was transferring its missile system division from Van Nuys to a 275-acre site at Sunnyvale,
with a research laboratory for advanced studies in missiles and un-
manned aircraft on a 22-acre site in the Stanford Industrial Park. [50] In
selecting the Stanford location, Gross stressed the university's reputation in electronics rather than aeronautics. With the increasing complexity and sophistication of guidance and avionics systems, Lockheed felt it could no longer rely on outside electronics expertise and
would have to develop its own. "To handle these big defense systems
involving billions not millions of dollars and covering a multitude of
sciences, we must broaden and deepen our competence into fields
related to ours," noted Gross. "The one I think of as most logical and
natural is electronics."[51]

Although attracted initially by Stanford's expertise in electronics,
Lockheed management also recognized the potential advantages of a
revitalized program in aeronautical engineering. To rebuild Stanford's faltering program in aeronautics to its own advantage, Lockheed initiated negotiations with the university that would ultimately
change the character and direction of both the company and the university's research programs.

Lockheed's plans centered on Nicholas Hoff, head of the aeronautical engineering department at Brooklyn Polytechnic Institute
and one of the company's top missile consultants. A generation younger than his fellow Hungarian aeronautical engineer Theodore von
Karman, whom he idolized, Hoff spent a decade as a designer for
Hungarian and German aircraft firms before coming to Stanford in
1939 to study with the famous Russian structural engineer Stephen
Timoshenko. At Stanford, he worked also with Niles and the aeronautical engineers and completed his degree in 1942. Thanks to a
recommendation from von Karman, who had been watching his career with growing interest, Hoff promptly landed a job teaching structures in a new department of aeronautical engineering at Brooklyn
Polytechnic Institute. [52]

Hoff proved himself a skilled administrator and aggressive department builder at Brooklyn. During the war he expanded his previous
research on monocoque structures for the NACA, testing scale mod-

els and developing new methods for calculating stress, and served on the NACA technical committee responsible for coordinating university and industry research on structures.

He later parlayed his wartime contacts and contracts into a top-flight academic research program, winning contracts from the NACA, the Navy, and the Air Force for studies of aircraft structures, and from the Bureau of Ships for confidential analyses of submarine design. Using those contracts he recruited a dozen faculty members and several dozen graduate students. Some of the best students he hired back into the department and sent others on to distinguished careers at Cornell, Rutgers, George Washington, and other universities, and in industry. Many eventually found their way onto advisory panels at ONR and the Air Force Office of Scientific Research (AFOSR). "It was even nicer to talk to former students when I needed money," Hoff recalled.[53]

Hoff's own research graphically plotted the shifting priorities of the aerospace industry across the sound barrier into hypersonics. From wartime studies of general instability in monocoques with cutouts (knowledge useful for building large conventional bombers) Hoff moved toward thermal buckling of wing panels at supersonic speeds (vital in the design of high-speed fighters).[54] Under contract to the Wright Air Development Center (the successor to McCook Field), he devised techniques for calculating thermal stresses on wing structures, in the hope, he said, that they "will be of some practical help to designers of supersonic aircraft."[55] He urged his colleagues in structures to pay serious attention to the new challenges of time and temperature lest they surrender their field to "thermodynamicists, physicists, and progressive aerodynamicists."[56] Hoff campaigned vigorously for an updated aircraft structures curriculum. He continued to serve on important military advisory panels and as consultant to a number of companies, notably Lockheed, on aerodynamic heating during missile reentry.

Impressed by Hoff's contributions on that consulting assignment, Willis Hawkins, temporarily in charge of Lockheed's missiles program, offered him a full-time job. When Hoff declined, Hawkins came back with a counteroffer. Would Hoff consider going to Stanford as professor and Lockheed consultant, with Lockheed paying half his salary over the first five years and offering some significant consulting opportunities as well? Hawkins explained Lockheed's new corporate strategy, especially its increasing need for well-trained research engineers, and offered to discuss the proposal with Terman, whom he usually saw once a week.[57]

Liftoff

Lockheed's initiative could not have been more timely. As dean, Terman had watched aeronautical engineering slide from distinction to insignificance. By 1954 it was attracting only a couple of students a year, bringing in no contract money, and was, in Terman's words, "essentially dead."[58] Even the head of mechanical engineering agreed that "during the next five years we must either have improved our *aeronautical division* greatly, as measured by student interest, or else we should abandon it altogether since we cannot afford to support an unpopular division in that field."[59] Terman laid the blame for Stanford's decline directly on "a staff inherited from the prewar period that has not kept up with the developments of the past fifteen years," and who "lacked the type of leadership that could find money to finance the modern facilities and the new staff required to keep Stanford in the forefront of aeronautical developments."[60]

Terman was about to deliver the final blow when a group of alumni, hearing rumors of the decision, offered to raise a "war chest" from the aircraft industry to save the program. Led by John Buckwalter of Douglas and Philip Coleman of Lockheed, they asked each major western airframe company to pledge $5,000 a year for five years to put the program back on its feet and into a position to once again attract outside support.[61]

With a backlog of orders and a critical shortage of trained aeronautical engineers, the industry responded quite differently to this campaign than it had to Reid and Niles's virtually identical appeal ten years before. Douglas, Boeing, Convair, Northrop, North American, Hughes, and Lockheed all promised support. Although not much by later standards, at the time Terman called the $130,000 pledged "mighty big."

With industrial funding in hand, and the prospect of Lockheed

paying for Hoff, Terman saw an opportunity he could not pass up—
the chance to build a steeple of excellence in aeronautical engineering
essentially for nothing. After negotiating (chiefly over whether Hoff
would get his own department), Terman reported back to Hawkins:
"Because Hoff has a demonstrated ability to provide the type of leadership that results in sound growth, we are setting up Aeronautical
Engineering at Stanford as an autonomous division of the School of
Engineering, and it will be given departmental status when its enrollment, research activities, etc. have established a sufficiently sound
basis to justify this step."[62] Looking back, Hoff recalled, "Lockheed
really brought me to Stanford," conceding though that "they didn't
have to twist my arm very much."[63]

To solidify its ties with the university, Lockheed loaned Stanford
Daniel Bershader, the head of its gas dynamics research program, to
teach part-time for free.[64] A specialist in high-temperature gas dynamics, Bershader had earned his doctorate in physics at Princeton
and taught there before joining Lockheed's Missile and Space Research Laboratory. His was the first of a number of joint appointments, several of which, like Bershader's, eventually led to full-time
faculty positions.

The academic program's resurgence strengthened collaboration
with the NACA's Ames Research Center as well. Though located
at nearby Sunnyvale and staffed top to bottom with Stanford graduates, Ames had contributed surprisingly little to Stanford's academic program. Much of the Center's best research in high-speed
aerodynamics—for instance, Julian Allen's breakthroughs on "blunt
body" designs for missile nose cones—was classified and therefore
not accessible to Stanford researchers. No one at Stanford was really
in a position to contribute much to the Center's work in any case.
When Ames tried to arrange advanced classes in aerodynamics
through the university, it discovered that Stanford's professors were
not prepared to teach them, and had to use in-house instructors instead. For advanced degrees it sent its best researchers all the way to
Caltech rather than just up the road to Stanford.[65]

With Lockheed's interest and Hoff's appointment, Stanford suddenly looked more attractive to Ames. To move the academic pro-

gram in aerodynamics along quickly, Hoff signed up Walter Vincenti, an old friend from student days who had gone on to earn a name for himself at Ames in transonic and supersonic aerodynamics. As head of the Center's new supersonic wind tunnel, Vincenti had supervised important research in supersonic wing design. Most recently, he had turned his attention toward aerothermodynamics, the behavior of flight surfaces at temperatures high enough to transform air from a mixture of inert gases into chemically reactive compounds. Winning the prestigious Rockefeller Public Service Award in 1955, Vincenti took a sabbatical at Cambridge University to study high-temperature gas physics. Convinced by Hoff that Stanford now offered a real chance to become the leading edge, Vincenti, who had turned down a previous offer, accepted a faculty appointment in January 1957, with funding from the industry "warchest."[66] Vincenti later brought along his former Ames colleague Milton van Dyke, a Caltech theoretician who had worked out some of the complex mathematics on the "blunt body" problem.[67]

"These appointments," Terman remarked, "have completely changed the character of the Division of Aeronautical Engineering, and have insured that Aeronautical Engineering will be a vigorous and important branch of the School of Engineering."[68] They completed the essential triangle of academic (Hoff), industrial (Bershader), and governmental (Vincenti and Van Dyke) experience and expertise at the heart of Stanford's subsequent success in aeronautics. Some indication of just how quickly these appointments turned things around was evident in the program's enrollment and budget statistics. In 1956 the department had two faculty members, twelve students (including undergraduates), and $4,500 in contracts, and awarded two engineering degrees. Two years later it had four and a half faculty, sixty-one students (all graduate), and $207,000 in contracts, and awarded nine degrees. A year after that it had ten faculty, ninety-two graduate students, and $460,000 in contracts, and awarded nineteen degrees.[69]

Lockheed's investment in Stanford (and in the region) amply confirmed the wisdom of relocating the Missiles Systems (renamed Missiles and Space in 1959) division. In 1956 Lockheed won the prime contracts both for the Navy's Polaris missile system (initially worth $62 million) and for the Air Force's Advanced Reconnaissance [Satellite] System (initially worth $12 million).

The satellite program, despite some early difficulties, quickly established itself as a substantial part of the missiles and space business, accounting for a third of the new division's revenues. The political fallout from Sputnik (in October 1957) immediately quadrupled the initial satellite contract (to $48 million), then tripled it again during the following year (to $150 million). [70] Although beaten to the punch by Sputnik, Discoverer—as Lockheed's CIA photo-reconnaissance satellite was known—offered technical capabilities the Soviet satellites would not be able match for years to come. [71] It could take high-resolution photographs and eject the film so that it could be recovered in midair, by plane, and then developed back on the ground. After a dozen failures, Discoverer 13 successfully returned its payload on August 10, 1960. Some thirty Discoverer flights followed over the next year, some of them crucial in assessing, and debunking, the so-called missile gap. [72]

While the CIA gained experience in photo-reconnaissance with Discoverer, the Air Force funded a separate Lockheed program known as SAMOS (for Satellite and Missile Observation System). Unlike the Discoverer, SAMOS employed electronic line-scanning technology to read photographic images in space and transmit them back to earth. The resulting photographs were not as high quality, but they could be obtained much more quickly. SAMOS was first launched in late 1960 and put to work watching Soviet ICBM sites and possible antiballistic missile installations. [73] In tandem, the Air Force sponsored MIDAS (for Missile Alarm Defense System). This Lockheed-designed satellite was equipped with extremely sensitive infrared detectors and placed in very high orbit, where it could continually search for the telltale heat plumes of a Soviet missile attack. [74] After two tries, a MIDAS was successfully put into orbit in late 1961, at a total estimated program cost of $423 million. [75]

On the strength of these efforts, Lockheed won a $25 million contract in 1959 to design and build the Air Force Satellite Control Facility. First put into service in the early 1960s, the Blue Cube (as it was popularly known for its modernist architecture) provided the nerve center for a worldwide system of satellites and tracking stations. Though officially an Air Force operation, the Control Facility was located on the Lockheed property in Sunnyvale and staffed largely with Lockheed employees.[76]

Lockheed dominated the imaging-satellite business until TRW began challenging it in the early 1970s. Lockheed's satellites, including successive generations of the famous Keyhole series, supplied the bulk of American photographic surveillance throughout some of the worst crises of the Cold War.[77]

Lockheed did even better in the missiles business. Success with the original Polaris system led to multimillion-dollar follow-up contracts for upgraded versions of the Polaris with increased range and accuracy, and later to billion-dollar contracts for the second- and third-generation fleet ballistic missiles, the Poseidon and Trident.[78] Lockheed served as prime contractor and systems integrator for all these programs and designed and built the special reentry vehicles for them as well.

By the late 1960s the Missiles and Space division was carrying the rest of the corporation, accounting for slightly more than a third of Lockheed's overall sales and an even greater share of its profits. Employment at the division soared from just 200 in 1956, to 9,000 in 1958, to 25,000 in 1964, with 1,200 in the Stanford Industrial Park laboratories alone, making Lockheed, by an order of magnitude, the biggest industrial employer in the region.[79]

Not surprisingly, given their relative sizes and financial strength, Lockheed had a far greater impact on Stanford than Stanford would ever have on Lockheed. Stanford, by itself, could not even begin to supply Lockheed's insatiable demand for technical expertise, though it could and did help fill some key positions. But Lockheed, as a member of aeronautics corporate associates programs, as a source of adjunct professors, as a participant in the honors cooperative program (sending up to fifty engineers a year), and perhaps most crucially, as the predominant local employer of graduating aeronautics engineers, exerted a powerful pull on Stanford's aeronautical engineering program. Lockheed's scientists and engineers, especially those at the corporate research laboratories, worked closely with their Stanford colleagues in setting the research and teaching agenda for aeronautical engineering in the space age. Lockheed's emerging priorities—in high-temperature gas dynamics, in orbital mechanics, in space vehicle design, in hypersonic structures, in guidance systems, and in plasma physics—thus became Stanford's priorities.

Virtually all of Stanford's growth in aeronautics (like Lockheed's) depended on military contracts. Hoff's first Stanford contract, $220,000 from the ONR for studies of high-temperature effects on structures, actually arrived before he did. By the fall of 1959 the department had research contracts with the Air Force's Office of Scientific Research, the ONR, the Arnold Engineering Development Center in Tullahoma, Tennessee (the Air Force's central aerodynamics and propulsion laboratory), and the Convair division of General Dynamics, totaling some $31,000 a month.[80]

More important than the sheer numbers, however, was what they signaled about the changing character of aeronautics research. Increasingly, the department's research and teaching program reflected the specific technical agendas of the missile age. As Hoff pointed out, "The major portion of this research is concerned with the effects of very high temperatures on structures, gas flow, and heat transfer as encountered in the re-entry of strategic missiles."[81]

Hoff extended his earlier studies of the behavior of structures at extreme temperatures. He developed original techniques for calculating the heat distribution and thermal stresses on different kinds of cylindrical structures, and devised methods for testing them experimentally. As Hoff began to recognize that supersonic and hypersonic speeds called into play new parameters of time and temperature, he turned his attention to creep, the gradual elongation of structures under elevated temperatures and loads.[82] After Niles retired in 1959, Hoff updated the old structures curriculum, adding classes that he said would "reflect the trend toward higher temperatures in aircraft and missiles."[83] He brought a specialist on missile structures from the Royal Aircraft Establishment in Britain to run a complementary structures laboratory, and later added the former head of applied mechanics for Lockheed's Polaris program to the structures team.

It was Vincenti who finally brought the department's aerodynamics program into the space age. Working with Lockheed engineer Ronald Smelt, Vincenti developed the so-called "hot shot" wind tunnel for studying very high temperature aerodynamics. Heating the air with a huge electric discharge, the tunnel could generate temperatures of 14,000 degrees Fahrenheit at speeds up to eighteen times the speed of sound. Vincenti and Smelt each built one for their respective institutions, Lockheed's to be used for applied research and Stanford's for more basic studies. [84] With Smelt's help, Vincenti also won a five-year contract from the Air Force for gas dynamics research with his new wind tunnel.

As a research tool, the "hot shot" tunnel was disappointing. The gigantic sparks contaminated the air, keeping the tunnel from becoming the precision instrument Vincenti and Smelt had expected. But as a teaching tool it laid the foundation for a series of courses in gas dynamics that were unique. Although undeniably "basic" in one sense, it was the industrial applications that gave these courses, like their counterparts in microwave electronics, their real importance. Hoff once described them as "dealing with the fundamentals of those particular aspects of physics and physical chemistry, such as kinetic theory, statistical mechanics and chemical kinetics, which knowledge is indispensable for a thorough understanding of the state of the air at very high altitudes when it is disturbed by a very rapidly moving object such as a re-entry missile."[85] As in structures, Lockheed had a strong corporate interest in the program. Several Lockheed employees earned degrees doing theses on the tunnel, and when Vincenti took a sabbatical on a Guggenheim Fellowship to write up his course notes as a textbook, their work contributed to his text. *An Introduction to Physical Gas Dynamics* became a standard teaching text in the field and continued to sell a quarter century later. It was a text, he admitted, in a "form dictated by the current . . . industry needs."[86]

Van Dyke, too, found himself drawn to the high-speed frontier. "Essentially, my career was sort of the Mach number increasing," he reflected. "I was subsonic when I was an undergraduate, and supersonic when I was a graduate student, and after that I went hypersonic."[87] Hoff helped him arrange an Air Force contract for studies of hypersonic flow theory. The contract was renewed in each of the next fifteen years. Building on that research, Van Dyke introduced new courses in hypersonic flow and related mathematical methods, culminating in his *Perturbation Methods in Fluid Mechanics*. "This book is the outgrowth of a succession of notes prepared for a graduate course that I have taught since 1959 in the Department of Aeronautics and Astronautics at Stanford University," he acknowledged. "It naturally draws heavily on my own research and that of my students, much of which has been supported by the Air Force Office of Scientific Research."[88] Like Hoff and Vincenti, Van Dyke became a Lockheed consultant, primarily on problems of boundary layer theory.

To move the department into the increasingly competitive field of guidance and control, Hoff hired Robert Cannon, an inertial guidance specialist from MIT with industrial experience at North American. Though as a graduate student Cannon had worked in the Instrumentation Laboratory, he had not taken his degree with Draper. The two had actually been in competition. One of Cannon's inertial guidance navigation systems had beaten out Draper's for the honor of guiding the USS *Nautilus* under the North Pole. In 1957 Cannon returned to MIT, where his research convinced Hoff that he was the person Stanford needed to round out its research and teaching program. The western aerospace industry agreed. Cannon's former supervisor at North American explained to Vincenti why a strong appointment in guidance and control was so crucial: "So far, especially in the West, the science and technology of guidance and control have grown up perforce largely in industrial laboratories. A serious need has been felt for more attention to be given to the field, in the universities and technical institutions. This applies in part to deficiencies in the curricula, which in effect make necessary a good deal of 'graduate study' on company time. Much more importantly, it applies to the lack of basic research and development which alone is best carried on in universities and technical institutions."[89]

Under Air Force sponsorship, Cannon rapidly built up a program in guidance and control in the early 1960s that rivaled those in structures and aerodynamics. He understood the necessity of keeping basic research oriented toward industrial and military needs. "There is a keen awareness to the important stimulation for basic research to be had in real problem areas and to the important need to couple research results back to the using agencies," he told his Air Force sponsors. "This will be particularly true in the contemplated guidance program."[90]

Cannon's twenty-year quest to build a gyroscope good enough to provide experimental confirmation of Einstein's theory of general relativity illustrated the subtle intertwining of Air Force and academic objectives in even the most "basic" research in guidance and control. Stanford physicist Leonard Schiff had calculated that an extremely precise gyroscope could reveal two precession effects predicted by Einstein but not by classical mechanics, and thereby provide an independent test of general relativity. Schiff talked the idea over with Cannon and with physics colleague William Fairbank, a low-temperature specialist. In the fall of 1959 the three of them began working on a gyroscope of unprecedented performance, six orders of magnitude better than anything then available.[91]

While intended to confirm one of the most esoteric theories in modern physics—"the experiment of the half century," Schiff called it—the relativity gyro attracted as much interest from the military as from the scientific community. A military scientist had in fact already proposed virtually the same experiment in a secret memorandum. For the military, confirming Einstein was not an end in itself but a critical step toward improving ballistic missile accuracy by accounting for minute gravitational effects. Such an experiment, a Pentagon official later told Cannon, "could be very useful to the Air Force, since precise knowledge of geodetic effects on ballistic missile trajectories are now becoming the key factor in accuracy."[92]

The relativity gyro grew into a major research effort employing a half dozen faculty and several dozen graduate students as well as entailing six-figure annual budgets, divided between the physics department and Cannon's Guidance and Control Laboratory. As predicted, the project had significant practical aspects for the military. Benjamin Lange, at the time a Cannon graduate student on leave from (and supported by) Lockheed, worked out the details of the so-called "drag free" satellite as part of the project, and Daniel DeBra, another Lockheed employee completing an advanced degree at Stanford, put the idea to work for the Navy's family of Transit navigation satellites.[93]

Like Hoff and Vincenti, Cannon established close relationships with Lockheed, then starting its major push into military satellites and therefore having a vital interest in advanced guidance systems.[94]

DeBra (supervisor of dynamics and control analysis), Ronald Smelt (later chief scientist), and Lange (a member of the Discoverer satellite group), all wrote theses for Cannon while working at Lockheed. DeBra and Lange later joined the faculty, as did John Breakwell, one of Lockheed's experts in orbital mechanics. Cannon's expansive *Dynamics of Physical Systems* brought together much of this research and teaching into one text. [95]

Building an Aerospace Complex

Lockheed provided a catalyst for the growth of an aerospace complex surrounding, and intersecting with, Stanford. Lured by the prospects of lucrative subcontracts for the ground support and tracking network for the Air Force's Satellite Control Facility, Philco broke ground for its Western Development Laboratories in Palo Alto in 1957. Philco was then a leading consumer electronics manufacturer, tops in radio and third in television sales. [96] Like the other electronics giants, however, it was looking to diversify into the defense business. In 1957 it purchased Sierra Electronics Corporation in San Carlos as what Philco's president called "a small stepping stone into the booming California electronics and aircraft industries."[97] Later that year Philco sent a small contingent of scientists and engineers West to found the Western Development Laboratories (WDL) as a subcontractor to Lockheed on the Discoverer program. [98] The new division immediately won major contracts on the electronic tracking stations, communications relays, and control stations for Discoverer, MIDAS, and SAMOS. About 90 percent of its revenues in the early days came from work for the Satellite Control Facility. But WDL subsequently won independent contracts for modernizing the Air Force's worldwide communications system ($19 million), [99] for developing a teletype and high-speed digital data communications system for the Army ($31 million), and for designing and building the first active-repeater communications satellite, Courier, for the Signal Corps. [100] These and other contracts boosted WDL employment to 2,500 by 1960.

Ford, also looking for a toehold in the defense and space business, bought Philco in 1961 and combined WDL with its existing Aeronutronics division (the original spinoff from Lockheed's Missiles Systems founded by Krause and the other disaffected scientists). Under Ford, WDL continued to prosper, winning a $25 million contract for a DOD communications satellite network and a $36 million contract for NASA's Integrated Mission Control Center in Houston. [101]

This rain of defense contracts on Lockheed and WDL encouraged the growth of smaller aerospace companies in their shadows. Itek, the Massachusetts-based optics, sensor, and antenna supplier for spy satellites, bought out Applied Technology to give it a West Coast presence. Link Aviation, a manufacturer of flight simulators headquartered in Binghamton, New York, shifted its advanced engineering laboratory to Palo Alto. Kaiser Aerospace opened a laboratory in the Stanford Industrial Park. United Aircraft put a branch of its research division in Menlo Park. And even local magnetic tape–maker Ampex found a booming new market for its recording systems in reconnaissance satellites. Local entrepreneurs also saw their opportunities and made the most of them: four scientists founded the Vidya Corporation to conduct supersonic wind tunnel tests on Polaris nose cones.

Whenever possible, Stanford took advantage of this local expertise to keep its aeronautics department up to date in particular specialties. Employees from Lockheed taught a range of courses. An officer of Vidya offered a course on aerodynamic heating, two researchers from the Hiller Helicopter Company taught vertical take-off and landing classes, and Howard Seifert, from United Research Corporation, organized a new rocket propulsion laboratory under an arrangement whereby his company continued to pay his salary. [102] Such courses gave students a taste for real-life engineering and at the same time offered local aerospace companies a good look at prospective consultants and employees.

Following the example of electronics, Hoff established his own industrial affiliates program, partly to tap industrial money but mostly to keep Stanford faculty and students in touch with industrial interests and opportunities. In February 1959 he drew up "A Plan of Industrial Liaison in Aero- and Astronautical Engineering at Stanford University" and sent it around to selected friends in the industry. In return for an annual pledge of $5,000–$10,000 a year for five years, each company was offered an opportunity to meet with department faculty and graduate students during an annual spring review, to receive copies of all the department's publications and theses, and to have its own faculty liaison officer. Hoff recognized that the department had at least as much to gain as the affiliates. "With the extremely rapid changes now taking place in the development and the design of airplanes, missiles and spacecraft, it is most important to the department to foresee new trends as fully as humanly possible and to adapt its teaching and research programs to the changing needs of industry," he said. [103]

With a foot in the door from the earlier appeal, Hoff had little difficulty lining up participants, including Lockheed, Northrop, Hughes, Aerojet, and others. Lockheed was the most generous contributor, giving $10,000 a year, not including its pledges to affiliates programs in electronics and fluid mechanics. [104] Altogether, the yearly total of pledges from affiliates came to about $100,000, about as much as one good defense contract. But for both the university and the company, the affiliates program was always more about jobs than money. The annual conference, usually a two-day affair in May, gave the member companies a chance to look over the current crop of students and hear brief summaries of their research. One faculty member jokingly likened the affiliates meeting to a "slave market."[105] And the affiliates, especially Lockheed, did in fact end up hiring many of the graduates. In thanking Lockheed for its generous support over the years, Terman suggested that since "a significant fraction of the graduate students we recruit from all over the country will some day work for Lockheed . . . your investment in Stanford Aeronautical Engineering has been justified."[106] Affiliate support also gave the department a discretionary fund for hiring promising new faculty who might otherwise be lost for lack of money or for purchasing equipment not included in the contract budgets. That meant, Hoff explained, that "worthwhile research projects can be begun before their usefulness can be demonstrated sufficiently to persuade the armed forces to grant research contracts for them."[107]

Local aerospace companies also sent employees to improve their technical expertise through the honors cooperative program. As in its sister program in electronics, the participants had to be nominated by their companies and then go through the university's normal admission process. They paid a tuition, and their companies paid a matching tuition, which went back to the department into a fund outside the normal academic budget. The honors coop students enrolled in regular daytime classes during work hours, although unlike other students they were permitted to complete the program on a class-by-class basis. The first year, the department attracted fourteen coop students out of a total enrollment of twenty-one. The following years it was thirty-nine of sixty-one, forty-nine of eighty-six, and seventy-six of 112. The military also sent students, up to eighteen officers at a time. [108] Those students (like their counterparts in electronics) and their ideas may ultimately have been Stanford's most vital contribution to the success of the local aerospace industry. Terman recognized the significant impact of the department's teaching. He told Hoff, "It is often said in writings about higher education that one of the problems of the university is that the professors are so busy doing their own research that they have no time to pay any attention to students. This is certainly not the case in the Aero Department that you have developed at Stanford; your professors are obviously busy with students and are turning out a steady stream of disciples who after leaving Stanford will carry with them the attitudes and viewpoints that you created at Stanford."[109]

The Durand Centennial Conference in August 1959 marked a milestone in the history of Stanford aeronautical engineering. Memorializing its founder, who had died the summer before at the age of ninety-nine, it pointed also toward the shape of things to come. Speaking for the AFOSR, one of the cosponsors, Colonel Raymond Gilbert summarized the technical agenda of the conference and with it the striking convergence of military and academic interests in contemporary aeronautics:

> The distinguished advisory committee for the conference selected several technical areas to illustrate the problems and progress in aeronautics and astronautics. The field of rarefied gas dynamics is pertinent to missile and satellite trajectories. Heat transfer, gas dynamics and material properties at hypersonic speeds are critical problems for manned aircraft, missiles, and reentering spacecraft. Plasma dynamics is a relatively new field, at least for aerodynamicists, which offers promise for trajectory control and propulsion in space. The problem of accurately

and quickly calculating orbits and trajectories has not been solved for many cases of interest to us. And lastly, this conference is concerned with new problems which have arisen in the design of flight structures occasioned by high temperatures and high speeds. [110]

All the American papers at the conference acknowledged support from Air Force contracts. Representatives from leading defense contractors —Boeing, Lockheed, McDonnell, Convair, North American, and Bell Aircraft—played prominent roles in the conference as presenters and commentators.

The conference also underscored the aeronautical engineering division's new independence, at least within the university. Having proven itself quite capable of standing on its own financially, the division was given formal approval as a separate, graduate-only department beginning in September 1959. With a hundred students and $460,000 in contracts, the department already ranked among Stanford's largest and was ready to join MIT, Caltech, and Princeton in the major leagues. [111]

As in electronics, Stanford's faculty moved easily among academia, industry, and the military. Many of them had come from industry in the first place and continued to consult for Lockheed and other aerospace companies. Many of their best students came from local firms, and the majority of the others went to work there after graduation. A number of department members served on military advisory panels. Hoff did two tours of duty on the AFOSR's Science Advisory Board. Cannon spent two years as chief scientist for the Air Force, so impressing his superiors that one high-ranking officer paid a special visit to Stanford's president just to thank him personally for Cannon's contributions. [112]

From the Air Force's perspective, Stanford's most important product was its students, not its research or its faculty advisers. The AFOSR considered its university programs a long-term investment, with the dividends paid in graduate students trained in scientific and engineering fields of special interest to the Air Force and its corporate contractors. The head of AFOSR explained:

These students are among the top strata of the nation's graduate students and they are receiving their education in areas particularly rele-

vant to the Department of Defense. Many have gone on to work in Air
Force contractor or in-house activities, equipped with knowledge and
skills particularly pertinent to their work, because of the previous Air
Force association. . . . We also find that many scientists supported by
AFOSR are consulting for the Department of Defense contractor and
in-house research and development activities. In a very real sense,
AFOSR support helps these persons achieve and maintain their exper-
tise while they contribute direct practical help to the Department of
Defense.[113]

Stanford's center for space science and engineering, completed in
1969 and named for founder William Durand, appropriately capped
the program's decade-long climb from obscurity to the summit of
academic aeronautics. Like the department it housed, the center
brought together military, industrial, and academic interests to a
common purpose.[114] Roger Lewis, who coordinated the fund-raising
campaign and whose own career as Secretary of the Air Force, president of General Dynamics, and university trustee neatly encompassed the golden triangle behind the center, dubbed it "a landmark
in the field of Government-industry-academic relations."[115]

The center was funded by a partnership of the Air Force, NASA,
and a consortium of industrial affiliates. The Air Force was looking to
expand Cannon's Guidance and Control Laboratory as rapidly as
possible, and willing to give Stanford $1 million (as accelerated de-
preciation on contracts) toward a new facility.[116] NASA administrator James Webb, anxious to tie Stanford researchers and their corporate allies more closely to NASA projects, authorized $2 million from
his Sustaining University Program budget in hopes that Stanford
might continue to "act as a focal point for the development of a regional scientific-technological-industrial complex."[117] And Roger
Lewis, building on earlier university appeals, sold yet another corporate affiliates program with promises of what such a center could offer
West Coast aerospace companies. In making his pitch, Lewis was not
shy about reminding potential contributors of what Stanford had already done for them, as his notes for a meeting with North American
suggest: "Professor Hoff of the Department of Aeronautics and Astronautics was an original member of North American's Scientific Ad-

visory Committee and knows [president] Lee Atwood very well. It should be noted that Hoff testified before a Defense Department committee on a project involving the B-70 and in so doing put in a good word for North American. Apparently Mr. Atwood is aware of this and holds the Stanford Department in high esteem."[118] Lewis got his money from North American, Lockheed, Northrup, and the other usual suspects, $1 million in all. When the campaign came up a little short, Lewis generously kicked in $100,000 of his own money to put it over the top.[119]

From Lesley's old test propellers in the lobby to Cannon's state-of-the-art guidance and control laboratory downstairs, the Durand Building symbolized the history and heritage of Stanford aeronautics. With two hundred students, a million-dollar-a-year contract budget, and thirty-nine master's and twenty-six Ph.D. graduates, Stanford surpassed MIT in 1970 (the year Hoff retired) as the country's leading producer of Ph.D.s in aeronautics.[120]

No one better appreciated the full measure of Stanford's achievement, or its costs, than the men who had made it happen. Earlier in his career, Hoff had publicly questioned the long-term implications of such heavy federal domination of aeronautics R&D. (For most of his career the military funded about 90 percent of university research in aeronautics, an even higher percentage than in electronics.) "By far the greatest part of the research funds is provided by government agencies," wrote Hoff. "The question arises, therefore, whether the restrictions imposed upon research sponsored by government or industry are likely to lead to a loss of our academic ideals? Is it desirable that the colleges become less dependent upon contractual work or should the contracts be modified in spirit in order to make them more suitable for promoting true academic work?"[121] If the answer seemed obvious to Hoff at the time—that academics could take these contracts without compromising their academic integrity—perhaps that was because neither he nor anyone else could foresee just how far those contracts, and the even larger industrial defense contracts behind them, would eventually redefine "true academic work" in postwar aeronautical engineering.

5 | The Power of the Nucleus

At a time "when the academic people of the country are finding increased reason to apply themselves to problems ordinarily considered to be military or political," what was going to happen to MIT and to physics? Jerrold Zacharias asked.[1] His own career revealed some of the answers as well as the possibilities and the limitations of extending into peacetime the wartime alliance of university physics and the military. The war brought Zacharias out of relative obscurity at Hunter College and into the heated activity of the Rad Lab and Los Alamos. With his colleagues there, he acquired a distinctive way of doing and seeing physics. It was a physics shaped by new instruments (largely from microwave electronics), new organizations (interdisciplinary laboratories), and a new patron (the military).

As director for ten years (1946–55) of the Laboratory for Nuclear Science and Engineering (LNSE), Zacharias transferred that legacy to MIT. LNSE trained hundreds of graduate students during his tenure, who then went on to university teaching (117), industry (106), and government laboratories and military agencies (fifty-seven). A thousand undergraduates did senior theses projects there.[2] The textbooks written there virtually defined physics for a whole generation of undergraduate and graduate students. MIT's physics department, thanks in large measure to LNSE, became by the mid-1950s the biggest graduate training program in the country, graduating thirty to forty Ph.D.s a year, twice as many as second-place Harvard, and as many as Berkeley and UCLA combined.[3] By 1964 LSNE had a $3.4 million budget and included fifty faculty members, thirty-eight post-doctorals, 110 graduate students, and 114 undergraduates.[4] Half of the Ph.D. candidates in a department that had moved into the elite of American physics programs, with Berkeley, Harvard, Princeton, and Stanford, came out of LNSE.

LNSE changed not only how (and how much) physics was done at MIT, but why it was done and for whom. Where prewar physics drew primarily on corporate and private philanthropic support, and so acquired something of an industrial flavor, postwar physics drew overwhelmingly on military support, acquiring quite a different flavor.[5] The two kinds of physics did share a dependence on techniques and applications, which was always characteristic of the Institute. What distinguished them was the increasingly narrow concentration of postwar physics on those fields, like nuclear science, thought to have promising military implications. Like its sister laboratory the Research Laboratory of Electronics, LNSE both reflected and reinforced the new federal agenda for science and the military priorities behind it. If it did not entirely confirm the early fears of long-time department member Philip Morse that "if the military controlled most of the funds, the directions of research would inevitably be bent away from peacetime goals," it certainly did suggest how far the military had redefined those peacetime goals.[6]

A Center for American Physics

Karl Compton took over as president of MIT in 1930, determined to make the sciences, and particularly physics, the "backbone" of a revitalized Institute.[7] During the 1920s, MIT physics had suffered with heavy undergraduate teaching loads, small budgets, and little encouragement for original research. In 1925 its program did not even rank among the top fifteen in the country.[8] As head of the Princeton physics department, Compton had built one of the top programs in the field, and his intention was to do the same at MIT. His vision for the Institute was closely patterned on Caltech—a technical institute supported by first-rate departments in the natural sciences, with physics as the keystone. "M.I.T. on the Atlantic and C.I.T. on the Pacific Coast, both emphasizing fundamental science in engineering, should have a profound influence not only in science itself but in developing a more progressive and effective attitude in engineering, industry, and business," he predicted.[9]

To head the physics department, Compton turned to John Slater, then a rising young star at Harvard. Just twenty-nine years old and looking "more like a gangly undergraduate than a full professor," Slater personified the competence and confidence of a new generation of American physicists.[10] He had done his graduate work at Harvard in the early 1920s, and then, like most top American physics students in those days, had gone to Europe to study with the masters of quantum mechanics. Like so many of them, Slater returned convinced that American physics needed to assert its independence from Europe by establishing its own centers for graduate education in the new physics.

Back at Harvard by 1924, Slater rapidly earned a name for himself applying wave mechanics to problems of atomic structure, notably the theory of atomic spectra. His research caught the eye of Compton, who tried to lure him to Princeton in 1927, and again in 1929, before asking him to take the chairmanship at MIT. Slater's Harvard colleagues thought moving to MIT was risky. Slater told Compton, "That of course was the conservative New England attitude, which I expected and do not appreciate. I am, as far as I know, the only person at Harvard who has been enthusiastic about your appointment, who has not merely thought that you were crazy and there was another good physicist gone wrong."[11] Finding the challenges of creating his own center for American physics irresistible, Slater accepted Compton's offer in June 1930.

"During those first years we had a situation that would never be duplicated again," Slater recalled, referring to the direct access he had to the president's office. "There were no deans. Deans hadn't been invented. At least they hadn't been invented there. The result was that when I wanted to settle something, I went directly to Karl Compton's office and we talked things over; and we talked them over as if the two of us were trying to develop physics at MIT. That's all there was to it. Then when we came to a conclusion, we carried it out."[12] Compton immediately asked the Institute trustees for, and got, a fivefold increase in the physics department's budget. He eased out the old chairman and five other senior faculty members and brought in several former Princeton colleagues and graduate students, including Philip Morse (who had coauthored the first American textbook on quantum mechanics), Wayne Nottingham (a specialist in physical electronics), and Robert van de Graaff (inventor of a powerful new electrostatic particle accelerator).[13]

Slater added one important recruit of his own, spectroscopist George Harrison from Stanford. They had gotten to know one another at Harvard, where they had both become interested in the measurement and interpretation of atomic spectra and had coauthored a 1925 paper on the subject. Harrison, feeling isolated at Stanford and discouraged by its stingy budgets, jumped at the chance to come East to head his own spectroscopy laboratory. "With you and [Edward] Condon [who eventually decided to stay at Princeton] and others to help me on the theoretical side, and Nottingham on the electrical side, I can see endless vistas of important problems for the spectroscopy lab. Gosh, I would be a fool to stay here!" he told Slater. "I feel like a tree that is being pulled up by the roots. But the plain fact of the matter is that Stanford hasn't the money, and never will have to do things on the scale that you plan. Also, it hasn't the location, nor the men. So I have the choice of rusticating here in comparative comfort, or bustling out into the world and doing something. And I guess the thing to do is to bustle."[14]

A bustling attitude encouraged ambitious assistant professors to stay and convinced others to join. Within a few years Slater and Compton had brought together one of the best-balanced young teams in American physics.

"What impressed me most, in my first meeting with Slater, was his determination to recast the physics curriculum at MIT so the young physicist would not need to go abroad to finish his education," Morse recalled.[15] And recast it he did, overhauling the curriculum from top to bottom. He made advanced mathematics an integral part of even beginning courses. He encouraged his faculty to write textbooks incorporating up-to-date theory and practice, and set an example by writing two texts of his own, *Introduction to Theoretical Physics* (with

N. H. Frank) for senior physics majors, and *Introduction to Chemical Physics* for graduate students. Somehow, he wrote them a page or two at a time during odd moments in the office routine, with one draft and very few revisions. Like the lectures on which they were based, they were models of good teaching—to the point, with an eye for the telling example and the challenging problem.

Slater put most of his effort into the graduate program. In the entire decade before he arrived, the department had awarded only six doctoral degrees. From 1934 to 1936 alone it granted thirty-three doctorates, placing it second among American universities, just behind Caltech (thirty-four) and well ahead of traditional leaders Berkeley, Chicago, and Harvard.[16]

Despite its new sophistication, the department's teaching and research programs continued to reflect MIT's long-standing commitments to engineering and industry. Slater explained, "We felt it almost a duty in a technical institution to carry on work in various applications of physics which do not usually attract interest in an arts college. Thus our work in electronics, in x-rays, in optics, in acoustics, was in each case in a field pursued in only a very few institutions in the country, and consequently not well known by the physicists of the country. Our department was often looked down on, to some extent, by those who felt that no physicist of any initiative would be in any field but nuclear physics. And yet in each of these less popular fields, our department was looked up to by the industrial leaders as the leading department in the country, and we were constantly urged to turn out more students in each of these fields."[17]

George Harrison's spectroscopy laboratory exemplified the distinctive industrial style of MIT physics. Its surpassing achievement was the "automatic comparator," an instrument capable of measuring, computing, and recording a thousand wavelengths an hour (compared with twenty or so by hand). As Slater put it, the comparator transformed spectroscopy from a "retail" to a "wholesale" science.[18] The laboratory's outstanding publication was the *M.I.T. Wavelength Tables*, a massive compilation of 110,000 spectral lines ground out by the comparator and an army of WPA conscripts. Completed in 1939, it immediately became an authoritative reference standard for analytical spectroscopy.

Nottingham's electronics program exhibited a similar commercial bent. Research problems like the behavior of tungsten electrodes or the use of phosphors in oscilloscopes, were frequently chosen with industrial applications in mind. Following Harrison's example, Nottingham inaugurated an annual electronics conference that drew hundreds of participants from RCA, GE, and other firms. "These conferences established the place of the Institute as a leader in the field of physical electronics, a field of very great technical importance in the electrical industry, but one which oddly enough is pursued in very few universities," Slater commented. "As a result of our concern with this field, and the number of good graduates whom we have had, we find that a number of the most important industrial laboratories now have a very liberal representation of M.I.T. graduates on their staffs."[19]

Robert van de Graaff's "Colossus of Volts," as someone dubbed it, perhaps epitomized the blend of scientific and industrial motives behind MIT physics in those years.[20] Invented by Van de Graaff at Princeton, it was really little more than a conventional electrostatic generator with some clever engineering refinements, though on a decidedly massive scale. Compton immediately recognized its possibilities in the high-stakes game of high-energy physics and brought Van de Graaff with him to MIT.[21]

Van de Graaff's machine literally dwarfed the competition, with 15-foot-diameter electrodes mounted on 25-foot-high insulating columns, housed in the only place big enough to accommodate it, an old dirigible hangar at Round Hill. On a good day it could crank out 5 million volts. One awestruck visitor described the scene: "As the motors in the bases of the two units began driving the great paper belts which carried the charges of electricity up to the spheres there was a faint humming sound. The hum grew more intense as the speed increased. Suddenly there was a blinding horizontal flash between the huge aluminum globes followed by a sharp report followed by repeated flashing and heavy crackling and sharper staccato reports. Dr. Van de Graaff's voice shouted through the din, 'Widen the gaps.' As the spheres separated the sounds of the blinding electrical discharge became deafening. It was like being in the center of an intense electrical storm—brittle cracks of lightning, crackling deep thunder claps, but no rolling echoes as heard from the skies."[22]

Compton envisioned a number of markets for these machines. As he explained to the president of the Research Corporation, a non-profit venture-capital group that developed and patented university research and then plowed back the proceeds, Van de Graaff generators could not only be put to work exploring the nucleus but also as X-ray devices, electric generators and motors, and other practical things. Impressed by Compton's pitch, the Research Corporation awarded Van de Graaff $10,000 in 1931 (twice what it initially gave Ernest Lawrence at Berkeley for his cyclotron), and followed up with a series of smaller grants. A year later Van de Graaff patented a "vacuum electrostatic power system" based on his generators and tried, unsuccessfully, to sell it to the TVA as a high-voltage power-generating-and-transmission system. He and graduate student John Trump later designed and built smaller generators as clinical X-ray machines, and eventually went into business as the High Voltage Engineering Corporation, developing electrostatic generators for government, corporate, university, and medical laboratories.[23]

MIT's success with industry did cost it something in philanthropic support. Just before Compton arrived, the Rockefeller Foundation had turned down a proposal from MIT for an endowment for the physics program on the grounds that MIT, as an engineering school, should look to business for its money. Even Compton's progress in remaking MIT as a science-based university did not entirely convince foundation officials. Instead of the major grant for the physical sciences that MIT was seeking, the foundation awarded $170,000 as a "fluid research fund" to be divided among physics, chemistry, and geology.[24] The department's program in radioactive isotopes production and analysis, however, was able to attract several large grants from medically oriented foundations.

By the eve of war, Slater and his colleagues had transformed physics from a service department for undergraduate engineers into an equal partner in the new, science-oriented MIT. They had doubled the size of the faculty, tripled the graduate enrollments, and quadrupled the research budget. By 1938 the faculty boasted nine "starred" physicists in *American Men of Science*, more than any other department except Caltech (eleven) and Harvard (nine).[25]

Meeting the Wartime Challenge

The war revealed the one flaw in Slater's strategy. In attempting to do everything well, he had not built up enough strength in nuclear physics, the one field destined to play the crucial role in both wartime and postwar research. By contrast, Berkeley had put its effort in the 1930s into developing Ernest Lawrence's cyclotron and built a top-notch team in nuclear physics around it.[26] During the war, Berkeley's physicists either stayed at home or took key positions with the Manhattan Engineering District laboratories at Chicago, Oak Ridge, and Los Alamos, where the best and brightest of American physics were gathering to build the atomic bomb, and in the process set the research agenda for postwar physics.

MIT was conspicuous by its absence. The Manhattan Project requisitioned one of Van de Graaff's machines for radiation-damage studies at Chicago's Metallurgical Laboratory, put Harrison's spectroscopy laboratory under contract to analyze uranium and other crucial bomb materials, and sponsored work on purifying uranium ores and casting uranium for the famous atomic pile in Chicago. But MIT neither sponsored any major nuclear laboratory of its own nor sent its best people to Chicago, Oak Ridge, or Los Alamos. Instead, MIT's physicists spent the war studying submarine and mine detection, bomb guidance, camouflage, and other critical but not highly visible projects.[27]

Slater and his colleagues recognized that the war had opened new vistas in nuclear physics as well as in microwave electronics. They also understood that MIT would have to make up ground quickly. "Physics during the war achieved an importance which has probably never before been attained by any other science," Slater noted. "The Institute, as the leading technical institution of the country and probably the world, should properly have a physics department unequaled anywhere."[28] In the postwar world that meant a major commitment to nuclear physics.

With their direct access to the Manhattan Project, MIT's competitors at Berkeley, Cornell, and Chicago had already started putting nuclear physics programs in place and making offers to the best people. At Los Alamos, Hans Bethe collared enough top nuclear specialists for Cornell to be able to hold a department meeting in exile.[29] At Chicago, Arthur Compton (Karl's brother) raided the Metallurgical Laboratory for the "nucleus" of a new Institute of Nuclear Studies. And at Berkeley, Lawrence had turned his close ties with the Manhattan Engineering District and its commanding officer Leslie Groves into hundreds of thousands of dollars in surplus equipment and postwar financing for his Radiation Laboratory.

The extent of the military's interest in nuclear science still gave MIT a chance to catch up, despite an initial disadvantage. The Navy, looking for a way to break the Army's nuclear monopoly, suggested that MIT consider establishing a new laboratory in nuclear science and engineering. In response, Slater and Harrison convened a special Nuclear Committee in September 1945 to position MIT "to meet new opportunities created by the atomic energy program."[30] Its members outlined areas of mutual technical interest, reviewed the programs being planned at Chicago, Berkeley, and elsewhere, and agreed on the importance of "having a strong nucleus at M.I.T. to attract subsidization by industry and government, if and when this becomes possible and desirable." Playing in this new league was going to take money, they realized. Slater and Harrison had heard through the grapevine that Chicago had guaranteed Harold Urey $100,000 a year in research support to stay and head its postwar program, and had made a comparable offer to Enrico Fermi.[31] By these standards, Slater and Harrison estimated that putting together a competitive nuclear program would cost twice as much as the electronics laboratory, perhaps as much as $370,000 a year.

MIT's first priority was signing up "young 'cream of the crop' men" as quickly as possible, even though wartime commitments might keep them from actually joining the Institute for some time. The Nuclear Committee persuaded MIT's administration to ante up $400,000 as a revolving appointment fund.[32] "This revolving fund made all the difference between success and failure in our program," Slater recalled. "We made a great many appointments, which were eventually covered by government financing, but which we certainly should never have been able to make if we had had to wait for the government contracts to be set up first. In fact, if the appointments had not been made in advance, we might not have had sufficiently good staff to justify the government contracts at all."[33]

Slater got lucky when Jerrold Zacharias, who had already accepted a postwar appointment, was sent from the Rad Lab on a six-month stint to Los Alamos to supervise the pilot plant production program. That gave him an ample opportunity to look over the uncommitted physicists and to recruit the best for MIT. Despite a late start, Zacharias did surprisingly well. He signed two distinguished émigrés, Victor Weisskopf, second only to Bethe in the theory group, and Bruno Rossi, a former Fermi student and cosmic-ray specialist. The three of them then went hunting junior appointments, research associates, and postdoctorates.[34] They proved to have exceptionally good eyes for spotting young talent. In all they landed a dozen physicists, including such prominent future department members as Bernard Feld, M. L. Sands, and David Frisch.[35] Zacharias also kept an eye out for surplus equipment and classified technical reports.

In his New Year's greeting for 1946, Karl Compton assured Alfred Sloan, one of the Institute's most generous benefactors: "We are delighted with the group of atomic scientists whom we have assembled during the past few months. In fact, outside of a few of the older Nobel Prize men and perhaps one other, I think they are the pick of the country."[36] The nuclear program got a further boost when Charles Coryell, head of the chemistry division at the Metallurgical Laboratories and later chief of research in radiochemistry at Oak Ridge, and John Chipman, former director of the metallurgy division at the Metallurgy Laboratories, decided to join the Institute.

The Laboratory for Nuclear Science and Engineering

Meanwhile, Slater and his colleagues began thinking about how to organize all this talent. "The research program in Nuclear Physics in the Physics Department has grown so great and so varied that there is a serious danger of its splitting up into a number of unrelated groups, if positive steps are not taken to correlate it," Slater admitted.[37] As a first step he suggested bringing together all the physics department's nuclear programs, from cosmic rays to nuclear theory, in some sort of "holding company." After some discussion, an interdepartmental laboratory along the lines of the recently created Research Laboratory for Electronics sounded especially attractive. Everyone recognized the political, as well as intellectual, advantages of bringing the chemists and engineers on board. Nuclear science overlapped strict department lines anyway, Slater pointed out, and so really demanded a new type of organization.[38] The Laboratory for Nuclear Science and Engineering was formally organized on December 19, 1945, with Zacharias as director and a steering committee representing each of five departments (physics, chemistry, chemical engineering, electrical engineering, and metallurgy) affiliated with the laboratory. It had three major divisions—accelerator building, radioactive isotope chemistry, and nuclear power—and an estimated annual budget of $600,000.[39] Zacharias's big thinking earned him a humorous tribute from the staff. A "Zach" ($250,000) became a local contract yardstick, because Zacharias would ask for nothing less.[40]

As at RLE, the immediate challenge was figuring out where the money would come from once the Institute's initial funding ran out. Slater had not given much thought to the finances, beyond expressing his hope that new sources of funding might, for the radioactivity center at least, "free it from the emphasis on biological and medical applications which has been necessary in order to get financial support in the past."[41] Zacharias was more concerned about the funding issues. From the start, he stressed that "collaboration with industry will be welcomed, and sought."[42] Hearing rumors that Rochester had attracted sizable funding from Eastman Kodak for nuclear science, and that Chicago had talked a consortium of oil companies into pledging $1,250,000 toward the support of its nuclear science program, Zacharias initiated a similar campaign at MIT.[43] He targeted oil companies, which he thought would be anxious to keep up with competitive energy sources, and chemical companies like Union Carbide, Du Pont, and Monsanto, which had held wartime contracts at Oak Ridge. The program asked companies for $50,000 a year for five years, in return for technical reports, special access to students and faculty, and the chance to send corporate representatives to work in MIT's laboratories.[44] But MIT's offer came too late. Standard Oil of Indiana, headed by Robert E. Wilson, the former director of MIT's Research Laboratory of Applied Chemistry, signed on, with the stipulation that three other oil companies also join. [45] But the other companies, already committed to Chicago's program, turned it down. All that Zacharias could arrange was a cooperative education program with Union Carbide's Oak Ridge facility and some corporate fellowships and grants-in-aid.

LNSE also tried the Rockefeller Foundation. During the war, Van de Graaff and his associates had substantially refined their generators. "When the war contracts stop, however, we shall be left with much experience, but no machine of our own," Slater explained to foundation officials. "The Institute has been too conscientious in its government financing to end up with funds so that we can hold our team together long enough after the termination of the contracts to construct one machine for our own research, embodying all the advances in the art which we know about," he said. [46] Van de Graaff machines might not have the power of new cyclotrons or betatrons, but they offered compensating advantages in precision, control, and versatility. In June 1945 the foundation awarded a two-year, $50,000 grant for designing and building a new Van de Graaff generator exclusively for nuclear physics. [47]

But neither industry nor private foundations would ultimately underwrite most of the postwar university research in nuclear science and engineering. As in electronics, the military would provide the lion's share of funding. Even before the official founding of LNSE, Admiral Bowen at the Navy's Office of Research and Inventions (ORI) was already talking with MIT officials about a "partnership agreement" in nuclear science and engineering. He emphasized that the Navy had as much of a stake in education as in research. "It is furthermore expected that you will integrate work under this contract with your educational program," he said. "Insofar as economy and efficient progress permit, the more students who can use this opportunity for credit toward a degree, the better will the Navy's ultimate interests be served in acquainting young men with our programs." [48]

In April 1946 the Navy and LSNE signed an initial contract for $600,000 a year for "a program of research with a view to extending the fundamental understanding of the constitution of atomic nuclei

William Radford and Henry Zimmerman (center and right) tweak the controls on the Project Meteor radar system, a top secret guided missile program funded by the Navy at MIT beginning in 1946. The missile fizzled, put Project Meteor trained dozens of MIT graduate students and contributed to phased array radar and other advanced defense systems. Radford later served as director at Lincoln Laboratory, while Zimmerman headed the Research Laboratory of Electronics from 1961 to 1976. *The MIT Museum Collections.*

Jay Forrester and Robert Everett (second and third from left) feed a computational problem to Whirlwind I in 1952. Funded by the Office of Naval Research and later by the Air Force, Whirlwind set the standards for the first generation of digital computers and became the "brains" of SAGE, Lincoln Laboratory's first continental air defense system. *The MIT Museum Collections.*

The Wright Brothers Wind Tunnel, completed in 1938, was the first of MIT's large-scale facilities for advanced research in aerodynamics. Funded with contributions from aviation companies and corporate executives, many of them MIT alumni, the wind tunnel paid for itself with industrial contracts and became an important center for aeronautics research and testing during World War II. *The MIT Museum Collections.*

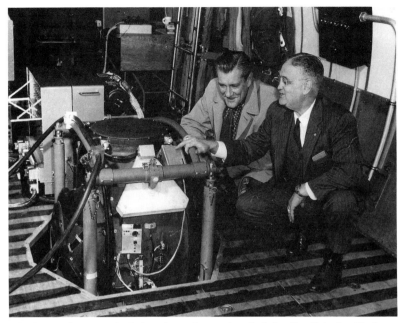

Charles Stark Draper (right) explains the unclassified details of his classified SPIRE, Jr. to CBS reporter Eric Sevareid during a demonstration flight on March 7, 1958. Though crude and bulky by later standards, SPIRE, Jr. served as a prototype for the internal guidance systems Draper would later design for several generations of Navy and Air Force ballistic missiles, including Polaris, Poseidon, Trident, Titan, and Minuteman. *The MIT Museum Collections.*

Jerome Hunsaker (left), founder of the MIT aeronautics program, dedicates the Naval Supersonic Wind Tunnel in 1949, while laboratory director John Markham (seated left) and MIT president James Killian (seated right) look on. Originally built for Project Meteor, the Naval Supersonic Wind Tunnel became a center for classified research on aerodynamic heating of missiles and advanced aircraft, and undertook tests on the B-58 bomber and the BOMARC and Sidewinder missiles, among other programs. *The MIT Museum Collections.*

Frederick Terman, as professor, dean of engineering, and provost, made Stanford into a world center for research and teaching in electronics. By shrewdly anticipating and cultivating the changing postwar market for defense electronics, Terman built up what he called "steeples of excellence" in such crucial fields as microwaves, radio propagation, and solid state. *Stanford University News and Publications Service.*

Lester Field shows off one of his pioneering traveling
wave tubes, the essential component in a number of
electronic countermeasures devices developed at Stanford during the Korean War era. Field trained the first
generation of traveling wave tube specialists at Stanford,
including Dean Watkins, before leaving for an industrial
career with Hughes Aircraft. *Stanford University News
and Publications Service.*

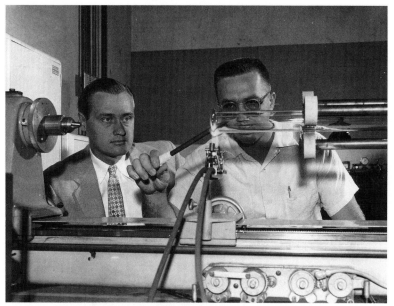

Dean Watkins supervises one of his graduate students as he puts the finishing touches on a microwave tube in the Stanford Electronics Laboratories. Watkins made crucial contributions to traveling wave tube design while at SEL, and later founded his own company, Watkins-Johnson, to put some of those ideas into practice. Still located in the Stanford Industrial Park, Watkins-Johnson was typical of the early companies spun off from Stanford laboratories in its close ties with the university and with the military market. *Stanford University Archives.*

Stanford Electronics Laboratories members (left to right) Oswald Villard, Laurence Manning, and Allen Peterson trying
out an experimental antenna design. Villard and Peterson's radio propagation studies made significant contributions to over-
the-horizon radar and jam-resistant communications systems.
Villard later left Stanford for the Stanford Research Institute in
the wake of protests against classified research on campus and
restrictions on those programs. *Stanford University Archives.*

Terman, the father of Silicon Valley, greets two of his
most famous former students, David Packard (left) and
William Hewlett (right). Terman wanted to build up an
independent West Coast electronics industry and strongly
encouraged his students to go into business for themselves.
He often invested in these start-up companies and served
on their boards of directors. Terman's investments, personal and financial, paid big dividends for the economic
growth of the region and for the university, where the
names on the buildings read like a who's who of Stanford
engineering alumni. *Stanford University News and Publications Service.*

Walter Vincenti (left) helped bring Stanford aeronautics into the missile age, both with his research on gas dynamics and with his teaching. Here he and co-author Charles Kruger go over some of the equations in their *Introduction to Physical Gas Dynamics*. Vincenti joined the Stanford program in 1957 after a distinguished career at the NACA's Ames Research Center. Like so many of his aeronautical engineering colleagues, Vincenti worked closely with his corporate counterparts in the emerging aerospace industry of the Santa Clara Valley. *Stanford University News and Publications Service.*

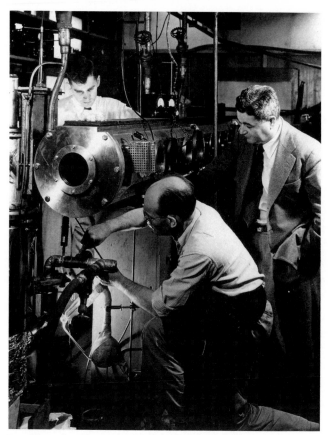

Jerrold Zacharias (right) oversees some adjustments on his molecular beam apparatus. Though intended as tools for exploring fundamental physics, Zacharias's beam experiments, like his parallel work on atomic clocks, exemplified a new kind of postwar physics that blurred conventional distinctions of theory and practice, unclassified and classified, and civilian and military. Zacharias was the founding director of MIT's Laboratory for Nuclear Science and Engineering and a tireless advocate for rethinking science education. *The MIT Museum Collections.*

Longtime physics department chairman John Slater (seated at far left) grills a graduate student during a doctoral examination. Slater, an influential teacher as well as researcher, built MIT's physics program into one of the nation's biggest and best, and helped initiate MIT's Center for Materials Science and Engineering. *The MIT Museum Collections.*

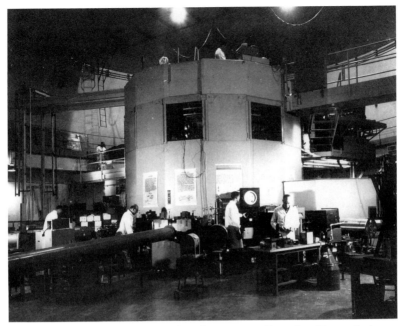

The interior of MIT's experimental nuclear reactor. Completed in 1958, the reactor was the centerpiece of MIT's program in nuclear engineering, the country's largest. MIT's nuclear engineers worked closely with the Navy in developing the first generation of submarine power plants, and with the Atomic Energy Commission's national laboratories in improving nuclear reactor design. *The MIT Museum Collections.*

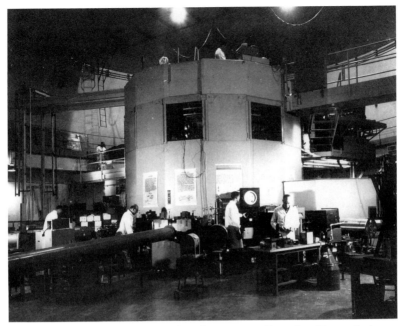

Francis Bitter (left) highlights some of the design features of a solenoid magnet for Benjamin Lax. Bitter invented the high power solenoid magnet which now bears his name. Lax, first at Lincoln Laboratory and later as founding director of the National Magnet Laboratory, made MIT an internationally recognized center of high power magnet design and research. *The MIT Museum Collections*.

The inventors of the klystron (clockwise from the lower left), Russell Varian, Sigurd Varian, David Webster, William Hansen, and John Woodyard, gather around an early version in 1939. Developed in the Stanford physics department on a shoestring budget, the klystron transformed radar and communications technology during the war, and helped make Stanford an important center of postwar electronics. In 1948 the Varians and Hansen founded Varian Associates to exploit the klystron and associated microwave technologies commercially. *Stanford University Archives.*

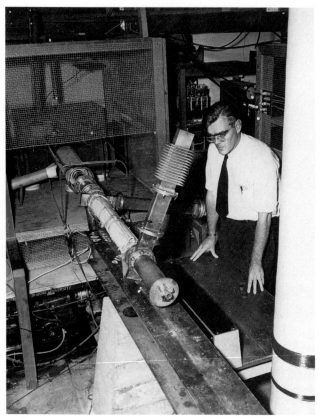

William Hansen assembling a section of Stanford's first linear electron accelerator in 1949. Hansen embodied the synergism of physics and electrical engineering behind so much of Stanford's postwar success in both fields. Tragically, Hansen died only a few months later, but his ideas lived on in a series of increasingly powerful linear accelerators, culminating, in 1966, in the Stanford Linear Accelerator Center, the biggest and most expensive "atom smasher" of its kind. *Stanford University Archives.*

Instrumentation Laboratory workers watch as Cambridge police clear the streets of antiwar protesters on November 5, 1969. Though police quickly routed the demonstrators, sit-ins, teach-ins, and similar events focused national attention on military-funded research at MIT, and ultimately led to MIT's divestment of the Instrumentation Laboratory. *The MIT Museum Collections.*

Robert Hofstadter (right) with one of his giant detectors in the Stanford High Energy Physics Laboratory. Though one of the primary beneficiaries of the new style of Stanford physics, and a Nobel Laureate in 1960 for his studies of nuclear dimensions done with the first large linear accelerator, Hofstadter eventually became a stubborn critic of Big Science. *Stanford University Archives.*

By the spring of 1969 the mood of campus protest turned ugly as police and students repeatedly clashed in front of the Stanford Research Institute's university annex. The April 3rd Movement also led an occupation of Stanford's Applied Electronics Laboratory to protest classified research programs there. In response to student and faculty unrest, Stanford divested itself of SRI and banned classified research from campus. *Stanford University Archives.*

and of nuclear processes, and of developing techniques and ideas to facilitate the practical application to other fields of the achievements of nuclear science."[49] Within a year that figure was increased to $1.5 million, while the staff grew from twenty to 155, which included fifty professors.[50]

Slater and his colleagues hoped that the laboratory would "carry on into peacetime the collaboration between the Radiation Laboratory and the Los Alamos laboratory which has been so fruitful during the war."[51] What they did not fully recognize was how far the postwar pattern would replicate the political expectations (for tools of war) as well as the social circumstances (a close working relationship of theorists and experimentalists) of that collaboration.

Clearly Bruno Rossi's and George Valley's cosmic-ray research came directly out of their wartime experiences. Rossi spent the war at Los Alamos designing improved particle detectors for the atomic bomb program. Valley worked in advanced electronics at the Rad Lab. At LNSE they designed and built a series of highly specialized cloud and ionization chambers and associated detectors that borrowed heavily from the techniques they had perfected during the war. Rossi's *Ionization Chambers and Counters* (1949) declassified many of the Los Alamos breakthroughs and made them available to the rest of the physics community for the first time. One of their younger collaborators coauthored a related text on applying new electronics techniques to nuclear physics.[52]

LNSE's electron synchrotron offered what MIT officials chose to call "an example of the reharnessing of scientists into pure research after war work in other fields."[53] It was actually a better example of continuing war work in a new kind of physics that made traditional definitions of "pure research" increasingly irrelevant. Edwin McMillan brought the fundamental idea of the electron synchrotron—phase stability—back to Berkeley with him from the Rad Lab and Los Alamos, along with $430,000 in promised funding and surplus equipment from the Manhattan Engineering District.[54] Ivan Getting, chief designer of the MIT machine, also came out of the Rad Lab. Several of his close collaborators, including M. L. Sands and J. Earl Thomas, came from Los Alamos. Their experiences with sophisticated wartime electronics proved decisive in, among other things, designing the accelerator's crucial timing and control circuitry. Completed in 1950, the 300-MeV machine gave MIT researchers access to a high-energy frontier previously accessible only through cosmic-ray studies. It also gave them the experience and confidence to move on to much bigger accelerators like the 6-GeV electron synchrotron they collaboratively designed and built with Harvard, which was completed in 1962. The ONR sponsored the original MIT synchrotron, as it did similar ones at Cornell, Berkeley, and Michigan, only partly because it was interested in what they might reveal about the fundamental forces binding the nucleus. It sponsored them because building and using such machines created the reservoir of talent that Bowen had emphasized, scientists and engineers trained in fields of particular interest to the Navy.[55] Getting's subsequent career certainly exemplified the favored path. He left MIT in 1950 for a top advisory post with the Air Force, then went to Raytheon as vice president for engineering and research, and ended up as president of Aerospace Corporation, another major defense contractor.[56]

New patterns of funding and new expectations reoriented even long-standing MIT programs toward military priorities. In the 1930s, Van de Graaff and Trump, largely with support from private philanthropies, designed and built high-power electrostatic generators for medical applications.[57] In the 1940s the Rockefeller Foundation and the Research Corporation could no longer match the enormous funding flowing in from the military. Rockefeller's $50,000 for a 5-MeV Van de Graaff generator was dwarfed by the ONR's nearly $300,000 for a 12-MeV machine. But it was not simply a matter of size and power. It was also a question of research direction.[58] Such machines had already proven their value at Los Alamos, which was building a copy for precise studies of neutron scattering.[59] Nor did Trump have any difficulty highlighting more direct applications of the 12-MeV machine in an appendix to his ONR contract proposal, "Portions of the High-Voltage Research Program Which Would Benefit the U.S. Navy."[60]

Zacharias's own research on atomic clocks revealed the military expectation behind even the most apparently esoteric postwar physics.[61] In the 1930s Zacharias had studied and collaborated with Rabi on his Nobel Prize–winning work with molecular beams. In the early 1940s and 1950s, he put what he had learned in the Rad Lab about microwave electronics (notably, sophisticated techniques of frequency control) to work updating Rabi's methods into an advanced atomic frequency standard. But far more than sophisticated time measurement was involved here. Zacharias often cited this research "as a good example of how it is possible to go directly from laboratory work to something the military want."[62] The military wanted atomic frequency standards both for in-house research and for applied work in missile guidance and tracking. Various Army, Navy, and Air Force contracts provided nearly all the money for Zacharias's research. Through development contracts with the National Company, a small electronics firm outside Boston, the military subsidized the transfer of this technology to industry. Zacharias was a key consultant for the company, and several of his graduate students went to work there. Military agencies further coordinated the academic and industrial sides of the atomic clock program by organizing joint conferences and seminars. And they purchased virtually all the early atomic clocks. With Jerome Wiesner (RLE director, and National Company board member and technical adviser), Zacharias founded Hermes Electronics "as more lucrative outlet for some of our military technological ideas."[63]

LNSE-trained graduate students in fairly large numbers poured into their chosen fields, sustaining the institution's impact on postwar physics. From 1948 to 1955, MIT graduated 283 Ph.D.s in physics, placing it first among American universities, with 8.8 percent of the total. By contrast, Harvard, which ranked second, graduated 136 Ph.D.s in that period, while Berkeley and UCLA together graduated 289.[64] MIT kept up that pace into the early 1960s.[65] About half of MIT's students did their graduate work in LNSE. Moreover, LNSE staff members, like their counterparts in RLE, were prolific textbook writers, and as Slater observed, "there is good reason for thinking that our influence is as widely felt through these texts as in any other way."[66]

A new pattern for the social as well as the technical practice of physics gradually emerged at LNSE, with far-reaching consequences for the development of new talent. Professors taught their students by example what and who really counted. The senior professors set the tone. The kinds of research projects they chose, the sorts of government and industrial consulting they did, provided the role models for junior faculty and graduate students alike. Younger people could see who got ahead and who did not, and that more often than not the fast track ran toward big defense projects, military advisory boards, and consulting for major defense contractors. Studying military problems, whether in the classroom, the laboratory, or in industry, became a natural part of the culture of physics at MIT in those years. From their first days in graduate school, would-be physicists found themselves in a world infused with military priorities. S. S. Schweber, who came of age as a physicist in the early 1950s, has remarked, "These outstanding scientists helped create a social reality in which working on military problems was an accepted norm for scientists at universities; more than that, their involvement suggested that one aspect of being the very best was participation in defense projects."[67]

LSNE strengthened its claims as being among "the very best" in this sense through its ongoing role as formal military adviser. In 1950, at the Navy's initiative, Zacharias coordinated a summer study of antisubmarine warfare code-named Project Hartwell. Like MIT's other summer studies (some are studies and some are not, Zacharias liked to say), it brought together representatives from academe (including six prominent members of LNSE and RLE), industry, and the military for a top-secret, three-month survey of a pressing defense priority, combating the increasing threat of Soviet submarines.[68] Its major recommendations—improved radar, acoustic and magnetic detection systems, and tactical nuclear weapons—all drew heavily on the ideas and techniques being perfected in places like LNSE and RLE. The ONR later called Project Hartwell "exemplary for the studies of the next ten years."[69]

Atomic Piles

Of the major postwar academic centers for nuclear research—including Cornell's Laboratory for Nuclear Studies, Chicago's Institute for Nuclear Studies, and Berkeley's Radiation Laboratory—only MIT's program gave prominence, in name and in fact, to nuclear engineering.[70] Atomic power was intended to be an integral aspect of the laboratory's agenda from the beginning. Early in the negotiations, Slater reminded the Navy's Office of Research and Inventions that one of the key reasons MIT had assembled such a strong team of nuclear specialists in the first place was "its conviction that atomic power is going to be of surpassing importance in the engineering of the future, and its belief that, as a leading scientific and engineering institution, it should take a commanding place in the study and development of atomic power."[71]

Fermi's prototype reactor at Chicago had set off a chain reaction of another kind within the scientific community; suddenly everyone wanted his own. Unfortunately for the scientists, the nuclear reactor was the American military's most carefully guarded secret, and one that General Leslie Groves had no intention of releasing without the tightest security and control.[72]

The Army could restrict access to atomic technology, but it could not, by itself, train the new scientists and engineers who would have to continue developing it. Seeing an opening, Zacharias proposed that the Manhattan District relocate part of the Oak Ridge laboratories to Cambridge. "Frankly stated," he explained, "our objective had been to try to persuade an appropriate committee . . . to plan a removal of the Clinton Laboratories to the vicinity of Cambridge for the purpose of collaborating with M.I.T. and Harvard in the matter of fission-pile research and design."[73] He urged the Army to circulate classified Manhattan Project documents among properly cleared LNSE members.[74] "Full cooperation between the Manhattan Project and the Laboratory of Nuclear Science and Engineering would be mutually advantageous and would serve as a means of bridging the gap between the present program and future developments," John Chipman agreed.[75] He also tried to interest the Army in building a reactor at nearby Fort Devens, either as a national facility or as a separate laboratory for the Cambridge community.[76]

MIT's competitors had similar ideas. At Columbia, I. I. Rabi was already plotting his own reactor program. Having lost so many of his best physicists to the Manhattan Project, and then to the University of Chicago, Rabi now believed that the Manhattan District owed him something, specifically a reactor. To strengthen his case, he sought out allies from Princeton, Yale, and other nearby universities. In late 1945 they sent a joint proposal to the Manhattan District for a nuclear reactor in the New York metropolitan area.[77]

MIT responded with a "Proposal for the Establishment of a Northeastern Regional Laboratory for Nuclear Science and Engineering," specifying its purposes in some detail but leaving its place open to further negotiation. "With the war . . . and the undertakings of the Manhattan District, nuclear research has entered an altogether new order of magnitude," Slater wrote.[78] Individual universities could no longer do it alone. Instead, they thought they needed a Rad Lab for nuclear physics, a center funded by the government but managed by, and for, academics.

Slater envisioned the laboratory "essentially as a part of the M.I.T. facilities, at a distance from Cambridge, though under a distinct business management of its own." The reactor would be an important tool (as a source of neutrons) for studies of nuclear and crystal structure, for radiochemistry and metallurgy, even for biology and medicine. It would become, Slater predicted, an important object of study in its own right. "Whether it is intended for producing a neutron beam, for generating plutonium, for producing fission fragments, or for producing heat and power," he wrote, "the pile is a machine whose operation must be studied by scientists and engineers." The potential impact on the whole discipline of physics was clear to Slater: "Even one man from a small college, spending part of his time in such a laboratory, would change the whole tone of that college, from one of comparative isolation, to one of taking part in the main current of scientific research."[79]

The MIT and Columbia groups met in February 1946 to draft a compromise proposal for the Manhattan Engineering District. While they agreed "that every effort should be made to obtain a chain reacting pile in an accessible location in the northeastern part of the United States," they spent the rest of the time arguing about exactly where to put it. Afterward, Rabi shrewdly tipped the geographical balance his way by adding Penn and Hopkins to the group, virtually assuring something close to New York City.[80] In the summer of 1946 a central Long Island site was chosen for the Brookhaven National Laboratory. MIT's physicists would have important roles to play there—Philip Morse as first director, Stanley Livingston as chief designer of the first big accelerator, Slater as visiting expert in solid-state research—but Brookhaven was simply too far from Cambridge to help develop and promote the kind of nuclear science and engineering program LNSE members had in mind.

MIT got a second chance for an independent nuclear program when the Navy launched its own nuclear initiative. Slater immediately appreciated the implications of new players in the game. "The Air Forces may well be interested in supporting a reactor program looking toward utilization of nuclear power for aircraft engines, and the possibility should be explored that the Bureau of Ships might be interested in joining in such a program, looking to nuclear power for naval vessels. . . . I believe we should get support from the Air Forces and the Bureau of Ships, with the approval of the Manhattan District, to start a pile development program at Devens, directed largely toward nuclear power for naval and aircraft propulsion," he wrote.[81]

The Navy's interest in nuclear propulsion was no secret around MIT. Early in their negotiations over LNSE, Karl Compton and Admiral Bowen explicitly discussed nuclear power for the fleet. Compton reassured him, "It is of course one of the major objectives of our M.I.T. project . . . to tackle problems fundamental to this type of application just as soon as we can acquire the necessary basic knowledge and facilities."[82]

Researchers at the Naval Research Laboratory had been thinking about atomic-powered submarines since news of the first fission experiments in 1938. A year later a Navy physicist drafted a secret report for Bowen on the advantages of using a "fission chamber" for submarines. But the Navy had to await the armistice before getting its nuclear fleet off the drawing board. In 1946 it detailed five officers and three civilians to Oak Ridge to gain some firsthand experience with reactor engineering, among them an ambitious young captain from the Bureau of Ships named Hyman Rickover, who would shortly thereafter take charge of the Navy's nuclear submarine program.[83]

Rickover immediately distinguished himself by his energy and by the way he took advantage of opportunity. He earned his "DOPE" (doctor of pile engineering), as it was called, by attending seminars with Edward Teller and other famous Manhattan Project veterans.

He made a point of getting to know the representatives from GE, Westinghouse, and other companies who, like himself, had also been sent to Oak Ridge to learn the latest advances in reactor technology. And he began pressuring his superiors for a 'full speed ahead' on nuclear propulsion. "Since there is no economic or other reason which would impel the electric-power industry to invest in the development of atomic power, and since the AEC has other immediate primary concerns [weapons development]," he said, "it would appear that if we are to have atomic power plants in naval vessels the inspiration, the program and the drive must come from the navy itself."[84]

One of the visiting scientists Rickover met at Oak Ridge was MIT physicist Clark Goodman. As an MIT physics graduate student in the 1930s, Goodman had worked on radioactive dating of petroleum deposits, and then joined the department. Like so many of his colleagues, he was drawn into wartime projects and then sent to Oak Ridge to learn reactor physics. Rickover, who was already worrying about how to cram a reactor into a submarine, offered him a Bureau of Ships contract to study light-weight neutron and gamma-ray shielding.[85]

Back at MIT as a charter member of LNSE, Goodman started the nation's first academic program in reactor design. His own research on neutron and gamma-ray shielding was supported by the ONR and the Bureau of Ships, and aimed at decreasing the weight and volume of mobile reactor shields so that they could be used in submarines. Five naval officers wrote theses under Goodman on neutron and gamma-ray shielding. Goodman taught a classified course on nuclear reactors in the fall of 1946 and organized an unclassified follow-up seminar to focus attention on nuclear power.[86] It featured contributions from a number of prominent LNSE experimentalists and theorists. Goodman chose for his topic the "Construction of Nuclear Reactors." He later edited the proceedings as *The Science and Engineering of Nuclear Power*, perhaps the first textbook on atomic reactor design.[87] Goodman put together a second seminar series the following year, with greater attention to the details of shielding, materials, and heat transfer, and published it as a sequel. Those seminars became also the basis for a graduate course in nuclear engineering which Goodman taught for some years before taking a job with industry.

Even the more purely science-oriented parts of the LNSE program were expected to have "a direct bearing on a program of nuclear engineering." Instruments developed for nuclear science, for instance, would "provide essential tools for problems associated with nuclear power," from electrostatic generators for nuclear cross-section measurements to radiochemical techniques for "chemical processing and reprocessing of nuclear fuel materials." The theorists, too, were enlisted in the course. "Those engaged in the scientific programs are not only willing to teach but also to calculate, criticize, and recommend new approaches, and otherwise assist the engineering group," the laboratory's administrators promised.[88] Robley Evans made a place for nuclear fission in his nuclear physics sequence and later retitled the course "Nuclear Physics for Engineers."

LNSE provided much-needed links between government, university, and industry as well as between theory and practice. In the rush to train nuclear scientists, other university programs had more or less forgotten about training engineers, but not MIT. It inaugurated a cooperative education program with Union Carbide's nuclear division at Oak Ridge. The dean of engineering explained the benefits: "The establishment of a station at Oak Ridge would supply a certain number of trained engineers urgently needed in the plants of the Atomic Energy Commission, and would build up a reserve of men trained in the field who might be called into such work in case of national emergency."[89] To transfer the latest advances to industry, MIT's industrial liaison office organized a classified summer conference on nuclear power for corporate representatives.[90]

After Rickover took charge of the Navy's Nuclear Power Branch, or Code 390, he began sending his top officers to MIT for advanced training in nuclear physics and engineering. He personally selected all the officers and kept close tabs on them, "both to see that they were making satisfactory progress and to check on thesis work which he expected to have a practical application to the activities of Code 390."[91] Rickover also made occasional suggestions for updating the curriculum to reflect current Navy interest. After graduation, Rickover's students went on to supervise the design and construction of the Navy's first nuclear fleet, starting with the USS *Nautilus* in 1950.

The Navy's reactor program also had close ties to LNSE's secret "Metallurgical Project," under Albert Kaufmann. Kaufmann spent the war at MIT fabricating special uranium castings for the atomic pile at the University of Chicago. He stayed on to run a large ($800,000 a year), classified metallurgical program for the Manhattan District, studying ways of working zirconium, beryllium, and other exotic metals either into fuel elements or reactor shields. Kaufmann supervised a number of classified theses by naval officers detailed to MIT and taught classified graduate seminars in nuclear metallurgy for them as well. When declassified, these seminars became a regular part of the nuclear engineering curriculum.[92] The dean of engineering gave Kaufmann's project an "A" for technical merit and called it one of the "building stones" of MIT's educational program in nuclear engineering.[93] Eventually, the work became too process-oriented even for MIT and was spun off into a private company, Nuclear Metals, under AEC contract. Kaufmann went along as vice president and technical director.[94]

LNSE also had a hand in getting the nuclear airplane off the ground, if only figuratively.[95] Air Force generals, like Navy admirals, dreamed of a weapon whose range would be limited, as someone put it, only by coffee and sandwiches for the crew. So in May 1946, the Air Force created a Nuclear Energy for Propulsion of Aircraft project at Oak Ridge. But designing a reactor that was small, light, and well shielded enough for a bomber made Rickover's job look easy, and the project quickly stalled amid questions of technical feasibility and charges of strategic irrelevance. To answer the critics, the Air Force and the AEC asked MIT to coordinate an "independent" evaluation of nuclear aircraft propulsion. Code-named Project Lexington, for the Army field station where the participants gathered, it included forty leading nuclear and aviation experts, among them several members of LNSE. Walter Whitman, chairman of MIT's chemical engineering department, served as director, and Zacharias as associate director. Under their leadership, the project members spent the summer of 1948 on a classified study of nuclear flight.[96] Project Lexington cost the AEC half a million dollars, which, from the perspec-

tive of nuclear flight enthusiasts, was money well spent. Refuting
many skeptics, the Lexington report argued that given enough time,
money, and ingenuity, a nuclear plane would fly. The Air Force, the
AEC, and their industrial contractors (GE, Pratt & Whitney, Lockheed, and Convair) spent a decade and more than a billion dollars
trying to make that happen, but it never did.[97] Without the academic
respectability conferred by the Lexington study, the nuclear flight
program would probably have been canceled years and millions of
dollars sooner. There was a fine line between advice and advocacy
and in this case, as in Project Hartwell and others, LNSE may have
strayed dangerously from one to the other.

Nuclear Engineering

In 1951 MIT created a separate graduate degree program in nuclear
engineering, initially for the increasing numbers of military officers
detailed to the Institute for advanced training. Manson Benedict, former head of process design for Kellex Corporation's uranium separa-
tion plant at Oak Ridge, was named program head. Although officially a member of the chemical engineering department, Benedict
held the title of professor of nuclear engineering. Benedict then
brought in Thomas Pigford from Oak Ridge, where he had been running MIT's School of Engineering Practice with Union Carbide's nuclear division.[98]

Benedict and Pigford organized a series of summer studies for the
AEC in order to educate themselves before taking on the greater challenge of educating anyone else. The AEC had for some time been
pushing MIT to build up a reactor design group under contract. It
hoped in that way to stimulate broader awareness of and interest in
particular problems of reactor design and thereby "provide a nucleus
for a planned program of graduate study in nuclear engineering at
MIT." Getting faculty involved was expected to "give various A.E.C.
applied research programs at M.I.T. more directness of purpose
through first-hand contact with the problems of reactor design" and
"make it possible for M.I.T. to train a selected group of cleared graduate students for work in reactor engineering, with a thoroughness not
now possible in educational institutions. This would be accom-

plished by interesting and developing faculty members in the field of reactor engineering and by providing classified information and reports for student work on real problems."[99] The summer studies initially focused on designing reactors for improved plutonium production and recovering uranium and plutonium from spent fuel cells. The AEC expected, in fact, "to integrate M.I.T.'s work in this field [reactor design] with the program for the improvement of plutonium reactors now being undertaken by the A.E.C."[100] Only later did they branch out into the economics of nuclear power and other civilian problems.[101] "The results of these projects were useful to the AEC in steering its reactor development program, and the experience gained in working on these projects was valuable professionally to staff and students alike," Benedict would later write.[102]

President Eisenhower's "Atoms for Peace" initiative of 1953 declassified certain details of reactor design and finally gave MIT the chance to build its own reactor.[103] Determined that MIT build a "research reactor second to none," the administration appropriated $1.5 million of internal funds to enter the reactor sweepstakes along with North Carolina State, Michigan, and Penn State.[104]

The declassified documents may now have been in the hands of the academics, but the detailed knowledge of how to design and construct a full-scale reactor was still in the heads of AEC engineers. Benedict found both his machine (Argonne National Laboratory's new heavy-water reactor) and his designer (Theos Thompson of Los Alamos) at AEC laboratories.

MIT's reactor, completed in 1958 at a cost $2.4 million, became a university-wide facility for studies in neutron diffraction, nuclear chemistry, ferromagnetics, and even experimental cancer therapy. The reactor research program, however, was always as much about building better reactors as about advancing fundamental science. Its biggest single source of support came from an eight-year AEC project intended to provide "definitive correlations of the effect of uranium enrichment, rod diameter, and rod spacing in reactor lattice parameters." A follow-up "Reactor Lattice Project" provided parallel measurements for improving the performance of plutonium-fueled reactors.[105]

Starting with only seven graduate students, Benedict rapidly built up the biggest program in the country, first as part of chemical engineering and, starting in 1958, as a separate department.[106] The curriculum expanded from a single course in the fall of 1952 on nuclear reactor theory to include advanced courses in reactor theory and reactor engineering, in nuclear chemical engineering, and in the biological effects of radiation. Enrollment soared to ninety-four students in 1957, not including several hundred from other departments attending courses in nuclear reactor engineering, the nuclear engineering laboratory, and advanced reactor theory.[107] By 1962 enrollment leveled off at about 125 total students, with forty graduates a year, plus an additional thirty-five special AEC Fellows.[108] Continuing an earlier pattern, Benedict drew many of his faculty members from AEC or military laboratories—Livermore, Oak Ridge, and the AEC's Naval Reactors Branch. Where industry had the edge, he arranged visiting lecturers, like the specialist from General Atomic (a division of General Dynamics), who taught the first courses in nuclear metallurgy and materials.[109]

By the early 1960s the department was awarding as many doctoral degrees (about eighteen a year) as its parent Laboratory of Nuclear Science (which had been renamed in 1951 to reflect the new intellectual division of labor). It was also granting twenty or so master's degrees a year. The subsequent careers of those students, even more than their theses, attested to the predominant direction of nuclear engineering in America in those years. By 1964, of the department's 192 graduates (excluding foreign students and joint degree candidates), forty-six were still in the armed forces, nineteen were working at Savannah River, Oak Ridge, Los Alamos, or other AEC laboratories, and most of the rest (115) had jobs with one or another of the Navy's nuclear contractors. Only twelve had accepted academic appointments, a third of them with MIT.[110]

After a careful review in 1962, the department's visiting committee concluded: "The Department of Nuclear Engineering could be considered a case history in the contemporary times of education in the United States. It draws on several disciplines and cuts across Department lines. The money for its support comes largely from the government. Fundamental research and application go hand in hand and there is no time lag between a fundamental discovery and its applica-

tion. The need catalyzes the work in basic science. The old concep-
tion of the 'Ivory Tower' is absent in this Department as many of the
men therein have to spend a great deal of time in Washington selling
their wares."[111]

What the department was selling, however, depended entirely on
what the military establishment was buying. In the program's formative years it was reactor technology for submarine propulsion, plutonium production, and other specific defense applications.

To a disturbing extent, military requirements determined the direction taken for civilian nuclear power. Rickover insisted on a light
(or pressurized) water design for his submarine fleet because, as a
proven technology, it offered quicker results. The AEC's promise that
"there will be no subordination of the primary civilian power objective to military considerations" in commercial nuclear power
was soon forgotten, or more likely, dismissed. When Eisenhower's
"Atoms for Peace" program needed a civilian reactor in a hurry, it had
nowhere else to turn except Rickover's Naval Reactors Branch. Rickover's engineers took a light-water reactor intended for a nuclear aircraft carrier, modified it for electric power generation, and put it into
service at Shippingport, Pennsylvania, for the Duquesne Light Company. Rickover's engineers oversaw the design and installation. Westinghouse, a prime contractor for nuclear submarine reactors, served
as the prime contractor for the Shippingport reactor. The Shippingport reactor, in turn, became the prototype for most later commercial nuclear power plants, as well as the training ground for the
nuclear engineers who designed and built them.[112] It set the pattern
for the entire American nuclear power industry, with virtually no debate over the appropriateness of the reactor design for the commercial
market. The industry's subsequent economic and safety record would
raise serious questions about that choice.[113]

Pausing for a moment amidst the bustle of postwar program building,
Slater thought about where MIT physics had been and contemplated
where it might be going in the years ahead. "The department has
lived a hectic life since the war," he said. "Everybody for almost ten
years has been much busier than he ever was before. This makes for

conspicuous and impressive programs, but perhaps not for the deep thought that is needed to make real and fundamental advances."[114]

Yet the military projects that had kept everyone so busy, and that would continue to do so over the next two decades, were not distractions from some fundamental scientific mission but rather a natural and expected extension of it. LNSE was literally a contract between the military and MIT. Part of the bargain was a new kind of physics that easily blended theory and experiment, science and engineering, understanding and application, unclassified and classified, research and policy advocacy.

The question was not whether MIT's physicists were thinking deeply, but what they were thinking deeply about. Working for and with the military gave MIT's physicists unprecedented resources and status, with which they fashioned a nationally acclaimed program. But it cost them something too—if not their self-image, then their independence.

6 | Accelerating Physics

Perhaps the most visible symbol of Stanford's push to postwar prominence was the Stanford Linear Accelerator Center (SLAC). Completed in 1966, it was the biggest (two miles long), most powerful (20 GeV), and most expensive ($114 million) scientific instrument of its day. Another towering steeple of excellence (albeit laid on its side), it made Stanford a world center of high-energy physics.

SLAC was the legacy of Stanford physicist William W. Hansen, who conceived the innovative microwave physics behind it, and his students and collaborators, who brought it to life after Hansen died tragically in 1949 at the age of forty. But it was also a legacy of the subtle blurring of ends and means in a postwar physics dominated by military money and expectations. Not simply a triumph of big physics—big money, big machines, and big teams of researchers—it evidenced a physics that owed its character as well as its funding to the military agencies that supported it. As one of SLAC's designers acknowledged, "Research in the microwave field must, of necessity, be *applied research*, always directed toward a useful goal in some other field."[1] At Stanford that "other field" was the high-powered microwave tubes that drove Stanford physics literally (as a source of energy to accelerate electrons) and financially (as a way of attracting government and industrial interest). The same kind of tubes and techniques that could power giant accelerators, and so suggest answers to the most fundamental questions of nature, could (and did) power sophisticated new radars and other vital defense systems. Stanford physicists worked on both with equal success. In the process, they set a pattern for postwar physics dependent upon, and aimed toward, military applications.[2]

The Klystron

Hansen came to Stanford as an undergraduate in 1925, just as the physics department was beginning its climb out of the academic minor leagues.[3] David L. Webster, a Harvard-trained experimentalist with a growing reputation in X-ray physics and an intense ambition to challenge established programs at Berkeley and Caltech, had recently been hired as chairman. Webster brought the quantum revolution to Stanford with his studies of atomic structure and the Compton effect and with his *General Physics for Colleges* (1923), one of the earliest undergraduate treatments of the new physics. He also hired young faculty members from Berkeley and Harvard and recruited some outstanding graduate students, including Hansen, who earned his doctorate in 1932 with a thesis on X-ray excitation.[4] Hansen then spent two years as a National Research Council Fellow, mostly at MIT with Julius Stratton and the other radio pioneers. Stratton recalled that Hansen "proved to be an enormously stimulating influence on our early thinking about microwaves," and acknowledged Hansen's contributions in his famous text on electromagnetic theory.[5] In 1934 Hansen returned to Stanford as an assistant professor.

By that time Webster had exhausted the research possibilities of the department's relatively low-power (200,000 volts) X-ray apparatus and was looking for new worlds to conquer. Ernest Lawrence at Berkeley had just invented the cyclotron, Richard Lauristen at Caltech had recently built a million-volt X-ray tube, and Robert Van de Graaff at MIT was completing an electrostatic generator promising 5 million volts. So Webster and his colleagues formed a special "Supervoltage X-ray Committee" to consider the possibilities for building something similar for X-ray and nuclear research. Without a strong medical angle, however, they were not able to interest either the Rockefeller or the Carnegie foundations, the two major sponsors of high-energy physics research in those years.[6]

Depression budgets and lack of foundation support thus made certain that any Stanford "atom smasher" would have to be long on ingenuity and short on cost. Rather than trying to compete directly with cyclotrons and Van de Graaff generators, Hansen suggested approaching the challenge of high voltage from a completely different perspective, using a tunable cavity resonator as a source of microwave energy to accelerate electrons gradually up to high energy. In January 1936, Hansen gave a talk to the physics journal club entitled "How To Get 10^n Volts Cheap," outlining ways of putting the cavity resonator to work as an electron accelerator. With a \$1,000 grant from the National Research Council, Hansen spent the better part of 1936–37 elaborating his ideas, only to see them surpassed at the prototype stage by a powerful new electron accelerator, the betatron, at Illinois.[7]

If the "rhumbatron," as Hansen dubbed his cavity resonator, never became a serious competitor as a particle accelerator (at least in its original form), it did become a crucial component in a more successful microwave tube, the klystron. In March 1937, Russell Varian, a friend from college days, told Hansen about an invention he and his brother, a commercial pilot, had been thinking about for locating and navigating airplanes with a microwave radio beam. The Varians, having run out of money to develop the idea on their own, were looking for collaborators and a place to work. Intrigued by both the idea and its commercial prospects, Hansen, with Webster's approval, arranged to have the Varians join the department as unpaid research associates, with access to faculty, laboratory space, and \$100 in materials, in return for half interest in any resulting patents.[8]

The new partnership paid surprisingly quick dividends. Russell Varian hatched "schemes," as he called them, at the rate of a couple a week and sent them off to Hansen and Webster for their evaluation. Webster occasionally lost patience with Varian's unrestrained enthusiasm: "He was so full of ideas that when he was helping in research, I'd have to say, 'For God's sake shut up, I want to concentrate on my work and not on this idea. But he was full of them. He sat around in the office with Hansen and swapped ideas. Hansen would say that most of them were no good, and show why. But eventually Russell came up with this idea of bunching the electrons. . . . That, we all recognized instantly as a grand idea."[9] Essentially, Varian took Hansen's original idea and turned it on its head, using the rhumbatron to amplify an oscillating field with an electron beam rather than to accelerate an electron beam with an oscillating field.[10] By early fall they had an improved version which, at the suggestion of a classics professor, they christened the klystron, for a breaking wave (of electrons).

As the Varians had hoped, the klystron quickly attracted commercial interest. The Sperry Gyroscope Company, a major naval defense contractor (by prewar standards, at least) recognized that a practical klystron could be a serious threat to its searchlight and acoustical airplane-detection business.[11] It could also be an entrée into a potentially vast new market for aerial detection and guidance. To gain some control over the invention, Sperry negotiated a contract with Stanford giving the university between $5,000 and $25,000 a year for klystron research, and a 5 percent royalty, in return for an exclusive license to make, use, and sell any high-frequency equipment developed by the Stanford physicists.[12] Though not much compared with later contracts, that money was twice what the department had spent for capital equipment over the past half century.[13]

In signing on with Sperry, Stanford's department fell comfortably into a pattern of appeasement toward military-industrial physics which, like the politics it paralleled, held fateful implications for the future. To protect its patent position, Sperry insisted on a measure of secrecy, negotiating a special agreement with Stanford's president so that "the University would recognize for academic purposes, outstanding work being done in the Department in the field of applied physics represented by work on the Klystron," even if some of it could not be published.[14] To speed up the conversion of the klystron from a physics curiosity into a practical radio device, Sperry brought electrical engineers into the picture. Arrangements were made for several of Terman's graduate students to join the project, including John Woodyard, who wrote his doctoral thesis on one aspect of it, and Edward Ginzton, who became a research associate.[15] Sperry also set up a separate prototype production facility staffed with its own engineers in nearby San Carlos.[16]

With war on the horizon, Sperry stepped up its klystron work and transferred the Stanford group, including Hansen, Ginzton, and Woodyard, to its Long Island research center in December 1940. The combination of academic specialties and corporate discipline clicked instantly. As Ginzton recalled, "Soon the klystron became not just an individual tube, but a circuit component, and we could explore its utility in a number of conventional combinations. Almost everything we tried—amplifiers, receivers, superheterodyne detectors, etc.— worked immediately and quite well. We were able to demonstrate that almost anything one could do with conventional radio tubes could be done by the klystron at microwave frequencies."[17] During the war the Sperry team developed a number of variations on the original klystron idea—with single cavities, as local oscillators for magnetron-powered radar, for Doppler radar.

The Microwave Laboratory

Hansen's wartime experiences at Sperry, and as a consultant on microwaves for the Rad Lab (the so-called "Hansen Notes" became an underground classic among the radar researchers), convinced him that the collaboration of physics and electronics that had proved so fruitful during the war would have equally significant implications afterward. At Sperry he had watched his protégé Ginzton rise to head an entire klystron division, with a staff of 150 engineers and technicians and an annual budget of $1.4 million.[18] Sperry's engineers, in turn, had transformed the improved klystron into a family of anti-aircraft tracking radar, searchlight control radar, aircraft interception radar, and microwave bombsights.[19]

Looking ahead, Hansen proposed to his dispersed colleagues in the physics department that they set up a special microwave laboratory after the war to follow up on the extraordinary progress made during the war. Thanks to the early klystron project, Hansen emphasized, Stanford already had a head start in multidisciplinary research. "The Micro-Wave Laboratory, in addition to any direct benefits it may bring, will also act powerfully to strengthen and reinforce the related activities of Physics and Radio Engineering," he explained. "It is hard to overemphasize this mutual benefit."[20] Thanks to the klystron royalties ($30,000 a year by the end of the war), Stanford also had adequate financial resources to support such a venture.

Compared with the schemes being hatched at MIT, Hansen's plans were quite modest. He anticipated that the Microwave Laboratory would have just two full-time faculty members, a machinist, a few research associates, a dozen or so graduate students, and an annual budget of maybe $25,000. Like his MIT counterparts, Hansen had his eyes on the Rad Lab's equipment, which he realized would go to "those who can show that they have a definite use for it as opposed to those who merely want it because it's cheap" (though in the end he was not close enough to get his hands on it).[21] Beyond the accumulated klystron royalties, Hansen felt confident that he could line up new industrial contracts. "It seems to me," he told Stanford's president, "that we have something to sell that Sperry and/or others will want, although just exactly what, how to go about selling it, and how much we can get is not known in detail."[22] As a start, it looked like Sperry, GE, and other companies coming out of the war with experience in the microwave field would want consulting, patents, access to state-of-the-art microwave research, and, most important of all, trained students.

For Hansen, the critical thing was speed. "Stanford has what seems a unique opportunity to get a Microwave Laboratory into effective operation soon after the war ends," he argued. "Eventually other schools will enter the field but it will take them time to plan, to find personnel, etc. Stanford, on the other hand, by planning now, can have a first class establishment operating a few months after the war— all the essentials are at hand."[23] Moving ahead quickly was crucial, Hansen knew, because MIT would be planning a microwave laboratory of its own, with government and industrial connections that he could not hope to match, at least right away.

Hansen's proposal immediately sparked a vigorous debate about the future direction of physics at Stanford.[24] Webster, disillusioned by his early experiences with Sperry, pronounced it nothing less than selling out the department to industrial and engineering interests. He recalled Hansen's earlier disputes with Sperry and how he "used to express his aversion to having his papers censored and often suppressed by the patent department of a company to whom God's laws were merely pawns, to be played or killed, according to whose side they were on."[25] He reminded his colleagues that "Money talks very loud in a privately endowed university after a big war. So it may be necessary to help finance the University by hiring part of it out. It may be argued that it is better for us all to become engineers with lots of money to spend than to remain physicists with little. That, possibly, is a matter for each individual to decide for himself."[26]

Hansen had already decided. For him the only real question was how to exploit most fully the opportunities of the postwar world, with its new collaborations, new patrons, new intellectual challenges, and new disciplinary contours. Whether the proposed Microwave Laboratory would be doing "pure" physics was, for Hansen, entirely a matter of definition, and in defining "pure physics" as in discovering new laws of nature, Webster had set his sights "terribly high." In any case, whatever money would be coming in from royalty checks had already been earned, "So we don't have to sell our souls for it. In principle, we don't have to do another lick of work to keep collecting it forever."[27]

Hansen found an unexpected ally in Felix Bloch, the brilliant émigré theorist who had joined the department in 1934 as part of the Rockefeller Foundation's relocation program. Although Bloch had started out as an engineering major, his theoretical studies of the magnetic scattering of slow neutrons and his measurements of the magnetic moment of the neutron in the 1930s owed little to the kind of industrial physics being pursued on the klystron project. He had, he admitted, "snobbishly maintained the principle of 'l'art pour l'art'" during the early klystron days, but changed his mind after spending some time at Los Alamos and RRL. By striving to remain too pure, he argued, the department might actually cut itself off from important opportunities. "If, by denying even the possibility of its value for physics, you would force the lab over to the electrical engineering department—where, no doubt, it would be received with open arms—I feel you would deprive our science and particularly our department of a chance the like of which will not come soon again," he told Webster.[28]

Hansen found an even more powerful ally in Terman. Returning to Stanford as dean of engineering, Terman was also a close friend of the university's incoming president. "Trust Terman to know the right

people!" Hansen told Bloch. Such a laboratory, Terman assured the
president, would be a "jewel in Stanford's crown" and would, along
with the Communications Laboratory, attract the best students and
defense project scientists heading back to school for advanced work in
electronics.[29] Terman also gave Hansen a few public relations point-
ers. Call it the Microwave Laboratory rather than the Stanford Microwave Laboratory, to emphasize its uniqueness, he counseled.
Hansen got the administrative go-ahead in December 1944, with the
promise of $12,500 for microwave equipment and supplies plus addi-
tional money for a second faculty appointment.

Hansen's choice of Ginzton as associate director of the Microwave
Laboratory confirmed the new direction of Stanford physics. Ginzton had solid research and administrative credentials from Sperry,
but a degree in electrical engineering, not physics. After caucusing,
the department granted him the title, "associate professor of applied
physics," which, like his subsequent work, pointed to the future. On
the bottom of a memorandum announcing the final arrangement for
the Microwave Laboratory, acting chairman Paul Kirkpatrick jotted
down a set of challenging questions: "1. Is this work physics? 2. Is it all
right to do work for Sperry and like outfits? 3. Is there any objection to
the financial arrangements whereby a staff member has what is in
effect a private presidential budget?"[30] The department's subsequent
work in high-power klystrons and linear accelerators would provide
the answers.

From the start, the Microwave Laboratory had two primary but
essentially divergent goals—to create a linear accelerator of unprecedented scale and to design and build powerful new microwave tubes
to drive it. In achieving them, it would simultaneously confirm
Hansen's most sanguine predictions about the scientific payoffs of microwave research, and Webster's deepest fears about a discipline increasingly dominated by corporate and military patrons, by engineering methods, and by quasi-independent laboratories.[31]

Sperry played an important, though diminishing, role in the Microwave Laboratory. Ginzton returned from Sperry in the spring of
1946 with a $25,000 contract for advanced klystron research in addi-
tion to the previous $20,000 commitment for more general micro-
wave research at the laboratory. The company negotiated a separate

contract with Terman's Electronics Research Laboratories, $10,000 a year in return for patent rights to any klystron or traveling-wave tubes developed there on the JSEP contract.[32] It also funded several graduate fellowships until it discovered that most of the students were taking jobs with competitors nearer to campus.[33]

To finance the long-stalled electron accelerator project, however, Hansen had to look elsewhere. Only the military had the kind of money he was looking for, and would be willing to spend it. He had little difficulty selling the ONR on the linear accelerator. After all, it offered the attraction of both nuclear physics (science's most glamorous specialty in those years) plus state-of-the-art microwave technology (engineering's most glamorous postwar specialty). One was connected in the public and the military mind with the triumphs of Los Alamos, and the other with the miracles of the Rad Lab. In June 1946 the ONR signed an initial $26,000 contract for accelerator research. Within a year Hansen had worked out a general theory for a linear electron accelerator and built a small, magnetron-driven prototype.[34]

What he really needed was a microwave driver more powerful and easier to synchronize than the magnetron. Hansen and Ginzton had already been thinking about very high-power klystrons as a way around some of the limitations of the magnetron. They brought in Marvin Chodorow, a former Slater student and Sperry colleague, to help design and build one in 1947. With a second $90,000 contract from ONR, Ginzton, Chodorow, several research associates, and a dozen graduate students set to work on a klystron a thousand times more powerful than anything yet built.[35] Although they knew of no theoretical reasons that would preclude their building such a tube, actually doing it proved more challenging than expected. Reviewing a frustrating history of cracked tuning diaphragms, fouled cathodes, leaky vacuums, and busted "windows," Hansen lamented, "We see now that the job is much bigger than we had imagined—every bit and piece is 100 times bigger than standard, and that makes a research job of it. I conclude we'll come out O.K. but will take longer to do it than we had thought."[36]

With a practical driver at least on the drawing board, Hansen and his colleagues set themselves the unprecedented, and admittedly arbitrary, goal of one billion electron volts. In the spring of 1948, Hansen sent the ONR a proposal for a 160-foot accelerator powered by sixteen 30-megawatt klystrons, at an estimated cost of $1 million. The ONR approved it that June. Hansen died of chronic lung disease (brought on by beryllium exposure during the war) in May 1949, only months after the first successful demonstration of a 14-megawatt pulsed klystron. Though virtually bedridden near the end, he rigged up an oxygen system in his car so he could still visit his accelerator and watch the progress being made by his colleagues and students.

Ginzton took over as director of the Microwave Laboratory following Hansen's death and continued the drive toward a billion volts. Under Ginzton's leadership, some forty graduate students and a dozen research associates, with $400,000 a year in support from ONR, gradually increased the length and performance of the accelerator, section by section, until the entire project ran out of room in early 1952 and literally came up against a wall in the laboratory building—eighty feet and several million volts short of the magic billion, but long and powerful enough to lay claim as the world's most powerful electron accelerator.[37]

With the accelerator virtually completed, Ginzton took a hard look at the future of the laboratory. He, Chodorow, and their students were not, and had no intentions of becoming, nuclear specialists. Their expertise and interests were in designing and building advanced microwave tubes. "What, then, shall become of the present staff and students and activities, other than physics, of the Microwave Laboratory?" Ginzton asked, referring to the staff of two professors, six research associates, and fifteen graduate students working on microwave tubes. "Having spent many years of their lives in establishing the microwave art, the present staff of the Laboratory would like to continue their efforts in the research and training of students in the same general directions as in the recent past. The successful development by this staff of the high power klystron and the linear accelerator insure continued interest in Stanford's microwave activities on the part of graduate students and of government circles that supply research funds. It is reasonable to believe that the microwave staff will be as successful in its teaching and research program in the future as it has been in the past."[38]

The tube researchers already had plenty to keep them busy. Looking down the road, Ginzton predicted that "The klystron and other related devices will provide an almost unlimited field of activity for engineering students. In this field, we can not only train graduate students and do work of general scientific interest but can also make significant contributions to the national defense program."[39] For despite Ginzton's earlier assertion that "our klystron, as it exists today, is not of practical importance to the Military Establishment," the defense department (and Stanford physicists) fully recognized the military implications of high-powered klystrons for advanced radar systems.[40] The early versions for the accelerator had been continuously pumped to hold their vacuum. But simply by sealing them off, such tubes were perfectly suitable for radar applications. "It was obvious," the researchers recalled, "that klystron amplifiers of this kind even at much lower power levels would be of value in radar systems; it was also apparent in the Laboratory that sealed-off tubes of this kind could be easily developed on the basis of information accumulated in the design of the 14 megawatt tubes."[41] The laboratory's military sponsors knew that, too. In August 1949 the ONR and the Microwave Laboratory sponsored a conference on high-power klystrons at Stanford, restricted to participants with security clearances.

The Korean mobilization gave the high-power klystron effort a strong push toward the applied, just as it had for Terman's electronics program. JSEP negotiated with the Microwave Laboratory an unprecedented parallel contract for investigating sealed, high-power klystrons that rivaled in scale the contract for the linear accelerator itself. Initially JSEP funded basic research in physical electronics aimed at extending the power and range, and reducing the size, of high-power klystrons. But once again "basic" research led directly to separate classified contracts for particular tube applications for the Signal Corps, Air Force, and the Navy, a total sponsored program of $700,000 a year that dwarfed the $100,000 "basic" contract.[42]

Under Ginzton and Chodorow, the Microwave Laboratory adapted its growing expertise in physical electronics to new tube configurations, notably very high-powered TWTs. At high voltage, Field's helical TWTs literally could not take the heat, and so were only good for receivers and other low-power applications. Borrowing from his accelerator experience, Chodorow developed the coupled-cavity TWT for radar, a completely different design, conceptually similar to a linear accelerator with special slots to produce beam/wave interaction. Although Chodorow's TWTs did not have the extraordinary bandwidth of Field's helical tubes, they compensated with far greater power—megawatts rather than watts. Offering longer range, more difficult to jam, and with a high rate of scanning, they became the heart of advanced radar systems like the Safeguard ABM and the Aegis.[43] The laboratory later boasted, with some justification, "Every multi-megawatt traveling-wave tube in use in military radar systems, the TWTs used in almost every phased array under development in this country, the TWTs in all ground transmitters for satellite communications, all use either a circuit first invented or first investigated in the Microwave Laboratory."[44]

At first the prospect of classified research raised serious questions, especially about the impact on students. "Any method that might be adopted which would allow only certain students to take Microwave Laboratory courses or work on ONR-sponsored research would create a very difficult and very artificial situation," Ginzton and Chodorow complained to their ONR sponsors. "One group of students would not be able to discuss freely their activities with another group within the walls of the same building."[45] Like their counterparts and frequent collaborators in SEL, the microwave physicists got around those restrictions by placing the classified portions of the contracts in AEL, and keeping the rest under the Microwave Laboratory itself. Graduate students could still contribute to and learn from the work being done on the applied contracts. Several, for example, wrote theses on high-power TWT design and circuits under the actual, if not formal, supervision of research associates in AEL.

Corporate Connections

The high-power klystron and TWT research contracts reinforced an already close collaboration between microwave electronics companies and the university. To convert their experimental designs into practical hardware, the Stanford researchers worked closely with the engineering staffs at the companies awarded defense contracts to produce high-power klystrons and TWTs for radar applications. Chodorow worked with Litton Industries developing a high-power L-band klystron for military radar, and with Varian Associates on an X-band version. As with electronic countermeasures tubes, Stanford researchers designed, built, and tested the prototypes, and then helped transfer the technology to industry. Litton's L3035 tube became the workhorse of advanced Air Force radar systems and, according to the laboratory's sponsors, "revolutionized radar technology."[46] Ginzton and Chodorow's graduates in corporate, military, and academic laboratories soon read like a who's who in microwave engineering. By the early 1960s, about half the world's supply of high-power klystron tubes was being built within ten miles of Stanford.[47]

Expanding from that one major corporate affiliation with Sperry, the Microwave Laboratory developed new partnerships, some with companies spun off from its own laboratory. Varian Associates literally got its start at Stanford, holding its first board meeting at the university in April 1948. Its founders, including the Varians, Hansen, and Ginzton, had all worked on the original klystron project. Varian's first products were based on Stanford-owned patents, and Stanford graduates and faculty members, including Hansen, Ginzton, and Terman, served as the company's first directors.[48]

While the company's stated purpose was to "conduct general research in the fields of physical science of every kind and nature," for the first years at least Varian was really a microwave tube defense contractor, with 95 percent of its tube business (and 80 percent overall) with the military. Its first large contract was for a reflex klystron designed by Chodorow as a proximity fuse for guided missiles. "Varian's growth during the first decade or so was rapid, primarily military based, and tied in closely with the growth of the aerospace industry," recalled the head of its tube division.[49] Its product line expanded into a full range of klystrons, from low-power models for airborne radar and guided missiles through medium-power versions for mobile communications systems and radar jamming, to very high-powered outfits for radar transmitters. Official marketing projections at the time correctly predicted a tiny commercial market for the company's microwave tubes and acknowledged that "even this minor fraction is adaptable to defense applications."[50] The company did develop UHF television transmitters and other commercial microwave systems, and a line of analytical instruments based on Felix Bloch's nuclear magnetic resonance research and patents. But still, it made most of its money on defense contracts. With a strong boost from the Korean War buildup, Varian's sales climbed from $200,000 in 1949 to $1.5 million two years later, to $20 million by the end of the company's first decade in business.

Varian kept up its close relationship with the Microwave Laboratory while its independent corporate and military connections expanded. Beginning with modest grants to Ginzton for microwave studies, it gradually increased its support of Stanford research until by 1960 it was providing $5,000 a year for solid-state research, $12,000 for microwave research, $50,000 for an expansion of the Microwave Laboratory building (the "Varian Associates" wing), and $250,000 for a new physics building. Including klystron royalties and personal gifts from the Varian family, the company's total contribution to the university exceeded $4.5 million.[51] Ginzton sat on the company's executive committee, and he and Chodorow sat on the technical committee, charged with charting new research directions. Such ties were vital in keeping Varian on the leading edge of high-power klystron and TWT research and design throughout the 1950s.

Varian further strengthened those ties to Stanford by signing on as the first tenant of the Stanford Industrial Park. For its first few years the company had struggled along in cramped quarters in San Carlos, until the increasing size of their defense orders forced them to look for more space. Seeking a location nearer to Stanford for a new research and development laboratory, Varian negotiated a lease for ten acres of university-owned land that had been set aside just south of campus for light industrial development. Construction began in 1951. Varian later leased additional acreage for a corporate headquarters and several specialized laboratories.[52]

Heartened by Varian's example, Terman, as a member of the Advisory Committee on Land and Building Development, urged the university to reconsider its development plans so as to encourage other companies to relocate near campus. When he learned of General

Electric's interest in high-power klystrons and TWTs, Terman wrote the manager of its electronics division, talking up the advantages of a research and development facility close to campus. "Employees could readily work towards advanced degrees from Stanford without serious loss of time from the job," he noted. "This could be used to aid G.E. recruiting the most promising of the young men coming out of college with Bachelor's and Master's degrees. . . . Still further, a considerable number of Stanford doctoral candidates might choose to carry on their research activities at such a laboratory under the direction of selected G.E. people. This contact with the policies and operation of the company should be helpful in securing their services when they later decide upon permanent employment."[53] Terman specifically mentioned Ginzton and Chodorow's pioneering studies on high-power klystons for S-band radar as the kind of work GE might wish to exploit. Impressed by the pitch, GE relocated its microwave electronics laboratory to the industrial park in 1954.

Stanford promoters also pointed out for RCA chairman David Sarnoff the benefits of the industrial park, notably its proximity to the Microwave Laboratory and its continuing supply of top-notch graduate students.[54] Betting instead on closer ties between its new research center in Princeton and that university's program, RCA declined, but that was the exception. By 1960 Stanford Industrial Park had twenty-seven tenants, with 8,595 employees, including Varian (2,200), Hewlett-Packard (2,700), and GE (400).[55] Most took full advantage of the cooperative education program, faculty consultants, and Stanford graduates. Chodorow's chief collaborator on the closed-cavity TWT went to work for GE, as did a number of his students. Ginzton left to become chairman of the board of Varian Associates in 1959, following the death of Russell Varian. He retained his academic title at Stanford, however, and continued to work closely with his former colleagues. The university later renamed the Microwave Laboratory wing of the physics building in honor of his intellectual and financial contributions to the department. Stanford earned enough royalties on the sales of the high-power klystrons and TWTs developed in the classified programs to pay for a new physics building, the (what else?) Varian Laboratory of Physics.[56]

Applied Physics

By the early 1960s the Microwave Laboratory had grown into the largest division in the physics department, with eight faculty members, eight senior nonfaculty researchers, twelve research associates, and fifty graduate students. When Chodorow took over as director in 1959, he expanded the faculty by promoting the best research associates into professorial positions, and by bringing in top people from outside. He hired Calvin Quate, a former student of Field's in low-noise TWTs and Arthur Schalow, a pioneer in quantum electronics, both out of Bell Labs, to replace Ginzton.

With each new appointment, however, Chodorow faced growing resistance from the physics department, which remained fiercely jealous of its right to define the scope of its academic discipline and which had become increasingly concerned about the rising tide of applied physicists. Under chairman Leonard Schiff and Nobel laureate Felix Bloch, the department had chosen to remain an independent island of little science in an ocean of big federal contracts. While other Stanford faculty, including Chodorow and the Microwave Laboratory staff, routinely drew half their salaries from contracts, the core physics faculty stubbornly insisted on supporting themselves and their graduate students on "hard" money. They recognized the contributions of "applied physics" but had no intention of granting it equal status within the department. [57]

Stymied by departmental politics, and eager to move into quantum electronics, plasmas, lasers, and other newer fields in applied physics, Chodorow in November 1961 proposed creation of a separate and equal department of applied physics. [58] Such a department, he suggested, would provide a stronger organizational identity for applied physics, make room for additional faculty appointments, encourage further interdisciplinary collaboration across traditional department boundaries, and offer physics graduate students greater opportunities to participate in the research programs of other departments. Even Bloch saw merit in the idea as a way of extending the applied programs while preserving the balance of specialties (and power) within the department. [59]

Outsiders were not so sure. The electrical engineers regarded any independent department of applied physics as a potential rival. Compared with science enrollments, engineering enrollments had begun to slip in recent years. And further, the areas Chodorow expressed interest in were the very same glamour fields where electrical engineering had staked a claim with its recent recruiting and research efforts. The physicists had worried after the war about losing interesting fields to the electrical engineers, but by the early 1960s the engineers were alarmed by the entrepreneurialism of the applied physicists.

Led by chairman Hugh Skilling and former chairman and dean of engineering Joseph Pettit, the electrical engineers expressed grave reservations and outright hostility to Chodorow's plan. Skilling protested: "I feel very strongly that nothing should be done that would tend to reduce the Electrical Engineering department to a second-class operation. . . . I particularly would be unhappy to see new and interesting ventures into unknown territory taken out of the realm of the Electrical Engineering department, with only routine and uninteresting subjects left."[60] After reviewing Chodorow's plan, Pettit told Terman: "I guess it is time to call a spade a spade. His program proposed is almost completely competitive with Engineering, adding virtually nothing we cannot do already except educating 60 new graduate students in the University. . . . It must be completely clear that the prestige value of solid state, quantum electronics and plasmas must in no way be *transferred* from EE to Applied Physics. The ability of EE to attract top students and faculty has derived largely from its involvement and identification with new and different fields. I am not willing for this to be substantially diluted, unless so instructed by the University to achieve some larger goal."[61] Sensing that perhaps Chodorow had been emboldened by poor public relations on the part of the engineers, Pettit seriously suggested claiming the fields for electrical engineering and changing the name of his area of responsibility to the School of Engineering and Applied Science.

As provost, Terman took a longer view than his former colleagues. He had actually foreseen just this possibility some years before. One of his long-standing fears had been that if engineers did not move aggressively into interesting new fields, scientists would. If engineers did not take care to prevent it, he had cautioned in 1955, "colleges of

Applied Science will develop on campus and insulate engineering from pure science while taking over the interesting and creative areas," leaving engineers with "dull trade school subjects."[62] At the time he had been confident that his colleagues would never allow such a catastrophe to occur. Only six years later, though, it appeared that the physicists were positioning themselves to make it happen. Terman, however, had come to believe that applied physics represented an extension and redefinition of science rather than an erosion of engineering. In fact, he favored closer ties between applied and "pure" physics on the model of the Microwave Laboratory. "We don't want Physics to insulate themselves from the Applied Physics activity," he said, "and this can be best avoided by keeping the present joint appointments so that the voice of Applied Physics can be heard inside the Physics Department at least for the present."[63] He had no doubts that the applied physics program would be able to make it on its own, and felt that it would not in any way detract from parallel efforts in the engineering school. With enough students—sixty by Terman's count—the new department would pay for itself.[64] The dean of graduate studies, acknowledging that "A high level of work in applied science has been extremely important to Stanford, and this trend is likely to be intensified," voted with Terman.[65] In the fall of 1962 the administration approved a new graduate division of applied physics within the School of Humanities and Sciences.

Applied Physics opened for business in the fall of 1963, with six faculty members, including Chodorow, Quate, Peter Sturrock, and Hubert Heffner (all former microwave tube specialists), and offering a full range of graduate courses in microwave electronics and measurement, plasma physics, and solid state. Rather than duplicating classes already on the books, the new division sought "to offer physics courses which are of value to the research program of Applied Physics or various engineering departments and which are either not being given by the Physics Department or not being given in a form and with the emphasis that is of optimum value for these University research activities."[66] So even though the initial course titles overlapped considerably with physics offerings, the actual instruction and laboratory work represented a significant intellectual departure. Chodorow, for instance, wanted new courses "whose emphasis and pace is better matched to the needs of the solid-state research activities than the present Physics courses," and complementary laboratory work able "to provide some training in basic experimental techniques selected with particular areas of research in mind."[67] Heffner, recognizing that "quantum effects are now beginning to be important in practical electronic devices," argued that the "present quantum mechanics courses taught in the physics department do not serve our purpose, for they are concerned largely with the problems of atomic and nuclear physics rather than with electromagnetic fields. No adequate course or text exists on quantum theory as applied to electronics, but in view of its relevance to the future of electrical engineering, it is important that we develop such material." In other words, applied physics meant not only putting theory to work on practical devices but redefining theory itself in terms of applications—microwave tubes, solid-state devices, and parametric amplifiers. Perhaps Chodorow's catalog description best summarized the distinction between applied physics and its parent: "Although there is no sharp division between the interests of the two organizations, work of the Division centers on those areas of physics which are significant more for their applications in technology than for their intrinsic interest as natural phenomena."[68]

The subsequent success of the division's research and teaching program amply confirmed Chodorow's sense of the changing character of academic physics. Starting with ten students, all supported with fellowships or teaching assistantships, the division expanded to sixty-five degree candidates by the end of its first five years, two-thirds of them on contract money. Most of them came with undergraduate physics degrees, not electrical engineering degrees, from MIT, Berkeley, Princeton, Cornell, and other top schools. In fact, the division rapidly outstripped the physics department as a center for doctoral training, graduating its first Ph.D. in 1966, four more the following year, six the next, and a dozen or so annually after that.[69]

With more than half its contract budget coming from defense agencies, the department's research program understandably reflected the changing military agenda for applied physics. Chodorow and his colleagues began by extending the concepts and calculations they had pioneered in the tube research into solid-state technology. Under

JSEP and Air Force sponsorship, they made the division a leading center for research and teaching in microwave acoustics (essentially ways of converting microwave signals into sound waves through specially designed crystals and associated circuitry).[70] They trained most of the early graduate students in this important new field, and one of them, Bertram Auld, wrote an important textbook on the subject, *Acoustic Fields and Waves in Solids*. Stanford was so dominant in microwave acoustics that Chodorow argued for a sabbatical year abroad by suggesting that "the best place for me to digest what we have done is somewhere away from the scene of battle."[71]

As in the microwave tube program, Stanford's success in basic research led to a family of practical devices for communications and radar and to a series of follow-up contracts to perfect them with individual service agencies.[72] The Air Force negotiated a $210,000 annual contract for advanced research in microwave acoustics, and a contract with the Rome Air Development Center for studies of acoustic delay lines in electronic countermeasures (useful, among other things, for confusing radar by duplicating and delaying the return signal). The Army supported Quate's research on acoustic crystals because it offered a new kind of radar filtering system, separating out the original signal from jamming and other noise. Perhaps the laboratory's biggest breakthrough in microwave acoustics was the "interdigital transducer." By dramatically increasing the efficiency of transferring energy from an electromagnetic source to an acoustic wave system, it suddenly made microwave acoustic devices practical.[73] Intrigued by the prospects, the military services quickly arranged complementary industrial contracts for acoustic signal processing and imaging systems. In microwave acoustics Stanford researchers did not actually build prototypes, but the Air Force contracts generally specified that such studies should be carried to the point that further improvement could be done by industrial laboratories.

The division's plasma program followed much the same pattern, getting its start when Chodorow hired Gordon Kino from Bell Labs in 1957 to strengthen the Microwave Laboratory's experimental plasma physics group. Kino's subsequent research, largely under Air Force sponsorship, built directly on the laboratory's strengths in microwave tubes and electron beam devices by exploring ways of generating, transmitting, and amplifying microwave power using the special properties of plasmas. He and Chodorow devised an entire family of "two stream" amplifiers which, though resembling their klystron and TWT ancestors, offered significant improvements in certain applications. They also worked on parametric amplifiers (extremely low-noise amplifiers for highly sensitive microwave receivers, as in radar and countermeasures).[74]

As in the microwave electronics research that preceded it, the plasma program maintained close ties with SEL, especially with Dean Watkins and his group in electron beams. Sturrock collaborated with SEL people in the Radio Science Laboratory. Chodorow worked there on parametric amplifiers. Staff members from both laboratories participated in an early plasma physics seminar run by Stanford Research Institute and coordinated by the director of Boeing's plasma physics laboratory. Sturrock, for one, certainly understood how the laboratory's plasma physics program depended upon the larger world of military and industrial science and engineering around it: "In the development of a new area of scientific activity, such as plasma physics, there is a very strong interaction between universities on the one hand and the scientific centers of industry and the nation on the other. Whether such an area develops, and the rate at which it develops, depends partially upon its intrinsic scientific interests, but also upon its industrial (and regrettably, military) significance. The great surge in development of plasma physics which we are now witnessing began (in secret) in national laboratories; further unclassified research in these laboratories and now also in industrial laboratories is an important stimulus to similar research in universities."[75]

The division's later research in lasers certainly mirrored larger military and industrial agendas, just as earlier research had. By the early 1960s, the DOD was seriously talking about lasers as "the biggest breakthrough in the weapons area since the atomic bomb," and was spending millions of dollars a year for research and development in hopes of turning out new kinds of rangefinders, missile guidance systems, and similar hardware.[76] In Applied Physics that money primarily supported studies of tunable lasers, with a view toward communications applications, and ring lasers, with a view toward sophisticated missile guidance and control systems. Stanford's laser researchers later insisted that military interests and funding made no difference for their research programs. Their contract monitors, however, took a different view. "The DOD plays a powerful role in shaping the profile of engineering research at Stanford," one explained. "In the absence of DOD interest laser physics would not enjoy the level of support it now receives at Stanford; funding by another agency, such as the NSF, would probably be allocated to different types of projects."[77] As one Stanford laser scientist explained, "Nobody likes DOD support less than we do. . . . The problem is, when the military supports everything, they're the people who come around with the problems, and so you think about those problems."[78]

Taking up the SLAC

Meanwhile, Stanford's High Energy Physics Laboratory (HEPL), which split off from the tube portion of the Microwave Laboratory in 1954, found itself moving toward a new kind of physics which, if more "basic" (in the sense that it had fewer direct military and industrial applications than microwave tubes and acoustics), still depended on the same financial, technological, and intellectual infrastructure. The Mark III accelerator and its successor, SLAC, were as much products of the new postwar physics as the high-power klystrons that drove them, and just as instrumental in setting the future direction of the department.

Although chairman Leonard Schiff, like his colleagues, initially regarded the Mark III as "just another research tool of the Department: much larger than but in principle on a par with the existing cyclotron, nuclear induction equipment, x-ray apparatus, and microwave equipment," subsequent events suggested otherwise.[79] Only days after Hansen's death, Karl Spangenberg, as a representative of the ONR, asked what was going to happen to the Navy's accelerator investment at Stanford and pressed the department to demonstrate its commitment to the machine by appointing some experimentalists to use it.[80] To move beyond machine building, the department added Robert Hofstadter, a former colleague of Schiff's from the University of Pennsylvania, and Wolfgang Panofsky, a refugee from the recent loyalty oath crisis at Berkeley, who launched an ambitious experimental program on the not-yet-completed Mark III. Hofstadter's electron-scattering experiments, revealing that subatomic particles like protons have finite dimension, eventually won him the Nobel Prize. Panofsky's research won similar acclaim. The two rapidly built their own stables of graduate students and won their own contracts, mostly from the ONR and the Air Force.

Having sampled the scientific rewards of an increasingly powerful machine, HEPL set its sights in 1955 on a truly giant linear accelerator, two miles long with 50 billion electron volts of power. Among other names for the project, the committee considered MOLE (for MOnster Linear Electron Accelerator) and SEAL (for Stanford Electron AcceLerator)—"The authors of these wish to remain, perhaps understandably, anonymous," Schiff quipped—before settling simply on Project M (for Monster).[81] After a series of preliminary meetings, an informal committee of Ginzton, Hofstadter, Panofsky, and Schiff forwarded a proposal for Project M to Stanford's administration, along with a warning that growing competition from Brookhaven, MIT, and the Europeans meant that "If we at Stanford are to remain in the high-energy field, it is necessary to start making preparations now for the construction of a new large accelerator to take place in the next five years or so."[82]

Though the scientific potential of such a machine was obvious (extremely high-energy electrons offered unique advantages as probes for elementary particles, as sources of strong gamma rays, and as a way of creating certain kinds of new particles), its scope and character raised serious questions about the future course of Stanford physics.[83] Felix Bloch, who had already seen big machine physics up close as acting director of CERN (the central European laboratory for nuclear physics), was openly skeptical. "10^8 bucks means administrators, personnel managers, foremen, auditors, navy contract men, prolonged sojourns in Washington, etc., etc. . . . 10^2 klystrons with their attachments means mass production—and I think that sufficiently characterizes this aspect of the thing," he warned his colleagues.[84] He urged them to resist the pressures of keeping up with the Berkeleys, and instead to put their effort into the kind of small-scale, high-quality physics that had secured the department's reputation in the first place. When asked if that meant going ahead with the accelerator over his "dead body," Bloch replied that building such a machine would not so much mark his own funeral as the department's.[85]

Even Hofstadter, an early supporter of the project as a way of opening up some "fun and challenging" problems, eventually came around to Bloch's point of view. His experiences at CERN had left a similarly bitter aftertaste. "My enthusiasm for it [Project M] has flagged considerably because I realize that it is soul destroying in the sense that one's personality (in physics) disappears in the merging that goes into its fabrication," he told Bloch.[86]

Behind Project M, however, was a powerful coalition led by Ginzton and Panofsky with the experience, connections, and political savvy to push the accelerator through roadblocks at home and in Washington.[87] Locally, the tide was running with the machine builders. Terman had recently been named provost and immediately saw how M would fit into his steeple-building schemes. Nationally, fears about Soviet success in space and weapons research, coupled with a growing concern about having an adequate number of future American physicists and engineers, ensured a receptive audience in Congress. Perhaps Stanford's strongest selling point in Washington was its proven record in microwave tube research and development. Unlike rival accelerators, Stanford's was backed by a decade of research and development on high-power klystrons and related microwave hardware. The accelerator may have been "brute force" technology, as someone dubbed it, but it was a technology that had been proven in practice to produce significant scientific and engineering payoffs. In 1961, after several years of political negotiations, Congress approved $114 million for the accelerator, the largest single appropriation for a scientific project up to that time.[88]

Although funded as a federal laboratory under university management, SLAC's designers and prospective users always considered it an integral part of Stanford. Panofsky recalled that "a main justification to have such a machine at Stanford rested on the argument that SLAC would have strong ties to the University community and contribute to its educational potential. In particular, SLAC would not have to be a complete laboratory like national centers isolated from academic communities."[89] In selling the project to the university's board of trustees, the physicists argued strongly that the facility would add to, as well as draw from, Stanford's research and teaching programs.

That objective was immediately threatened by an increasingly bitter controversy pitting self-proclaimed purists like Bloch, Schiff, and Hofstadter against their own colleagues, and against much of the rest of the university as well. Just as they had previously worried about unbalancing the department by appointing too many "applied physicists," the traditionalists now feared being drowned in a flood of high-energy specialists. By 1960 half the faculty and more than half the graduate students were already concentrated in the high-energy field. To reassert control, the core members of the department restricted the number of new joint appointments with SLAC and limited the number of graduate students those appointees could supervise to 10 percent of the number of graduate students currently enrolled in the department.[90] Terman, for one, was incensed by the 10 percent rule, complaining, "This is a mighty small contribution for a research facility costing $114 million to build, and $20 million a year to operate."[91]

SLAC quickly became a lightning rod for a campuswide debate on the relative merits of center- and department-oriented research, and it represented a classic confrontation between the old and new styles in research. The purists, led by Hofstadter, Bloch, and Schiff, found most of their support coming from colleagues in biochemistry, chemistry, and other departments still operating on traditional patterns of small science. Chemist Paul Flory, for instance, urged the administration "to support the muted pleadings of an excellent department against the strident demands of ambition and bigness."[92]

Yet even department supporters recognized that isolating SLAC from the rest of the campus would end up being counterproductive. "The attitude of the Blochs and Schiffs will help make real the Big Science they fear," one sympathetic critic suggested, "because if their position prevails Big Science will tend to be devoid of academic content and academic types. It is ironic that they will contribute in a major way to the development they are so anxious to prevent."[93] Many faculty members seemed to agree with Panofsky, who dismissed Bloch's objections to SLAC as a "romantic view that experimental physics today means setting up a few magnets in the basement of the building," a not-so-veiled reference to Bloch's nuclear induction experiments.[94] Most others concluded that SLAC was simply far too important to be hobbled by any one department, however distinguished.

For a time the controversy paralyzed both SLAC and the physics department. The department had trouble making appointments—courting and losing several eminent candidates—while SLAC had trouble holding on to theirs. "This controversy has long ago reached the dimensions of a national scandal," Heffner lamented. "For two years now, on every trip I make on which I talk with a colleague in physics, I am asked about the latest developments in the raging controversy."[95]

SLAC (which came on line in 1966) certainly did not end up being "devoid of academic content and academic types." Panofsky eventually won most of his earlier demands for graduate students, joint appointments, and collaborative research and built up his own steeple of excellence on the far edge of the high-energy frontier. If anything, it displaced the department as the intellectual center of Stanford physics.[96]

Although overshadowed by its giant neighbor and the controversy surrounding it, HEPL could not resist the attraction of machine physics, either. Its Mark III, where Hofstadter had chosen to continue his electron-scattering research, had scarcely reached its stated goal of a billion electron volts before it became essentially obsolete. Only by making it superconducting, and thereby effectively doubling its power, could he and his collaborators hope to compete with newer machines coming on line in France and the Soviet Union, and of course at SLAC itself.

As so often before, means, not scientific ends, caught the eye of potential sponsors. Just as the ONR had supported early Stanford accelerators as much for their potential contributions to high-power klystrons as for their contributions to high-energy physics, it now offered a $22 million contract (that doubled the laboratory's financial support) for upgrading the old Mark III into a state-of-the-art superconducting accelerator. In awarding the contract, the Navy emphasized that it "was extending support primarily for the purpose of

stimulating research and development on cryogenic systems," not esoteric physics.[97] The researchers themselves also emphasized the
practical implications of superconducting microwave cavities and the
"possibilities for new kinds of very stable oscillators and frequency systems which might have use in Navy communications and guidance."[98] An assistant secretary of the Navy later cited the HEPL's
cryogenic research as a particularly good example of the relevance of
the ONR's basic research program to the Navy's larger mission: "This
large scale refrigerator for operating at very, very low temperatures
means that we can build electronic systems which will be very much
more compact, reliable, and efficient. The cryogenic technique
would permit a great advance in certain kinds of radar and electronic
warfare systems. The fact that we can build this refrigerator on this
scale means that it will probably become a practical matter to obtain
high efficiency in the transfer of electromagnetic radiation on board
ship."[99] In fact the accelerator project led to follow-up contracts with
the Air Force for basic research on superconducting accelerometers,
with an eye toward advanced guidance and control systems.

With an uncanny sense of what lay ahead, Paul Kirkpatrick predicted
as early as 1946: "The postwar future of Stanford is subject to our control to only a minor degree. World and national economic, political,
and social conditions will take the ball away from us and carry it."[100]
Events would prove him right. In those years physics became less an
end in itself than a means to other ends, most of them military. Like
their colleagues elsewhere, Stanford's physicists came out of the
war not only with new tools but with a new sense of direction and
purpose. What had been thought to be a temporary aberration of
wartime—making applied science the center of their discipline—
became business as usual. Even when applications did not become
ends in themselves, they established the intellectual contours of inquiry, thus setting limits on their users.

   Though he had benefited as much as anyone from the new physics, Hofstadter also recognized its high cost—restricting the opportunity to follow an independent course. In a commencement address
entitled "The Free Spirit in the Free University," he warned of the
growing dangers of research institutes and centers: "We must be care-

ful to see that the growth of these large semi-independent research organizations within the university does not result in control by these organizations—or even partial control—of the administrative and academic functions of the university—even for what may seem at the time to be well-motivated reasons. These research organizations have narrow purposes compared to the main functions of the university which is to teach, to allow its staff to study, and to encourage the thinking process. Though bigness is of the essence of the research organizations, the thoughts they produce fall into various small corners of the universities' range of knowledge."[101] At Stanford, as in other top American university departments of physics, it was all too clear that those small corners had moved rapidly to the center.

7 | A Matter of State

John Slater's career spanned a transformation in the materials science field—from its esoteric origins in the quantum revolution of the 1920s to its maturation in the 1960s as the most practical of scientific disciplines. Starting out at MIT as the head of a small, financially struggling program in what one of his students called the "sharecropper" science days of the Depression, he ended up as a leader of one of the nation's best, and best funded, academic research empires. In the early days, working with only a few students and a blackboard, he had to beg four-figure grants from private foundations just to keep going. Three decades later, he was in charge of MIT's Center for Materials Science and Engineering (CMSE), perhaps the leading institution of its kind in the world. Along the way, he helped invent the techniques, train the students (including William Shockley), and write the texts—including a four-volume series on the quantum theory of solids—that revolutionized the science and technology of materials and that made their properties of far more than academic interest. His career, like CMSE itself, depicted the intellectual and organizational reorientation of postwar MIT as well as the military's pivotal role in that process.

A Quantum Leap

Slater first studied the properties of materials as a graduate student at Harvard, measuring the compressibility of sodium chloride crystals and trying theoretically to account for their behavior.[1] Convinced that contemporary quantum theory, still in its formative stage, did not adequately address these questions, he set out to extend the range of its applications to solids. He pursued that interest abroad in the mid-1920s, working with many of the pioneers in solid-state physics in Copenhagen and Leipzig and adding some significant contributions of his own, including a simplified method for calculating molecular binding energies. Back at Harvard as a professor in the late 1920s, he pushed for an interdisciplinary approach to solid state using refined tools of quantum mechanics, which, he said, could now, at least in principle, "explain all the properties of matter."[2] His proposal received a polite hearing from his Harvard colleagues, but no action.

Slater found a more receptive audience when he moved on to MIT in 1930 to head Karl Compton's physics department. In 1934 he persuaded Vannevar Bush to appoint him chair of a special Joint Committee on the Properties of Matter, which was to survey teaching and research in the field throughout the Institute and explore ways of coordinating it more effectively.[3] "In my investigations I have discovered a number of fields in which work is being done in a number of departments with comparatively little interchange of ideas," he reported. "This is not desirable either for the individuals and departments concerned, or in the Institute as a whole."[4] To facilitate discussion, he organized a joint colloquium series on materials sponsored by the physics department. Attendance, he had to admit, was rather disappointing.[5]

With no clear mandate from the rest of the Institute for a major interdisciplinary initiative in materials research, Slater simply went ahead on his own. First simplifying the recently devised "cellular method" for calculating the energy bands of solids (which, according to quantum theory, accounted for the particular behavior of conductors, semiconductors, and insulators), he applied it to new families of crystals.[6] He put several of his best graduate students to work on this problem, including William Shockley and Marvin Chodorow. Both would leave shortly after—Shockley moving to Bell Laboratories and Chodorow to Sperry and Stanford. Only the relatively primitive calculating devices of the day kept Slater and his students from perfecting their techniques. By the late 1930s Slater had earned an international reputation not only for clever computational methods but for innovative teaching and textbooks as well. As chairman, he put quantum theory and its applications to solids in both the undergraduate and graduate curricula, and included it in his *Introduction to Chemical Physics* (1939).

Slater's plan for interdisciplinary materials research also took shape, though not, as it turned out, through his own department. Learning of the Rockefeller Foundation's interest in placing German refugee Arthur von Hippel, and its willingness to carry a substantial share of his salary, Compton offered an appointment in electrical engineering in 1936.[7] "We definitely desire to give increasing emphasis to the field of applied physics in which Dr. von Hippel has been most active, namely the physical explanation of phenomena of high voltage and insulation," Compton told the Rockefeller board.[8] He planned that von Hippel would join the Institute's rapidly expanding program set up to commercialize Van de Graaff generators for electrostatic power systems.

Von Hippel brought to MIT a commitment to building a new science of materials as strong as Slater's.[9] His Laboratory for Insulation Research (LIR), which Slater liked to call an experimental solid-state laboratory, emphasized the "bridges between physics and electrical engineering." With a $5,500 annual budget, and a small interdisciplinary staff, LIR almost single-handedly transformed a specialty dominated by empiricism into one "based upon knowledge of the structure of matter and directed towards a real understanding of the dielectric phenomena involved."[10]

The war gave a tremendous boost to materials science, as it did to other scientific and engineering fields. Building on the theoretical insights of the 1930s to which Slater and his students had contributed, wartime researchers at Bell Labs and elsewhere learned to purify and crystallize silicon and germanium, and to identify the crucial importance of trace impurities in semiconductors. Out of this research

came such important electronics applications as silicon crystal rec-
tifiers for microwave radar receivers.[11] Von Hippel's laboratory also
made significant contributions. Under contracts from industry and
the government, it devised improved manufacturing techniques for
selenium photocells that dramatically cut production time, developed new instruments and reference standards for radar dielectrics,
and compiled a classified "Tables of Dielectric Materials."[12]

Reconversion

Slater and von Hippel looked forward to a postwar boom in materials
science. In his "Reconversion Plan for the Laboratory for Insulation
Research," von Hippel stated his hope that industrial contracts would
cover the bulk of LIR's future expenses, with foundation support
picking up the rest.[13] "If the properties of materials can be designed
and the phenomena steered judiciously by an understanding of the
underlying molecular causes," he later argued, "engineers can become creators where at present they are empiricists."[14] Slater too expected big things ahead for solid-state physics.

The Institute had some initial success with several creative schemes
for enlisting industrial and foundation support for materials research.
The Plastics Materials Manufacturers Association gave $30,000 a
year for a program in polymer research and teaching.[15] The Sloan
Foundation built a Metals Processing Laboratory aimed at applying
the latest breakthroughs in materials science to "machining, finishing, casting, forging, welding, forming, powdered metallurgy, and
related techniques of modern manufacturing."[16] A corporate liaison
program backed by Phelps Dodge, U.S. Steel, and other industry giants contributed $70,000 a year for metallurgical research.[17] LIR also
managed to arrange some small industrial contracts for its work.

Right from the start, however, those civilian contracts were simply
dwarfed by military money. One classified contract for metallurgical
studies of reactor fuel–element fabrication and radiation shielding
alone brought the Institute $800,000 a year.[18] Even laboratories
founded for commercial ends came to depend on military contacts
and contracts. At the dedication of the Metals Processing Laboratory,

the keynote speaker was the chairman of the Joint Research and Development Board, who chose as his topic, "Policies in Defense Research."[19]

LIR was shaped as much by the "macro" interests of its sponsors as by the "micro" interests of its staff. A joint services contract similar in character to RLE's (though smaller in scale) provided most of LIR's postwar funding. As part of his first summer symposium on dielectrics, von Hippel invited representatives from each of his military sponsors to explain their specific interests in dielectric research to each other and to the laboratory staff. Each service understandably emphasized somewhat different technical requirements, such as high-temperature radome materials for Air Force fighters, and improved piezoelectric crystals for Navy sonar. What they shared was a strong general commitment to increased miniaturization and reliability of electronics across a range of temperatures and environmental conditions. LIR's research programs increasingly reflected these military interests in microelectronics materials, notably research on silicon crystal growing (for heat and radiation resistant transistors), ferroelectrics (for computer memory applications), and gaseous breakdown (for radar switching tubes).[20]

Slater also found himself caught up in a new set of military problems. In the summer of 1949 the AEC asked him to head a special committee charged with investigating reactor materials.[21] Radiation damage had become a real threat to the AEC's weapons program, and was already delaying expansion at the Hanford plutonium facility. Slater's committee, which included several past and present MIT colleagues as well as industry and government representatives, spent several weeks reading the classified literature, touring AEC and industrial facilities, and talking with reactor specialists.[22] Their secret report urged the AEC "to encourage the general development of solid state physics, with particular application to the materials concerned in present fast reactor design," by supporting collaboration between AEC-sponsored facilities and university researchers and by supporting academic materials research directly.[23] To get started, Slater helped organize a conference on radiation damage later that summer at Brookhaven, with participants from the AEC laboratories (Oak

Ridge and Los Alamos), contractors (Westinghouse and North American Aviation), and military clients (Hyman Rickover and his nuclear engineers).[24]

Slater recognized that whatever intellectual rewards he might personally derive, the driving force behind solid-state physics, both theoretical and experimental, was going to be the promise of practical, and preferably military, applications. In a talk on solid-state physics for a military conference at MIT in the fall of 1949, he highlighted recent advances in the field and warned that despite its importance, "very few institutions in this country . . . pay adequate attention to the training of solid state scientists, and it is our hope that we may be able to make this an interesting enough field to attract many students, and give them the broad training necessary to work in different aspects of the solid state." With its research program spread across so many departments, materials science was not developing along a broad and coordinated front. "It seems to me not impossible that at some future date it may be a good idea to centralize a larger fraction of the work," he said.[25]

Slater was already thinking about a common focus for solid-state research at the Institute. In September 1950 he proposed the formation of a Molecular Theory Group within the physics department. Despite all that solid-state theory had contributed to practical developments during and after the war, the entire field, in Slater's words, "gives the impression of having fallen into a state of disrepute," at least among physicists. "Industrial and government laboratories are clamoring for solid-state physicists," he wrote. "What they find, when they look for them, is that experimental solid-state physicists are hard to find, and theoreticians in the field, particularly those with a good understanding of practical problems, are almost unobtainable."[26] To remedy that shortage, Slater planned to establish a small team, perhaps fifteen graduate students and a few postdoctorates, and immerse them in both theoretical and experimental solid-state physics. Properly directed, the program could provide an impetus for materials research throughout the Institute.

Predictably, Slater found the armed services his most receptive audience. Slater's emphasis on making the Solid State and Molecular

Theory Group (SSMTG) "a unifying influence in the whole field of the science of materials" appealed to the ONR, which started to provide significant funding in 1951.[27] Technically, SSMTG picked up where Slater's own research in solid state had left off in the late 1930s—calculating energy bands in solids, though now with the incomparably greater power of the Whirlwind I computer.[28]

As promised, Slater kept SSMTG in close touch with real-world problems. He took about half the members of SSMTG with him to Brookhaven in 1951 to take advantage of the experimental possibilities of the new reactor as a source of high-energy neutrons. He made a point of taking the students on "field trips" to IBM and Bell Laboratories. "I felt that in this way the students would get some idea of what was going on in industrial and government laboratories, and at the same time would let the people in charge of those laboratories know of our plans for the SSMTG," he recalled.[29]

Slater hoped to establish especially close ties with Lincoln Laboratory. Though the SSMTG's work was still quite theoretical, Slater saw real possibilities for it in Lincoln's growing solid-state program. He told Stratton: "The sort of work the boys are doing now is too fundamental, too far from experiment, to be much use to a practical laboratory. But in a couple of years we should be able to learn enough about the nature of energy bands in such materials as germanium to be highly valuable for practical purposes. . . . That being the case, it seemed to me a good investment for Lincoln to take on a number of my boys (they are all good), and to regard them as an investment for a couple of years, hoping the investment would pay off later. I'd actually keep them right in my group, though presumably on the Lincoln payroll: and we'd begin in that way to build up a theoretical group for Lincoln. I'd keep my hand on them right along, so that I would be able to turn their interests more in the direction of experiment when that seemed to pay, and in the meantime of course we would start right away to make such connection with experimental work as we could."[30] Slater worked most of the summer of 1952 at Lincoln. Several of his best students joined full time, including George Koster, who spent four years there before returning to the physics department as a faculty member. Throughout the 1950s, Lincoln provided slightly less than half of SSMTG's annual budget, and ONR the rest.[31]

The National Magnet Laboratory

Lincoln repaid some of its debt to solid-state physics on the campus in 1958 with the creation of the National Magnet Laboratory. The original proposal for a high-power magnet facility came from Benjamin Lax, a onetime Slater student who had gone on to head Lincoln's solid-state physics group. A Rad Lab veteran, like many of his Lincoln colleagues, Lax took a job after the war as a liaison officer with the Air Force Cambridge Research Laboratory and studied for his doctorate part-time at RLE. He intended to do a theoretical dissertation and collaborated with Slater for a time on magnetron theory. But Slater suggested that, at thirty-one, Lax might be too old for a theoretical career. (Twenty years later, with the advantage of hindsight, Slater suggested that perhaps Lax was not yet quite old enough!)[32] In looking for a more experimentally oriented topic, Lax became interested in Brown and Allis's gas discharge and plasma program at RLE and finished his degree under them in 1949. He transferred to the solid-state physics group at Lincoln in 1951. Over the next few years, Lax earned a reputation as a master of cyclotron resonance techniques for unraveling the band structure of semiconductor materials, specifically germanium and silicon. As he broadened the scope of his resonance studies toward the infrared region, he felt increasingly handicapped by the limits of his magnets.

Under Francis Bitter, MIT had been an acknowledged center of magnet research before the war. Bitter had worked with Peter Kapitza at Cambridge University developing powerful pulsed magnets before he joined the Institute in 1934.[33] In recruiting him, Compton had mentioned to Bitter that MIT was "extremely anxious to get some good work started on the properties of materials," and thought his research might encourage interdisciplinary efforts in that direction.[34] Bitter's prewar research culminated in an electromagnet (which now bears his name) capable of continuous fields of 100,000 gauss. Its secret was a way of cooling the solenoid, thereby preventing it from melting under the heat of massive electrical currents. Bitter founded a separate Magnet Laboratory in 1938, but both he and his laboratory were drafted for defense work before he could carry any new projects very far. [35]

Bitter returned to the Institute in 1945 with an appointment in the physics department and an ambitious plan to transform the magnet laboratory into a nationally recognized center for the study of the properties of matter. By taking advantage of the new microwave and cryogenics techniques developed during the war, Bitter hoped to dramatically improve the measurement of nuclear spins and magnetic moments. But his relatively modest proposals got lost in the bustle of postwar empire building, and most of his colleagues considered the laboratory "out of the mainstream." [36]

Instead, Lax and his Lincoln group took the initiative in using high-power magnets for solid-state research. They pushed their commercial magnets to 40 kilogauss, and their own pulsed versions up to 800 kilogauss, but could not achieve consistent or accurate measurements. "It now appears certain," they concluded, "that future research in these [cyclotron resonance and magneto-absorption phenomena] and many other branches of solid-state physics will depend increasingly upon the availability of suitable, high-field DC magnets." [37] The best around were in Bitter's laboratory, and Lax made arrangements to use them four hours a week in 1957. But even Bitter's best were not up to the demands of solid-state research in the infrared region, which demanded field strengths several times that of anything yet built. "If a million gauss magnet was developed by Division 7 and actually constructed as a result of our efforts, this would represent an exceptional engineering achievement," one of Lax's researchers told him. "The magnet would be invaluable in many areas of scientific research and the personnel involved and Lincoln Laboratory would gain world wide professional recognition." [38]

Lax's solid-state group already had a number of specific experiments in mind. A high-power, continuous field magnet would improve the accuracy of their present cyclotron, ferromagnetic, and paramagnetic resonance measurements and at the same time extend those measurements to new classes of materials. While the team envisioned a number of intriguing possibilities, from confirming the recently observed violation of the conservation of parity to new ways of identifying strange particles, no one had any doubts about the practical dimensions of such an instrument: "From these experiments come data on the internal structure and properties of semiconductors, and magnetic properties and composition of magnetic materials. These experiments are vital in the design of semiconduction devices and a large class of electronic equipment."[39]

With such appealing prospects for state-of-the-art science and technology, Lax began the process of arranging big-time support of the project. In the fall of 1957 he outlined his plans for a high-field magnet for Lincoln's director Carl Overhage that highlighted the "tremendous opportunities" it would open up for the laboratory's solid-state effort. Lax recognized that something with a likely price tag of $5 million would not be easy to sell, even to the Air Force, as an exclusive tool for Lincoln. He told Overhage, "Such an investment can only be justified on a basis similar to that of a large accelerator or cyclotron which is available to a community of scientists representing different organizations and a diversity of scientific interests."[40]

To build support, Lax organized a meeting in November 1957 with interested researchers from Lincoln, MIT, and Harvard, along with representatives from the Air Force Cambridge Research Center (AFCRC), the ONR, and the Signal Corps.[41] The group then appointed Lax, Bitter, and Harvey Brooks (dean of applied science at Harvard) as a committee to draw up a formal proposal and push it through the "proper channels" of the defense department.

Their proposal, which underscored the laboratory's potential contributions to solid-state electronics, generated considerable interest around MIT.[42] Slater became an early and vocal advocate of finding a place for the facility on campus rather than at Lincoln. To Slater, the magnet laboratory looked like an important opportunity to focus the Institute's solid-state research effort. He considered it "just as important as the Electronics and Nuclear laboratories," and told provost Stratton that it would be "of great value not only to M.I.T. and the educational program, but to the services and the country as a whole."[43]

Lax submitted the final proposal in the fall of 1958 and then took up the vital job of lobbying on its behalf. He gave the chief of the DOD's physical science division a personal tour of Lincoln's facilities, detailing what progress had been made and also where it was being held back by a lack of better magnets. He especially stressed the need for high-power continuous magnets of the type specified in the proposal. Without them, he explained, making sense of the band structure and other properties of semiconductors and semimetals "might be likened to the mapping of the Carlsbad Caverns with a surveyor's transit using only the light from photographic flashbulbs."[44] In briefing George Valley for his statement to the Air Force on the need for the magnet laboratory, Lax said that he expected the optical, millimeter wave, and infrared techniques made possible by the high-power magnet "to contribute as much to our basic knowledge of physics as the powerful microwave techniques which came into use after World War II."[45] He also emphasized the laboratory's potential role, as DOD's first large-scale university facility for solid-state research, as a training center for graduate students, postdoctorates, and visiting faculty members.

Lax and his colleagues thought they knew what the facility could do for basic physics, but they recognized as well as anyone that such "basic" research depended on eventual applications nearly as much as it contributed to them. Stratton acknowledged it outright when he told Herbert York, newly appointed head of the entire R&D effort for the Pentagon, that the magnet laboratory would "be of great importance to our national defense effort, as well as to the advancement of our civilian economy."[46] The Air Force approved the project in 1960, awarding MIT $6 million to construct the laboratory, $3 million to staff and get it running, and an annual research budget of $2 million.[47]

Although located just a few blocks from the main campus, next to the MIT reactor, the National Magnet Laboratory (NML) seemed in some ways closer to Lexington than to Cambridge. Lax was named director but retained his Lincoln appointment as head of solid-state physics. He brought along a number of his top people to design and build the magnets, recruit the staff, and plan the research program. The laboratory's assistant director, Donald Stevenson, kept his post at Lincoln as group leader of solid-state physics. The laboratory's chief magnet designers, Henry Kolm and Bruce Montgomery, also kept up their Lincoln appointments. Just as NML was coming on line in

1964, Lax was offered a promotion to associate director of Lincoln. He decided to retain both positions, explaining to his Air Force superiors that "Such an arrangement would clearly have many advantages . . . namely any practical developments and applications which are evolved at NML could then be readily put into practice by members of the Lincoln Laboratory who are more directly concerned with applications to components and systems on behalf of the Air Force."[48] Even after officially resigning his Lincoln post, Lax remained a valued consultant in Lexington.

As expected, NML quickly became a world center for magnetics research, making some impressive contributions to solid-state theory and experiment. With the capability of creating continuous fields of up to 250 kilogauss, and pulsed fields up to 750 kilogauss, its facilities offered unprecedented opportunities for detecting ferromagnetic, antiferromagnetic, and electron spin resonance across a broad range of frequencies, for studying superconductivity and transport phenomena, and for pushing the limits of low-temperature physics. NML staff grew to a couple of dozen in-house researchers and a dozen graduate students, along with distinguished visiting scientists from the United States and Europe.

At the same time, NML's research proved to have many of the practical implications its sponsors had anticipated. In planning the laboratory's experimental program, its administrators prepared a long list of "practical devices and applications which might result from basic research at the National Magnet Laboratory."[49] To no one's surprise, it was a list heavily slanted toward military technologies, from refined delay lines for radar and communications systems, miniaturized electronics, and improved microwave components to sophisticated inertial guidance systems, radiation shields, and new types of masers and lasers. They pointed to several devices based on NML research that had already reached the prototype stage, such as the infrared semiconductor laser for radar systems, superconductivity, and magnetic shielding.[50]

Long before Senator Mike Mansfield's 1970 amendment and its requirements for the military "relevance" of DOD-sponsored research, NML's directors had little difficulty coming up with an inventory of "Activities of the AFOSR Sponsored National Magnet

Laboratory That Have Had Identifiable Value to the DOD."[51] The low-temperature research had pointed toward new types of high-gain/low-noise amplifiers. Superconductivity techniques had suggested a host of applications from tunable lasers and infrared detectors to frictionless accelerometers and gyroscopes. In addition to their own work, NML researchers gave valuable technical assistance to military projects in other laboratories. Kenneth Button consulted with Lincoln on its phased-array antenna designs. Other staff members worked with the Naval Ordnance Laboratory and the Wright Field Air Development Command. Some served as visiting scientists at military laboratories or on military advisory panels. Convair developed and put into practice a magnetic metal-forming system based on NML ideas. Other aerospace companies took advantage of new NML metal-cutting techniques, an innovation that tripled production rates.

Despite such well-documented successes, NML, like most other on-campus centers in those years, eventually found itself formally threatened by the Mansfield amendment and the relevancy controversy. The AFOSR, facing substantial budget cuts of its own, and under considerable pressure to reduce its university obligations, trimmed its support of NML by 10 percent for 1969 and placed it on a list of facilities to be turned over to the NSF. This despite the fact that both NML's administrators and its sponsors remained thoroughly convinced of the laboratory's "relevance" for advanced surveillance, reconnaissance and communications systems, radiation-hardened electronics, and other defense technologies. Lax, in an ironic postscript to a letter seeking support for the laboratory from the Institute president, actually validated those claims. Apologizing for missing a meeting to discuss NML's contributions to the Institute, Lax wrote, "I am sorry . . . but I have a very important commitment to keep with the Air Force people at Kirtland Air Force Base to discuss some classified ideas which have evolved from our work on high magnetic field technology. As much as I would like to be here in view of the circumstances, I feel it is too important at this time for me to cancel my trip."[52] Lax eventually lost the fight over NML's "relevance." The NSF took over the laboratory's support in 1970 and promptly put it on a budgetary diet.

Though it never regained its former prominence, NML had a lasting impact on solid-state research at MIT. Lax supervised two dozen graduate theses at NML, and many of those students either went on to Lincoln, to faculty appointments at the Institute or elsewhere, or to jobs with local high-tech companies like Raytheon. Lax also managed to publish an influential text, *Microwave Ferrites and Ferrimagnetics*, begun, appropriately enough, as a lecture series on the theory of ferrites and ferrite devices for Sylvania's corporate laboratory.[53] In an important sense, Lax never really left Lincoln. Asked to choose between Lincoln and the Institute proper, he recalled being told, "Well, if you want to be a member of the faculty, leave Lincoln and come to the campus." Reflecting on his decision to move to Cambridge full time, Lax commented, "Well, I didn't leave Lincoln, I brought part of Lincoln over here, and then joined the faculty."[54]

The Center for Materials Science and Engineering

Slater, through his membership on several important advisory committees, was aware of a growing concern at the highest levels of the defense establishment about America's preparedness in materials science. Critical weapons technologies from jet turbines to radiation-hardened electronics were being held back by inferior materials and by a shortage of materials specialists to fabricate them. In late 1955, T. H. Johnson, director of research for the AEC and an old friend of Slater's from Brookhaven days, asked Slater to serve on a blue-ribbon panel "to guide us in increasing our effectiveness in the fields of metallurgy, ceramics, and solid state physics."[55] Chaired by Frederick Seitz, the panel included two former members of Slater's AEC radiation damage committee, one of whom had headed a classified project on radiation shielding for the AEC at MIT before launching his own company. Seitz's panel strongly recommended that the AEC fund interdisciplinary centers at leading universities where the next generation of scientists and engineers would be trained. The panel also got Slater and his MIT colleagues talking about doing something in materials along the lines of RLE or LNSE. At Johnson's urging, Slater submitted a proposal to the AEC for a dramatically enlarged effort in materials science at MIT.[56] At $5.5 million up front and $1.5 million a year, however, it was more than the AEC thought it could afford at the time.

Meanwhile, Slater talked the NSF into funding a Laboratory of Chemical and Solid State Physics. Though certainly not on the same scale as his original vision, it was still an important step, in Slater's opinion, toward "organizing the work now spread through many departments in the form of many small research projects into a few large interdisciplinary research groups."[57] Like the molecular theory group, it concentrated on X-ray and neutron diffraction studies of crystals, magnetic resonance techniques, and the properties of materials at low temperature.

Fearing that their colleagues in the sciences might steal materials science out from under them, the engineers set up their own interdepartmental committee on materials engineering.[58] They canvassed friends and colleagues in the aerospace, automotive, electrical, chemical, and other industries and uncovered substantial support for such an academic program.[59] Most everyone seemed to agree with J. Herbert Hollomon, an MIT-trained engineer then heading GE's metallurgical and ceramics research division (and later Under Secretary of Commerce), who argued that high-tech companies could not long afford to keep training their own materials scientists. "It seems to me," he said, "that MIT must take a leading role in establishing this new trend."[60])

Encouraged by the response, the committee officially approved a separate curriculum and degree program for materials engineering in 1959. They found a strong ally in Slater. "He seems eager to participate in this program, and is willing to govern his teaching of the relevant physics courses accordingly," they reported to the dean of engineering. "This is a wonderful step. Slater also thinks that the new curriculum might prove attractive to science students who wish to lean towards solid state physics and chemistry. Perhaps the program has interschool as well as interdepartmental potentialities."[61]

Where the money would have to come from to support such an effort was no secret. "A laboratory on this scale would be a very large undertaking, and would form a major item in the research program of the country," Slater explained. "It could be supported only by an agency of the breadth of the Department of Defense."[62] Indeed, by the late 1950s MIT was receiving slightly less than $4 million a year for materials research, about four-fifths of it from the military or the AEC. Of that, the Air Force was putting in more than $1 million (most of it from applied research centers like Wright Air Development Division and AFCRC), the Navy slightly less than a million, and the Army half a million. The AEC's share was $560,000. By contrast, the total NSF contribution was $425,760 and total nongovernment support, including industry, just $459,195.[63]

As it had in other fields of science and engineering, Sputnik added a sense of urgency to the "materials gap." The federal defense budget for 1958 included $55 million in "emergency funds" for materials research. The following year the Federal Council for Science and Technology appointed a high-ranking committee with representatives from the AEC, DOD, and NASA to draft a blueprint for advancing American materials science. After surveying the state of the art in industrial, academic, and government laboratories, the committee concluded that the real crisis was educational. Too few students were being trained in the field, and they were being taught to view the discipline too narrowly. The committee's final report endorsed a plan to increase the nation's output of Ph.D.s by 75 per cent within the decade by funding a number of interdisciplinary laboratories at leading universities.[64]

Control of materials science quickly fell into the hands of the (Defense) Advanced Research Projects Agency (ARPA), the newest and most aggressive member of the defense establishment.[65] First set up as the Pentagon's space agency in the wake of the Sputnik humiliation, with a sky's-the-limit budget and ambitions to match, ARPA had lost most of its original budget and programs to the Air Force and NASA and was looking for something to complement its remaining missions in ballistic missile defense and military satellites. To Herbert York, newly appointed research director for the DOD (and former chief scientist at ARPA), materials science seemed ideally suited to ARPA's redefined mission as a "rapid strike force" in science and technology. York assigned ARPA $17 million in emergency appropriations "to obtain at the earliest practicable date a major improvement in structural and power conversion materials required to satisfy the military requirements of the several U.S. surface, air or missile programs," including "super strength materials, radiation resistant materials, and materials intended for very high temperature service," and "electric and electronic circuitry capable of operation at high temperatures."[66]

Instead of spreading the wealth, York and ARPA thought they could more effectively strengthen military materials research by funding a few interdisciplinary laboratories (IDLs) at selected universities. These centers would not only undertake important research projects of their own but train the next generation of materials scientists and engineers for industry, government, and other universities. Though administratively distinct from conventional DOD materials research contracts, the IDLs were expected to build upon, and contribute to, them. As Charles Yost, ARPA's assistant director for materials science, explained, "The IDL program is intended to be an integral part of the total Department of Defense program in materials science and is planned to complement existing research programs now under way with the sponsorship of the Office of Naval Research, the Air Force Office of Scientific Research, the Army Research Office in Durham, N.C., and the other Service agencies. . . . One of the goals of the program is to achieve the maximum interaction between the IDL program and these other service programs."[67]

In the spring of 1959, ARPA sent a delegation to study MIT's materials science programs. They talked with Slater and others, assembled detailed figures on contract support, numbers of faculty, postdoctorates, and students, and so on, and asked for specific estimates about what ARPA funding would mean for MIT's overall materials science effort. Slater particularly highlighted the proposed Magnet Laboratory's place in any future MIT materials program, arguing that it would be "as useful for solid-state work as the large accelerators are for nuclear and high-energy research." With Lincoln, the National Magnet Laboratory, and the Center for Materials Science and Engineering, MIT would have an opportunity to consolidate its position as the leading American academic center in solid-state research.[68]

Impressed by what it saw and heard, ARPA invited MIT to submit a formal proposal for one of the new IDL centers. Slater took the lead in drafting it. Understandably, he emphasized the size and diversity of the Institute's materials science and engineering effort, as well as

MIT's pioneering tradition of interdisciplinary enterprises. Instead of starting from scratch, a Materials Center at MIT would draw together a coalition from existing laboratories or the local available work force: von Hippel's LIR (renamed the Laboratories for Molecular Science and Molecular Engineering), with fifteen senior staff and eighty postdoctorates and graduate students; RLE's twelve senior staff and fifty postdoctorates and graduate students in microwave spectroscopy, gas discharge, and plasma dynamics; a proposed Laboratory of Materials Engineering that would include most of the people involved with the materials engineering program, some fifty senior staff and 230 postdoctorates and graduate students in all; selected specialists from Lincoln and the National Magnet Laboratory; and Slater's own Laboratory of Chemical and Solid State Physics, with twenty senior staff and ninety postdoctorates and graduate students.[69]

Figuring that a little advertising might strengthen MIT's chances, the Institute's industrial liaison office began planning a national conference on materials science and engineering for the spring of 1960. By showcasing recent breakthroughs for an invited audience of government and industry leaders, the conference was expected "to attract national attention and support for the proposed Materials Center at M.I.T." and "to demonstrate M.I.T.'s leadership in this critical field, including the strategic array of existing programs and the readiness of the M.I.T. faculty to join in this expanded effort."[70] At the same time, it would highlight the Institute's commitment to the industrial side of the materials science equation—something that ARPA could obviously not afford to ignore.

To the astonishment of Slater and his colleagues, MIT lost out in the first round to Cornell, Northwestern, and Pennsylvania, all programs heavily stocked with Institute graduates. ARPA acknowledged that the IDL program had been modeled on MIT's program in the first place, but argued that since the Institute was already something of "the General Motors in the materials field," and since its program was going to be strengthened substantially by NML, then ARPA should spend its limited resources elsewhere. The ARPA committee did have to admit that it was "genuinely embarrassed to have turned down M.I.T.," and invited it to reapply for the next round of centers the following year.[71]

MIT's administration took several steps to bolster their chances the second time around. Slater, von Hippel, and Nicholas Grant (from metallurgy) redrafted the ARPA proposal. "I think it highly important for us to show that we are making real progress toward a true inter-disciplinary program of the type envisioned by the Department of Defense and by us," Julius Stratton told Slater. "M.I.T. has a great deal at stake in these plans, and I shall rely heavily upon your leadership."[72] The new proposal reemphasized the teaching side of the program and the role of the Center in coordinating materials science and engineering throughout the Institute. Slater personally presented it at the Pentagon in January 1961.[73]

A materials research center was also a focus of the Institute's Second Century Fund, the biggest capital drive in MIT's history. The fund secured pledges from the Sloan Foundation and a number of corporations for half the cost of a new laboratory building for materials research.[74] That was the kind of financial leverage ARPA administrators appreciated. Naming Charles Townes as MIT provost in the spring of 1961 was further insurance. His breakthroughs with the maser and laser had been frequently praised as outstanding examples of what basic research could contribute to the military's mission. Putting Townes in administrative charge of any future interdepartmental materials laboratory, as Stratton later admitted, "weighed substantially in our favor in the final decision of ARPA to support M.I.T."[75]

Only von Hippel seemed unhappy with the final arrangements for the center. Frustrated by the politics of coalition building and by his own diminishing influence over the center, he resigned from the materials science and engineering committee and pulled his Laboratory for Insulation Research out of the coalition.[76] A number of von Hippel's staff members did move their laboratories into the center, including the crystal-growing and magnetics groups, but von Hippel himself stubbornly held out at the LIR until his retirement.

MIT's artful maneuvering paid off. ARPA announced in the fall a $3.3 million award to MIT for a Center for Materials Science and Engineering. The Institute, through the Second Century Fund, would kick in an additional $3 million for the laboratory complex.[77]

Although the ARPA contract increased MIT's total budget for materials science and engineering by only about 25 percent, it had far greater implications than the dollar figures alone might imply. By drawing together similar efforts from RLE, the Laboratory of Chemical and Solid State Physics, Lincoln, and elsewhere in low-temperature physics, solid-state materials, magnetic resonance, and related fields, and providing them with equipment too specialized or expensive for any one group, the CMSE served as a financial catalyst for materials studies throughout the Institute. In its first year the center signed on 115 professors, 126 postdoctorates, and 395 graduate students representing a dozen departments plus RLE, Lincoln, and the National Magnet Laboratory.[78] As Nicholas Grant bluntly put it, ARPA's money was the glue that held everything together.[79]

While there were limits to the CMSE's power to dictate specific research agendas ("We must remember that M.I.T. is an educational institution, and that one of the most valued prerogatives of a man in academic life is the privilege of choosing his own field of research"), its leaders recognized that selecting staff and allocating the money gave them considerable control. "By choosing to make new appointments in one field or in another, and by supporting one area generously, another less so, out of funds for the common purpose, it is possible to exercise a great deal of pressure, without dictating to any professor what he or his students should work on," they reassured their ARPA sponsors.[80]

Slater, as chairman of a steering committee, ran the center for the first year. As his successor, he nominated Robert A. Smith, head of the physics section of the Radar Research Establishment (RRE), Britain's foremost laboratory for military electronics. In many respects RRE was a British equivalent of RLE, without the distinctively American academic affiliation. Paralleling American experience, RRE's physics program initially specialized in microwave and electronic circuit techniques closely related to radar, including research on klystrons and TWTs, and then later branched out into solid-state, low temperature, digital computers, and other newer fields. Under Smith, the physics department earned an international reputation for its research in semiconductor materials, notably its studies on the properties and performance of silicon.[81]

Slater had gotten to know Smith through their mutual wartime research on the magnetron, and later through joint consulting for high-tech companies in Boston. He admired Smith's technical contributions in semiconductor and infrared detection technology, and his talent, rare among British scientists, for bridging the worlds of pure and applied physics. "He would fill in very well a serious gap which we have in our program, that in the general field of semiconductors," Slater told Townes. [82]

Slater briefed Smith in the spring of 1961 about MIT's plans for CMSE and asked if he would be interested in becoming part of them. [83] Smith found the prospects appealing. "It has always surprised me a bit that M. I. T. itself had not done more to make itself an academic center of 'Solid State' and more particularly semiconductor research," he replied. "There is a great need for such an academic centre and I am not convinced that either Cornell or Univ. of Penn. where a lot of money has been allocated are the right places."[84] Like Slater, Smith was committed to "a close marriage of pure research and technological development and a mustering of research workers from different disciplines—physicists, chemists and metallurgists in particular."[85] At RRE his efforts had been hampered by the boom and bust of British defense budgets, and by having no graduate students to replicate his program elsewhere. And so even with Slater's warnings about the distractions of life at MIT ("where a faculty member must concern himself not only with doing research, but with finding financing for it, with teaching, with contributing to teaching methods, including writing books and preparing courses, and setting up teaching laboratories, with cooperating in many ways with the government, and with helping the development of scientific industries"), [86] Smith accepted the appointment as director of CMSE starting in the fall of 1962.

Lincoln Laboratory continued to provide leadership and direction for the center. Harry Gatos came over from Lincoln, where he had been associate head of the solid-state division, to take charge of the center's materials preparation effort. He brought with him an active research program in crystal growing and on-the-surface behavior of semiconductors. Richard Adler, the center's authority on semiconductor applications, had earlier headed Lincoln's solid-state and transistor group. [87] The head of the center's first low-temperature physics group had also been at Lincoln. As late as 1977, following Smith's resignation and a decade under Grant, the center again turned to Lincoln, selecting Mildred Dresselhaus, a former Lax protégé, as director.

Although CMSE's research encompassed a broad range of scientific and engineering specialties, its core programs—chemical and solid-state physics; electronic, magnetic, and optical properties of materials and device applications; and metallurgy—clearly supported ARPA's technical agenda.[88] If anything, the center's programs confirmed the opinion of one of Yost's counterparts in the ONR materials science office, that "it is not exactly a secret that the interest of these Government agencies [DOD and the AEC] in research does not stem from philanthropic emotions, but from inseparable connection between modern warfare and scientific-technological development."[89] Some of the center's research, like high-temperature metallurgy under Grant, electronic materials under Gatos, semiconductor materials and devices under Adler, and the metallurgy of high-field superconductors under John Wulff, had obvious technology applications. Even what seemed to be the more basic studies in optical spectroscopy and low-temperature physics had some practical objectives, for example understanding microwave acoustics or the behavior of specific kinds of semiconductors. As Slater explained, "This fundamental research will be closely tied to work on the development of new solid-state devices for use in electronics and on the study of materials of particular electronics interest."[90] The center's studies of thin films and active thin-film devices exemplified that commitment, ranging from basic research on high-vacuum technology (for controlling the composition of the films) to new ways of fabricating multilayer devices.

Understandably, the center's programs were of great interest to industry. Its inaugural industrial symposium in the spring of 1962 drew 145 corporate representatives from fifty companies, making it one of the largest meetings ever held by the industrial liaison office.[91] Later symposia, like one on semiconductors organized by Gatos, attracted similar attention. Thirty companies supported the center directly, through research contracts or graduate fellowships, many of them (e.g., GE, Pratt & Whitney, Raytheon, and United Technologies) interested mostly in the defense applications of materials science.[92]

Industrial demand for graduates was so strong that the center found it difficult to hang on to enough of them to expand its own programs. Faculty members also found plenty of opportunities for putting their ideas into practice. One candidate for chair of the metallurgy department was surprised to learn just how much time his prospective colleagues spent on consulting or running their own companies. "In obtaining sponsored research, some faculty have difficulty distinguishing between what is sent them as a Professor at M.I.T. with students to support and what is sent them as the head of a Route 128 enterprise," he told the dean of engineering, and turned down the offer.[93]

The completion of the CMSE's own building in 1965 further illustrated the impact of its programs. Appropriately dedicated to Vannevar Bush, whose committee had started things moving thirty years before, it united MIT's research efforts in physics, chemistry, metallurgy, and electrical engineering both literally and symbolically.[94] Its laboratories provided space for some forty professors and their research teams, and its strategic placement (just behind the main building and dome) put the center's specialized equipment and preparation facilities within easy reach of the rest of the campus.

Ironically, neither Slater nor von Hippel, both of whom had done so much to make the center possible, ever got a chance to work there. Facing mandatory retirement at MIT, and convinced in any case that his own department "had been literally captured by the nuclear physicists," Slater accepted an appointment at the University of Florida where he continued to explore energy bands, magnetism, and other aspects of solid-state physics up until his death in 1976.[95] Von Hippel stayed in voluntary exile in the LIR until his retirement. The center's only public acknowledgment of its debt to von Hippel's early vision of materials science was its Arthur R. von Hippel Reading Room.

The Center for Materials Science and Engineering more than fulfilled its promises to ARPA. "Clearly, there is no academic equivalent to the Center in the United States, and the over-all size of the materials effort at M.I.T. rivals the largest industrial and government laboratories," one MIT administrator boasted, with considerable justification. With 132 professors (17.5 percent of the Institute's total),

170 postdoctorates, and 419 graduate students (15 percent of the total), CMSE was MIT's largest single intellectual enterprise almost from the start.[96]

But what made it important was far more than size. CMSE marked the emergence of materials science as a distinct academic discipline, not merely at MIT but within the American university. Its graduates went on to staff and direct programs in materials science and engineering at other ARPA centers and in government and industrial laboratories as well. Its faculty members assumed leading roles on the Semiconductor Electronics Education Committee, an industry-funded project aimed at making solid-state electronics an integral part of the electrical engineering curriculum through textbooks, symposia, films, and the like.[97] Through its graduates and texts, and certainly by its example, MIT helped give materials science its distinctive character, oriented in large measure toward electronics and electronics applications. This orientation inescapably defined the field far beyond the boundaries of the Institute. CMSE was ultimately far more than a catalyst for research in materials at MIT. It virtually created and then set the direction for an entirely new academic discipline, one that bore the signs of its origins long after the center itself had been turned over to the NSF in 1972.

It was von Hippel, always something of an outsider, who perhaps most clearly recognized the finality of the change. In an essay entitled "The University in Transition," he penned what almost sounded like an epitaph for his generation of university scientists and engineers: "What has happened to the old ivory tower! Telephones ring incessantly; visitors swarm in droves through the laboratories; meetings crowd meetings; an ocean of papers blots out the horizon; and the wise men, once quietly guided by the star of Bethlehem, now frantically count time by the star of Moscow. Yet this turmoil is of our own doing. Universities showed that research pays, and huge laboratories sprang up for profit; universities devised new weapons, and the countries bristle with laboratories for defense. What an outcome of a search for understanding of nature and for peace in our times."[98]

8 | Materiel Science

Despite Stanford's growing reputation in most other science and engineering fields, it lagged far behind in materials science. When MIT-trained metallurgist Robert Huggins came to Stanford in 1954, he joined a two-man department of metallurgical engineering suspended in time in the days of legendary mining school graduate Herbert Hoover. The department was part of the School of Mineral Sciences, and still had a dozen furnaces in the back room, where an earlier generation of engineers had learned assaying and blacksmithing.[1] The metallurgy program had only a handful of undergraduate and graduate students, and a single research contract.

Yet within two decades Huggins built a program in materials sciences second in size only to MIT's—with sixty-five faculty members, four hundred graduate students, $7 million in contracts, and seventy Ph.D. degrees a year—and second to none in reputation.[2] The Vincent Bendix Award from the American Society for Engineering Education later recognized that achievement: "By combining technical prescience with administrative acumen he took a relatively small, conventional metallurgical department with rather prosaic research interests and almost single-handedly converted it into a dynamic, expansive materials science research organization."[3]

At the heart of Huggins's steeple-building campaign was Stanford's Center for Materials Research (CMR), which he founded in 1961 and directed for a decade and a half. By 1970 CMR had fifty-nine faculty members (fifty-one under direct support), seventy-nine research associates, 293 graduate students (sixty under direct salary support), and a total annual budget of $1.4 million.[4] Perhaps even more importantly, CMR served as the essential catalyst in a university-wide materials effort ($5.5 million in contracts) that was making Stanford a world leader in materials science and Silicon Valley a world center in microelectronics.

Huggins, like so many of his Stanford colleagues in other fields, fully appreciated the changing politics of postwar science. He anticipated and exploited changing national priorities for materials science, and fashioned an academic powerhouse. And, clearly, the national priorities in defense and space technology that made CMR so successful channeled materials science in certain directions (toward electronics and aerospace applications) rather than others.

The defense establishment virtually created materials science as an academic discipline, funding all but a tiny fraction of American materials research during the Cold War years. The DOD, through its Advanced Research Projects Agency (ARPA), established and supported a network of interdisciplinary laboratories at Stanford, MIT, and elsewhere that still dominate the field. Although the NSF has taken a more active role in recent years, the intellectual contours and direction of materials science were set in those formative years, with fateful implications.[5]

The Materials Revolution

Stanford very nearly sat out the materials revolution of the 1950s. Where other scientific revolutions were playing themselves out largely within the walls of the academy, the transformation of materials science took place in industry and government laboratories. As William Baker, who played a key role in the materials revolution in Bell Laboratories and in government policy circles recalled, "The National Materials Program in both its federal and independent forms is probably the only example of a major scientific frontier in which the initiative for study came from technological and engineering efforts outside of academic centers."[6]

The unique challenges of defense electronics and aerospace engineering fueled the advancing materials effort. Wartime work on high-frequency radar, with its demands for improved dielectrics (for microwave windows), semiconductors (for microwave detectors), and conductors (for waveguides), stimulated intense interest in the properties of materials with specific microwave applications. Benjamin Lax at Lincoln called the science of materials the "silent but indispensable partner of microwave science and technology."[7] At Bell Labs, wartime research led to new methods for preparing pure semiconductor materials and "doping" them with specific impurities, making possible the first point-contact transistor in 1948. Subsequent Bell breakthroughs in so-called zone refining and diffusion techniques opened the way to the dramatically improved junction transistor, inaugurating the microelectronics revolution. Bell originally intended the transistor as a substitute for its mechanical telephone relays. The Army Signal Corps, recognizing the dramatic implications of electronics miniaturization for military communications, immediately took sponsorship of the program and subsequently subsidized about half of Bell's transistor research and development effort through the mid-1950s, and a substantial share of the production costs as well.[8] Predictably, commercial transistor research and development at Bell and other American electronics companies quickly fell behind the military counterpart. In the aerospace industry, too, the leading edge of materials science in the 1950s encompassed high-temperature jet turbine fans, lightweight skin alloys, fibrous composites, heat-resistant nose cones, ballistic missile motor cases, and similar high-performance products with primarily military applications.[9]

Huggins recognized that Stanford had some catching up to do. As he pointed out to Terman, Stanford's program simply had "not kept pace with the numerous technical and scientific advances in metallurgy during and just after the second world war" and "did not reflect the very significant change in approach and emphasis that had been taking place in metallurgical education away from descriptive material relating to specific groups of materials (e.g., tool steels, light metals, etc.), their manufacture, treatment, and properties." At the leading schools in the field, Huggins explained, such an approach had long since given way to "an integrated program emphasizing an analytical treatment of fundamentals relating to all metallurgical systems."[10] In other words, rather than considering each kind of material and its related industrial processes in isolation, the best academic programs were now looking for general theories (e.g., equilibrium and diffusion) and analytical techniques (e.g., X-ray diffraction, electron microscopy) that could be applied across a range of materials. Stanford's metallurgists, by contrast, still focused most of their attention on such classic problems as metal fatigue and continued to draw most of their research problems from industrial consulting, on questions about improving the heat treatment of gears or limiting corrosion in steam boilers.[11]

Having learned something about the advantages of government funding from his graduate student days at MIT, Huggins set about reinvigorating Stanford metallurgy with some contracts. He quickly landed one from the Air Force Office of Scientific Research for studies of the mechanical behavior of aluminum at very high temperatures.[12] His contract monitor was Charles Yost, who, as head of the materials science program at ARPA, would soon play a key role in the development of materials science at Stanford. In this project, Huggins was interested in the properties of the so-called grain boundary—the abutment of two crystals within a metal marking a change in orientation but not in chemistry. His principal challenge was in isolating the grain boundary so its effects could be more precisely measured and understood. To accomplish this, Huggins devised new techniques for growing foot-long crystals of very pure aluminum with a single grain boundary down the middle, a bicrystal. He could then cut samples from the bicrystal and evaluate them in a high-temperature furnace under controlled conditions of stress and strain. Those measurements, in turn, could reveal important information about the high-temperature performance of the metal.

The Air Force contract gave the metallurgy program the momentum it needed. Huggins and his colleague Cutler Shepard (who had hired him in the first place) won several other contracts with defense agencies, industry, and the NSF. Huggins extended his studies of crystalline imperfections and the mechanical behavior of solids with support from the Air Force and the Navy.[13] Titanium Metals Corporation sponsored an investigation of diffusion in titanium, a metal of increasing importance for high-temperature alloys for the aerospace industry. The NSF concurrently supported research on high-temperature creep.[14] Huggins and Shepard also negotiated a contract from the atomic division of American Standard for a study of alloys with promising properties for nuclear shielding.[15] Shepard followed up his interest in nuclear materials by taking his sabbatical in 1957 with the atomics division of North American Aviation. In his absence, Huggins took charge of the metallurgical engineering program.

Even as acting head, Huggins demonstrated ability to size up promising new opportunities and then make the most of them. His careful planning would carry Stanford materials science right to the top. In arguing with the administration for new appointments, Huggins stressed what metallurgical engineering could contribute to Stanford's burgeoning efforts in aeronautical engineering and microwave and solid-state electronics. He specifically mentioned Nicholas Hoff's interest in having an experienced physical metallurgist join his high-temperature structures research team in aeronautics.[16] Before making any appointments, Huggins sent letters to every prominent metallurgy department, government laboratory, and corporate research laboratory in the country soliciting advice and nominations, and assembled a list of forty prospects. He then targeted several candidates whose backgrounds and experience seemed to fit especially well into his blueprint for the future of the department, men whose specialties, whether in instrumentation or theory, best complemented Stanford's strengths in other engineering fields. One candidate had designed and built at MIT an electron-probe microanalyzer, a unique and powerful tool for studying solid-state kinetics, an instrument with particular value to Huggins and Hoff. Another had a keen interest in semiconductor materials and applications. A third was an expert on the theory of the mechanical behavior of solids and had done a stint with the ONR. Huggins got all three of his first choices, more than doubling the size of his department at a stroke and insuring a close fit with related efforts in neighboring departments.

Huggins revitalized the instructional program as well. Compared with students at the best programs, Stanford's metallurgy students simply did not take enough courses in fundamental physics and chemistry, he insisted. Nor did they take enough mathematics. "As a matter of fact," Huggins lamented, "it is doubtful if an integral sign appeared in any undergraduate courses."[17] To bring the curriculum up to date, Huggins drastically cut the undergraduate course offerings in such traditional areas as mineral dressing (from seven to no units) and industrial metallurgy (from eleven to three units), and expanded those in newer specialties such as analytical physical metallurgy (from none to seventeen units) and chemical metallurgy (from none to eleven units). He implemented parallel reforms on the graduate level as well.

Huggins then launched an aggressive marketing campaign so that the rest of the world would know what Stanford was up to. He sent copies of a pamphlet he wrote, *Metallurgy at Stanford*, to two thousand high school science teachers. He mailed posters on graduate work in metallurgical engineering at Stanford to the heads of every metallurgy department in the country and to one hundred chairs of chemistry and physics departments in the western half of the country.[18] For greater exposure at home, he taught a popular undergraduate survey on the science of materials.

Departmental leadership meant hands-on management to Huggins. According to Terman, the department's research program was "largely of his making, in that Huggins helped each principal investigator organize his plans, assisted him in writing proposals, and handled some of the contacts with potential sponsors."[19] By 1959 Huggins had his program well positioned for the opportunities of the future. Three faculty members, all recent graduates of top programs, had been added. He had built up the sponsored research effort from scratch to $215,000 a year, primarily with Air Force and Navy contracts. He had revamped both the undergraduate and graduate curricula, with serious attention to advanced science and mathematics, and added new graduate courses in powder metallurgy, thermoelectric materials, properties of surfaces, crystal growth, and other state-of-the-art areas. In physical metallurgy, at least, he believed that Stanford's program was "now comparable to those at the best schools in the country."[20] Enrollments had increased to twenty-seven undergraduate students and twenty-five graduate students, up from just four three years earlier.[21] Finally, Huggins convinced the administration to change the name of the department from Metallurgical Engineering to Materials Science, to reflect its new orientation and to move the department out of the School of Mineral Sciences and into the School of Engineering, where it could seek more natural and profitable alliances.

The Materials Gap

Meanwhile, Soviet achievements in space and nuclear weapons had focused the attention of defense analysts and policy planners on materials science as a dangerous soft spot along the advancing front of military technology. Independent studies by the AEC's Metallurgy and Materials Branch, the ONR's Solid State Sciences Advisory Panel, and a National Academy of Sciences Committee on Materials (under the sponsorship of the Air Force) all recommended immediate action to coordinate materials research at the national level, either through a national materials laboratory or through some kind of "materials research institutes."[22] The newly organized President's Science Advisory Committee (PSAC) likewise singled out materials science as an urgent national priority. Its background paper, "Coordinating Materials Research in the United States," prepared by William Baker and presented in March 1958, called for a large-scale effort to build up the infrastructure of materials science and engineering by funding equipment and building grants and by providing support for interdepartmental and interdisciplinary research teams. "While the problems of high temperature materials, and materials having a high strength to weight ratio, are very urgent matters for Federal agencies, they are of little significance in the civilian economy today," the PSAC report acknowledged. "It thus becomes clear that the Federal Government will have to play a leading role in encouraging the research and development which is needed."[23] Just as clear was the fact that the federal government in this case meant defense agencies, which had the money and the incentive to spend it on this kind of research.

PSAC's landmark study, *Strengthening American Science*, submitted to the President in December 1958, seconded the earlier conclusions about the importance of mobilizing materials science, but with a twist. Concerned that relying too heavily on industrial and government laboratories, with their primary focus on applied research, might ultimately lead to "an impoverished science and a second-rate technology," PSAC strongly urged more attention to the university side of the materials effort. It recommended a major capital support program for academic materials science, including money for new laboratories and the instruments to equip them, plus longer-term research contracts (rather than typical year-to-year contracts) to ensure greater stability and continuity.[24] The report led James Killian, the President's Special Assistant for Science and Technology, to appoint a top-level Coordinating Committee on Materials Research and Development to follow up on the PSAC proposals.[25] The committee, in turn, designated ARPA as the lead federal agency for implementing the materials program.

To get the materials program started, DOD authorized a special $17 million appropriation for fiscal year 1960 (a 25 percent increase in the overall DOD materials science budget),[26] with $6 million targeted for equipment grants to university laboratories.[27] Universities could only contribute their share to closing the materials gap, ARPA administrators reasoned, if faculty and student researchers had ready access to the latest analytical instruments and processing techniques. ARPA saw the equipment grants program not as a government handout but as an investment in DOD's ongoing materials science interests. A panel of military scientists was asked to recommend specific instrumentation needs that would best strengthen current DOD university research.[28] Beyond its short-run payback in better university research and teaching, the equipment grants program was expected to build a political constituency, both in the universities and in Washington, for the bigger initiatives to follow.

ARPA's larger goal was to establish the interdisciplinary university laboratories that, by educating the materials science leaders of the future, would become the foundation for a real National Materials Program.[29] The architects of the interdisciplinary laboratories program had backgrounds in industrial and government laboratories (Bell Labs, GE, Los Alamos), where multidisciplinary research was the rule rather than the exception. They had seen for themselves the advantages of a problem- (rather than discipline-) oriented approach in the development of integrated circuits, hard semiconductors, very high-temperature alloys, and other materials breakthroughs, and so wanted to foster a similar spirit in the universities. In the spring of 1959 a team of ARPA representatives and outside consultants visited leading academic centers of DOD and AEC materials research looking for possible locations for interdisciplinary centers, places that offered promise of "a truly joint, cooperative attack on materials research across disciplines," and made plans for a national competition. [30]

Huggins generally kept a close eye on Washington, but this time he was caught off guard. He only learned about the ARPA initiative late in the summer of 1959 through a telephone call from the ONR representative on the equipment grants panel, who wanted a detailed instrument wish-list from Stanford. [31] Huggins hurriedly canvassed his colleagues in electrical engineering, physics, chemistry and chemical engineering, and materials science and sent back a detailed catalog with everything from an electron microscope ($42,000) and crystal-growing apparatus ($22,000) down to jet etching equipment ($500)—nearly $500,000 altogether, [32] virtually all of it directly tied to current military contracts. In explaining his own department's shopping list, Huggins pointed out, "Because of both a change in emphasis and the growth of these research activities, there are several items of equipment that are urgently needed in connection with existing Department of Defense contracts." He subsequently trimmed his original budget to a more realistic $85,000, primarily for crystal-growing equipment, an electron microscope, and ultraclean evaporation equipment for thin-film and surface studies. "The equipment requested in this proposal will significantly enhance the ability of the University to carry out investigations on currently active basic research contracts in Materials Science sponsored by the various agencies in the Department of Defense," Huggins reassured his ONR contact. "None of these items are currently budgeted in any Department of Defense contract in the field of Materials Science at Stanford." [33] Along with sixty other universities, Stanford received a one-time equipment grant in June 1960, but its materials science program was not yet considered strong enough by the ARPA evaluating committee to merit a site visit or an invitation to compete for the interdisciplinary laboratories.

Stanford's materials scientists began positioning themselves for potential follow-up programs to the ARPA initiative. Provost Terman appointed an interdepartmental faculty committee on materials science, with Huggins as chairman, and charged it with more effectively coordinating the university's scattered materials research effort.[34] Huggins learned through some high-level Washington connections that ARPA was in fact planning a second and perhaps even a third round of competition for interdisciplinary laboratories, and that universities that could demonstrate both strong existing materials research and training programs and a commitment to interdisciplinary collaboration would have the inside track. "This may be a once-in-a-lifetime type of opportunity to get a large amount of research funding in materials science," Huggins told his dean of graduate studies. "If Stanford were to be one of a limited number of institutions so supported it would very quickly be looked upon as one of the leaders in the field." On the other hand, he stressed, "if Stanford were not selected it might be increasingly difficult to obtain research support, since it is possible that a number of agencies might decrease their level of support for smaller individual programs in favor of the larger integrated ones."[35]

Stanford almost missed out on the second round when the ARPA announcement was apparently misplaced somewhere in the president's office. Huggins heard about the competition from his ONR contract monitor. One of the aeronautical engineers heard similar rumors and wrote for details.[36] ARPA dispatched a representative to Stanford in late July to meet with Huggins, Hoff, Hubert Heffner (of Electrical Engineering), and other interested faculty and administrators. He outlined for them the interdisciplinary laboratory initiative and the recent contracts negotiated with Northwestern, Pennsylvania, and Cornell and explained how ARPA had made its decisions. What counted, he said, was not only the scientific caliber of the faculty and the demonstrated support of the administration but also "the distribution of effort among the pertinent fields of science and technology such as to best meet the needs of the Department of Defense."[37] The interdisciplinary centers, he emphasized, were in no way intended to replace ongoing DOD materials research programs. "On the contrary," he told them, "it is expected that the present type of support will expand around the strong center provided by the proposed [interdisciplinary laboratory] contracts. In this way, the program can help provide the desired substantial addition to the present level of materials research supported by the Department of Defense." Fifty schools had already expressed interest in the program, he said, and if Stanford wished to be considered, it had to submit a preliminary proposal by the end of October.

Huggins and his colleagues managed somehow to pull together a prospectus by the deadline. They played up not only the progress they had made in transforming materials science from an adjunct of the mining school into a strong and independent department but also their success in reinforcing the bridges between materials science and other strong Stanford research programs in aeronautics and electronics. "The overlap of interests between faculty and students working on the fundamental behavior of materials and those interested in the applications of materials to particular engineering systems can be very fruitful," they stressed. [38]

Stanford made the first cut. In January 1961 an ARPA site-visit team came to campus for a firsthand look at the faculty and facilities. Terman gave them a well-rehearsed sales pitch highlighting Stanford's long tradition of interdepartmental and interschool collaboration, exemplified by the success of the Microwave Laboratory and the university's "demonstrated ability to get results from $." He likewise promoted the industrial spinoff that could be expected from a Stanford program in materials. Stanford's location at the center of an expanding industrial complex, he said, was "no accident."[39]

Huggins, as prospective director, had already given considerable thought to how he would organize and run an interdisciplinary materials laboratory. He insisted on calling it a "center," instead of an "institute," to underscore its complementary rather than competitive role in relation to departmental research. He saw its principal value as an institutional catalyst, providing central processing facilities and analytical instruments too costly for individual contracts, seed money for new research projects, salary support for graduate students and research associates, and a common meeting ground for materials specialists from different disciplines. He appreciated that getting people to talk with each other was half the battle. After all, Robert Sproull, head of Cornell's materials laboratory and later director of ARPA, was only half joking when he said that the lunchroom had been the key to success in materials research at Bell Laboratories.[40]

Stanford's final proposal in April 1961 made it clear how the ARPA center was expected to function. Of slightly under $1 million in contract support for materials science, $335,750 was coming from the Air Force, $270,500 from the Navy, $189,000 from the Army, and $72,000 from the AEC.[41] "The proposed ARPA program will be closely allied with those activities," the researchers promised. "It is proposed to use ARPA funds to amortize approximately half of a new laboratory building. It is expected that the other half, to be paid from university funds, will house a good fraction of the other government supported research in the materials field. The ARPA program will thus serve as a center of focus for all of the research in Materials Science."[42]

Impressed, ARPA officials invited a group of Stanford representatives, including Huggins and Terman, to Washington in early June 1961 to hammer out the contractual details. They took home a four-year, $2.6 million contract, one of only five materials centers contracts awarded that year among forty-two contenders. The other winners were MIT, Harvard, Chicago, and Brown, leaving Stanford as the lone center in the West.[43] Huggins relayed the good news to Heffner, on leave with the ONR office in London. "Evidently this was the year in which it paid to be successful," Huggins remarked, aware through government contacts that this was to be the final round of ARPA contracts. He told Heffner to keep his eye out for possible faculty prospects in Europe, and closed with a characteristically spirited "Tallyho!"[44]

The Center for Materials Research

Winning the ARPA contract only accentuated Stanford's desperate lack of laboratory space. The CMR contract provided about $1 million for bricks and mortar, but that still left the university far short of the state-of-the-art facilities the materials scientists had in mind.

With the center's organizers predicting that "the activities within this building will have significant impact on the industry of the west, and particularly on industry in the San Francisco Bay and Peninsula areas," they obviously hoped some local entrepreneur would come forward to foot the rest of the bill.

Terman had in mind Jack McCullough, cofounder of Eitel-McCullough, the oldest electronics firm in the valley. For years, Terman had been after him to consider making a major gift to Stanford. McCullough was not a graduate (although his son was), but he had worked closely with Stanford faculty, hired many Stanford graduates, and even sent one of his company's ceramists to teach in the department of materials science. Despite occasional grumbling about faculty members who spent too much time consulting for competing companies, McCullough had given $25,000 for the new Varian Laboratory of Physics in 1960.[45] Now he was thinking about something bigger, and with a little smooth talking from Terman, McCullough donated $1.5 million for the CMR.[46]

By design, the McCullough Building reflected the center's interdisciplinary commitment. Completed in 1965 on a site between the engineering and science quads, with an open-air arcade to the physics lecture hall, the building itself was a symbolic bridge between disciplines. Huggins had watched how scientists and engineers communicated with one another—along halls rather than up and down the stairwells—and took account of those patterns in planning the interior architecture. To encourage mingling, he arranged the laboratories and offices around a central core of preparation and processing facilities, with neighboring specialties—semiconductor electronics and semiconductor materials, for instance—located next door to each other.[47]

In keeping with his original strategy, Huggins reserved the lion's share of the center's $1 million annual budget for core facilities for crystal synthesis and preparation, X-ray analysis, thin-film preparation, electron microscopy, and the like. The rest he spent on research, generally to attract new professors and to help get their programs up and running to the point where they could attract independent contracts. Over the initial three years of the center's contract, five professors were brought in that way, four of them with joint appointments in materials science and electrical engineering.[48] The center also funded research proposals from present faculty members on a competitive basis, but encouraged researchers to consider center support as seed money, not long-term support.

That strategy paid off handsomely in new faculty, new contracts, and new students, just as Huggins had promised. By 1963 overall contract support for materials science at Stanford had risen to $1.3 million (up from $996,000 before the CMR contract), exclusive of ARPA, reflecting across-the-board increases from the Air Force (from $365,000 to $448,691), the Navy ($271,000 to $349,918), the Army ($189,000 to $195,985), the AEC ($72,000 to $143,700), and the NSF ($77,000 to $235,850). Non-ARPA-supported research in materials science continued to grow at about the same rate, tripling from 1961 to 1968 to more than $4 million.[49] The numbers of faculty and graduate students kept pace. CMR membership expanded from twenty-two to fifty-eight faculty, and of the thirty-six new faculty members in materials science recruited to the university, half received primary start-up support from the center.[50] The graduate student population exploded, from sixty-two at the opening of the center to 304 by 1968, and from eleven Ph.D. and fourteen M.S. degrees a year to fifty-nine Ph.D. and twenty-six M.S. degrees. Altogether, Stanford's materials scientists published thirty-one technical papers in 1961, and 196 in 1968.[51]

The center also enhanced Stanford's ongoing campaign to strengthen the engineering school through private support. In 1959 the Ford Foundation, the richest philanthropic trust in the world, had redefined its mission as "banking partner to higher education" and announced a $71 million program of challenge grants to build national "centers of excellence" in engineering.[52] Stanford missed out on the first round, in which MIT received $9 million for developing a more science-based and interdisciplinary engineering curriculum, including substantial support for materials science. Stanford received only $200,000 for student fellowships and loans. Stanford's faculty and administration, already sensitized to such curricular issues in part because of the ARPA initiative, studied MIT's experience, learned from it, and came back to Ford the next year with a much stronger proposal and won $3.4 million. The next year Ford gave the Stanford engineering school an additional $1.2 million grant specifically for the support of graduate education in materials science and chemical engineering. One important reason for shifting materials science to the engineering school was in fact to take advantage of the Ford grant, which specified support for engineering departments only.[53] In principle, Ford money for materials research was completely separate from contract support, but in fact the lines were not quite so distinct. "An important feature of the projects incorporated in this [Ford] proposal are that they are not directly supportable as extensions of our normal program of Defense Department research," engineering dean Pettit explained. "Some of them may be later, and indeed the prospect of this lends encouragement to our expecting continued operation following the ten-year program of Ford support."[54]

The ARPA contract defined only the broadest objectives for the materials research program. But the center in practice and by design actually served to strengthen Stanford's expertise in strategic specialties such as microwave acoustics, semiconductor electronics, lasers, and infrared optics.[55] Marvin Chodorow's group in applied physics could not have achieved its breakthroughs in microwave acoustics, including the crucial miniature delay lines and electromagnetic amplifiers, without CMR facilities for preparing single crystals of yttrium iron garnet and for fabricating acoustic transducers. James Gibbon's integrated circuits group built on center expertise in ion implantation to get around the limitations of conventional doping techniques. G. L. Pearson's electronics group looked to the center for assistance in growing gallium arsenide crystals with improved high-temperature electrical properties, with important applications for space technology and for solid-state microwave electronics devices. William Spicer's infrared team depended on center resources for studying the electronic structure of semiconductors using photoemission techniques, leading to photocathodes an order of magnitude more sensitive than commercial infrared detectors. The center's crystal-growing laboratory—specifically its expertise in lithium niobate—gave Steven Harris and his laser researchers an enviable edge in developing rapidly tunable lasers. Center researchers were also instrumental in developing new epitaxy (for growing pure crystals), thin-film (for forming multilayer connection patterns on silicon chips), and the other technologies at the heart of the micro-electronics revolution, and of Silicon Valley.

Industry Coupling

From ARPA's perspective, the interdisciplinary materials laboratories still fell short of expectations in getting new ideas out of the laboratory and into the defense industry. Shortly after taking over as ARPA director in the fall of 1963, Robert Sproull, former head of Cornell's materials science laboratory, announced a new program to "couple" universities with industrial and defense laboratories. Sproull had concluded that DOD, despite spending millions of dollars a year on materials science, was not entirely getting its money's worth. Six years after Sputnik, a "materials bottleneck" was still hampering the development of key military technologies. In Sproull's opinion, the basic problem was that university scientists did not spend enough time talking with their industrial and government counterparts. As a start, he inaugurated an exchange program between DOD and university laboratories, and a series of seminars to introduce university researchers to DOD's most pressing materials challenges.[56]

Sproull's larger agenda, however, was attracting "and training . . . a new generation of engineers and scientists in materials technology who have acquired respect for applied problems."[57] Industrial and DOD laboratories could not encourage such practical orientation by themselves because they did not catch materials scientists early enough in their careers. Only by reaching future materials researchers while they were still in school could ARPA help break down some of the snobbish attitudes of many graduate students toward real-world problems and persuade some of the better students "that technological problems [could] be as exciting as scientific problems, and that even a first-rate scientific graduate might find a more productive career in applied science or engineering than he could find in pure science."[58] Instead of simply waiting for serendipitous fallout from academic research, Sproull intended to bring together industrial, university, and military R&D in a common assault on composites, high-temperature polymers, refractory metal coatings, thermal protection, and other specific DOD objectives.[59]

Sproull's initiative struck a responsive chord around Stanford. William Rambo, dean of engineering research, and Wayland Griffith, director of research for Lockheed Missiles and Space, attended ARPA's briefing on the industrial coupling program in May 1964 and returned enthusiastic about its possibilities. Griffith vigorously seconded Sproull's assessment that for all of ARPA's success in advancing materials science as a discipline, its efforts had "fallen far short of our potential capability in coming up with new materials which will help solve existing real problems."[60] Moreover, he concurred that too many "highly capable graduate students complete their work without either sympathy for, or fascination with, the challenges of applied problems" and that a proper academic education should be "preparing them emotionally and intellectually for useful professional careers in applied science."

Stanford at least seemed to be doing better than other universities. As evidence, Griffith pointed to the close ties between Stanford and Lockheed—the honors cooperative programs, consulting arrangements, university courses taught by Lockheed researchers, and joint seminars and symposia. Individual Stanford materials researchers were in fact already actively collaborating with their Lockheed counterparts. For instance, in an effort to improve the performance of the tellurium-lead alloys used on its satellites, Lockheed had sent one of its employees back to school in the honors cooperative program to study the degradation of tellurium-lead materials.[61] With a little long-range planning, Lockheed executives reasoned, that kind of interaction could be significantly expanded. Rambo agreed that the program "represents an excellent opportunity for Stanford and Lockheed,"[62] though he cautioned that forging an effective partnership between several university departments and several corporate divisions presented some formidable logistical challenges.[63]

Over the summer of 1964, Lockheed and Stanford drafted a joint proposal for an industrial coupling effort in composites and refractory (heat-resistant) metals and coatings.[64] For Lockheed, the challenge was clear: "With re-entry maneuvers, hypersonic flight, and other high heat flux input flight operations becoming increasingly important, new materials must be developed which can withstand the extreme environmental conditions engendered by such operations. . . .

Experience with previous and current materials development programs suggests that conventional individual materials cannot be readily improved to the point of satisfying the above mentioned requirements. It appears that a more promising approach to meeting these requirements is the development of selected materials in combination—composites—tailored to meet particular needs in specific applications."[65] To move ahead, Lockheed's missiles and satellites programs needed new materials—and the expertise to create them. And one of the best sources of that expertise was right next door. By identifying specific targets, the Lockheed-Stanford partnership would "stimulate basic research investigations at Stanford University on technologically important materials" and at the same time "acquaint talented young scientists in universities with the challenging opportunities associated with translating results of material science to innovations in materials engineering."

In the end, the Lockheed-Stanford proposal lost out to some more ambitious-sounding competitors. "We're all very disappointed, as I'm sure you are," Griffith consoled Rambo after hearing the news. "Let's keep after other similar opportunities—we'll win one together yet."[66] They did too, but not by winning a competition for a single large contract. As Stanford and its corporate partners had always done, informal "coupling" through contacts between individual faculty members, graduate students, and corporate researchers was the key to success. Ironically, their competitors never found ways to link university and corporate research as effectively, and so failed to deliver on many of their promises.

The Center for Materials Research, like Stanford's other steeples, encouraged informal exchange among faculty members from different disciplines and among faculty and corporate researchers. Many new center members had industrial experience and contacts. Richard Bube came from RCA, where he had spent a decade studying dislocation theory and the mechanical properties of crystals. William Spicer, a specialist in electronic structure and the optical properties of solids, also came from RCA. Robert White had worked at Hughes Aircraft and GTE in microwave spectroscopy and magnetics, as had Kenneth Wickersheim. Center members did consulting work for local high-tech companies such as Varian and Lockheed. A few even started their own companies. About half the center's graduates went to industry, many to firms in Stanford's own backyard.

Stanford's laser research program exemplified the pattern of academic/industrial/military interaction fostered by CMR. A. E. Siegman's studies of microwave photodevices in the mid-1960s (itself growing out of an earlier tradition of Stanford microwave electronics) led to Air Force contracts for microwave photodevices and systems.[67] Siegman, in turn, encouraged students like Steve Harris, who went on to invent the traveling-wave–microwave phototube, another idea picked up and developed by the Air Force at Sylvania Electro-Optics and Lockheed. As a Stanford faculty member, Harris subsequently made major contributions to tunable laser technology, drawing on the center's expertise in nonlinear materials. Stanford's tunable laser technology was then transferred to Sylvania, Martin-Marietta, and other corporate and military laboratories. Harris's mode-locking laser found a corporate sponsor with Sylvania, and his tunable optical filter (for tuning dye lasers) with Chromatix.[68]

Stanford graduates played key roles in transferring these and other laser technologies to industrial and government laboratories. One former student became director of research for Sylvania Electro-Optics, in neighboring Mountain View, and hired several later graduates for his staff. Another became director of research for Chromatix, while a third cofounded Rolm, a leading manufacturer of military-hardened computer systems. Others went on to prominent positions in laser research at Lawrence Livermore, Lincoln, and Bell Laboratories.[69]

Despite its enviable record of successfully turning basic materials into practical concepts and devices, Stanford's Center for Materials Research, along with its counterparts at MIT and other universities, came under fire in the late 1960s from an ARPA leadership increasingly squeezed between demands from top DOD officials for "relevance" and demands from radical students and sympathetic academic administrators for reducing the military presence on campus.[70]

Huggins, on leave as director of ARPA's materials science program from 1968 to 1970, found himself caught in the middle. Like most of his Stanford colleagues, he had no doubts about the military relevance of the center's research in the broader sense. But he also recognized the potential political liability of the ARPA connection in an atmosphere of growing hostility to even unclassified DOD research. Too weak a claim of relevance would leave the center vulnerable to charges of malfeasance from its sponsors. Too strong a claim would leave it equally vulnerable to criticism of complicity from radical students and faculty.

Huggins did his best to protect the materials science program from a basically antagonistic ARPA director, who seemed to feel "very strongly that universities have stabbed him in the back."[71] But by the time Huggins returned from his stint in Washington, the decision had already been made to transfer the interdisciplinary laboratories to the NSF and concentrate ARPA resources on direct mission-oriented work in industry and government laboratories.[72] In 1972 the NSF formally took over the university centers and renamed them the Materials Research Laboratories (MRL), cutting their overall budget from $17.2 to $12.1 million in the process.[73]

The NSF inherited the elite of academic materials science—the programs with the biggest budgets (up to about $2 million in core funding alone), the latest equipment, the most sought after faculty and students, and the best results.[74] Altogether, the twelve NSF centers included six hundred faculty members and accounted for 350 doctoral degrees a year, better than triple the number of materials science degrees awarded before the ARPA initiative began.[75] Although there was some shift in emphasis under the NSF, the research trajectories of these centers had already been set. An early MRL policy directive acknowledged as much: "Encouraged by national aerospace, electronic and defense requirements, the ARPA laboratories developed extensive expertise in the electronic and optical properties of materials, primarily through the efforts of solid state physicists, physical chemists, and electrical engineers. By contrast, relatively little fundamental emphasis was given to mechanical, structural and other relevant properties of materials or to equally important classes of materials such as polymers, composites, alloy and bimaterials."[76]

Huggins as well was having second thoughts about the imbalance between military and commercial funding of the nation's materials science program. Just after the shift of the Stanford center from ARPA to the NSF in 1972, he set out his ideas for future directions for his discipline. "Particularly important at the present time," he emphasized, "is the desire to make use of the already strong base in materials science to assist progress in some of the civilian technologies that have lain comparatively dormant in recent years, when primary attention was heavily concentrated upon those oriented primarily toward defense- and space-related matters."[77]

Huggins followed his own advice and reoriented his personal research program toward energy and environmental issues, studying, for instance, high-tech batteries as an alternative automotive power source. But redirecting an entire discipline would not be so easy, he acknowledged, especially given "the momentum in other directions that has been established over the last several decades."[78] Only when policymakers and scientists themselves figured out how "to interest and excite a community that has been oriented in a different direction and marching to a different drummer" would materials science be able to break out of yesterday's paradigm—the paradigm of space and defense—and move on to the civilian challenges of tomorrow.[79]

9 | The Days of Reckoning: March 4 and April 3

MIT faculty members stunned the academic world in January 1969 by calling a strike.[1] Not a strike against MIT itself, the organizers stressed, but rather a symbolic gesture intended to provoke "a public discussion of problems and dangers related to the present role of science and technology in the life of our nation."[2] Instead of business as usual, they urged their colleagues and students to join them in a day of reflection on the uses and abuses of science.[3] Forty-eight MIT faculty members, most of them scientists and engineers, signed the March 4 manifesto, including three department chairs.

Behind their call to action was a growing alarm over the militarization of American science, underscored by the proposed antiballistic missile system and the war in Vietnam. The signers issued a challenge for themselves and their colleagues "to devise means for turning research applications away from the present emphasis on military technology toward the solution of pressing environmental and social problems" and "to convey to our students the hope that they will devote themselves to bringing the benefits of science and technology to mankind and to ask them to scrutinize the issues raised here before participating in the construction of destructive weapons systems."[4]

March 4 sparked the liberal imagination. The press applauded the organizers for "starting to behave like citizens as well as scientists"[5] and for "summoning up the courage to bite the hand that has been feeding them."[6] Sympathizers at two dozen other campuses, including Stanford, announced similar plans.

Predictably enough, perhaps, most MIT students and faculty spent the big day in their classrooms and laboratories.[7] A few hardliners even organized a "work-in" as a counterprotest. Still, an estimated 1,400 people jammed Kresge Auditorium to hear panel discussions on military conversion, arms control, academic-government relations, and the responsibility of intellectuals.[8] "We're not attacking M.I.T.," one prominent organizer explained. "What we're concerned about is the misuse of national talents and resources, and about our students."[9] All the same, linguist Noam Chomsky brought the issues of March 4 uncomfortably close to home by reminding his audience: "The universities, by becoming inferior, contracted members of the defense establishment can only increase their participation as the intellectual advocates and architects of the war machine."[10]

March 4 touched off a national debate over the military presence on campus and the university's ultimate responsibility to the public interest. It inspired protest marches and sit-ins, "teach-ins" and special faculty investigations, restrictions on classified research, calls for conversion to civilian research, and even led to the divestment of a few key university laboratories. But in the end, the well-intentioned speeches and faculty senate resolutions were not enough to break an iron triangle between the military, the defense industry, and higher education that had taken so many powerful constituencies three decades to build. Reflecting on the willingness of American higher education in general, and MIT in particular, to sell itself to the highest bidder, whatever the long-term costs, one liberal critic complained, "Thus the great splurge of military spending not only created the illusion of affluence and distorted the economy generally; it debauched the bookkeeping and fiscal policies of a fine institution. M.I.T must now sober up. . . . The lesson of the present crisis is that while the military Mephistopheles can make life pleasant for a time, in the end he demands his due, simply by withholding a part of what his victim covets."[11]

Pentagon East

Critics in the spring of 1969 were calling MIT "Pentagon East" or "Pentagon on the Charles." With $119 million in military research contracts for fiscal 1968, MIT ranked first among university defense contractors, with twice the total of second-ranked Johns Hopkins and seven times more than fourth-ranked Stanford.[12] There had been scattered protests against CIA funding for the Center for International Studies in April 1966,[13] a Students for a Democratic Society (SDS)-led sit-in against Dow ("Napalm") Chemical's campus recruiting in November 1967,[14] and a weeklong "sanctuary" for an Army deserter in October 1968. But compared with Columbia, where students fought pitched battles with police over the university's affiliation with the Institute for Defense Analysis,[15] or Harvard, where students protesting ROTC (the Reserve Officer Training Corps program) held a university building until evicted by the police,[16] MIT was relatively quiet. The essential contradictions of MIT radicalism were captured in a cartoon showing a scruffy MIT student carrying a placard filled with equations, over the caption, "Man, that's really telling it like it is . . . !"[17]

March 4 put "war research" and "conversion" on the MIT agenda. Mobilized as the Science Action Coordinating Committee (SACC), radical students took to the streets with their demands for an end to cooperative education courses with the defense industry, an end to academic credit for classified research and theses, an end to "war-related research" at the Institute, and the establishment of new, "socially constructive" priorities for Lincoln Laboratory and the Instrumentation Laboratory.[18] The Instrumentation Laboratory, just a few blocks off the main campus, was a vulnerable target. "The students could gin up a march on the steps of [Building] 77 in the sun, put themselves in a frenzy, and be over here in two or three minutes," Draper ruefully recalled.[19] On April 22, fifty radical students led by SACC rallied in front of MIT's famous dome to protest ongoing Poseidon missile guidance research in the Instrumentation Laboratory and then marched over for a direct confrontation. Draper caught them off balance by meeting them at the door and invited some of them into the laboratory for a firsthand look at the "military-industrial complex" in action. After a brief verbal exchange, in which Draper said he had been able "to give them hell on their own bullhorn several times," the protestors returned to campus to press their demands with the administration. Draper, pugnacious as ever, later showed up for a free-swinging afternoon debate. [20]

The Instrumentation Laboratory demonstration, mild enough compared with disorders on other campuses that spring, still alarmed the administration, already edgy over recent events at Harvard. Anxious to forestall further confrontations and to reassert some control over the "war research" issue, MIT president Howard Johnson hastily convened a Review Panel on Special Laboratories on April 25. [21] Popularly dubbed the Pounds Panel, for chairman William Pounds (dean of the Sloan School of Management), its charge was to reassess the role of Lincoln and the Instrumentation Laboratory in the overall teaching and research mission of MIT. [22] Its preliminary report, released just two weeks later, generally reaffirmed the laboratories' place at MIT, though it criticized a few specific programs. It recommended diversifying the laboratories' research programs, reducing the level of classified research, fostering more collaboration with the main campus, and appointing an oversight committee to monitor future laboratory contracts. [23] Only two panel members, a professor of chemical engineering and a graduate student in electrical engineering, called for "the Institute to divest itself of all or part of these laboratories during the next few years," fearing that these giants were "changing the character of the Institute." [24]

Draper sensed the trouble was far from over. His homespun testimony had charmed the Pounds Panel, but privately he called it an "inquisition" and hinted to the press that if pushed too hard, he would take his laboratory elsewhere. [25] The Pounds Panel also had Draper's sponsors worried. Fearing that any oversight committee was "likely to be responsive to the interests of the faculty or even worse, the radical faculty/students' 'vocal demands,'" the Air Force liaison officer assigned to the laboratory immediately drew up contingency plans for transferring vital research programs to industry, or for transforming the entire laboratory into an independent, nonprofit corporation along the lines of MITRE (MIT REsearch). [26]

The pressure intensified as students and faculty returned to campus after the summer recess. In September Johnson named the oversight committee recommended by the Pounds Panel and announced that civil engineer Charles Miller, head of MIT's Urban Systems Laboratory, would take over as director of the Instrumentation Laboratory on the first of the year. Draper would stay on as senior advisor and technical director, with the assignment of correcting the present imbalance between civilian and military contracts in the laboratory.[27]

Draper made no attempt to disguise his feeling that Miller's appointment was a stab in the back. "I got fired," he told the press.[28] He blamed the events and aftermath of March 4 for his predicament and dismissed conversion as so much wishful thinking. "The weakness of all these gentlemen who talk [about conversion] is that they are completely devoid of ideas," he said. "They're not about to do anything. They're only making noises about how other people should do it. They have no practical suggestions to offer from the standpoint of financing, of organization, of subject matter."[29] Veteran staffers wondered how MIT was going to raise $10 or $15 million a year for civilian technology in a time of dramatically shrinking federal R&D budgets. "All the Alumni Organization together, working for a whole year, can only raise two weeks worth of funding for this Lab," associate director William Denhard pointed out.[30]

Emboldened, radical students continued to push for a more rapid reordering of MIT's priorities and even started talking about shutting down the "war machine" by force.[31] Draper took these threats seriously and warned his staff to prepare for an impending "time of troubles."[32] The MIT administration also readied itself. President Johnson obtained a temporary restraining order prohibiting demonstrators from the use or even the threatened use of force.

On November 5 the students struck. About 350 demonstrators began picketing the Instrumentation Laboratory at dawn. Waving Viet Cong flags and shouting "Shut it down!" at the technicians inside, they scuffled with laboratory workers arriving for the morning shift. At 9:00 A.M., with dogs and tear gas at the ready, the police moved in and promptly routed the protesters down the back alleys of Cambridge. Within the hour, the street had been cleared and the laboratory reopened for business. Ten people were injured and one arrested.[33]

Laboratory workers were surprisingly apathetic. "What I'm designing may one day be used to kill millions of people," one graduate student employee told a reporter. "I don't care. That's not my responsibility. I'm given an interesting technological problem and I get enjoyment out of solving it."[34] Most blamed the trouble on outside agitators with no sense of the laboratory's real mission or accomplishments.

The radicals vowed to fight military research at MIT "until the cost of keeping it is higher than the cost of ending it."[35] For MIT's administration, the November demonstration escalated the potential political costs of either alternative—keeping or divesting the special laboratories—and raised tough questions that MIT could no longer evade. The "siege" at the Instrumentation Laboratory provoked widespread comment and public debate. To conservatives, the promises of conversion and Draper's impending "retirement" signaled a pattern of appeasement to student radicals[36] and led them to recommend putting the laboratory under direct federal control.[37] To liberals, the episode demonstrated how misguided national priorities had once again corrupted an American institution.[38]

With student activism narrowing the debate over defense research to these two options—conversion or divestment—the radicals held out for conversion, arguing that divesting the laboratories without realigning their research priorities would only strengthen the military's grip over American science and technology. "By working almost solely for the military," they contended, "M.I.T. has trained its students in military technology and thereby induced them to continue in DOD work after graduation. In addition, by accepting military contracts, M.I.T. inculcates in its students a positive attitude concerning war research."[39]

The proponents of conversion drew inspiration from the example of the Fluid Mechanics Laboratory. Founded in 1962 as part of the mechanical engineering department, the laboratory initially specialized in reentry physics. Though unclassified, its research clearly had a strong military orientation. By 1966 the laboratory had six professors, twenty graduate students, and a $300,000 budget, all of it from defense agencies.[40] "Almost all of our graduate students who didn't go into university teaching wound up in the missile and aircraft industries," recalled one professor. "We were churning out defense-oriented graduate students."[41] At that point its leaders—including Ascher Shapiro, head of the mechanical engineering department and an expert on jet engines, and Ronald Probstein, an expert on ballistic and antiballistic missile systems—deliberately shifted the laboratory's research agenda toward civilian technology. Shapiro put his knowledge of fluid mechanics to work studying bladder infections and heart valves. Probstein launched a new research program on desalinating sea water. Other laboratory members looked at smokestack design and its effects on air pollution, nitric oxide emissions from automobile engines, and ways of containing and collecting oil spills.[42] Although the laboratory had to rebuild its networks of sponsors and colleagues and its scientific reputation virtually from scratch, by 1969 two-thirds of its $600,000 annual budget went for nondefense research, and half its graduates to civilian industry.[43]

Despite his own experience, however, Shapiro delivered an unequivocal call for divestment at a general faculty meeting on the special laboratories on March 11, 1970. The idea of converting the special laboratories was futile and misguided, he argued: "The target is the wrong one. As long as the military budget is high, and the powers of the Pentagon are unchecked, the military research the DOD wants to get done will get done. The only way to bring the military back into reasonable balance is to attack the problem at the national level: through reduction of budgetary allocations, and through exposure of the symbiotic relationship that exists between the military, certain segments of industry, and certain segments of national and state politics."[44] New priorities demanded new people, new laboratories, new perspectives. Even if the special laboratories could somehow be "converted," he said, they would only end up competing for scarce civilian funding with other MIT laboratories, like his own. Although the faculty tabled Shapiro's motion for divestment, Instrumentation Laboratory members left the meeting convinced that divestment was inevitable. "This brings the month of May into bright focus," associate director William Denhard told a Pentagon contact afterward, "since that is when the Sheehan [oversight] Committee will report to

Johnson, Dr. Hill [MIT's vice president for research] will report to Johnson, Johnson will report to the faculty, and—lacking a fix on any financial problems—the rest of us will report to the unemployment office."[45]

The administration had in fact already decided. Before he took office in January 1970, Miller had been told that the Instrumentation Laboratory would be divested.[46] President Johnson made it official on May 20 in a special faculty meeting. Starting June 1, 1970, the Charles Stark Draper Laboratory would become an independent division of MIT under its own board, with full divestment coming as soon as the financial details could be worked out.[47]

Draper never really understood why his former colleagues had seemed to turn against him. Years later he still suspected a conspiracy. "Very curiously, Howard Johnson made the decision, but I don't think he made the decision all by himself," he recalled. "I've never belonged to the gun club around here, so I don't know who was in on making the decision."[48]

Draper's lieutenants were apparently better informed. MIT needed a scapegoat. Deputy assistant director Charles Broxmeyer told the Pounds Panel: "For MIT it appears that such [a scapegoat] has been found. . . . The special laboratories, which every shred of evidence indicates have nothing whatever to do [with the genesis] of the Vietnam War, have been selected to be destroyed. Only then will the collective guilt of the MIT community, that part of it which remains, be expiated. Only then will the students and professors feel cleansed and purified. Once the laboratories are destroyed, everything will then obviously be all right and everyone will feel much better."[49] With its single, long-standing Air Force contract and somewhat protected by its distance from Cambridge, Lincoln Laboratory survived. The Instrumentation Laboratory, despite being part of an academic department and despite its long tradition of faculty/staff interchange, despite the dozens of courses it had offered and hundreds of students it had trained, despite a better balance of civilian and military funding than many on-campus laboratories, got the ax. It was too visible and too close to home.

One of the student members of the oversight committee showed perhaps the keenest insight into the consequences and causes of the divestment decision. "Education will only suffer as a result of this action," he told the faculty. "We are losing a close tie with a valuable educational resource." But given the "senseless ordering of national priorities," the choice was all but inevitable. "We should all do our utmost to try to influence our political system to bring some rationality to our national priorities."[50] In July 1973, after a transition period to sort out contractual obligations, the Charles Stark Draper Laboratory, Inc., officially declared its independence from MIT and became a nonprofit research corporation.[51]

Pentagon West

At Stanford, March 4 seemed more a day of dispassionate accounting than personal accountability. According to one reporter, "The March 4 observance at Stanford was not much of a setback for the military- industrial complex. But it was perhaps the first infusion of a comparatively large and public interest into questions of scientific policy-making that had occurred in a long time, and it may be that it is a portent."[52]

Home to the Hoover Institution and to a largely conservative faculty and student body, Stanford had slumbered through the early years of the antiwar movement. While its cross-bay rival, the University of California at Berkeley, became synonymous with student activism, Stanford remained, as it always had, a staunchly conservative campus better known for its fraternity parties than its student politics.[53]

That began to change in May 1966. Stung by disclosures of covert CIA contracts with other universities,[54] Stanford's faculty and students began asking some embarrassing questions about confidential research on their own campus. Under pressure, the administration admitted that the Stanford Electronics Laboratories (SEL) had been running a CIA-sponsored study of electronic communications and surveillance for eight years, in addition to a number of classified contracts for the armed services. On May 2, fifty students and faculty members picketed Stanford's administrative offices, protesting secret contracts and classified research as violations of academic freedom and integrity.[55]

The extent of Stanford's classified research program, although common knowledge among the engineers, shocked an academic community still coming to terms with the Vietnam War. President J. E. Wallace Sterling demanded a full accounting of classified research at Stanford, while the academic council announced public hearings. Terman and Rambo vigorously defended the classified contracts. Academic freedom, they maintained, cut both ways. It also included the rights of individual faculty members to undertake classified research if they chose. Terman pointed out that even Harvard, which had publicly banned classified research, generally turned a blind eye to violations, either by allowing classified projects to be done as part of consulting work or by arranging cooperative programs with MIT. "Some would call this hypocrisy, others expediency," he said.[56] Rambo denied that there was anything all that secret about the SEL contracts anyway, since virtually all the faculty and a third of the students held security clearances. He dismissed the security issue as a red herring: "The bulk of the [classified] work is in the Applied Electronics Laboratory Building. This building has a sinister reputation not fully deserved; most of it is freely accessible to all. This is well known to many faculty, staff, and students outside of EE, in large part because the Sergeant of the Guard, a slightly built man in his seventies who does not carry a gun, makes what is reputed to be the best coffee on campus."[57]

Their spirited defense did not entirely satisfy their colleagues. In response to faculty and student pressure, the academic council appointed a special subcommittee on classified research, which spent the next year surveying classified projects on campus and drafting a carefully worded report. It found little evidence that security restrictions had eroded traditional academic values, and largely reaffirmed the status quo. It even defended full student participation in classified contracts. Anything less, it argued, "constitutes a most objectionable form of paternalism that forces upon students a priority by which the faculty is unwilling to live."[58]

Meanwhile, the escalating war abroad and the feverish debates at home threatened to make the faculty deliberations irrelevant. On April 4, 1967, The Experiment, a student-run alternative college, published a detailed account of "war research" on campus and called for a mass rally "to indict Stanford U. and its Board of Trustees for Complicity in War Crimes."[59]

At the top of The Experiment's hit list was the Stanford Research Institute (SRI), which, for many student radicals, symbolized the military's presence on campus. Incorporated by Stanford in 1946 as a nonprofit research institute similar to the more established Mellon and Battelle, SRI was originally intended to encourage regional economic growth by undertaking commercial contract research too specialized, expensive, or speculative for industry alone. At the same time, SRI was supposed "to promote the educational purposes of Stanford University."[60]

Fulfilling that commitment while preserving a businesslike bottom line proved more difficult than expected. Commercial clients simply did not bring in enough revenue to pay the bills, and SRI lost money in the early years. Only cash advances from the university totaling about $600,000 kept it afloat. To turn things around, SRI brought in an aggressive new director whose strategy was to go after the lucrative military R&D contracts. Under the new management, SRI researchers took on electronic miniaturization contracts for the Navy, electronic navigation and antenna systems design for the Air Force, communications research for the Army, and nuclear weapons testing and evaluation for the AEC. In just a few years SRI quintupled its contract revenues from $2 to $10 million and turned a $60,000-a-year loss into a $325,000 surplus. By 1955 SRI was earning half its income from defense contracts, many of them classified, and setting a pattern for the decade ahead. By 1965 government contracts accounted for 82 percent of SRI's revenues, with military contracts accounting for 78 percent of the government share.[61] Those contracts included some controversial studies of land reform in Vietnam, counterinsurgency surveillance in Thailand, and chemical weapons. By 1968 SRI's research program rivaled the university's, in numbers if not in reputation, with 1,500 professional staff members (compared with 1,000 university faculty members) and annual contract revenues of $64 million (compared with $76 million for the university).[62] SRI's military effort dwarfed the university's. In 1969 SRI held $28.7 million in military contracts, ranking it third among "think tanks" and nonprofit research corporations, just behind MITRE and just ahead of Rand. Stanford, by contrast, held $16.4 million in military contracts that year, fourth on the university list.[63]

SRI's size and visibility made it an obvious target. Starting in 1965, radical student and community groups (apparently with inside help) began leaking details of SRI's chemical weapons and counterinsurgency research through the underground press. These charges, culminating in lengthy exposés published by The Experiment and the local chapter of SDS, attracted widespread attention in the Stanford community. On April 14, 1967, the SDS organized the first of several antiwar marches on SRI's Menlo Park headquarters (a couple of miles from campus),[64] and then nailed a list of demands on the president's door: an end to war research at both the university and SRI; full disclosure of all corporate and government contracts; and the resignation of the three university trustees most closely associated in the students' minds with the military-industrial complex.[65]

Mindful of SDS success at Columbia and elsewhere, acting president Robert Glaser tried to head off further confrontations by appointing a joint faculty-student Stanford-SRI Study Committee to consider the proper relationship between SRI and the university.[66] Despite opposition from liberal members who wanted franker discussions of the moral issues, the committee spent most of its time on financial and legal questions. Seeking a compromise between complete conversion and complete independence, the majority of the members recommended selling SRI to itself, with restrictive covenants on chemical weapons, counterinsurgency, and other "morally offensive" research.[67] Some members argued that instead of trying to enforce "hazy" moral covenants, the university should simply seek to maximize the return on its investment, and then put the money where it would do the most good. A radical minority held out for conversion on the grounds that divesting SRI, with or without restrictions, would not address the most crucial issue. They wanted Stanford to seize control and turn SRI in what they considered more socially responsible directions.[68]

Convinced that official bodies like the faculty committee would only end up preserving vested interests, radical students took more direct action. They marched on the Systems Techniques Laboratory (STL), broke up a trustee luncheon with demands for an end to all university research related to the war, momentarily occupied the Applied Electronics Laboratory (AEL), and picketed the SRI annex in the Industrial Park, home to the counterinsurgency contracts.[69]

On April 3, 1969, in a massive "town meeting," the various factions of the Stanford antiwar movement reorganized as the April 3 Coalition. Their demands were sweeping: that the university trustees draft stricter guidelines for SRI; end all classified research at the university and at SRI; end all chemical warfare and counterinsurgency research at both institutions, whether classified or not; and schedule a public trustees' meeting on the war research issue.[70]

Backing up their demands with more direct action, the radicals seized AEL on April 9, vowing to hold it until the administration capitulated.[71] Clearly relishing the prospects of a long siege, they set up a child care center in one laboratory, the Red Guard Book Store in a second, the Eldridge Cleaver Room in a third, the Che Guevara Room in a fourth, and the United Student Movement (for the high school auxiliary) in the basement.[72] They turned the laboratory printshop into an underground press and began distributing "The Goods on AEL," "Declassified," and other sensational exposés on AEL.[73] Surprisingly, they managed to hold out for nine days until Stanford's president, armed with emergency powers from the university's judicial council, threatened to suspend them. He then closed the laboratory to everyone, including its own staff, for a week of cooling off.

Stanford's cruelest month climaxed with a massive outdoor rally on April 18 where some 8,000 members of the community gathered to debate the moral and practical dilemmas of classified research and the Stanford-SRI connection. They voted overwhelmingly to commend the April 3 Movement for "helping focus attention of the campus upon the nature of research being conducted at the University and SRI" and to suspend classes on April 22 as a "Day of Concern." About half the participants pledged to reoccupy AEL or otherwise force the administration's hand if the trustees did not acceptably respond to the crisis by the middle of May.[74]

The AEL sit-in added renewed urgency to the ongoing faculty debate over classified research. Seeking to head off "hasty," "unworkable," or "repressive" restrictions, engineering dean Joseph Petitt announced that his school would no longer accept classified contracts and would terminate present ones as rapidly as possible."[75] It was not enough to silence the opposition. On April 24, in what Rambo described as a mood of "near hysteria,"[76] the academic senate passed guidelines that effectively banished classified research from campus.

The new policy left dozens of faculty members, research associates and graduate students in the lurch. SEL held about $2 million worth of classified contracts that no longer qualified under the guidelines. Many researchers talked about leaving the university altogether and taking their contracts with them.[77] Pettit, trying to minimize the damage, sent a letter to the alumni explaining recent events and pleading for continued understanding and support, financial and otherwise. He got hundreds of replies, virtually all sympathetic and most urging a harder line with the students. "Very nice letter— but when I was a kid if I pulled this stuff you would have kicked my *ass* clean out of school forever," said one. "We are on your side. It is our belief that if the 'loud mouthed arts and letters types' were given enough Lab courses and reports to write they would become better citizens and not bother those of us who are trying to build something better," suggested another.[78]

The senate resolution and the faculty report on SRI-university relations infuriated SRI staffers. They considered the majority recommendation for selling SRI to itself financially unattainable, and the minority recommendation for conversion under an oversight committee downright insulting.[79] A poll of SRI employees revealed little sympathy for any restrictions on contracts, and considerable support for breaking away from the university altogether.[80]

Stanford president Kenneth Pitzer (who had only taken the job in December 1968) braced for the worst. He obtained a restraining order against potentially violent demonstrations, and ordered in the police to break up a sit-in on April 30 at the main administration building.[81]

In mid-May, as everyone awaited the trustees' final decision on SRI, campus protest momentarily took on a carnival air. Students called a boycott of classes—though no one seems to have missed midterms—and held an outdoor fair featuring the chance to knock over effigies of the trustees with tennis balls or batter an old police car with a sledge hammer.[82]

On May 13, the trustees announced that after careful consideration they had voted to divest SRI without restrictions, though with the hope that an independent SRI would commit itself to a stronger social agenda. They concluded that imposing special restraints on SRI or trying to reform it by fiat would only cripple a top-notch research facility. Merging it in some manner with the university would go against the strong and explicit wishes of the SRI staff and "would embark Stanford upon a program of applied contract research in manner and scale completely foreign to our concept of an educational institution of high quality."[83]

With no higher forum for appeal, the students again took to the streets, blocking the entrance to the SRI annex in the Industrial Park, letting air out of car tires, and barricading intersections. This time, town police drove them back to campus with clubs and tear gas.[84] "We didn't want to hurt them," one officer explained. "We just wanted to open their minds."[85] Sixteen people were arrested. Perhaps it was the prospect of criminal prosecution or maybe the approach of final examinations, but student activism fell off dramatically. For the moment the movement had apparently worn itself out.

By fall, the mood of the campus had changed. STL shut its doors. Twenty-five members of the staff left for SRI, taking $800,000 in contracts and $300,000 in overhead with them. Six others went into business for themselves.[86] SRI closed the Industrial Park annex, thus eliminating a major target. In January 1970 the trustees presented their blueprint for divesting SRI. It would be sold to itself for 1 percent of its gross operating revenues ($58 million for 1969) up to $25 million and become simply SRI, International.[87] The campus community seemed to greet the announcement with a collective sigh of relief. Drained by more than a year of angry speeches, sit-ins, teach-ins, resolutions, and constant turmoil, most faculty and students now seemed more interested in peace at home than in Indochina.

Some turned their scrutiny inward, examining what the military-industrial complex was doing to their own university. In October 1969 the students initiated the Stanford Workshops on Political and Social Issues (SWOPSI), an experiment in alternative education intended to encourage research and teaching on current affairs. Under faculty sponsorship, one group of graduate students organized a course on sponsored research at Stanford premised on understanding "how a generation of close interaction with the Department of Defense has affected Stanford as an academic institution."[88] They surveyed faculty members, talked with graduate and undergraduate students, interviewed military officials, examined contracts, and searched the computer files of the Defense Documentation Center for descriptions of research contracts. The end result was a detailed file of approximately one hundred DOD contracts at Stanford along with comments from the principal faculty investigators.[89] What struck the students most were the apparent discrepancies between what faculty investigators said they were doing and what DOD contract monitors said the faculty investigators were doing. Where the professors emphasized a broad range of fundamental questions in science, their sponsors stressed a narrower band of military applications. "Basic research, like beauty, is in the eye of the beholder," the Army's chief scientist explained to the students.[90]

Hard-core activists, having lost faith in mass democracy itself following the American invasion of Cambodia and the subsequent shootings of student protesters by National Guardsmen at Kent State in the spring of 1970, resorted to rock throwing and vandalism, or "trashing" as they called it. Lacking clearer targets, they lashed out at ROTC, a symbolic though scarcely essential part of the war machine. Idealistic questions about the university's larger responsibility got lost amidst the clubbings, tear gassings, broken windows and broken heads. During April and May of 1970, police and students clashed a half dozen times, with scores of injuries and arrests and tens of thousands of dollars in property damage.[91]

Faculty liberals sometimes seemed as lost as the students. They passed predictable resolutions against the war and against academic credit for ROTC, but the easy confidence that remaking Stanford would remake the world had been largely replaced by cynicism and despair.

Rambo's assessment of the AEL sit-in ("Whatever the noble beginnings, the affair itself achieved the eventual moral stature of a car theft"),[92] seemed a fair epitaph for the Stanford student movement. The radicals, enraged as much by the apparent indifference of those around them as by the ceaseless escalation of the war, seemed to run out of constructive ideas and resorted to throwing stones. There was further "trashing" following the bombing of Hanoi, taking out most of the windows in the newly completed Durand Building, and again following the American invasion of Laos. But the number of demonstrators dwindled to insignificance, and the biggest cheers at a campus rally protesting the Laos invasion went to black students complaining that breaking windows was not stopping the war and was draining money from their scholarship fund. [93]

President Pitzer's resignation in June 1970 and the firing of tenured English professor H. Bruce Franklin the next year seemed somehow a fitting finale to Stanford's days of rage. Pitzer, an avowed liberal and an outspoken opponent of the war, found himself, like so many college presidents in those days, squeezed between radical demands for instant reform and reactionary demands for complete repression. The radicals caused Pitzer more day-to-day trouble, picketing his house at all hours, showering him with verbal abuse at every opportunity, and even pouring paint over his head at a formal dinner. But it was the reactionaries who ultimately cost him his job, threatening to withhold all-important financial support. [94] Franklin lost his job for heckling Henry Cabot Lodge and allegedly trying to incite a "people's war" against the Stanford Computation Center as part of the Laos demonstration. [95] Linus Pauling called it "a political firing," [96] which it obviously was. By that point, however, the antiwar movement had degenerated into guerrilla theater, with Franklin's wife waving an empty carbine at the press conference following the firing, and Franklin hinting at retribution from Stanford's version of the Red Guards. In the end, there were just threats. Like the war itself, the movement finally exhausted itself (and anyone connected with it) into apathy and recrimination.

Military Redux

Draper Laboratory prospered in its new role. In a handsome new headquarters in Technology Square, just down the street from its original home in the old shoe-polish factory, it maintained its reputation as a leading center for inertial guidance technology, winning contracts for updating the older Polaris and Minuteman systems and for developing their successors on the Navy Trident and the Air Force MX missiles. Annual contract revenues climbed from $71 million at divestment to $206 million in 1984. The laboratory even kept up most of the old ties with MIT. It sponsored about fifty MIT graduate students a year as Draper Fellows, who completed their course work at MIT and their thesis research at the laboratory. A similar option was extended to undergraduates through the MIT Undergraduate Research Opportunities Program. In addition, it offered seminars for undergraduates, attracting as many as 131 students a year. The laboratory's professional summer seminars brought in an additional 170 MIT students.[97] Even without the formal MIT connection, Draper Laboratory continued to enroll about twenty special military students a year for classified classes and thesis research, plus 130 or so resident engineers from industrial contractors.[98] Whatever the new formal administrative arrangements between MIT and Draper Laboratory, a recent internal MIT report concluded, "Its campus influence remains essentially the same."[99] In every way that mattered, nothing had changed except on paper.

Lincoln likewise maintained close campus affiliations despite its change of status to a federally funded research and development center. In 1985 twenty-six MIT graduate students were doing thesis research at Lincoln for master's or doctoral degrees and twenty-four research assistants and twelve coop students were working there. At the same time, twenty-three MIT faculty members were consultants to Lincoln, all but three of them on stipends, and three Lincoln staff members were teaching on campus,[100] about the same numbers as two decades before. If anything, Lincoln's research program had tilted even further toward applied research and direct military applications in the intervening years. A 1986 Lincoln study committee noted "that current opportunities for research overwhelmingly have military applications as an end-goal."[101] In recent years about a quarter of Lincoln's budget has come from the Strategic Defense Initiative.

SRI, Inc., never really suffered from losing its university connection either. Contract revenues dropped from $65 to $59 million immediately following the divestment decision, reflecting national defense cuts.[102] But after that, revenues steadily increased to $82 million in 1987, making SRI one of the largest independent research institutes in the world.[103]

As many critics had predicted, divestment only strengthened Draper Laboratory's and SRI's reliance on defense contracts. As an independent, Draper instantly vaulted to the top of the nonprofit federal contractor chart, with twice the R&D contracts ($83 million in 1974) of second-ranked SRI ($40 million the same year).[104] Draper's federal contracts declined somewhat through the mid-1970s and then rebounded dramatically with the defense buildup of the Reagan years, to $65 million in 1983 and $250 million by 1986. DOD obligations consistently represented more than 90 percent of those totals, with NASA making up the difference.

SRI followed a similar pattern. It consistently ranked second to Draper among nonprofit federal R&D contractors throughout the 1970s and 1980s. Its defense contract revenues also leveled off during the 1970s and then soared to $59 million in 1988.[105] The DOD share of those figures was 74 percent, just about what it had been at divestment.

In the 1980s MIT and Stanford largely retraced, in constant dollars, the pattern of the 1960s. They led a national resurgence of DOD spending for university science and engineering that climbed from a post–World War II low of 8 percent of total federal R&D spending in 1975 back to 18 percent by 1983.[106] Even without Draper and Lincoln, MIT retained its spot on top of the university defense contractor list, with $56 million in on-campus defense contracts in 1983.[107] Stanford kept pace, though at a respectable distance back, with $32 million in on-campus DOD contracts in 1983, or 23 percent of total federal contracts, just slightly less than in 1970.[108]

As always, however, the big picture obscures some crucial distinctions. A closer look at exactly where that money was going demonstrates that some fields of science and engineering depended far more heavily on defense funding than others. So although DOD support for academic science and engineering never exceeded a fifth overall (about the same as the NSF contribution), its presence in selected fields was felt far more strongly. In 1983, DOD funded 82 percent of the academic research budget in electrical engineering, 54 percent in aeronautics, 29 percent in computer science, 29 percent in materials science, and 14 percent in physics. [109] Including funding from NASA and the Department of Energy, much of it defense oriented, would produce even higher figures.

Once again, MIT exemplified national patterns. From a 1977 low of 20 percent, DOD's share of the MIT engineering research budget climbed back to 36 percent by 1984, accounting for 50 percent of the sponsored support for electrical engineering, 46 percent for aeronautics, and 18 percent for materials science. For some laboratories, the figures were higher. DOD contributed 71 percent of the financial support for the Laboratory for Computer Science, 62 percent for the Artificial Intelligence Laboratory, 40 percent for the Research Laboratory of Electronics, and 31 percent for the Materials Processing Center. [110]

Among some scientists and engineers, at least, the military instauration of the 1980s reopened some long-repressed questions about the university's commitment to the public interest. What were the subtle lessons for students, they wondered, of putting contracts ahead of conscience and disciplinary advancement ahead of wider social vision? Were they training a generation of scientists and engineers so addicted to the wasteful culture of military procurement that they could never flourish in the cost-conscious world of civilian technology? [111]

Back in 1965, at the high watermark of postwar defense spending, distinguished electrical engineer John Pierce of the Bell Laboratories in an article in *Science* pointedly asked his colleagues, "What Are We Doing to Engineering?" By pressing so many of the nation's best young minds into the service of national defense without fully considering the long-term consequences, he argued, America had been "alienating engineering education from the civilian economy" for so long that the country's future social and economic health were at risk. Pierce offered no easy prescriptions, but he did point to educational reform as an important part of the solution: "Undergraduate engineering is a reflection of the ideas and attitudes of leaders in engineering education. These are men who have been leaders in university engineering research and teaching. Their attitudes reflect the research they have done. In turn, the research and attitudes of the graduate student reflect the research and attitudes of his professor. And the graduate students supply the universities with a new generation of professors, as well as supplying industry with some of its best-trained and intellectually most capable engineers."[112] Only when the federal research establishment, with the help of its industrial partners, was able to break the self-reinforcing cycle of defense and space R&D spending would the nation be able to move on to new priorities for science and engineering education. "If we are to remain strong and prosperous," Pierce warned, "we must take thought and action to draw engineering education and civilian industry closer together."

Pierce's boss, Bell Laboratories president James Fisk, also saw earlier and more clearly than federal policymakers the implications of letting military agencies set American high technology policy. As head of the nation's premier corporate laboratory, one primarily devoted to commercial technologies but not without its own substantial defense contracts, Fisk had witnessed firsthand some of the limitations of that policy. (From 1960 to 1967, AT&T ranked eighth among all firms in prime military contract awards, with $4 billion. That total, however, represented only about 10 percent of sales, compared with about 60 percent for typical aerospace companies.)[113] Despite some spectacular success stories to the contrary, Fisk cautioned against placing too much confidence in a model of industrial competitiveness driven by military funding and expectations. Especially pernicious, in Fisk's view, was the assumption that defense spending actually contributed to American economic competitiveness, by fostering high technology innovations. Thanks to "intense federal subsidy of electronics, space vehicle and guidance operations, communications and computer programs," Fisk pointed out, places like Silicon Valley and Route 128 might appear to be breeding grounds for innovation. But the innovations spawned there, however important for the national defense, would not necessarily translate into "the sort of enduring, economically productive high employment industries which are the backbone of this nation," he warned. "We believe it would be inaccurate and probably eventually dangerous to persist in the presumption that this is the way to start and maintain important industrial innovation."[114] What America really needed to compete, Fisk insisted, were policies aimed at strengthening and revitalizing established, commercially oriented industries, not creating new, militarily oriented ones. And that could not be done by following a model of industrial development that "depends so heavily on federal subsidy as do these classic spinoffs from the university."

The subsequent histories of Route 128 and Silicon Valley bore out Fisk's predictions. As many entrepreneurs, workers, and politicians learned the hard way, defense spending put the heat in "Silicon Valley Fever" and the magic in the "Massachusetts Miracle."[115] The electronics/aerospace complex prospered only at the cost of increased isolation from the commercial world outside. Few of these companies ever broke their essential dependence on defense contracts. Many, like Lockheed, virtually abandoned the civilian market altogether. Others, like General Electric, Sylvania, and Ford, which had looked to their defense divisions to reinvigorate their commercial business with a dose of high tech, discovered that the innovations spun off from military R&D were generally too specialized and expensive to be of any competitive significance in the civilian sector.

Whether by design or simply by default, the Pentagon continued to set the American high technology agenda,[116] with unfortunate consequences for the civilian economy.[117] Whatever good such policies may have done in assuring the national defense, they have done nothing to reverse America's decline in the face of a very different kind of international competition. As Fisk had foreseen, the Silicon Valleys and Route 128s could not revitalize America's basic industries nor restore America's sagging competitiveness. Even Frederick Terman eventually had to acknowledge that the balance had tipped too far. In 1970 he shared with the Stanford faculty his private hopes that "in the education of engineers towards the Ph.D. degree, engineering faculties would cease turning out people in their own image but would rather educate engineers attuned to the needs of non-aerospace, non-defense industries by working on research related to the problems of the world."[118]

For a brief moment that vision seemed genuinely possible. In the 1970s new federal policy initiatives in energy, biomedical and environmental sciences, and civilian manufacturing technology pointed a number of academic scientists and engineers in fresh directions, though without offering them anything like the financial support they had once enjoyed from defense agencies. But the scales tipped back toward defense priorities in the 1980s, closing off many of those options and encouraging a return to earlier patterns of the military/industry/university partnership.

Symbolic of that renewed partnership was the DOD-University Forum, an alliance created in 1983 by the Pentagon and the strongest lobbying arms of American higher education to rebuild the connections between defense agencies and top universities that had lapsed in the wake of the Vietnam War.[119] Among other achievements, it has been credited with pushing through the University Research Initiative, a $125 million program aimed at stimulating interdisciplinary research in high technology fields of particular military interest, including electro-optical systems, materials, propulsion technology, and submicron electronics, and with revitalizing the graduate fellowships, faculty exchanges, and other reciprocal training programs that once linked the defense agencies with leading universities.[120] Thanks to the DOD-University Forum and related efforts, the military's presence has even been felt in high technology fields generally considered to be of primarily commercial importance. For instance, Stanford's Center for Integrated Systems, founded in 1980 with pledges totaling some $15 million from a consortium of microelectronics companies and aimed at recapturing the commercial market for Very Large Scale Integration from the Japanese, received $9 million in start-up funds from DARPA. Follow-up initiatives in Very High Speed Integration and in computer science have relied even more heavily on DOD participation.[121]

In a conscious effort to emulate the earlier examples of MIT and Stanford, aggressively hungry institutions like Carnegie-Mellon and Georgia Tech turned to military money to carry them to the top. Georgia Tech hired Terman protégé Joseph Pettit away from Stanford to lead its drive to national prominence, and he did so largely by remaking Georgia Tech in Stanford's image. In 1987 Georgia Tech temporarily surpassed MIT as the largest recipient of defense funding for academic science and engineering. Carnegie-Mellon made itself into a national powerhouse in computer science and artificial intelligence largely with defense dollars. Its Air Force–sponsored Software Engineering Institute and its Robotics Institute, cosponsored by Westinghouse, DARPA and ONR, in this sense represent as much a return to the past as a glimpse of the future.[122] Penn State, Southern Cal, and Texas have similarly made defense contracts the cornerstone of their recent steeple-building strategies.

Postwar events largely proved out the fears of Cornell (and later MIT) physicist Philip Morrison and others that the military would end up buying American science and engineering on the "installment plan."[123] But the full costs of mortgaging the nation's high technology policy to the Pentagon can only be measured by the lost opportunities to have done things differently. No one now can go back to the beginning of the Cold War and follow those paths not taken. No one can assert with any confidence exactly where a science and engineering driven by other assumptions and priorities would have taken us. No one can even blame more than a portion of the economic difficulties of the early 1990s on the willingness to let the military set industrial policy for industries and universities alike.[124]

Yet for too long the master architects of our high technology policy have assumed, with a nod to former Secretary of Defense Charles Wilson, that what was good for the Pentagon was good for American business and good for American universities. While the "benefits" of the military/industrial/academic complex have been amply demonstrated in successive generations of sophisticated weapons systems, so have the costs, in an American science and engineering dominated by the same mindset that made those weapons possible in the first place. Breaking out of that mindset will take time, determination, and not least of all money—money that will be exceptionally hard to come by in an era of continuing high military expenditures now coupled with tightening federal budgets. But if America can muster the political and moral will to put its science and engineering to work on behalf of a more worthy national agenda and to take advantage of a long overdue "peace dividend," then the nation should consider reallocating substantial funds to rebuilding the infrastructure of civilian science and technology that more than two generations of war, and preparing for war, has so badly depleted.

Notes

Introduction

1. House Committee on Science and Technology, *Science Support by the Department of Defense*, Science Policy Study Background Report No. 8, 99th Cong., 2d sess., December 1986, pp. 34–35.

2. David A. Wilson, ed., "Universities and the Military" (Special Issue) *Annals of the American Academy of Political and Social Science* 502 (March 1989): 11. Wilson's collection includes a balanced cross section of contributors, including those who helped shape the military-university partnership and those who were shaped by it.

3. Thomas Misa, "Military Needs, Commercial Realities, and the Development of the the Transistor, 1948–1958," in Merritt Roe Smith, ed., *Military Enterprise and Technological Change: Perspectives on the American Experience* (Cambridge: MIT Press, 1985), pp. 253–88, convincingly makes this point, as do the contributors to John Tirman, ed., *The Militarization of High Technology* (Cambridge: Ballinger, 1984).

4. *Science Support by the Department of Defense*, pp. 280–83.

5. Carl Kaysen, "Can Universities Cooperate with the Defense Establishment," in Wilson, ed., "Universities and the Military," p. 30. Official estimates in the early 1950s placed the figure closer to three-quarters of the nation's scientific manpower.

6. J. William Fulbright, "The War and Its Effects: The Military-Industrial-Academic Complex," in Herbert I. Schiller, ed., *Super-State: Readings in the Military-Industrial Complex* (Urbana: University of Illinois Press, 1970), pp. 171–78.

NOTE: A list of abbreviations appears on p. 315.

7. Paul Forman, "Behind Quantum Electronics: National Security as Basis for Physical Research in the United States, 1940–1960," *Historical Studies in the Physical and Biological Sciences* 18, no. 1 (1987): 149–229, is perhaps the most ambitious and successful effort to assess the implications of defense spending for academic science, though Forman generally limits his study to physics. Other important attempts to come to terms with the meaning of the postwar political economy for postwar academic science include Peter Galison, "Physics Between War and Peace," in Everett Mendelsohn, M. Roe Smith, and Peter Weingart, eds., *Science, Technology, and the Military* (Boston: Kluwer Academic, 1988), pp. 47–85; Paul Hoch, "The Crystallization of a Strategic Alliance: The American Physics Elite and the Military in the 1940s," also in Mendelsohn, Smith, and Weingart, pp. 87–116; S. S. Schweber, "The Empiricist Temper Regnant: Theoretical Physics in the United States, 1920–1950," *Historical Studies in the Physical Sciences* 17, no. 1 (1986): 55-98, and "Big Science in Context: Cornell and MIT," in Peter Galison and Bruce Hevly, eds., *Big Science: The Growth of Large-Scale Research* (Palo Alto: Stanford University Press, 1991), pp. 149–83; Allan Needell, "Preparing for the Space Age: University-based Research, 1946–1957," *Historical Studies in the Physical and Biological Sciences* 18, no. 1 (1987): 89-110; and Dan Kevles, "Cold War and Hot Physics: Science, Security, and the American State, 1945–56," *Historical Studies in the Physical and Biological Sciences* 20, no. 1 (1990): 239–64.

8. The classic study is Seymour Melman, *Pentagon Capitalism: The Political Economy of War* (New York: McGraw-Hill, 1971), which can be usefully updated by Tirman, ed., *The Militarization of High Technology*. David Noble, *Forces of Production: A Social History of Industrial Automation* (New York: Knopf, 1984), provides an invaluable study of the impact of the military on one crucial technology.

9. Dwight D. Eisenhower, "Farewell Address," in Carroll W. Pursell, Jr., ed., *The Military-Industrial Complex* (New York: Harper and Row, 1972), p. 207.

10. Randolph Bourne, "The State," in Carl Resek, ed., *War and the Intellectuals* (New York: Harper and Row, 1964), p. 154.

11. Carol S. Gruber, *Mars and Minerva: World War I and the Uses of the Higher Learning in America* (Baton Rouge: Louisiana State University Press, 1975), is the best account of the academic draft and the plight of those who resisted.

12. See Paul Koistinen, "The 'Industrial-Military Complex' in Historical Perspective: World War I," *Business History Review* (Winter 1967): 378–403, and *The Military-Industrial Complex: A Historical Perspective* (New York: Praeger, 1979). The definitive account of the WIB is Robert Cuff, *The War Industries Board: Business-Government Relations in World War I* (Baltimore: Johns Hopkins University Press, 1973).

13. Koistinen, *The Military-Industrial Complex*, pp. 47–61, details the in-

terwar planning and its implications for industrial mobilization during World War II.

14. Quoted in Daniel J. Kevles, *The Physicists: The History of a Scientific Community in Modern America* (New York: Knopf, 1977), p. 116. Kevles offers the best overview of scientific mobilization in World War I.

15. See Robert Kargon, "The New Era: Science and Individualism in the 1920's," in Kargon, ed., *The Maturing of American Science* (Washington, D.C.: American Association for the Advancement of Science, 1974), pp. 1–23, on the conservative slant of the NRC leadership.

16. Gruber, *Mars and Minerva*, pp. 213–52, details the genesis of the Students' Army Training Corps and its impact on the universities.

17. Kevles, *The Physicists*, pp. 147–48.

18. For a perceptive comparison of the research strategies of GE and AT&T, see Leonard S. Reich, *The Making of American Industrial Research: Science and Business at GE and Bell, 1876–1926* (New York: Cambridge University Press, 1985); for GE, George Wise, *Willis R. Whitney, GE, and the Origins of American Industrial Research* (New York: Columbia University Press, 1985); and for Du Pont, David Hounshell and John Kenly Smith, *Science and Corporate Strategy: DuPont R&D, 1902–1980* (New York: Cambridge University Press, 1988).

19. Lance E. Davis and Daniel J. Kevles, "The National Research Fund: A Case Study in the Industrial Support of Academic Science," *Minerva* 12 (April 1974): 213–20, analyzes the failure of academic scientists to mobilize corporate support for basic research. Carroll W. Pursell, "The Anatomy of a Failure: The Science Advisory Board, 1933–35," *Proceedings of the American Philosophical Society* 109 (December 1965): 344–49, and Lewis Auerbach, "Scientists in the New Deal: A Pre-War Episode in the Relations Between Science and Government in the United States," *Minerva* (Summer 1960): 457–82, highlight the failure of academics to gain prominent federal patronage.

20. Robert Kargon, "Temple to Science: Cooperative Research and the Birth of the California Institute of Technology," *Historical Studies in the Physical Sciences* 8 (1977): 3–31.

21. John Servos, "The Industrial Relations of Science: Chemical Engineering at MIT, 1900–1939," *Isis* 71 (1980): 531–49.

22. For the big picture, see Roger Geiger, *To Advance Knowledge: The Growth of American Research Universities, 1900–1948* (New York: Oxford University Press, 1986). For a closer look at the biological sciences, see Robert Kohler, "Warren Weaver and the Rockefeller Program in Molecular Biology: A Case Study in the Management of Science," in Nathan Reingold, ed., *The Sciences in the American Context: New Perspectives* (Washington, D.C.: Smithsonian Institution Press, 1979), pp. 249–94; R. Kohler, "Science, Foundations and American Universities in the 1920s," *Osiris* 3, 2d series (1987): 135–96, and *Partners in Science: Foundations and Natural Scientists, 1900–1945* (Chicago: University of Chicago Press, 1991).

23. See Servos, "The Industrial Relations of Science," and W. Bernard Carlson, "Academic Entrepreneurship and Engineering Education: Dugald Jackson and the MIT-GE Cooperative Engineering Course, 1907–1932," *Technology and Culture* 29, no. 3 (July 1988): 536–67.

24. Rebecca S. Lowen, "Transforming the University: Administrators, Physicists, and Industrial and Federal Patronage at Stanford, 1935–49," *History of Education Quarterly* 31, no. 3 (Fall 1991): 365–88.

25. Lowen, "Transforming the University," stresses the role of prewar industrial sponsorship in shaping the postwar university, as does Michael A. Dennis, "A Change of State: The Political Cultures of Technical Practice at the MIT Instrumentation Laboratory and the Johns Hopkins University Applied Physics Laboratory, 1930–1945" (Ph.D. diss., Johns Hopkins, 1990).

26. David F. Noble, *America By Design: Science, Technology, and the Rise of Corporate Capitalism* (New York: Knopf, 1977), looks at the evolution of chemical and electrical engineering at MIT in light of corporate expectations and influence. John Servos in "The Industrial Relations of Science" and W. Bernard Carlson in "Academic Entrepreneurship and Engineering Education" argue for a more even balance of power between corporate patrons and academic clients, without really undermining Noble's larger point about industrial interests setting the academic agenda.

27. A. Hunter Dupree, "The Great Instauration of 1940: The Organization of Scientific Research for War," in Gerald Holton, ed., *The Twentieth-Century Sciences: Studies in the Biography of Ideas* (New York: Norton, 1972), pp. 443–67.

28. Pursell, ed., *The Military-Industrial Complex*, p. 6. This book is an excellent introduction to the literature. Barton Bernstein, "The Debate on Industrial Reconversion: The Protection of Oligopoly and Military Control of the Economy," *American Journal of Economics and Sociology* 26 (April 1967): 159–72, and Gregory Hooks, *Forging the Military-Industrial Complex: World War II's Battle of the Potomac* (Urbana: University of Illinois Press, 1991), are the best studies of the reconversion controversy and its consequences. Hooks pays particular attention to how wartime and postwar mobilization at once undermined and reshaped the economic reforms and bureaucratic structures of the New Deal.

29. Pursell, ed., *The Military-Industrial Complex*, pp. 317, 338.

30. Larry Owens, "Vannevar Bush and the Differential Analyzer: The Text and Context of an Early Computer," *Technology and Culture* 27, no. 1 (January 1986): 63–95, gives an excellent summary of Bush's early career.

31. The best short study of the OSRD is Carroll W. Pursell, "Science Agencies in World War II: The OSRD and Its Challengers," in Reingold, ed., *The Sciences in the American Context*, pp. 287–301.

32. Nathan Reingold, "Vannevar Bush's New Deal for Research: Or the Tri-

umph of the Old Order," *Historical Studies in the Physical and Biological Sciences* 17, no. 2 (1987): 299–344.

33. Melman, *Pentagon Capitalism*, pp. 231–34.

34. Harvey M. Sapolsky, "Academic Science and the Military: The Years Since the Second World War," in Reingold, ed., *The Sciences in the American Context*, pp. 379–99.

35. For JPL see Clayton Koppes, *JPL and the American Space Program* (New Haven: Yale University Press, 1982); for APL see Dennis, "A Change of State"; for Lawrence Laboratory, John Heilbron, Robert Seidel, and Bruce Wheaton, *Lawrence and His Laboratory: Nuclear Science at Berkeley, 1931–1961* (Berkeley, 1981).

36. Forman, "Behind Quantum Electronics," pp. 153–57. Ralph B. Levering, *The Cold War, 1945–1972* (Arlington Heights, Ill.: Harlan Davidson, 1982), offers a guided tour of the vast literature on the Cold War. For the historian of science and technology, the most important study is Walter McDougall, *The Heavens and the Earth: A Political History of the Space Age* (New York: Basic Books, 1985), a challenging thesis on the causes and consequences of the space race, especially for American politics and values.

37. Kevles, "Cold War and Hot Physics," and Needell, "Preparing for the Space Age," both emphasize the Korean War as a watershed, in contrast to Walter McDougall, *The Heavens and the Earth*, who places the great "saltation," as he calls it, at Sputnik. Following Kevles, I will not try to draw precise distinctions between science and engineering, for their merger was an important feature of the postwar era.

38. Kevles, "Cold War and Hot Physics," offers an excellent overview of the reorganization of postwar science at the national level.

39. Robert Nisbet, *The Degradation of the Academic Dogma: The University in America, 1945–1970* (New York: Basic Books, 1970), pp. 71–72.

40. Thorstein Veblen, *The Higher Learning in America: A Memorandum on the Conduct of Universities by Business Men* (Viking Press, 1918; New York: Kelly Reprints of Economic Classics, 1965), p. 2.

41. Ian Hacking, "Weapons Research and the Form of Scientific Knowledge," *Canadian Journal of Philosophy*, supplementary vol. 12 (1986): 259.

42. See Crosbie Smith and M. Norton Wise, *Energy and Empire: A Biographical Study of Lord Kelvin* (Cambridge: Cambridge University Press, 1989), and Bruce Hunt, *The Maxwellians* (Ithaca, N.Y.: Cornell University Press, 1991), for a superb analysis of how telegraphy and heat engines shaped the specific content of physical theory in nineteenth-century Britain.

43. Eisenhower, as quoted in McDougall, *The Heavens and the Earth*, p. 230.

44. Wiebe Bijker, Thomas Hughes, and Trevor Pinch, eds., *The Social Construction of Technological Systems: New Directions in the Sociology and His-*

tory of Technology (Cambridge: MIT Press, 1987), offer an excellent introduction to recent studies aimed at constructing a theory of technological knowledge. In particular see Pinch and Bijker, "The Social Construction of Facts and Artifacts: Or How the Sociology of Science and the Sociology of Technology Might Benefit Each Other," pp. 17–50.

45. Donald MacKenzie, *Inventing Accuracy: A Historical Sociology of Nuclear Missile Guidance* (Cambridge: MIT Press, 1990), p. 381.

46. Noble, *Forces of Production.*

47. Charles Rosenberg, "Toward an Ecology of Knowledge: On Discipline, Context, and History," in Alexandra Oleson and John Voss, eds., *The Organization of Knowledge in Modern America, 1860-1920* (Baltimore: Johns Hopkins University Press, 1979), p. 448.

48. John W. Servos, *Physical Chemistry from Ostwald to Pauling: The Making of a Science in America* (Princeton: Princeton University Press, 1990).

49. Robert Kohler, *From Medical Chemistry to Biochemistry: The Making of a Biomedical Discipline* (New York: Cambridge University Press, 1982).

50. Langdon Winner, *The Whale and the Reactor: A Search for Limits in an Age of High Technology* (Chicago: University of Chicago Press, 1986), p. 23. Winner offers a compelling argument about the politics of artifacts, with important implications for historians.

51. Galison and Hevly, eds., *Big Science: The Growth of Large-Scale Research,* survey the state of the art. Recent examples of institutional history include John L. Heilbron and Robert W. Seidel, *Lawrence and His Laboratory: A History of the Lawrence Berkeley Laboratory* (Berkeley: University of California Press, 1989), and Necah S. Furman, *Sandia National Laboratories: The Postwar Decade* (Albuquerque: University of New Mexico Press, 1990). Robert Smith's *The Space Telescope: A Study of NASA, Science, Technology, and Politics* (New York: Cambridge University Press, 1989), though concerned with an ostensibly civilian technology, opens up the dense network of national and disciplinary politics behind large-scale science and technology of any sort.

52. Dupree, "The Great Instauration of 1940."

53. Dennis, "A Change of State," makes this connection explicitly in his insightful reading of these two laboratories as political artifacts.

54. In the last few years, Johns Hopkins has been ranked ahead of MIT in defense contracts, but only because its Navy-funded Applied Physics Laboratory has been counted as an on-campus facility (though it is actually located some miles away), while MIT's Air Force–funded Lincoln Laboratory (similarly situated in relation to the main campus and with much closer intellectual ties) has been counted under a separate category as a federally funded contract research center. For a good overview of MIT's changing position in the postwar years, see Henry Etzkowitz, "The Making of an Entrepreneurial University: The Traffic Among MIT, Industry, and the Military, 1860–1960," in Mendelsohn, Smith, and Weingart, eds., *Science, Technology, and the Military,* pp. 515–40.

55. James Clayton, ed., *The Economic Impact of the Cold War* (New York: Harcourt, Brace, and World, 1970), p. 42.

56. Roger Geiger's forthcoming history of the postwar American university *Research and Relevant Knowledge: American Research Universities Since 1940* (New York: Oxford University Press, forthcoming) will undoubtedly provide an important overview of the rise of the "multiversity." David A. Hollinger, "Academic Culture at Michigan, 1938–1988: The Apotheosis of Pluralism," *Rackham Reports* (Ann Arbor: Horace H. Rackham School of Graduate Studies, University of Michigan, 1989), pp. 58–101, offers a provocative model for assessing these changes.

57. David Webster, "America's Highest-ranked Graduate Schools, 1925–1982," *Change* (May–June 1982), pp. 14–23, gives a general indication of Stanford and MIT's rise to national prominence.

58. Randolph Bourne, "The Idea of the University," in Resek, ed., *War and the Intellectuals*, p. 154.

59. Fulbright, "The War and Its Effects," pp. 177–78.

1 | A University Polarized Around the Military

1. Weinberg, as quoted in Dorothy Nelkin, *The Military and the University: Moral Politics at M.I.T.* (Ithaca, N.Y.: Cornell University Press, 1972), p. 24.

2. Carroll W. Pursell, Jr., ed., *The Military-Industrial Complex* (New York: Harper and Row, 1972), p. 338.

3. Ralph Lapp, *The Weapons Culture* (New York: Norton, 1968), pp. 191–97.

4. Adam Yarmolinsky, *The Military Establishment: Its Impacts on American Society* (New York: Harper and Row, 1971, p. 62.

5. Pursell, *The Military-Industrial Complex*, p. 321.

6. Research Laboratory of Electronics, "Annual Report," July 7, 1965 (MIT Archives [MIT] AC 31 9/RLE). See also Karl Wildes and Nilo Lindgren, *A Century of Electrical Engineering and Computer Science at MIT, 1882–1982* (Cambridge: MIT Press, 1985), pp. 242–79; Stephen C. Ehrman, "Past, Present, Futures: A Study of the MIT Research Laboratory of Electronics" (unpublished manuscript, 1974); Robert P. Spindler, "Scientific Autonomy and the Funding of Basic Research: MIT's Research Laboratory of Electronics, 1944–1949" (unpublished manuscript, 1985).

7. Julius Stratton, "RLE: The Beginning of an Idea," in Stratton et al., *RLE: 1946 + 20* (Cambridge, 1966), p. 6.

8. Alex Soojung-Kim Pang, "Edward Bowles and Radio Engineering at MIT, 1920–1940," *Historical Studies in the Physical and Biological Sciences 20*, no. 2 (1990): 313–37, offers an excellent analysis of this episode. See also Wildes and Lindgren, *A Century of Electrical Engineering and Computer Science at MIT*, pp. 114-23.

9. Quoted in Wildes and Lindgren, *A Century of Electrical Engineering and Computer Science at MIT*, p. 122.

10. W. Bernard Carlson, "Academic Entrepreneurship and Engineering Education: Dugald C. Jackson and the MIT-GE Cooperative Engineering Course, 1907–1932," *Technology and Culture* 29, no. 3 (July 1988): 536–67, offers the best account of Jackson's career and his particular vision of engineering education. A. Michal McMahon, *The Making of a Profession: A Century of Electrical Engineering in America* (New York: IEEE Press, 1984), pp. 70–78, perceptively places Jackson's career into the context of the emerging profession of electrical engineering.

11. Edward L. Bowles, " 'There Followed 38 Years of Distinguished Contributions to MIT,' " *Technology Review* (July 1966): 61.

12. Larry Owens, "Vannevar Bush and the Differential Analyzer: The Text and Context of an Early Computer," *Technology and Culture* 27, no. 1 (January 1986): 63–95.

13. Wildes and Lindgren, *A Century of Electrical Engineering and Computer Science at MIT*, pp. 112–13.

14. Pang, "Edward Bowles and Radio Engineering at MIT," pp. 315–16.

15. Leonard S. Reich, *The Making of American Industrial Research: Science and Business at GE and Bell, 1876–1926* (New York: Cambridge University Press, 1985), pp. 218–38, details the struggle between these corporate giants to control radio. Hugh G. J. Aitken, *The Continuous Wave: Technology and American Radio, 1900–1932* (Princeton: Princeton University Press, 1985), sets the radio story into a business context, though with scant attention to academic developments.

16. D. C. Jackson to F. B. Jewett, April 15, 1925 (MIT AC 13 11/Jackson, D. C., 1923–28).

17. Wildes and Lindgren, *A Century of Electrical Engineering and Computer Science at MIT*, pp. 129–30.

18. Bowles, " 'There Followed 38 Years of Distinguished Contributions to MIT,' " p. 66.

19. Pang, "Edward Bowles and Radio Engineering at MIT," p. 316.

20. Bowles, " 'There Followed 38 Years of Distinguished Contributions to MIT,' " pp. 65–66.

21. Samuel Stratton to E. H. R. Green, Nov. 3, 1923 (MIT AC 13 9/Green, E. H. R., 1923–31).

22. Pang, "Edward Bowles and Radio Engineering at MIT," pp. 317–18.

23. "Outline for a Research Institution in Memory of Mrs. Hetty Green for Research on Electricity, Physics, and Electric Communication" (MIT MC 5 3/184).

24. Jackson to Samuel Stratton, "Memorandum on Possibilities of Research in Radio Communication at the Massachusetts Institute of Technology," March 31, 1925 (MIT AC 13 11/Jackson, D. C., 1923–28).

25. V. Bush to S. Stratton, July 7, 1926 (MIT AC 13 3/Bush, V., 1921–28).

26. Pang, "Edward Bowles and Radio Engineering at MIT," p. 326.

27. Edward Bowles, Summary of Round Hill activities, March 31, 1948 (MIT AC 4 205/Round Hill, December 1947–January 1948).

28. Wildes and Lindgren, A Century of Electrical Engineering and Computer Science at MIT, p. 121.

29. Ibid., p. 106.

30. Pang, "Edward Bowles and Radio Engineering at MIT," pp. 328–30.

31. Karl Compton to Chief, Bureau of Aeronautics, October 21, 1937 (MIT AC 4 205/Round Hill, 1937).

32. Karl Compton, Memorandum of discussion with Dean Moreland and Professor Bowles, January 5, 1940 (MIT AC 4 40/Bowles, 1933–45).

33. Ibid.

34. E. Bowles to K. Compton, June 11, 1940 (MIT AC 4 40/Bowles, 1933–45); H. Willis to K. Compton, December 31, 1945 (MIT AC 4 258/Willis, H. Hugh, 1939–47).

35. Bowles to K. Compton, "Ultrahigh Frequency Research Program," May 12, 1939 (AC 4 40/Bowles, 1933–45).

36. K. Compton, "Memo for Exec. Comm." May 20, 1940 (MIT AC 4 40/Bowles, 1933–45).

37. Ibid.

38. Daniel J. Kevles, The Physicists: The History of a Scientific Community in Modern America (New York: Knopf, 1977), pp. 293–97.

39. McMahon, The Making of a Profession, p. 199.

40. John S. Rigden, Rabi: Scientist and Citizen (New York: Basic Books, 1987), pp. 128–31.

41. Pang, "Edward Bowles and Radio Engineering at MIT," p. 334.

42. Kevles, The Physicists, p. 308. Kevles gives the best short account of the Rad Lab's history. Henry Guerlac, Radar in World War II (New York: American Institute of Physics, 1987), an official history of the laboratory, offers the definitive version.

43. Bowles to Sylvia Wilks, November 28, 1941 (MIT AC 4 205/Round Hill, July 1948–December 1948).

44. Harold Hazen, "Memoires: An Informal Story of My Life and Work" (unpublished manuscript, 1976; copy in MIT Archives).

45. Bowles to K. Compton, March 20, 1946 (MIT AC 4 40/Bowles, 1946–55).

46. John C. Slater, "History of the Physics Department at M.I.T., 1930–1948," p. 27 (Slater Papers [SP] "MIT, Physics Department History").

47. J. Slater to G. R. Harrison, March 23, 1942 (SP "Harrison, George R. #6").

48. John C. Slater, Solid State and Molecular Theory: A Scientific Biography (New York: John Wiley, 1975), p. 215.

49. Slater, "History of the Physics Department at M.I.T.," p. 37.

50. Slater to K. Compton, August 23, 1944 (SP "Compton, Karl T. #10").

51. Harold Hazen, "Note on Electrical Engineering Department's Fields of Interest in Research Laboratory of Electronics," December 6, 1944 (MIT AC 4 204/3).

52. Ibid.

53. J. Stratton to Slater, November 18, 1944 (SP "Stratton, Julius A. #2").

54. Slater, "History of the Physics Department at M.I.T.," p. 41.

55. J. Stratton to J. Slater, March 10, 1945 (SP "Stratton, Julius A. #2").

56. J. R. Killian to David Sarnoff, November 16, 1945 (MIT AC 4 204/3).

57. J. Stratton to J. R. Killian, October 23, 1944 (MIT AC 4 33/12).

58. Bowles, quoted in Michael S. Sherry, *Preparing for the Next War: American Plans for Postwar Defense, 1941–45* (New Haven: Yale University Press, 1977), p. 133.

59. General Dwight Eisenhower, "Memorandum for Directors and Chiefs of the War Department General and Special Staff Divisions and Bureaus and the Commanding Generals of the Major Commands," April 30, 1946 (MIT AC 4 44/5).

60. Paul Forman, "Behind Quantum Electronics: National Security as Basis for Physical Research in the United States, 1940–1960," *Historical Studies in the Physical and Biological Sciences* 18, no. 1 (1987): 155.

61. Harvey M. Sapolsky, "Academic Science and the Military: The Years Since the Second World War," in Nathan Reingold, ed., *The Sciences in the American Context: New Perspectives* (Washington, D.C.: Smithsonian Institution Press, 1979), pp. 379–99.

62. Shapley, quoted in Kevles, *The Physicists*, p. 355.

63. A. L. Gilbert and B. D. McCombe, "The Joint Services Electronics Program: An Historical Perspective," in David Robb and Arnold Shostak, eds., *Proceedings of the Fortieth Anniversary of the Joint Services Electronics Program* (ANSER, Arlington, Va.: 1986).

64. "The Research Laboratory of Electronics—A Review," December 15, 1946 (MIT AC 12/RLE, 1946–58).

65. J. Stratton, "Memorandum to Members of the Research Laboratory of Electronics," May 1, 1946 (MIT AC 12/RLE, 1946–58).

66. "The Research Laboratory of Electronics—A Review," December 15, 1946.

67. Albert Hill, "Why the Military?" *Technology Review* (May 1966): 68.

68. J. Stratton to J. R. Loofbourow, October 10, 1945 (MIT AC 4 232/Stratton, 1940–46).

69. Slater, "Proposed Physics Program for the Research Laboratory of Electronics," n.d. (SP MIT).

70. J. Stratton to Chief of the Bureau of Ordnance, January 7, 1946 (MIT AC 4 212/17).

71. Wildes and Lindgren, *A Century of Electrical Engineering and Computer Science at MIT*, p. 247.

72. Louis Smullin, interview with author, Cambridge, Mass. January 20, 1988.

73. William P. Allis, "Plama Research: A Case History," *Technology Review* (November 1960): 68.

74. Ibid.

75. A. G. Hill, Memo on first industrial conference, May 13, 1949 (MIT AC 4 204/6).

76. Conference with National Military Establishment, November 14–15, 1949 (MIT AC 4 204/7).

77. James A. Parrott, "Technological and Institutional Innovation in Massachusetts Electronics" (Ph.D. diss., MIT, 1985), p. 256. Parrott offers the best available analysis of the rise of Route 128 and its dependence on defense contracts. Otto J. Scott, *Creative Ordeal: The Story of Raytheon* (New York: Atheneum, 1974), provides a detailed account of one company's experience.

78. Dean A. Forseth, "The Role of Government-Sponsored Research Laboratories in the Generation of New Enterprises—A Comparative Analysis" (S.M. thesis, Sloan School of Management, MIT, 1966).

79. Arnold Shostak, "History of the Joint Services Electronics Program," in Robb and Shostak, eds., *Proceedings of the Fortieth Anniversary of the Joint Services Electronics Program*, p. 19.

80. Carl Barus, "Military Influence on the Electrical Engineering Curriculum Since World War II," *IEEE Technology and Society Magazine* 6, (June 1987): 5.

81. G. Brown to J. R. Killian, December 30, 1952 (MIT AC 4 100/12).

82. Wildes and Lindgren, *A Century of Electrical Engineering and Computer Science at MIT*, p. 315.

83. Barus, "Military Influence on the Electrical Engineering Curriculum Since World War II," p. 7.

84. Wildes and Lindgren, *A Century of Electrical Engineering and Computer Science at MIT*, pp. 310–25, discuss Brown's proposals in detail.

85. "Engineering Education at M.I.T.," Committee on Engineering Education, 1956 (MIT AC 12 5/Committee on Engineering Education).

86. Ehrmann, "Past, Present, Futures," pp. 11–13.

87. Harold Zahl, *Electrons Away: Or Tales of a Government Scientist* (New York: Vantage, 1968), p. 117.

88. Robert A. Scholtz, "The Origins of Spread-Spectrum Communications," *IEEE Transactions on Communications* 30, no. 5 (May 1982): 835–36.

89. George Valley, "How the SAGE Development Began," *Annals of the*

History of Computing 7, no. 3 (July 1985): 196–226. The SAGE (Semi-Automatic Ground Environment) system will be discussed shortly.

90. Ibid., p. 212.

91. H. W. Serig, "History of Project Lincoln, 1946–Sept., 1953" (Air Force History Office, Bolling AFB), p. 23. I would like to thank Patrick Harahan for making a copy of this document available to me.

92. J. Stratton to J. R. Killian, December 12, 1950 (MIT AC 132 4/Project Charles).

93. Ivan Getting, *All in a Lifetime: Science in the Defense of Democracy* (New York: Vantage, 1989), pp. 231–32.

94. Valley, "How the SAGE Development Began," p. 213.

95. Valley to Killian, April 10, 1952 (MIT AC 4 105/5).

96. J. Stratton to J. R. Killian, November 19, 1951 (MIT AC 132 3/Lincoln).

97. Carl Overhage, "Notes on Interactions between M.I.T. and Lincoln Laboratory," February 14, 1963 (MIT AC 134 19/Defense Laboratories).

98. Massachusetts Institute of Technology, Review Panel on Special Laboratories, Final Report, October 1969, p. 134 (MIT Museum, Charles Stark Draper Laboratory, Historical Collections [CSDL HC] Activism Reports).

99. William H. Radford, "M.I.T. Lincoln Laboratory: Its Origin and First Decade," *Technology Review* (January 1962): 15–18.

100. Wildes and Lindgren, *A Century of Electrical Engineering and Computer Science at MIT*, p. 115.

101. For a historical overview of SAGE and its technical contributions, see "Special Issue: SAGE," *Annals of the History of Computing* 5, no. 4 (October 1983).

102. Kent C. Redmond and Thomas M. Smith, *Project Whirlwind: The History of a Pioneer Computer* (Bedford, Mass.: Digital Press, 1980), provide the best account of the origins and development of this venture.

103. Valley, "How the SAGE Development Began," p. 207.

104. David Noble, *Forces of Production: A Social History of Industrial Automation* (New York: Knopf, 1984), p. 111. Noble perceptively places the Whirlwind story within the larger context of MIT's postwar engineering program, particularly the effort to develop numerically controlled machine tools.

105. Redmond and Smith, *Project Whirlwind*, detail these protracted negotiations. pp. 122ff.

106. J. Stratton to J. R. Killian, February 3, 1950 (MIT AC 132 4/Project Whirlwind).

107. Redmond and Smith, *Project Whirlwind*, pp. 153ff.; Valley, "How the SAGE Development Began," p. 210.

108. Parrott, "Technological and Institutional Innovations in Massachusetts Electronics," p. 185.

109. M. Astrahan and J. Jacobs, "History of the Design of the SAGE Computer—The AN/FSQ-7," *Annals of the History of Computing* 5, no. 4 (October 1983): 347–49.

110. Quoted in Parrott, "Technological and Institutional Innovation in Massachusetts Electronics," p. 185.

111. Claude Baum, *The Systems Builders: The Story of SDC* (Santa Monica, Calif.: Systems Development Corporation, 1981).

112. Carl Overhage, "Lincoln Laboratory and the Greater M.I.T. Community," *Technology Review* (January 1962): 24.

113. John Goodenough to Jay Forrester, March 14, 1955 (MIT AC 4 132/8).

114. J. Stratton, quoted in Wildes and Lindgren, *A Century of Electrical Engineering and Computer Science at MIT*, p. 300.

115. Overhage, "Notes on Interactions Between M.I.T. and Lincoln Laboratory," February 14, 1963.

116. Scholtz, "The Origins of Spread-Spectrum Communications," pp. 836–37.

117. Ibid., pp. 837–41; Wildes and Lindgren, *A Century of Electrical Engineering and Computer Science at MIT*, pp. 267–68.

118. Richard Morenus, *DEW Line* (New York: Rand McNally, 1957), p. 29.

119. Radford, "M.I.T. Lincoln Laboratory," pp. 15–16.

120. Overhage to James McCormack, October 1, 1962 (MIT AC 134 19/Defense Laboratories).

121. Valley to J. Stratton, November 17, 1958 (MIT AC 134 29/Linclon Laboratory).

122. Overhage to James McCormack, October 4, 1962 (MIT AC 134 19/Defense Laboratories).

123. Ibid.

124. Overhage, "Notes on Interactions between M.I.T. and Lincoln Laboratory," February 14, 1963.

125. Milton Clauser, "Retention or Divestiture of the Special Laboratories: A Reply," March 9, 1970 (MIT Museum, CSDL HC Activism Reports).

126. Massachusetts Institute of Technology, Review Panel on Special Laboratories, Final Report, October 1969, p. 147. This document contains an extremely helpful overview of Lincoln's history and technical achievements (pp. 131–48).

127. Parrott, "Technological and Institutional Innovation in Massachusetts Electronics," p. 261.

128. Herbert A. Wainer, "The Spin-Off of Technology from Government-Sponsored Research Laboratories" (S.M. thesis, Sloan School of Management, MIT, 1965), pp. 51–56.

129. Nancy Dorfman, "Route 128: The Development of a Regional High Technology Economy," *Research Policy* 12 (1983): 314.

130. Testimony of Edward Roberts, MIT Review Panel on Special Laboratories, May 7, 1969 (Reel 3), p. 16.

131. "Spin-Off Companies from MIT Lincoln Laboratory," April 1987, p. 17 (MIT Archives).

132. Dorfman, "Route 128," p. 310

133. J. Wiesner et. al., "Twelve Years of Basic Research—A Brief History of the Research Laboratory of Electronics," (RLE, March 1958), p. 1.

134. G. Brown to J. Stratton, October 16, 1958 (MIT AC 134 37/RLE).

135. Wildes and Lindgren reproduce a copy of this sketch in A *Century of Electrical Engineering and Computer Science at MIT*, p. 324.

136. Ibid., pp. 322–25.

137. Louis Smullin, "Proposal for a Study of Major Engineering Problems of the World," August 26, 1959 (MIT AC 134 21/Electrical Engineering).

138. Louis Smullin, *Technology Review* (July–August 1970): 51.

2 | Steeple Building in Electronics

1. Frederick E. Terman to Paul Davis, December 29, 1943 (Stanford Archives [SA] SC 160 I 1/2).

2. Ibid.

3. Terman, "Recipe for Distinction," 1958 (SA SC 160 III 19/6).

4. The university's campus newspaper, the *Stanford Campus Report*, October 5, 1977, offers an excellent summary of Terman's educational philosophy, largely in his own words.

5. The figures are drawn from Ralph Lapp, *The Weapons Culture* (New York: Norton, 1968), pp. 191–97.

6. For Terman's role in creating Silicon Valley see Michael Malone, *The Big Score: The Billion-Dollar Story of Silicon Valley* (Garden City, N.Y.: Doubleday, 1985); Everett Rogers and Judith Larsen, *Silicon Valley Fever: Growth and High Technology Culture* (New York: Basic Books, 1984); and Dirk Hanson, *The New Alchemists: Silicon Valley and the Microelectronics Revolution* (Boston: Little, Brown, 1982).

7. For Ryan's career see W. F. Durand, "Harris Joseph Ryan," *National Academy of Sciences: Biographical Memoirs*, vol. 19 (Washington, D.C.: National Academy of Sciences, 1938), pp. 285–306; and Thomas P. Hughes, *Networks of Power:Electrification in Western Society, 1880–1930* (Baltimore: Johns Hopkins University Press, 1984), pp. 158–60.

8. Terman to T. Hoover, April 26, 1926 (SA SC 160 II 4/4).

9. The best study of Terman's early career is A. Michal McMahon, *The*

Making of a Profession: A Century of Electrical Engineering in America (New York: IEEE Press, 1984), pp. 183–87.

10. H. Ryan to R. Wilbur, August 2, 1924 (SA SC 64A 57/"Electrical Engineering, 1923–1924"), discusses Terman's record at MIT, his illness, and his long road to recovery.

11. Terman to T. Hoover, April 26, 1926 (SA SC 160 II 4/4).

12. Terman, "The Electrical Engineering Research Situation in the American Universities," *Science* 65, no. 1686 (April 22, 1927): 386.

13. Terman to H. Ryan, April 27, 1927 (SA SC 160 II 6/3).

14. Terman to H. Ryan, ca. 1927 (SA SC 160 II 4/4).

15. For a contemporary description of the laboratory and its research program, see Terman to R. Swain, August 14, 1929 (SA SC 160 II 4/4).

16. Terman to W. Wells, October 20, 1932 (SA SC 160 II 2/7).

17. J. Pettit's recollections in *Stanford Engineering News* 17, no. 22 (July 1965) (SA SC 216 A32).

18. Terman to P. Davis, October 29, 1937 (SA SC 160 II 2/14).

19. Terman to R. Wilbur, January 3, 1934 (SA SC 160 II 1/7).

20. Terman, "Stanford and the Training of Future Leaders in Engineering," n.d. (SA SC 160 II 3/9).

21. Terman to P. Davis, October 29, 1937 (SA SC 160 II 2/14).

22. Terman to R. Wilbur, November 5, 1937 (SA SC 160 II 4/17).

23. Terman to M. Boring, December 1, 1937 (SA SC 160 II 2/10), lists the placement record for Terman's students.

24. See Leonard S. Reich, *The Making of American Industrial Research: Science and Business at GE and Bell, 1876–1926* (New York: Cambridge University Press, 1985), pp. 218–38.

25. David Packard's recollections in *Stanford Engineering News* 17, no. 22 (July, 1965) (SA SC 216 A32).

26. Terman's reply to Packard in ibid.

27. Arthur Norberg, "The Origins of the Electronics Industry on the Pacific Coast," *Proceedings of the IEEE* 64, no. 4 (September 1976): 1314–1322, perceptively sketches the prewar electronics industry in California.

28. Terman to S. Hollister, March 17, 1938 (SA SC 160 II 3/1).

29. McMahon, *The Making of a Profession*, pp. 201–06, recounts Terman's RRL experiences in detail.

30. S. Morris to Terman, January 12, 1942 (SA SC 160 I 4/2).

31. K. Compton to Terman, February 16, 1942 (SA SC 160 I 4/2).

32. Terman, notes (SA SC 160 I 4/2).

33. Terman, "Personnel: Final Report" (SA SC 160 I 3/3).

34. Terman to R. Wilbur, March 9, 1942 (SA SC 160 I 1/14).

35. Terman to P. Davis, November 10, 1942 (SA SC 160 I 1/2).

36. Terman to H. Skilling, August 27, 1942 (SA SC 160 I 1/11).

37. I am drawing this account of RRL's research from Oswald Villard, Jr.'s "Administrative History of the Radio Research Laboratory" (SA SC 160 I 9/1); and Guy Suits, *Applied Physics: Electronics* (Boston: Little, Brown, 1948), pp. 49–54.

38. Terman logbook (SA SC 160 I 4/3).

39. K. Spangenberg to H. Skilling, August 8, 1943 (SA SC 160 II 10/2).

40. Terman to H. Skilling, June 20, 1944 (SA SC 160 I 1/11).

41. Suits, *Applied Physics: Electronics*, pp. 49–54, details this effort.

42. Terman, quoted in McMahon, *The Making of a Profession*, p. 233.

43. Terman, Dean's Report, School of Engineering, 1946–47 (SA SC216 39/School of Engineering, '46–'47).

44. Terman to A. Eurich, October 30, 1944 (SA SC 160 I 1/12).

45. Terman to H. Skilling, June 20, 1944 (SA SC 160 I 1/11).

46. Terman to D. Tresidder, April 25, 1947 (SA SC 216 39/School of Engineering, '48–'49).

47. Terman, "Partners in Prosperity," in Carroll W. Pursell, Jr., *Readings in Technology and American Life* (New York: Oxford University Press, 1969), p. 437.

48. Charles Susskind, "Electron-Tube Research at Stanford University" (SA SC 160 II 15/11), recounts some of the history of TWT research at Stanford.

49. "Stanford Electronics Attracts National Attention: The Traveling Wave Tube," *Stanford Engineering News* 6 (May 1950).

50. "Summary of Sponsored Research Projects in Engineering Started Since May 1, 1946" (SA SC 165 I 3/3).

51. Terman to J. E. W. Sterling, November 8, 1950 (SA SC 216 39/School of Engineering, '50–'51).

52. H. Skilling to C. H. Faust, December 30, 1948 (SA SC 216 38/12).

53. "Summary of Sponsored Research Projects in Engineering School Since May 1, 1946."

54. Karl R. Spangenberg and Walter E. Greene, "Basic Research Projects Under ONR Contract," *Electronics* (June 1949): 66–69.

55. Karl R. Spangenberg, *Vacuum Tubes* (New York: McGraw-Hill, 1948).

56. Villard recounts the early history of Stanford radio research and its technical fallout in O. G. Villard and R. A. Helliwell, "Shortening the Time Between Inspiration and Application: One Engineering School's Experience with Radioscience, 1925–59" (URSI Conference, Boulder, Colorado, January 1989). See also "Proposal From Stanford University for a Research Project to Evaluate the Susceptibility to Jamming of Radio Communications in Reflections from Meteor Trails" (SA SC 160 II 15/6).

57. "Summary of Sponsored Research Projects in Engineering Started Since May 1, 1946."

58. Skilling to J. E. W. Sterling, December 29, 1949 (SA SC 216 38/14).

59. On the JSEP program at Stanford and its technical contributions, see S. E. Harris and J. S. Harris, "Stanford University Electronics Laboratory and Microwave-Ginzton Laboratory," in David Robb and Arnold Shostak, eds., *Proceedings of the Fortieth Anniversary of the Joint Services Electronics Program* (ANSER, Arlington, Va.: 1986), pp. 104ff. Brooking Tatum, "Stanford Electronics Laboratories" (SA SC 132 5/SEL), also details the early years of SEL.

60. L. Field, memorandum, October 17, 1951 (SA SC 160 II 15/12).

61. Terman, "Program of the School of Engineering," 1949 (SA SC 216 A12).

62. Terman to D. Tresidder, April 25, 1947 (SA SC 216 39/School of Engineering, '47–'48).

63. Terman to J. E. W. Sterling, January 3, 1950 (SA SC 216 39/School of Engineering '50–'51).

64. Terman to J. E. W. Sterling, April 13, 1953 (SA SC 216 39/School of Engineering, '52–'53).

65. Terman, "Program of the School of Engineering," 1949.

66. "Stanford University, Proposed Program for Applied Research and Development in Electronics," 1950 (SA SC 216 39/School of Engineering, '50–'51).

67. Terman to J. E. W. Sterling, "Proposed Project in Applied Electronics," September 12, 1950 (SA SC 160 II 13/18).

68. "Excerpts from Board of Trustees Minutes Re: Electronic Research Laboratory" (SA SC 160 II 17/8). E. S. Erwin to D. McFadden, May 6, 1952 (SA SC 160 II 14/14), details the contract extension.

69. Terman to J. E. W. Sterling, "Proposed Project in Applied Electronics," September 12, 1950.

70. Terman, Report to the President, School of Engineering, October 1, 1952 (SA SC 165 IV 1/2).

71. Terman, "Organization of the Stanford Electronics Laboratories" (SA SC 160 II 17/5).

72. "Remarks on Classified Research Presented by W. R. Rambo to the Academic Council on May 17, 1966" (SA SC 160 III 10/8).

73. Ibid.

74. Spangenberg to W. Steere, June 14, 1957 (SA SC 160 III 18/5).

75. "Electronics Research Laboratory at Stanford University: Proposal for Extension of Contract N6onr25(07)," July 29, 1954 (SA SC 160 II 14/17); Terman to AEL-ERL Personnel, January 16, 1956 (SA SC 160 II 17/5).

76. "Expenses and Overhead for Government Research in the School of Engineering," September 1, 1954–August 31, 1955 (SA SC 160 III 18/5).

77. Meeting of Senior Staff, AEL, May 21, 1951 (SA SC 160 II 17/2).

78. Terman to J. E. W. Sterling, May 6, 1966 (SA SC 160 III 10/8).

79. James Clayton, "Defense Spending: Key to California's Growth," *Western Political Quarterly* 15 (1962): 280–93.

80. Litton Industries, Quarterly Fiscal Report, 1956–57, Charles Litton Papers, Bancroft Library, University of California, Berkeley 75/7c.

81. "Eitel-McCullough, Inc.," *Microwave Journal* (August 1960): 86–87.

82. "Huggins Laboratories, Inc.," *Microwave Journal* (February 1961): 109–12.

83. Adelaide Paine, "Ray Stewart," *Microwave Journal* (November 1962): 35–39.

84. Adelaide Paine, "Stanley F. Kaisel," *Microwave Journal* (December 1962): 19–26.

85. Watkins-Johnson Company Prospectus, June 18, 1964.

86. William B. Harris, "The Electronics Business," *Fortune* (April 1957): 139–41.

87. "Briefing on Department of Army Quick Reaction Capability in Electronic Warfare," n.d., U.S. Army Communications-Electronics Command Archives, Fort Monmoth, N.J.

88. Donald Harris, "Countermeasures—Guided Missiles Signal Corps Contract," June 2, 1952 (SA SC 160 17/11).

89. F. F. Urhane to Chief, Engineering and Technical Division, Office of the Chief Signal Officer, September 17, 1953, U.S. Army Communications—Electronics Command, Fort Monmouth, N.J.

90. S. J. Schulman, "EDL—Yesterday and Today," September 14, 1953, U.S. Army Communications—Electronics Command, Fort Monmouth, N.J.

91. Robert A. Scholtz, "The Origins of Spread-Spectrum Communications," *IEEE Transactions on Communications* 30, no. 5 (May 1982): 822–54.

92. President's Report, School of Engineering, 1958–59 (SA SC 165 IV 1/4).

93. Terman to W. Cooley, May 2, 1954 (SA SC 160 V 7/5).

94. Hugh Enochs, "The First Fifty Years of Electronics Research," *The Tall Tree* 1, no. 9 (Palo Alto Chamber of Commerce, May 1958): 34.

95. Terman to W. Cooley, April 9, 1958 (SA SC 160 V 7/7).

96. Enochs, "The First Fifty Years of Electronics Research," p. 36.

97. Terman to W. Cooley, March 1, 1956 (SA SC 160 V 7/6).

98. Terman, "The University and Technology Utilization," March 1963 (SA SC 160 X 2/11).

99. Henry Lowood, "From Steeples of Excellence to Silicon Valley," *Stanford Campus Report*, March 9, 1988, pp. 11–13.

100. "Number of Employees and Value of Buildings in Stanford Industrial Park," December 7, 1960 (SA SC 160 III 32/10).

101. W. Rambo to J. Pettit and D. Bacon, October 15, 1958 (SA SC 132 18/Misc.), describes some of the problems of conflict of interest raised by these arrangements.

102. W. Rambo, notes for a speech for General LeMay, July 1955 (SA SC 132 17/1).

103. Susskind, "Electron-Tube Research at Stanford University."

104. C. Susskind, "College Training in Microwave Engineering in America," *Microwave Journal* (January 1954): 32–34.

105. O. Villard to J. E. W. Sterling, September 12, 1964 (SA SC 160 III 19/3).

106. David Simon, "Dr. John Van Nuys Granger," *Microwave Journal* (June 1960): 25–29.

107. O. Villard to W. Rambo, November 18, 1964 (SA SC 132 2/Aerospace Eng).

108. Terman to J. W. Paup, December 13, 1956 (SA SC 132 17/2).

109. W. Rambo, Speech at JSEP Technical Advisory Committee, University of Southern California, April 9, 1964 (SA SC 132 19/JSEP).

110. For a summary of STL's technical program, see "The Systems Techniques Laboratory of Stanford University" (SA SC 132 6/21); and for a description of the unclassified work, see *IEEE Spectrum* 1, no. 1 (January 1964).

111. Terman to W. Cooley, April 24, 1959 (SA SC 160 V 7/7); "Applied Technology, Inc." *Microwave Journal* (June 1961): 122–24.

112. Ernest Braun and Stuart MacDonald, *Revolution in Miniature: The History and Impact of Semiconductor Electronics* (New York: Cambridge University Press, 1978), is the standard account.

113. Tatum, "Stanford Electronics Laboratories."

114. Terman to W. Shockley, September 20, 1955 (SA SC 216 38/19).

115. Terman to J. E. W. Sterling, December 30, 1954 (SA SC 216 39/School of Engineering, '54–'55).

116. J. Linvill to L. McGhie, "Industrial Affiliates Program in Solid State Electronics," April 19, 1955 (SA SC 160 III 56/1), and Stanford University press release, December 3, 1959 (SA SC 160 III 18/1).

117. J. Linvill, "List of Possible Candidates for Solid State Electronics Program," November 12, 1958 (SA SC 160 III 17/4).

118. Linvill to Terman, "Summary of Pertinent Facts About Solid State Electronics Program at Stanford," June 6, 1963 (SA SC 160 III 18/3). *Stanford Electronics Newsletter* 47 (May 15, 1961) details the early research program, as does *Stanford Engineering News* 16, no. 4 (January 1963).

119. Linvill to J. Pettit and Terman, August 7, 1961 (SA SC 160 III 17/2).

120. Rambo to J. M. Bridges, October 31, 1960 (SA SC 132 18/ODDRE).

121. Rambo to J. Lanier, July 8, 1960 (SA SC 132 19/Corresp).

122. Spangenberg to Terman, January 28, 1957 (SA SC 160 III 18/5).

123. Quoted in Frank A. Medeiras, "The Sterling Years at Stanford: A Study in the Dynamics of Institutional Change" (Ph.D. diss., Stanford University, 1979), p. 140.

124. "Remarks on Classified Research presented by W. R. Rambo to the Academic Council on May 17, 1966."

125. Terman's remarks on receiving the Hoover Award Medal, April 29, 1970 (SA SC 165 VIII 4/2).

3 | Military Guidance and Control

1. Harold Reiche to Dean Burchard, October 10, 1958; John E. Burchard to C. Stark Draper, October 31, 1958 (MIT AC 43 2/35).

2. R. H. Miller, "The Draper Laboratory and the Department of Aeronautics and Astronautics," February 24, 1970 (MIT AC 43 11/35).

3. "Aeronautics and Astronautics at M.I.T.," February 1959 (MIT AC 43 12/2).

4. Instrumentation Laboratory, "Fiscal Annual Expenditures Total Laboratory" April 1965 (CSDL Historical Collection, 219).

5. "Teaching and Research in the Aeronautical Engineering Department, Present Sponsored Research Program," February 1, 1958 (MIT AC 43 11/43).

6. "Department of Aeronautics and Astronautics, Analysis of Graduate Students, 1958–59" (MIT AC 43 6/36).

7. Shatswell Ober, "The Story of Aeronautics at M.I.T., 1895-1960," 1965 (MIT AC 43 17/9), offers an invaluable overview of the department's founding and early history. See also Richard P. Hallion, *Legacy of Flight: The Guggenheim Contribution to American Aviation* (Seattle: University of Washington Press, 1977), pp. 56–59.

8. Jerome Hunsaker to Admiral R. M. Watt, April 22, 1913 (MIT MC 272 2/29).

9. Ivy Lee to Harry Guggenheim, January 13, 1927, Daniel Guggenheim Fund for the Promotion of Aeronautics, Box 11, Manuscripts Division, Library of Congress. [LC]

10. News clipping from the *Boston Evening Transcript*, June 4, 1928, in Daniel Guggenheim Fund, Box 11, LC.

11. Hallion, *Legacy of Flight*, offers the best account of the Daniel Guggenheim Fund and its impact on American aeronautical engineering education.

12. Samuel Stratton to H. Guggenheim, May 25, 1926, Daniel Guggenheim Fund, Box 11, LC.

13. J. Hunsaker to H. Guggenheim, January 28, 1939 (MIT AC 43 15/53).

14. Hallion, *Legacy of Flight*, p. 218; "Proposed Wright Brothers Memorial Wind Tunnel at the Massachusetts Institute of Technology," January 1, 1937 (MIT AC 43 14/18).

15. Karl Compton to J. Hunsaker, March 31, 1933 (MIT MC 272 2/21).

16. Shatswell Ober, "The Wright Brothers Memorial Wind Tunnel," March 15, 1963 (MIT AC 43 17/30).

17. "Proposed Wright Brothers Memorial Wind Tunnel at the Massachusetts Institute of Technology" January 1, 1937.

18. J. Hunsaker to H. Guggenheim, January 28, 1939 (MIT AC 43 15/53).

19. Michael A. Dennis, "A Change of State: The Political Cultures of Technical Practice at the MIT Instrumentation Laboratory and the Johns Hopkins University Applied Physics Laboratory, 1930–1945" (Ph.D. diss., Johns Hopkins University, 1990), offers the best account of Draper's career at MIT.

20. C. S. Draper, "Aircraft and Spacecraft Navigation," Seventeenth Lester D. Gardner Lecture, October 25, 1978. See also Barton Hacker's oral history interview with Draper, Cambridge Mass., January 19, 1976 (MIT MC 134 1).

21. C. S, Draper, "The New Instrument Laboratory at the Massachusetts Institute of Technology," *Journal of the Aeronautical Sciences* 1 (March 1936): 151–53. See also Shatswell Ober, "Development of Aeronautical Engineering at MIT, Departmental Laboratories, 1933–60," May 1965 (MIT AC 43 17/27).

22. Thomas P. Hughes, *American Genesis* (New York: Viking, 1989), pp. 106–37.

23. Draper, in oral history interview with Hacker, p. 10.

24. C. S. Draper and G. P. Bentley, "Measurement of Aircraft Vibration in Flight," *Journal of the Aeronautical Sciences* 3, no. 4 (February 1936).

25. Dennis, "A Change of State," p. 88.

26. Charles Stark Draper, "Inertial Guidance for the Age of Jets" (Dayton, Ohio: Delco Electronics Division of General Motors, 1970), p. 9 (CSDL Historical Collection, 228); see also C. S. Draper, "The Instrumentation Laboratory of the Massachusetts Institute of Technology: Remarks by Dr. C. S. Draper, Director of the Laboratory from Its Beginnings Until the Present Time (1969)" (J. Scott Ferguson, CSDL Historical Collection Projects, August 3, 1979, Appendix A, pp. 13–14).

27. Alex Soojung-Kim Pang, "Edward Bowles and Vannevar Bush at MIT: A Study in Research Styles and the Emergence of Analog Computing and Radio Communications" (B.S. thesis, University of Pennsylvania, 1986), pp. 43–44. Also see *Technology Review* 41, no. 3 (January 1939): 111–12, for a description of the system.

28. C. S. Draper, "Instrument Instruction at M.I.T.," *Instruments* 14 (1940): 278.

29. Draper, in oral history interview with Hacker, p. 93.

30. Draper, "Instrument Instruction at M.I.T."

31. Dennis, "A Change of State," p. 75.

32. Julius Stratton, "Charles Stark Draper—An Appreciation," in Sidney Lees, ed., *Air, Space, and Instruments* (New York: McGraw-Hill, 1963), p. 3.

33. Dennis, "A Change of State," p. 60.

34. Draper, "The Instrumentation Laboratory of the Massachusetts Institute of Technology: Remarks by Dr. C. S. Draper," pp. 14–16; "Inertial Guidance for the Age of Jets," pp. 9–10.

35. Karl Wildes and Nilo Lindgren, A Century of Electrical Engineering and Computer Science at MIT, 1882–1982 (Cambridge: MIT Press, 1985), pp. 214–15. See also David Noble, The Forces of Production: A Social History of Industrial Automation (New York: Knopf, 1984), pp. 106ff.

36. W. F. Raborn and John Craven, "The Significance of Draper's Work in the Development of Naval Weapons," in Lees, ed., Air, Space, and Instruments, pp. 16–18; Draper, "The Instrumentation Laboratory of the Massachusetts Institute of Technology: Remarks by Dr. C. S. Draper," pp. 15–16.

37. Raborn and Craven, "The Significance of Draper's Work in the Development of Naval Weapons," pp. 19–20; John E. Burchard, Q.E.D.: M.I.T. in World War II (New York: John Wiley, 1948), pp. 141–42.

38. Draper, in oral history interview with Hacker, p. 72.

39. J. R. Killian to C. S. Draper, December 20, 1943 (MIT AC 4 25/6).

40. Burchard, Q.E.D., pp. 167–70, 189; see also Ober, "Development of Aeronautical Engineering at MIT: Departmental Laboratories, 1933–60."

41. "Report on the Gas Turbine Laboratory: History," n.d. (MIT AC 4 211/9).

42. Edward W. Constant II, The Origins of the Turbojet Revolution (Baltimore: Johns Hopkins University Press, 1980), pp. 208–40.

43. Karl Compton, "Memorandum of conversation with A. P. Sloan," May 17, 1944 (MIT AC 4 211/9). Alfred P. Sloan, Jr., My Years with General Motors (New York: Doubleday, 1964), pp. 362–74, discusses GM's aviation investments and postwar plans.

44. K. Compton, "Memorandum of conversation with A. P. Sloan," May 17, 1944.

45. Hunsaker to Gordon Rentschler, September 13, 1944 (MIT AC 4 211/9).

46. "Report on the Gas Turbine Laboratory."

47. E. S. Taylor, "Research in the Gas Turbine Laboratory," c. 1960 (MIT AC 43 9/14).

48. J. P. Hartog to Richard Soderberg, September 26, 1955 (MIT AC 43 11/40).

49. E. S. Taylor, "List of Projects in the Gas Turbine Laboratory," January 1952 (MIT AC 43 9/11); Taylor, "Research in the Gas Turbine Laboratory," c. 1960.

50. Ibid.

51. "Assignment of Task 'A' Under Bureau of Ordnance Contract NOrd 9661," December 19, 1945 (MIT AC 4 212/17).

52. J. Stratton to Chief of the Bureau of Ordnance, "Subject: Project Meteor Budget Policy and Program," April 28, 1947 (MIT AC 4 212/17); J. R. Killian to Admiral G. F. Hussey, May 8, 1946 (MIT AC 4 212/17).

53. John Markam to C. S. Draper, July 1, 1954 (MIT AC 43 13/14).

54. Markham to C. S. Draper, June 14, 1956 (MIT AC 43 11/14).

55. Markham to C. S. Draper, "Report of Naval Supersonic Laboratory Operations During Fiscal '54," July 1, 1954 (MIT AC 43 13/14).

56. Markham to C. S. Draper, June 14, 1956 (MIT AC 43 11/41).

57. J. R. Markham, "Present and Future Operations of the Naval Supersonic Laboratory," November 1958 (AC 43 2/34).

58. J. R. Markham, "Aeronautical Engineering: Supersonic Laboratory, Expenditures for the Fiscal Year 1958" (MIT AC 43 7/26).

59. Markham, "Present and Future Operations of the Naval Supersonic Laboratory," November 1958.

60. "Tenth Annual Report of the Naval Supersonic Laboratory," October 1957 (MIT AC 43 10/27); Markam to C. S. Draper, June 5, 1955 (MIT AC 43 11/42).

61. J. R. Killian, "Remarks at Groundbreaking and Dedication of Navy Supersonic Lab" (MIT MC 272 4/38).

62. Recruiting poster for NSL, October 1957 (MIT AC 43 10/27).

63. J. R. Markham, "The Naval Supersonic Laboratory, Massachusetts Institute of Technology," May 1964 (MIT AC 43 14/22).

64. Markham to C. S. Draper, April 29, 1957 (MIT AC 43 13/14).

65. Markham to C. S. Draper, June 14, 1956 (MIT AC 43 11/41).

66. Ober, "Development of Aeronautical Engineering at MIT, Departmental Laboratories, 1933–60"; "M.I.T. 'Gadget' Tests A-Bomb Strain on Planes," unidentified news clipping (MIT AC 43 1/30).

67. R. L. Bisplinghoff to C. S. Draper, "Summary of Aeroelastic and Structures Research Activities from 1 July 1951 to 30 June 1952," July 23, 1952 (MIT AC 43 11/37).

68. Alvin Graves to Stark Draper, July 24, 1951 (MIT AC 43 1/23).

69. Bisplinghoff to C. S. Draper and J. C. Hunsaker, May 20, 1954 (MIT AC 43 1/24).

70. Bisplinghoff to C. S. Draper, "Summary of Aeroelastic and Structures Research Activities from 1 July 1951 to 30 June 1952," July 23, 1952; "Teaching and Research in the Aeronautical Engineering Department," October 1952 (MIT AC 43 11/38).

71. Bisplinghoff to C. S. Draper, "Activities in Structures and Aeroelasticity During the Past Year," February 1952 (MIT AC 43 1/23).

72. Holt Ashley to C. S. Draper, June 4, 1956 (MIT AC 43 11/41).

73. J. Bicknell, H. Stever, H. Ashley, M. Finston, L. Trilling to C. Draper, J. Hunsaker, and S. Ober, January 8, 1952 (MIT AC 43 8/48); S. Ober, "De-

scription of Course Revisions, Aeronautical Engineering Department," March 12, 1952 (MIT AC 43 6/48).

74. S. Ober, "Facts About the Graduate School," June 7, 1957 (MIT AC 43 11/42).

75. R. L. Bisplinghoff and J. W. Markam, "Outline of Proposed Shock and Vibration Course for Air Force Officers at M.I.T.," n.d. (MIT AC 43 6/46).

76. Paul Sandorff, "Curriculum," c. 1957 (MIT AC 43 11/42).

77. Ibid.

78. R. L. Bisplinghoff, "Remarks on Survey of Present and Projected Departmental Laboratory Facilities and Their Use in Graduate Teaching," May 2, 1952 (MIT AC 43 11/37).

79. "Fourth Industrial Liaison Symposium, Aeroelasticity and Aircraft Structures," April 26–27, 1955 (MIT AC 43 1/24).

80. R. L. Halfman, "Some Notes on the Activities of the Fluid Dynamics Research Group in the Academic Year 1956–57" (MIT AC 43 11/42).

81. Sandorff, "Curriculum," c. 1957.

82. Ashley to C. S. Draper, June 4, 1956 (MIT AC 43 11/41).

83. "Department of Aeronautics and Astronautics: Report to the Dean of Engineering, 1963–1964" (MIT AC 43 12/7).

84. J. Markham, "Placement Record," December 2, 1952 (MIT AC 43 11/3).

85. Bisplinghoff to C. S. Draper, "Activities in Structures and Aeroelasticity During the Past Year," February 1952.

86. Bisplinghoff, "Remarks on Survey of Present and Projected Departmental Laboratory Facilities and Their Use in Graduate Training," May 2, 1952.

87. L. E. Beckley to S. Ober, "Flutter Laboratory History," January 15, 1965 (MIT AC 43 17/30).

88. C. S. Draper, "Self-Contained Guidance Systems," IRE Transactions on Military Electronics (December 1958), 2(1): 25–35.

89. Donald MacKenzie, Inventing Accuracy: A Historical Sociology of Nuclear Missile Guidance (Cambridge: MIT Press, 1990), pp. 66ff., offers an excellent account of the objections to inertial guidance and how they were overcome.

90. Leighton Davis, "Military Significance of Draper's Work for the Air Force," in Lees, ed., Air, Space, and Instruments, pp. 6–8.

91. J. Scott Ferguson, "FEBE" (CSDL Historical Collection Projects, C–5249).

92. Draper, "The Instrumentation Laboratory of the Massachusetts Institute of Technology: Remarks by Dr. C. S. Draper," pp. 20–21.

93. The story of the flight appears in Donald MacKenzie, "Missile Accuracy: A Case Study in the Social Processes of Technological Change," in Wiebe

Bijker, Thomas Hughes, and Trevor Pinch, eds., *The Social Construction of Technological Systems* (Cambridge: MIT Press, 1987), p. 206; and in J. Scott Ferguson, "SPIRE" (CSDL Historical Collection Projects, C–5249).

94. Walter McDougall, *The Heavens and the Earth: A Political History of the Space Age* (New York: Basic Books, 1985), pp. 115–16.

95. Edmund Beard, *Developing the ICBM: A Study in Bureaucratic Politics* (New York: Columbia University Press, 1976), sets the political context for the ICBM program.

96. MacKenzie, *Inventing Accuracy*, pp. 148–50.

97. J. Scott Ferguson, "Titan II and III" (CSDL Historical Collection Projects, C–5249).

98. Instrumentation Laboratory, "Fiscal Annual Expenditures Total Laboratory," April 1965 (CSDL Historical Collection 219).

99. Memorandum for Dr. Draper, December 19, 1960 (CSDL Historical Collection).

100. C. S. Draper, "Submarine Inertial Navigation—A Review and Some Predictions," Polaris Steering Task Group, October 22, 1959 (CSDL Historical Collection 107).

101. R. A. Furhman, "The Fleet Ballistic Missile System: Polaris to Trident," *Journal of Spacecraft* 15, no. 5 (September–October 1978), offers a concise history of Polaris by one of the participants. Harvey Sapolsky, *The Polaris System Development: Bureaucratic and Programmatic Success in Government* (Cambridge: Harvard University Press, 1972), gives the political history of the fleet ballistic missile system.

102. MacKenzie, *Inventing Accuracy*, pp. 145–47.

103. J. Scott Ferguson, "Fleet Ballistic Missile" (CSDL Historical Collection Projects, C–5249).

104. "The Instrumentation Laboratory," April 1965 (CSDL Historical Collection).

105. Charles Stark Draper Laboratory, "Annual Expenditures and Commitments—Total Laboratory," July 1971 (CSDL Historical Collection).

106. Draper to Robert C. Seamans, Jr., November 21, 1961 (MIT Museum, CSDL P, Apollo Correspondence).

107. Charles Stark Draper Laboratory, "Annual Expenditures and Commitments—Total Laboratory," July 1971.

108. Draper, in oral history interview with Hacker, p. 93.

109. Julius A. Stratton, "Charles Stark Draper—An Appreciation," in Lees, ed., *Air, Space, and Instruments*, p. 4.

110. C. S. Draper, testimony, Review Panel on Special Laboratories, p. 58 (MIT AC 59, reel 2).

111. Shatswell Ober, "Material for the President's Report 1951-52, Graduate School Affairs 1951–52" (MIT AC 43 11/37); Walter McKay to C. S. Dra-

per, "Numbers of Students Specializing in Instrumentation and Control," December 11, 1951 (MIT AC 43 6/34).

112. "Service Groups Specializing in Instrumentation," September 6, 1951 (MIT AC 43 6/46); "Education and the Instrumentation Laboratory," April 1965 (MIT Museum, CSDL Historical Collection).

113. C. S. Draper, "Departmental Report to the Dean of Engineering Covering the Academic Year 1951–52," September 2, 1952 (MIT AC 43 11/38).

114. "Description of Courses Contained in Proposed Curriculum Leading to S.M. Degrees for Air Force Officers," May 22, 1952 (MIT AC 43 6/46).

115. Draper to Captain J. M. Hicks, April 9, 1953 (MIT AC 43 6/43); E. S. Lee to C. S. Draper, September 17, 1952 (MIT AC 43 6/46).

116. E. E. Patridge to J. R. Killian, August 11, 1952 (MIT AC 43 6/46).

117. Bisplinghoff to H. G. Stever, April 11, 1958 (MIT AC 43 11/43).

118. Laurence Young, testimony, Review Panel on Special Laboratories, p. 72 (MIT AC 54, reel 2).

119. Draper, "The Instrumentation Laboratory of the Massachusetts Institute of Technology: Remarks by Dr. C. S. Draper," pp. 23–24.

120. "Department Organization, 1956–57" (MIT AC 43 7/13).

121. W. Wrigley, "A Position Paper on the Educational Function of the Charles Stark Draper Laboratory," March 2, 1970 (MIT Museum, CSDL, Activism File).

122. Thomas Sherwood to J. R. Killian, August 7, 1952 (MIT AC 4 102/4).

123. Ibid.

124. C. S. Draper, W. Wrigley, S. Lees, *Instrument Engineering* (New York: McGraw-Hill, 1952).

125. C. S. Draper, "Instrumentation Activities of the Aeronautical Engineering Department at the Massachusetts Institute of Technology," March 1953 (MIT AC 43 9/26).

126. "Education and the Instrumentation Laboratory," April 1965 (MIT Museum, CSDL Historical Collection).

127. "Teaching and Research, Department of Aeronautics and Astronautics," March 1960 (MIT AC 43 112/2).

128. "Education and the Instrumentation Laboratory," April 1969 (MIT AC 43 11/35).

129. "68 Albany Street," Ross McElwee directed this short promotional film about the Instrumentation Laboratory, featuring interviews with a number of longtime engineers and other employees.

130. R. R. Ragan to D. Fraser, D. Driscoll, and J. O'Connor, January 21, 1987 (CSDL Historical Collection).

131. W. McKay, "Report on Course 16.351, Special Problems in Instrumentation and Control," September 26, 1951 (MIT AC 43 9/11).

132. C. S. Draper, "Aeronautical Engineering Department Activities for the Academic Year 1953–54" (MIT AC 43 11/39).

133. Instrumentation Laboratory, "Company Residents in Instrumentation Laboratory," April 1965 (CSDL Historical Collection).

134. Charles Stark Draper Laboratory, "Man-Days of Engineering Visits from 1954," July 1971 (CSDL Historical Collection).

135. Charles Stark Draper Laboratory, "Staff Member Turnover to Industry and Research Laboratories," July 1971 (CSDL Historical Collection).

136. "GM Builds Research Lab Near M.I.T. to Aid Research, Tap Pool of Engineers," *Wall Street Journal*, August 20, 1959, p. 22.

137. Paul V. Teplitz, "Spin-Off Enterprises from a Large Government-Sponsored Laboratory" (S. M. thesis, Sloan School of Management, June 1965).

138. "GM Builds Research Lab Near M.I.T. to Aid Research, Tap Pool of Engineers," *Wall Street Journal*.

139. *Technology Review* 61, no. 5 (March 1959): 224.

140. Teplitz, "Spin-Off Enterprises from a Large Government-Sponsored Laboratory" offers a detailed account of these firms up to 1965, based on a questionnaire and interviews with the founders. This thesis was part of the larger effort by MIT management professor Edward Roberts to evaluate the impact of MIT's laboratories on the economic development of the Boston region.

141. Charles Stark Draper Laboratory, "Staff Member Turnover to Industry and Research Laboratories," and "Man-Days of Engineering Visits From 1954," July 1971.

142. Ragan to D. N. Yates, September 2, 1963; R. R. Ragan, "Conversation with Dr. Bowles, and Instrumentation Laboratory Long-Range Plan, on 4 September 1963" (CSDL Historical Collection).

143. "Report of the 1967–68 Visiting Committee to the Department of Aeronautics and Astronautics" (MIT AC 43 12/9).

144. Leon Trilling to R. L. Bisplinghoff, December 8, 1967 (MIT AC 43 12/9).

145. C. S. Draper, "A Position Paper on the Special Laboratories," February 20, 1970.

146. J. Hunsaker, "Written for the Development Fund," 1948 (MIT AC 43 16/11).

4 | Sonic Boom

1. "Annual Research Support Funding for Stanford University Department of Aeronautics and Astronautics, 1957–1964" (SA SC 160 III 2/9).

2. F. Terman, "Department of Aeronautics and Astronautics, An Example of a Successful Graduate Program," 1963 (SA SC160 III 2/8).

3. F. Terman, "William Frederick Durand," *National Academy of Sciences: Biographical Memoirs,* vol. 48 (Washington, D.C.: National Academy Press, 1976), pp. 153–93, gives a valuable account of Durand's career and a list of his many publications. See also Durand's autobiography, *Adventures in the Navy, in Education, in Engineering, and in War* (New York: McGraw-Hill, 1953).

4. Alex Roland, *Model Research: The National Advisory Committee for Aeronautics, 1915–1958* (Washington, D.C.: NASA, 1985), is the standard history of the NACA and perceptively places Durand's research program into the larger context of American aviation.

5. Walter Vincenti, "The Air-Propeller Tests of W. F. Durand and E. P. Lesley: A Case Study in Technological Methodology," *Technology and Culture* 20, no. 4 (October 1979): 712–51, details this episode and draws some provocative conclusions about the differences between science and engineering.

6. Terman, "William Frederick Durand," p. 162.

7. Harry Guggenheim, "Safety and Economics in the Air," May 1927, Harry F. Guggenheim Papers, Box 6, Manuscripts Division, Library of Congress.

8. Richard P. Hallion, *Legacy of Flight: The Guggenheim Contribution to American Aviation* (Seattle: University of Washington Press, 1977), traces the impact of the Daniel Guggenheim Fund on American aeronautics research in the 1920s and 1930s.

9. Hallion, *Legacy of Flight,* pp. 49–51, details the negotiations. See also Paul Hanle, *Bringing Aerodynamics to America* (Cambridge: MIT Press, 1982), pp. 19–21, for an account of Durand's role. R. L. Wilbur to Trustees of the Daniel Guggenheim Fund, May 13, 1926, Harry Guggenheim Papers, LC, provides a good overview of Stanford's aeronautics program at the time.

10. A. Niles to W. Durand, February 23, 1927 (SA SC 165 I 4/1), highlights Niles's early career.

11. James R. Hansen, *Engineer in Charge: A History of the Langley Aeronautical Laboratory, 1917–1958* (Washington, D.C.: NASA, 1987), p. 53, discusses Reid's career at Langley.

12. T. Hoover to A. Roth, February 11, 1927 (SA SC 165 I 4/1).

13. E. Reid, "The Guggenheim Aeronautic Laboratory of Stanford University," *Aviation* (May 11, 1929): 1603ff., discusses the laboratory's equipment and research program.

14. "Summary of the Activities of the Daniel Guggenheim Aeronautic Laboratory at Stanford University from 1927–1938" (SA SC 165 I 4/1). See also Hallion, *Legacy of Flight,* pp. 211–15.

15. E. P. Lesley to H. Guggenheim, May 1, 1939 (SA SC 165 I 5/24).

16. Quoted by W. Vincenti, "From a Wooden Ship to Jet Propulsion, Prof. Durand Was Leader in Aeronautics," *Sandstone and Tile* (May 1986): 11.

17. Ibid.

18. Reginald M. Cleveland, *America Fledges Wings* (New York: Pitman, 1942), p. 145.

19. Lesley to S. B. Morris, June 9, 1937 (SA SC 165 I 4/1).

20. For an example, see Lesley to R. Wilbur, May 30 1928 (SA SC 165 I 4/1.

21. See Hansen, *Engineer in Charge*, p, 53, for the list.

22. "Stanford on the Job: Aviation," *Stanford Illustrated Review* (April 1939): 2–10 (SA SC 165 I 4/2).

23. H. Guggenheim to E. P. Lesley, May 9, 1939 (SA SC 165 I 5/24).

24. W. Durand to D. Tresidder, October 13, 1943 (SA SC 165 I 4/4).

25. Elliott Reid, "Memorandum on Commercial Testing, Guggenheim Aeronautic Laboratory—1940" (SA SC 165 I 4/2).

26. E. Reid to L. S. Jacobsen, February 3, 1941 (SA SC 165 I 4/2).

27. A. Domonoski to R. Wilbur, February 12, 1940 (SA SC 165 I 4/2).

28. Reid to L. S. Jacobsen, February 3, 1941 (SA SC 165 I 4/2).

29. S. Morris to F. Terman, December 18, 1943 (SA SC 165 I 4/3).

30. Morris to D. Tresidder, December 23, 1943 (SA SC 165 I 4/3).

31. Clayton Koppes, *JPL and the American Space Program* (New Haven: Yale University Press, 1982), pp. 18–29, describes the wartime roots of JPL.

32. "Postwar Aeronautical Engineering Training and Research Program for Stanford University," May 16, 1944 (SA SC 165 I 4/4).

33. Reid to C. L. Johnson, August 8, 1944 (SA SC 165 I 4/4).

34. C. L. Johnson to E. Reid, August 14, 1944 (SA SC 165 I 4/4).

35. A. E. Raymond to S. Morris, August 21, 1944 (SA SC 165 I 4/4).

36. E. Reid, "A Financial Study of the Commercial Operation of the Guggenheim Aeronautic Laboratory Between Sept. 1, 1939 and Oct. 31, 1947" (SA SC 165 I 4/3).

37. John B. Rae, *Climb to Greatness: The American Aircraft Industry, 1920–1960* (Cambridge: MIT Press, 1968), pp. 172ff., chronicles the industry's postwar crisis in some detail. See also G. R. Simonson, ed., *The History of the American Aircraft Industry* (Cambridge: MIT Press, 1968).

38. Walter McDougall, *The Heavens and the Earth: A Political History of the Space Age* (New York: Basic Books, 1985), pp. 97ff., analyzes the early ICBM program.

39. Roy A. Anderson, *A Look at Lockheed* (Newcomen Society of North America, 1983), p. 11.

40. Lockheed's official history can be traced in Lockheed, *Of Men and Stars* (New York: Arno Press, 1980). For a more critical perspective, see David Boulton, *The Grease Machine* (New York: Harper and Row, 1978).

41. For the impact of missiles on the airframe industry, see G. R. Simonson, "Missiles and Creative Destruction in the American Aircraft Industry, 1956–1961," *Business History Review* 38, no. 3 (Autumn 1964): 302–14.

42. McDougall, *The Heavens and the Earth*, pp. 116–17; Jeffrey Richelson,

American Espionage and the Soviet Target (New York: William Morrow, 1987), pp. 140–41.

43. Michael R. Beschloss, *Mayday: Eisenhower, Khrushchev and the U-2 Affair* (New York: Harper and Row, 1986), is the best account of the Powers episode and its political repercussions.

44. Herbert F. York and G. Allen Greb, "Strategic Reconnaissance," *Bulletin of the Atomic Scientists* (April 1977): 38.

45. Philip J. Klass, *Secret Sentries in Space* (New York: Random House, 1971), pp. 82ff., details the Lockheed program.

46. Donald MacKenzie, *Inventing Accuracy: A Historical Sociology of Nuclear Missile Guidance*, (Cambridge: MIT Press, 1990), pp. 134ff., summarizes the evolution of the Polaris system. See R. A. Fuhrman, "The Fleet Ballistic Missile System: Polaris to Trident," *Journal of Spacecraft* 15, no. 5 (September–October 1978), for an insider's perspective.

47. See *Of Men and Stars* for the history of the missiles and space division. See also "Lockheed Shifts New Missile Systems Group," *Aviation Week* 60, no. 15 (January 25, 1954).

48. Quesada, quoted in *Time*, August 23, 1954, p. 67.

49. "Scientists Take a Walk," *Newsweek*, December 26, 1955, and "Where Does the Lab End and the Plant Start?" *Business Week*, December 24, 1955, pp. 90–92.

50. A. W. Jessup, "Lockheed Moving Missiles Division into San Francisco Bay," *Aviation Week* 64, no. 34 (February 6, 1956): 29–30.

51. "Lockheed Atune to USAF Warning, Plans Expansion into Avionics," *Aviation Week* (July 8, 1957).

52. For a biographical sketch by a former student see B. A. Boley's essay in R. B. Testa, ed., *Aerostructure: Selected Papers of Nicholas J. Hoff* (New York: Pergamon, 1971).

53. N. J. Hoff, interview with author, Palo Alto, Calif., July 30, 1987.

54. N. J. Hoff, "Stress Analysis of Aircraft Frameworks," *Journal of the Aeronautical Sciences* 8, no. 8 (June 1941): 1–24, and "General Instability of Monocoque Cylinders," *Journal of the Aeronautical Sciences* 10, no. 4 (April 1943): 105–15.

55. N. J. Hoff, "Thermal Buckling of Supersonic Wing Panels," *Journal of the Aeronautical Sciences* 23, no. 11 (November 1956): 1019.

56. N. J. Hoff, ed., *High Temperature Effects in Aircraft Structures* (New York: Pergamon, 1958), p. 8.

57. F. Terman, Memo of phone conversation with Willis Hawkins, July 13, 1956 (SA SC 160 III 38/1), outlines these negotiations. Also, N. J. Hoff, interview with author, June 12, 1987.

58. F. Terman, "Recent Activities in the Department of Aeronautics of Stanford University" (SA SC 216 39/School of Engineering, '63–'64).

59. "Plans for the Next Five Years in Mechanical Engineering" (SA SC 216 A12/5).

60. F. Terman to A. Raymond, November 11, 1955 (SA SC 216 39/27).

61. Terman, "Department of Aeronautics and Astronautics, An Example of a Successful Graduate Program," 1963.

62. Terman to W. Hawkins, November 21, 1957 (SA SC 160 III 38/1).

63. N. J. Hoff, interview with author, July 30, 1987.

64. Department of Aeronautical Engineering, "Annual Report to the President for the Academic Year 1956–57" (SA SC 165 IV 1/3).

65. For the official history of Ames see Elizabeth A. Muenger, *Searching the Horizon: A History of Ames Research Center, 1940-1976* (Washington, D.C.: NASA, 1985). Edwin P. Hartman, *Adventures in Research: A History of Ames Research Center* (Washington, D.C.: NASA, 1970), offers more technical insight, though less context.

66. A brief biographical sketch appears in "Staff Backgrounds (Aeronautics and Astronautics)" in "Proposal to the National Aeronautics and Space Administration for a Research Facility in Space Engineering and Science," November 25, 1964 (SA SC 165 I 8/7). Also, W. Vincenti, interview with author, Palo Alto, Calif., June 9, 1987.

67. Hartman, *Adventures in Research*, pp. 200ff., describes some of Van Dyke's work.

68. President's Report, School of Engineering, 1956–57 (SA SC 165 IV 1/3).

69. Terman, "Department of Aeronautics and Astronautics, An Example of a Successful Graduate Program," 1963.

70. Klass, *Secret Sentries in Space*, p. 90.

71. William F. Burrows, *Deep Black: Space Espionage and National Security* (New York: Random House, 1986), p. 90.

72. Klass, *Secret Sentries in Space*, pp. 101–106.

73. Jeffrey Richelson, "The Keyhole Satellite Program," *Journal of Strategic Studies* 7 (June 1984): 128–29.

74. Burrows, *Deep Black*, pp. 84–85; Klass, *Secret Sentries in Space*, pp. 174–75.

75. Klass, *Secret Sentries in Space*, p. 175.

76. See James B. Schultz, "Inside the Blue Cube," *Defense Electronics* (April 1983): 52–59; and Burrows, *Deep Black*, pp. 200–201.

77. Richelson, *American Espionage and the Soviet Target*, pp. 173–95.

78. MacKenzie, *Inventing Accuracy*, pp. 240–96, offers an excellent summary of the fleet ballistic missile program, with special attention to its guidance systems. See also Fuhrman, "The Fleet Ballistic Missile System," pp. 265–86.

79. F. Terman's financial file on Lockheed Aircraft Corporation gives a chronological listing of Lockheed contracts, revenues, and employment com-

piled from newspaper clippings, annual reports, and the like (SA SC 160 V 10/Lockheed).

80. "Report of the Department of Aeronautical Engineering for the Academic Year 1959–60" (SA SC 165 IV 1/5).

81. Ibid.

82. N. J. Hoff and S. V. Nardo, *Structures, Ballistic Missile Series*, Ordnance Engineering Design Handbook, ORDp 20–286 (July 1960); Hoff, ed., *High Temperature Effects in Aircraft Structures*.

83. Department of Aeronautical Engineering, "Annual Report to the President for the Academic Year 1959–60" (SA SC 165 IV 1/6).

84. "A Plan of Industrial Liaison in Aero- and Astronautical Engineering at Stanford University," February 1, 1959 (SA SC 160 III 2/8); also, W. Vincenti, interview with author, Palo Alto, Calif., June 9, 1987.

85. "A Plan of Industrial Liaison in Aero- and Astronautical Engineering at Stanford University," February 1, 1959.

86. W. Vincenti, interview with author, Palo Alto, Calif., June 9, 1987.

87. Milton Van Dyke, interview with author, Palo Alto, Calif., June 16, 1988.

88. Milton Van Dyke, *Perturbation Methods in Fluid Mechanics* (New York: Academic Press, 1964), p. v.

89. J. M. Slater to W. Vincenti, September 29, 1958 (SA SC 216 38/2).

90. "Proposal for a Program of Advanced Research and Instruction in Guidance, Control, and Instrumentation," January 1964 (SA SC 160 III 2/10).

91. The best account of the relativity gyro is C. W. F. Everitt, "Background to History: The Transition from Little Physics to Big Physics in the Gravity Probe B Relativity Gyroscope Program," in Peter Galison and Bruce Hevly, eds., *Big Science: The Growth of Large-Scale Research* (Palo Alto: Stanford University Press, 1991), pp. 212–35. See also Donald Stokes, "Cannon Leads Test of Einstein's Work . . . ," *Stanford Campus Report*, February 29, 1984.

92. R. Cannon, Trip Report, Visit to DOD, December 7, 1964 (SA SC 132 16/Air Force Guidance.

93. "Is Einstein Right?" *Stanford Observor*, November 1980, p. 6. Benjamin Lange gives his own account in "The Drag-Free Satellite," *American Institute of Aeronautics and Astronautics Journal* 2, no. 19 (September 1964): 1590–1606.

94. See Burrows, *Deep Black*, pp. 85–111, for Lockheed's involvement with the Discoverer program.

95. R. H. Cannon, Jr., *Dynamics of Physical Systems* (New York: McGraw-Hill, 1967).

96. Edward T. Thompson, "The Upheaval at Philco," *Fortune*, February 1959, p. 210.

97. Terman to W. Cooley, April 1, 1957 (SA SC 160 V 7/6).

98. Robert Lindsey, "Philco Division Completes Reorientation," *Missiles and Rockets* 14 (June 15, 1964): 28–31.

99. *New York Times*, April 11, 1959, p. 5.

100. Philip Siekman, "Henry Ford and his Electronic Can of Worms," *Fortune*, Februay 1966, p. 119.

101. Ibid., p. 119; Lindsey, "Philco Division Completes Reorientation," p. 31.

102. "A Plan of Industrial Liaison in Aero- and Astronautical Engineering at Stanford University," February 1, 1960; N. Hoff to J. Pettit, January 6, 1960 (SA SC 216 38/2).

103. "A Plan of Industrial Liaison in Aero- and Astronautical Engineering at Stanford University," February 1, 1959.

104. Affiliates of Aeronautical Engineering Program, November 27, 1959 (SA SC 160 III 2/8).

105. M. van Dyke, interview with author, Palo Alto, Calif., June 16, 1988.

106. Terman to H. Hibbard, January 14, 1959 (SA SC 160 III 8/1).

107. "A Plan of Industrial Liaison in Aero- and Astronautical Engineering at Stanford University," February 1, 1959.

108. Department of Aeronautics and Astronautics, "Annual Report to the President for the Academic Year 1963–64" (SA SC 165 IV 1/6).

109. Terman to N. Hoff, November 12, 1970 (SA SC 160 III 2/9).

110. N. J. Hoff and W. Vincenti, eds., *Aeronautics and Astronautics* (New York: Pergamon, 1960), pp. 1–2.

111. Department of Aeronautics and Astronautics, "Annual Report to the President for the Academic Year 1960–61" (SA SC 165 IV 1/5).

112. J. E. W. Sterling to N. Hoff, June 14, 1967 (SA SC 2183/Aeronautics and Astronautics).

113. William J. Price, "The Key Role of Mission-Oriented Agency's Scientific Research Activities," in W. Dale Compton, ed., *The Interaction of Science and Technology* (Urbana: University of Illinois Press, 1964), p. 38.

114. "Proposal to the National Aeronautics and Space Administration for a Research Facility in Space Engineering and Science," November 25, 1964, gives the background for the venture.

115. R. Lewis to H. Brown, January 4, 1967 (SA SC 165 I 8/4).

116. See Hoff to J. Blair, November 8, 1967 (SA SC 165 I 8/5), and K. Creighton to A. Brandin, December 16, 1966 (SA SC 165 I 8/3), for some of the financial details.

117. "Memorandum of Understanding Between National Aeronautics and Space Administration and Leland Stanford Junior University Concerning Research Facilities Grant" (SA SC 165 I 7/6). A. Michal McMahon, "Shaping a 'Space-Oriented Complex': NASA and the Universities in the 1960s" (Paper presented to the Military and Academic Science Workshop, Johns Hopkins University, April 16–17, 1986), perceptively analyzes the NASA agenda.

118. Notes and worksheet on the fund drive for the space engineering building, October 22, 1965 (SA SC 165 I 8/6).

119. Space Engineering, Corporate Gift Projection, October 7, 1965 (SA SC 165 I 8/2), lists the contributors; A. D. Kirkland, "Record," details the fundraising effort.

120. Growth Statistics: School of Engineering, June 1969; Terman to N. J. Hoff, November 12, 1970 (SA SC 160 III 2/9).

121. N. J. Hoff and V. Salerno, "Graduate and Research Work in Universities and the Use of College Men in Industry and Government," *Journal of Engineering Education* 40, no. 10 (June 1950): 595.

5 | The Power of the Nucleus

1. Jerrold Zacharias to Lloyd V. Berkner, March 5, 1952 (MIT MC 31/1).

2. S. S. Schweber, "The Mutual Embrace of Science and the Military: ONR and the Growth of Physics in the United States After World War II," in Everett Mendelsohn, M. Roe Smith, and Peter Weingart, eds., *Science, Technology and the Military* (Boston: Kluwer Academic, 1988), pp. 3–45, provides a thoughtful account of the military's impact on academic physics, with particular attention to MIT.

3. George Harrison, "Memorandum Regarding Doctorates Granted in Physics in the U.S., 1948–1955," May 15, 1959 (MIT AC 134 35/Physics).

4. Bernard Feld, "Laboratory for Nuclear Science," *MIT Annual Report*, 1963–64, p. 289.

5. For a look at one part of that earlier tradition, see Finn Aaserud, *Redirecting Science: Niels Bohr, Philanthropy, and the Rise of Nuclear Physics* (New York: Cambridge University Press, 1990).

6. Philip M. Morse, *In at the Beginnings: A Physicist's Life* (Cambridge: MIT Press, 1977), p. 216.

7. For Compton's institution-building strategy, see John Servos, "The Industrial Relations of Science: Chemical Engineering at MIT, 1900–1939," *Isis* 71 (1980): 531–49.

8. Allan M. Cartter, *An Assessment of Quality in Graduate Education* (Washington, D.C.: American Council on Education, 1966), gives rankings for American physics departments back to 1925.

9. K. Compton, "Brief of Application to the Rockefeller Foundation or the General Education Board for Support of Fundamental Science at the Massachusetts Institute of Technology," November 12, 1930 (Rockefeller Foundation [RF] 1.1 224/4/42).

10. Philip M. Morse, "John Clarke Slater," *National Academy of Sciences: Biographical Memoirs*, vol. 53 (Washington, D.C.: National Academy Press, 1982), pp. 297–319, offers an overview of Slater's career by a close associate.

11. J. Slater to K. Compton, May 23 1930 (SP Compton, K. T. #1).

12. J. Slater, interview with Charles Weiner, February 23, 1970, p. 13, AIP History of Quantum Physics, American Philosophical Society.

13. John Slater, "History of the M.I.T. Physics Department, 1930–48 [1948]" (SP Slater/History of the MIT Physics Department).

14. G. Harrison to J. Slater, June 19, 1930 (SP Harrison, G. R. #7).

15. Morse, "John Clarke Slater," p. 302.

16. *Research—A National Resource: Relation of the Federal Government to Research* (Washington, D.C.: GPO, 1939), pp. 172–73.

17. Slater, "History of the M.I.T. Physics Department," p. 37.

18. Ibid., p. 7.

19. Ibid., p. 12.

20. See "Colossus of Volts," *Technology Review* 36 (December 1933).

21. Thomas Cornell, "Merle Tuve and His Program of Nuclear Studies at the Department of Terrestrial Magnetism" (Ph.D. diss, Johns Hopkins University, 1986), pp. 280ff., places Van de Graaff's work in the context of contemporary high-energy physics.

22. The High Voltage Research Laboratory, Massachusetts Institute of Technology, 1965 (MIT MC 45 2/159).

23. Larry Owens, "MIT and the Federal 'Angel': Academic R&D and Federal-Private Cooperation Before World War II," *Isis* 81 (June 1990): 189–213, details this fascinating episode. See also Frank T. Cameron, *Cottrell: Samaritan of Science* (New York: Doubleday, 1952), pp. 280ff.

24. Servos, "The Industrial Relations of Science," pp. 545–46.

25. *Research—A National Resource*, p. 174.

26. For Lawrence's prewar career, see John L. Heilbron and Robert W. Seidel, *Lawrence and His Laboratory: A History of the Lawrence Berkeley Laboratory*, vol. 1 (Berkeley: University of California Press, 1989).

27. See John E. Burchard, *Q.E.D.: M.I.T. in World War II* (New York: John Wiley, 1948).

28. J. Slater, "Physics," *MIT Annual Report*, 1945–46, p. 133.

29. See S. S. Schweber, "Big Science in Context: Cornell and MIT," in Peter Galison and Bruce Hevly, eds., *Big Science: The Growth of Large-Scale Research* (Palo Alto: Stanford University Press, 1991), pp. 3–45 for a revealing contrast of the postwar strategies of these two schools.

30. G. Harrison, "Minutes—Meeting #1 of M.I.T. Nuclear Committee," September 26, 1945 (SP MIT/Laboratory for Nuclear Science and Engineering).

31. Harrison to J. R. Killian, August 9, 1945 (MIT AC 4 236/12).

32. K. Compton to Alfred Sloan, January 5, 1946 (MIT AC 4 49/6).

33. Slater, "History of the M.I.T Physics Department," p. 41.

34. Ibid., pp. 44–46.

35. "Minutes—Meeting #2 of M.I.T. Nuclear Committee," October 9, 1945 (MIT AC 4 236/12).

36. K. Compton to Alfred Sloan, January 5, 1946 (MIT AC 4 49/6).

37. Slater to J. Zacharias, November 20, 1945 (MIT MC 31/2).

38. J. Slater, "Memorandum on the Relationship Between the Physics Department and the Laboratory of Nuclear Science and Engineering," December 10, 1945 (SP Slater, J. C./Relationship between physics department and laboratory of nuclear physics).

39. Zacharias to Commanding Officer at Office of Research and Invention, February 14, 1946 (MIT MC 31/1); "Memorandum Regarding Institute Program in Nuclear Science and Engineering," January 14, 1946 (MIT AC 4 236/14).

40. James R. Killian, *The Education of a College President* (Cambridge: MIT Press, 1985), p. 166.

41. Slater, "Memorandum of the Relationship Between the Physics Department and the Laboratory of Nuclear Science and Engineering," December 10, 1945.

42. Zacharias to Commanding Officer at Office of Research and Invention, February 14, 1946.

43. "Notice on Conference in President Compton's Office," November 18, 1946 (MIT MC 31/1).

44. Zacharias to Charles Thomas, November 24, 1945 (MIT MC 31/1).

45. K. Compton to Robert Wilson, July 15, 1947 (MIT MC 31/1).

46. Slater to Warren Weaver, April 2, 1945 (RF 1.1 224D 5/44).

47. N. Thompson to K. Compton, May 18, 1945 (RF 1.1 224D 5/44).

48. H. G. Bowen to K. Compton, November 8, 1945 (MIT MC 31/1).

49. Task Order for the Laboratory for Nuclear Science and Engineering of the Massachusetts Institute of Technology Under Navy Contract No. NSori-78, February 21, 1946 (MIT MC 31/1).

50. Fiscal Operations of the Laboratory for Nuclear Science and Engineering—1946 (MIT MC 31/1 "Budget").

51. "Statement of Prof. J. C. Slater," attached to K. Compton to H. G. Bowen, November 13, 1945 (MIT MC 31/1).

52. Peter Galison, "Physics Between War and Peace," in Mendelsohn, Smith, and Weingart, eds., *Science, Technology, and the Military*, pp. 66–67. Galison provides an insightful look at what the tools of peace owed to the tools of war.

53. MIT press release on the 300-volt synchrotron, January 19, 1950 (MIT MC 31/1).

54. See Robert Seidel, "Accelerating Science: The Postwar Transformation of the Lawrence Radiation Laboratory," *Historical Studies in the Physical Sciences* 13 (1983): 375–400, for a comparison with Berkeley.

55. Galison, "Physics Between War and Peace," p. 76, makes the same point with respect to the Army Air Force.

56. See Ivan Getting, *All in a Lifetime: Science in the Defense of Democracy* (New York: Vantage, 1989).

57. Karl Wildes and Nilo Lindgren, *A Century of Electrical Engineering and Computer Science at MIT, 1882–1982*, (Cambridge: MIT Press, 1985), pp. 160–65.

58. Slater to J. Killian, January 15, 1948 (MIT MC 31/1), sets out the department's expectations for the two machines.

59. Zacharias to Urner Liddel, July 3, 1947 (MIT MC 31/1).

60. John Trump, "Proposal for the Establishment of a Comparative High-Voltage Research Program in the Electrical Engineering Department at M.I.T." December 28, 1945 (MIT MC 31/1).

61. Paul Forman, "Atomichron: The Atomic Clock from Concept to Commercial Product," *Proceedings of the IEEE* 73 (July 1985): 1181–1204, convincingly places the atomic clock story into the context of Cold War priorities for physics.

62. "Dr. Jerrold Zacharias," *Microwave Journal* (December 1959): 17.

63. Ibid.

64. Harrison, "Memorandum Regarding Doctorates Granted in Physics in the U.S., 1948–1955," May 15, 1959.

65. H. W. Koch to G. Harrison, June 27, 1961 (MIT AC 31 6/LNSE).

66. Slater, "History of the M.I.T. Physics Department," p. 70.

67. Schweber, "The Mutual Embrace of Science and the Military," p. 33.

68. Ibid. Schweber carefully analyzes the summer studies within the larger context of postwar physics. See Killian, *The Education of a College President*, pp. 63ff., for an official view.

69. Quoted in Paul Forman, "Behind Quantum Electronics: National Security as Basis for Physical Research in the United States, 1940–1960," *Historical Studies in the Physical and Biological Sciences* 18, no. 1 (1987): 216.

70. "Laboratory for Nuclear Science and Engineering—Objectives," January 3, 1946 (SP MIT/Laboratory for Nuclear Science and Engineering).

71. Slater to Captain Conrad, October 23, 1945 (SP MIT/Proposed Research Program in Nuclear Physics).

72. Allan Needell, "Nuclear Reactors and the Founding of the Brookhaven National Laboratory," *Historical Studies in the Physical Sciences* 14 (1984): 93–122, offers the best account of the Brookhaven Laboratory.

73. Zacharias to Charles Thomas, January 21, 1946 (MIT MC 31/1).

74. "Minutes—Meeting #2 of M.I.T. Nuclear Committee," October 9, 1945.

75. John Chipman to K. D. Nichols, January 4, 1946 (MIT MC 31/2).

76. J. Slater, "Suggested M.I.T Policy Concerning a Field Station at Fort

Devens for the Laboratory for Nuclear Science and Engineering," May 27, 1946 (MIT AC 4 236/14).

77. John S. Rigden, *Rabi: Scientist and Citizen* (New York: Basic Books, 1987), pp. 182ff.

78. J. Slater, "Proposal for the Establishment of a Northeastern Regional Laboratory for Nuclear Science and Engineering," February 9, 1946 (MIT MC 45 2/164); see also Needell, "Nuclear Reactors and the Founding of the Brookhaven National Laboratory."

79. Ibid.

80. Rigden, *Rabi: Scientist and Citizen*, p. 184.

81. Slater, "Suggested M.I.T. Policy Concerning a Field Station at Fort Devens for the Laboratory for Nuclear Science and Engineering," May 27, 1946.

82. K. Compton to H. Bowen, March 21, 1946 (MIT AC 4 44/4).

83. See Norman Polmar and Thomas Allen, *Rickover* (New York: Simon and Schuster, 1982), pp. 118ff., for Rickover's involvement with the nuclear submarine effort.

84. Rickover, quoted in Polmar and Allen, *Rickover*, p. 131.

85. Clark Goodman to J. Slater, April 2, 1947 (MIT MC 31/1).

86. *Nuclear Engineering at M.I.T.: The First 25 Years* (Cambridge: MIT Press, 1984), p. 7; also see Schweber, "The Mutual Embrace of Science and the Military."

87. Clark Goodman et al., *The Science and Engineering of Nuclear Power* (Cambridge, Mass.: Addison Wesley, 1947).

88. Laboratory for Nuclear Science and Engineering of the Massachusetts Institute of Technology, 1946 (MIT MC 45 2/164).

89. Thomas Sherwood to J. Zacharias, October 24, 1947 (MIT MC 31/2).

90. R. V. Bartz to J. Stratton, August 8, 1949 (MIT MC 31/1).

91. Richard Hewlett and Francis Duncan, *Nuclear Navy, 1946–1962* (Chicago: University of Chicago Press, 1974), p. 123. Hewlett and Duncan offer the best history of Rickover's career.

92. *Nuclear Engineering at M.I,T.*, pp. 7–8.

93. Sherwood to A. R. Kaufmann, December 29, 1949 (MIT AC 12 12/Metallurgical Project).

94. *Wall Street Journal*, February 9, 1955, p. 9.

95. LNSE members discussed such a proposal as early as 1946, "Minutes— Meeting #4 of M.I.T. Nuclear Committee," May 29, 1946 (SP MIT/Nuclear Committee).

96. Richard Hewlett and Francis Duncan, *Atomic Shield, 1947–1952* (University Park, Pa.: Pennsylvania State University Press, 1972), pp. 190–211.

97. W. Henry Lambright, *Shooting Down the Nuclear Plane* (Indianapolis: Bobbs Merrill, 1966).

98. *Nuclear Engineering at M.I.T.*, pp. 7–9.

99. Sherwood to L. R. Hafstad, February 3, 1950 (MIT AC 4 184/7).

100. "Memorandum of Meeting, Nuclear Engineering Project," February 13, 1952 (MIT AC 12 14/Nuclear Engineering).

101. A. Shapiro, "Origins and Mode of Operation of Project Dynamo," September 2, 1953 (MIT AC 12 14/Nuclear Engineering).

102. Manson Benedict, "Nuclear Engineering at M.I.T.," December 1957 (MIT AC 134 34/Nuclear Engineering).

103. See Richard Hewlett and Jack Holl, *Atoms for Peace and War, 1953–1961* (Berkeley: University of California Press, 1989), pp. 209–70, for the larger context of the story.

104. "Proposal for a Nuclear Reactor at M.I.T.," May 25, 1954 (MIT AC 12 14/Nuclear Engineering); also see Manson Benedict, "Early Days of the MIT Reactor," July 27, 1978 (MIT Archives, TK 9202.B4). For a comparison with Penn State, see Michael Bezilla, *Engineering Education at Penn State* (University Park: Pennsylvania State University Press, 1981), pp. 165–68.

105. *Nuclear Engineering at M.I.T.*, p. 27.

106. C. Richard Soderberg to J. Stratton, November 18, 1957 (MIT AC 12 14/Nuclear Engineering); Benedict, "Nuclear Engineering at M.I.T.," December 1957.

107. M. Benedict to Richard Post, December 17, 1957 (MIT AC 12 14/Nuclear Engineering).

108. "Report of the 1961–62 Visiting Committee on the Department of Nuclear Engineering at M.I.T.," March 4, 1962 (MIT AC 31/6).

109. *Nuclear Engineering at M.I.T.*, p. 18.

110. "Activities of Graduates in Nuclear Engineering—June 1964" (MIT AC 31 8/Nuclear Engineering).

111. Report of the 1961–62 Visiting Committee on the Department of Nuclear Engineering (MIT AC 31/6).

112. Hewlett and Duncan, *Nuclear Navy*, and Polmar and Allen, *Rickover*, are the best sources for the Shippingport reactor and the early history of civilian power.

113. George Basalla, *The Evolution of Technology* (New York: Cambridge University Press, 1988), pp. 162–68, gives a concise account of the industry's dilemma. For a fuller account, see Gerard Clarfield and William Wiecek, *Nuclear America: Military and Civilian Power in the United States, 1940–1980* (New York: Harper and Row, 1984), pp. 273–86.

114. Slater, "History of the M.I.T. Physics Department, 1930–48," p. 73.

6 | Accelerating Physics

1. Edward L. Ginzton, "Microwaves," *Science* 127 (April 18, 1958): 841.

2. Rebecca S. Lowen, "Transforming the University: Administrators, Physicists, and Industrial and Federal Patronage at Stanford, 1935–49," *History of*

Education Quarterly 31, no. 3 (Fall 1991): 365–88, has recently used the story of Stanford physics to argue for industrial funding and administrative initiative as the keys to understanding the transformation of the postwar university. By bringing university administrators back into the picture, Lowen offers an important corrective to accounts (including this one) that perhaps place too much emphasis on entrepreneurially inclined professors at the expense of other actors. By stressing the conflict between various faculty factions and between the faculty and the administration, she also introduces an important new dynamic. At the same time, focusing on local politics may draw our attention away from the larger political patterns that were reshaping the attitudes and expectations of faculty and administrators alike.

3. For an overview of Hansen's career, see Felix Bloch, "William Webster Hansen," *National Academy of Sciences: Biographical Memoirs*, vol. 27 (Washington D.C.: National Academy of Sciences, 1952), pp. 121–37.

4. See Bruce Hevly, "David L. Webster," *Dictionary of Scientific Biography*, vol. 18, supp. 2, pp. 984–86; and Paul Kirkpatrick, "David Locke Webster II," *National Academy of Sciences: Biographical Memoirs*, vol. 53 (Washington D.C.: National Academy Press, 1982), pp. 367–400.

5. Julius Stratton et. al., *RLE: 1946 + 20* (Cambridge, 1966).

6. Peter Galison, Bruce Hevly, and Rebecca Lowen, "Controlling the Monster: Stanford and the Growth of Physics Research, 1935-1962," in Galison and Hevly, eds., *Big Science: The Growth of Large-Scale Research* (Palo Alto: Stanford University Press, 1992), pp. 46–77, offer the best history of Stanford physics, with particular attention to the local political context. See also "Prospectus on Supervoltage X-Ray Research Work at the Ryan Laboratory," March 12, 1935 (SA SC 197 1).

7. For Hansen's own account, see "Statement of William W. Hansen, U.S. Patent Office, William C. Hahn vs. Russell H. Varian vs. Frederick B. Llewellyn," p. 22 (Sperry Gyroscope Company Records [SpP], vol. 2, Hagley Museum and Library).

8. Edward L. Ginzton, "The $100 Idea," *IEEE Spectrum* 10 (February 1975): 30–39, offers the best account of the origins of the klystron. For another perspective, from the widow of one of the inventors, see Dorothy Varian, *The Pilot and the Inventor* (Palo Alto: (Pacific Books, 1983).

9. D. W. Webster, interview with Donald Shaunghnessy, January 26, 1963 (SA SC 197 9/AAPT History Project).

10. Paul Forman suggested this clever way of redefining the klystron.

11. Thomas P. Hughes, *Elmer Sperry: Inventor and Engineer* (Baltimore: Johns Hopkins University Press, 1971), pp. 201 ff.

12. For details of the patent agreement see Contract Between Stanford University and Sperry Gyroscope Company, April 27, 1938 (SA SC 160 I 8/14).

13. J. Hugh Jackson to R. Wilbur, September 10, 1938 (SA SC 330 3B/Stanford Corr, 1937–45).

14. One of the Sperry engineers details the university-corporate relationship from the company's perspective in H. Hugh Willis, "Ultra-High Frequency Radio Project," August 4, 1939 (SpP II).

15. F. Terman to H. Willis, October 21, 1941 (SA SC 160 II 3/6).

16. See John Bryant, "Microwave Technology and Careers in Transition: The Interests and Activities of Visitors to the Sperry Gyroscope Company's Klystron Plant in 1939–40," *IEEE Transactions on Microwave Theory and Techniques* 38 (November 1990): 1545–1558.

17. Ginzton, "The $100 Idea," p. 39.

18. W. Hansen to D. Tresidder, n.d. (SA SC 126 4/40).

19. William T. Cooke, "Microwave Development at Sperry," February 26, 1945 (SpP II), provides a convenient summary of Sperry's wartime accomplishments.

20. W. Hansen, "Proposed Microwave Laboratory at Stanford," November 17, 1943 (SA SC 126 4/40).

21. Ibid.

22. Hansen to D. Tresidder, September 27, 1944 (SA SC 126 4/41).

23. Hansen, "Proposed Microwave Laboratory at Stanford," November 17, 1943.

24. Galison, Hevly, and Lowen consider this debate in some detail in "Controlling the Monster."

25. D. Webster to P. Kirkpatrick, January 9, 1943 (SA SC 126 4/40).

26. Webster to W. Hansen, February 13, 1943 (SA SC 126 4/40).

27. Hansen to D. Webster, February 4, 1943 (SA SC 126 4/40).

28. F. Bloch to D. Webster, March 23, 1943 (SA SC 126 4/40).

29. Terman to D. Tressider, October 17, 1944 (SA SC 126 4/40).

30. P. Kirkpatrick to W. Hansen, May 2, 1945 (SA SC 126 4/40).

31. For an early administrative history of the Microwave Laboratory based on interviews with the prinicipals, see Ernest B. O'Byrne, "The Research Institutes of Stanford University" (Ph.D. diss., Stanford University, 1951).

32. Terman to W. Barrow, July 13, 1951 (SA SC 165 I 8/16).

33. Terman to Carl Frische, March 14, 1955 (SA SC 165 I 8/17).

34. See Galison, Hevly, and Lowen, "Controlling the Monster," for details of the first accelerator and its research program.

35. For a participant's eye view of the project, see Edward L. Ginzton, "An Informal History of SLAC: Early Accelerator Work at Stanford," *SLAC Beam Line* (April 1983): 2–16.

36. Hansen to D. W. Fry, March 7, 1949 (SA SC 126 3/28).

37. E. Ginzton to J. W. Sterling, January 8, 1952 (SA SC 160 II 18/14).

38. Ibid.

39. Ginzton to J. W. Sterling, May 20, 1953 (SA SC 216 24/508).

40. Ginzton, quoted in Galison, Hevly, and Lowen, "Controlling the Monster," p. 60.

41. "Research History of the Microwave Laboratory—W. W. Hansen Laboratories of Physics [c. 1963]" (SA SC 132 15/5).

42. Ginzton to Dean Hilgard, April 20, 1953 (SA SC 220 14/1).

43. "Research History of the Microwave Laboratory—W. W. Hansen Laboratories of Physics"; and Marvin Chodorow, interview with author, Palo Alto, Calif., April 9, 1989.

44. "Research History of the Microwave Laboratory—W. W. Hansen Laboratories of Physics."

45. Ginzton to W. Barkas, May 31, 1949 (SA SC 220 14/1).

46. S. E. Harris and J. S. Harris, "Stanford University Electronics Laboratory and Microwave-Ginzton Laboratory," in David Robb and Arnold Shostak, eds., *Proceedings of the Fortieth Anniversary of the Joint Services Electronics Program* (Arlington, Va.: ANSER, 1987), pp. 114–16.

47. F. Terman, "The University and Technology Utilization," March 1963, p. 294 (SA SC 160 X 2/11).

48. Varian Associates, *Varian: 25 Years, 1948–1973* (Palo Alto: Varian Associates, 1973), offers an official corporate history.

49. Ibid., p. 15.

50. Varian Associates, "Microwave and Electronic Research, Development, Production," October 1, 1951 (Varian Associates, Corporate Records).

51. Terman to W. Johnson, March 9, 1960 (SA SC 160 III 9/8); "Lists of Varian Gifts to 8/60" (SA SC 160 III 34/7).

52. Henry Lowood, "From Steeples of Excellence to Silicon Valley," *Stanford Campus Report*, March 9, 1988, pp. 11–13, provides the best history of the Stanford Industrial Park.

53. Terman to I. Kaar, July 2, 1953 (SA SC 160 III 27/3).

54. Alf Brandin to David Sarnoff, November 24, 1955 (SA SC 160 III 32/10).

55. "Number of Employees and Value of Buildings in Stanford Industrial Park," December 7, 1960 (SA SC 160 III 32/10).

56. Terman to J. W. Sterling, May 6, 1966 (SA SC 160 III 10/8).

57. Galison, Hevly, and Lowen, "Controlling the Monster," highlight the controversy within the department over cost sharing on contracts.

58. M. Chodorow to A. Bowker, n.d. (SA SC 160 III 41/14).

59. F. Bloch, "Plan for a Department of Applied Physics," November 6, 1961 (SA SC 303 II 14/2).

60. H. Skilling to J. Pettit, April 17, 1962 (SA SC 160 III 3/6).

61. J. Pettit to F. Terman, December 21, 1963 (SA SC 160 III 3/6).

62. Terman, quoted in A. Michal McMahon, *The Making of a Profession: A Century of Electrical Engineering in America* (New York: IEEE Press, 1984), p. 286.

63. Terman to A. Bowker, October 23, 1962 (SA SC 160 III 3/6).

64. Terman to J. W. Sterling, December 13, 1963 (SA SC 160 III 3/6).

65. A. Bowker to J. Pettit et. al., February 20, 1962 (SA SC 160 III 3/6).

66. Chodorow to F. Terman, December 19, 1963 (SA SC 160 III 3/6).

67. Ibid.

68. "Applied Physics at Stanford,"1966 (SA SC 3540/6).

69. Chodorow to Lincoln Moses, December 6, 1967 (SA SC 216 38D/Applied Physics).

70. See Harris and Harris, "Stanford University Electronics Laboratory and Microwave-Ginzton Laboratory," pp. 114–21.

71. Chodorow to H. Royden, January 2, 1968 (SA SC 99 13/21).

72. Stanton Glantz et al., *DOD-Sponsored Research at Stanford*, vol. 1, *Two Perceptions: The Investigator's and the Sponsor's* (Palo Alto: Stanford Workshop on Political and Social Issues, June 1971), pp. 68–72 and 215–16, detail some of these contracts.

73. The chairman of Applied Physics highlighted some of these breakthroughs for the department's visiting committee. See Calvin Quate, "Notes Concerning the Protest Movement Written for the Purpose of Briefing the Visiting Committee on Feb. 4, 1972" (SA SC 330 3/Physics).

74. Peter Sturrock, "Plasma Physics—Growth of a New Program at Stanford," January 30, 1963 (SA SC 160 III 22/8).

75. Peter Sturrock, "Ford Foundation Survey of the Training of Scientists and Engineers in Plasma Physics," March 21, 1963 (SA SC 160 III 3/6).

76. Robert Seidel, "From Glow to Flow: A History of Military Laser Research and Development," *Historical Studies in the Physical and Biological Sciences* 18, no. 1 (1987): 111–48.

77. Quoted in Norm V. Albers et al., *DOD-Sponsored Research at Stanford*, vol. 2, *Its Impact on the University* (Palo Alto: Stanford Workshop on Political and Social Issues, November 1971), pp. 17–18.

78. Quoted in Steven Ungar and Richard Miles, "Laser Scientists Discuss Support," *Stanford Daily*, April 1, 1971, p. 1.

79. L. Schiff to C. Faust, January 18, 1949 (SA SC 216 24/505).

80. K. Spangenberg to F. Terman, June 2, 1949 (SA SC 220 14/1).

81. "Minutes—Project M Meeting," November 21, 1958 (SC 220 14/18).

82. Ginzton, R. Hofstadter et al. to J. W. Sterling, October 8, 1954 (SA SC 220 14/19).

83. Galison, Hevly, and Lowen recount the controversy in some detail in "Controlling the Monster."

84. Bloch to R. Hofstadter, December 8, 1954 (SA SC 303 I 1/12).

85. "Report on Telephone Conversation Between Bloch and Schiff," December 17, 1954 (SA SC 220 14/19).

86. R. Hofstadter to F. Bloch, March 13, 1955 (SC 303 I 6/4).

87. See Daniel Greenberg, *The Politics of Pure Science* (New York: New

American Library, 1967), pp. 224ff., for a perceptive analysis of SLAC politics on the federal level.

88. See Robert H. Moulton, "The Linear Accelerator," *Per/Se* (Fall 1968): 16–20 (SA SC 220 14/20).

89. S. Drell, W. Panofsky, D. Ritson to A. Bowker, December 7, 1962 (SA SC 220 14/20).

90. Schiff to J. W. Sterling, March 18, 1964 (SA SC 216 B3/SLAC-Physics Dept. 1963–66).

91. Terman to J. W. Sterling, March 20, 1964 (SA SC 216 B3/SLAC-Physics Dept. 1963–66).

92. P. Flory to J. W. Sterling, September 28, 1965 (SA SC 216 SLAC-Physics Dept. 1963–66).

93. R. H. Moulton to J. W. Sterling, October 13, 1965 (SA SC 216 B3/SLAC-Physics Dept. 1963–66).

94. Bowker to F. Terman, October 13, 1960 (SA SC 160 III 45/10).

95. H. Heffner to J. W. Sterling, April 6, 1965 (SA SC 216 B3/SLAC-Physics Dept. 1963–66).

96. Michael Riordan, *The Hunting of the Quark* (New York: Simon and Schuster, 1987), offers a popular history of some of SLAC's later achievements.

97. H. Heffner to L. Schiff, R. Hofstadter et al., June 13, 1967 (SA SC 99 5/21).

98. "Revised Proposal for the Superconducting Accelerator Project (SCA) in the Stanford High Energy Physics Laboratory Nonr-225 (67)," December 1966 (SA SC 99 5/21).

99. Robert A. Frosch, as quoted in Stanton A. Glantz and Norm V. Albers, "Department of Defense R&D in the University," *Science* 186 (November 22, 1974): 708.

100. Kirkpatrick to D. Tresidder, November 22, 1943 (SA SC 158 1/2).

101. R. Hofstadter, "The Free Spirit in the Free University," June 13, 1962 (SA SC 160 III 3/4).

7 | A Matter of State

1. The best account of Slater's early career is S. S. Schweber, "The Young John Clarke Slater and the Development of Quantum Chemistry," *Historical Studies in the Physical and Biological Sciences* 20 (1990): 339–406. See also Philip M. Morse, "John Clarke Slater," *National Academy of Sciences: Biographical Memoirs*, vol. 53 (Washington, D.C.: National Academy Press, 1982) pp. 297–321.

2. J. Slater, "Memorandum on a Proposed Research Program for Jefferson Laboratory," May 15, 1929 (SP Harvard University/Memorandum on Jefferson).

3. V. Bush to J. Slater et al., "M.I.T. Project on Properties of Matter," May 12, 1934 (SP MIT/Joint Project Committee on Properties of Matter).

4. J. Slater to Keyes et al., May 14, 1935 (SP MIT/Joint Project Committee on Properties of Matter).

5. Slater to F. Keyes, October 17, 1934 (SP MIT/Joint Project Committee on Properties of Matter).

6. J. Slater, "Quantum Physics in America Between the Wars," *Physics Today* (January 1968): 43–51; John Slater, *Solid-State and Molecular Theory: A Scientific Biography* (New York: John Wiley, 1975), pp. 189ff.; and Schweber, "The Young John Clarke Slater and the Development of Quantum Chemistry."

7. K. Compton to S. Duggan, May 1, 1936 (RF 1.1 224D 5/50). On von Hippel's place in the larger refugee resettlement program, see Robin E. Rider, "Alarm and Opportunity: Emigration of Mathematicians and Physicists to Britain and the United States, 1937–1945," *Historical Studies in the Physical Sciences* 15, no. 1 (1984): 107–76, especially p. 163.

8. K. Compton to Rockefeller Foundation, June 5, 1936 (RF 1.1 224D 5/50).

9. For an overview of von Hippel's career, see Karl Wildes and Nilo Lindgren, *A Century of Electrical Engineering and Computer Science at MIT, 1882–1982* (Cambridge: MIT Press, 1985), pp. 166-77.

10. Arthur von Hippel, "Reconversion Plan of the Laboratory for Insulation Research," September 27, 1944 (MIT AC 4 31/18).

11. See Thomas J. Misa, "Military Needs, Commercial Realities, and the Invention of the Transistor, 1948–1958," in Merritt Roe Smith, ed., *Military Enterprise and Technological Change: Perspectives on the American Experience* (Cambridge: MIT Press, 1985), pp. 253–88, for a careful examination of one aspect of the military influence on wartime and postwar materials science.

12. Wildes and Lindgren, *A Century of Electrical Engineering and Computer Science at MIT*, pp. 169–70.

13. Von Hippel, "Reconversion Plan of the Laboratory for Insulation Research," September 27, 1944.

14. A. von Hippel, "The Molecular Designing of Materials," August 1963 (SP MIT/Department of Physics, #161).

15. "Proposed Plastics Research Program," September 27, 1945; F. J. McGarry to Gordon Brown, January 4, 1965 (MIT AC 12 16/Plastics Laboratory).

16. J. Killian to Alfred Sloan, August 21, 1953; Thomas Sherwood to Ralph Flanders, February 12, 1952 (MIT AC 12/Metals Processing, 1949–53).

17. R. V. Bartz to John Wulff, July 11, 1950 (MIT AC 12/Metals Processing, 1949–53).

18. E. L. Cochrane, "Alternatives for the M.I.T. Metallurgical Project," February 18, 1953 (MIT AC 12 12/Metallurgical Project).

19. Sherwood to W. G. Whitman, February 19, 1952 (MIT AC 12/Metals Processing, 1949–53).

20. See Arthur von Hippel, ed., *Dielectric Materials and Applications* (New York: John Wiley, 1954), pp. 283–90.

21. Slater, *Solid-State and Molecular Theory*, pp. 232ff.

22. Anthony Vallado, "Survey of Effects of Radiation on Materials" (SP Radiation Damage Survey). For the unclassified version, see J. Slater, "The Effects of Radiation on Materials," *Journal of Applied Physics* 22 (March 1951): 237–56.

23. J. Slater, "Radiation Damage," July 22, 1949 (SP Radiation Damage Survey).

24. "Brookhaven Conference on Radiation Damage," August 18, 1949 (SP Brookhaven Conference on Radiation Damage).

25. J. Slater, "Talk on Solid State Physics for Military Conference," November 15, 1949 (SP Slater/Talk on Solid State Physics).

26. J. Slater, "Proposal for a Molecular Theory Group in the Physics Department at M.I.T.," September 21, 1950 (SP Slater/Proposal for Molecular Theory Group).

27. Slater, *Solid-State and Molecular Theory*, p. 237.

28. Slater to F. Bitter, July 7, 1958 (SP Bitter, F.).

29. Slater, *Solid-State and Molecular Theory*, p. 241.

30. Slater to J. Stratton, January 29, 1952 (SP Stratton, J. A. #1).

31. "Final Report, Grant NSF-G10821," December 1959–October 1962 (SP MIT/Department of Physics, #160A).

32. Benjamin Lax, interview with author, Cambridge, Mass., January 19, 1988.

33. See Francis Bitter, *Magnets: The Education of a Physicist* (London: Heinemann, 1959; reprint, New York: Doubleday/Anchor, 1960).

34. K. Compton to F. Bitter, September 21, 1932 (MIT MC 77 1/MIT 1932–38).

35. "The Magnet Laboratory of the Massachusetts Institute of Technology," May 8, 1946 (MIT MC 77 5/Magnet Lab). Also see "The Greatest Magnet of All Will Be at M.I.T.," *Technology Review* (November 1960): 29ff.

36. Benjamin Lax, interview with author, Cambridge, Mass., January 19, 1988.

37. Henry Kolm, Memorandum, May 2, 1957 (MIT AC 152 1/48).

38. S. L. Hensel to M. Hannoosh, July 10, 1957 (MIT AC 152 1/48).

39. M. Askin to M. Hannoosh, September 20, 1951 (MIT AC 152 1/48).

40. B. Lax to C. Overhage, November 12, 1957 (MIT AC 152 1/48).

41. B. Lax, F. Bitter, H. Brooks to P. Foote, April 9, 1958 (MIT AC 152 1/49).

42. "Proposal for a High Field Magnet Laboratory," September 8, 1958 (MIT AC 152 1/48).

43. Slater to J. Stratton, August 8, 1958 (SP Stratton, J. A. #2).

44. Lax to John Holloway, May 7, 1959 (MIT AC 152 1/49).

45. Lax to G. Valley, July 31, 1959 (MIT AC 152 1/49).

46. J. Stratton to Herbert York, May 22, 1959 (MIT AC 152 1/56).

47. J. Stratton to Faculty and Staff, July 12, 1960 (MIT AC 12 11/Magnet Lab).

48. Lax to D. Ostrander, February 4, 1964 (MIT AC 31 7/National Magnet Lab).

49. "The National Magnet Laboratory and the Technology of the Future," February 20, 1963 (MIT AC 152 3/8).

50. D. T. Stevenson, "Accomplishments of the National Magnet Laboratory Which May Have a Direct Effect on the National Economy," November 4, 1963 (MIT AC 152 3/8).

51. "Activities of the AFOSR Sponsored National Magnet Laboratory That Have Identifiable Value to the DOD," March 1966 (MIT AC 152 3/8).

52. Lax to Howard Johnson, December 11, 1969 (MIT AC 152 3/42).

53. Benjamin Lax and Kenneth Button, *Microwave Ferrites and Ferrimagnetics* (New York: McGraw-Hill, 1962), p. iv.

54. Benjamin Lax, interview with author, Cambridge, Mass., January 19, 1988.

55. T. Johnson to J. Slater, November 1, 1955 (SP Johnson, T. H.).

56. "Proposal for an Expanded Program of Materials Research at the M.I.T.," January 12, 1956 (SP Materials Research #1); Slater, *Solid-State and Molecular Theory*, pp. 268ff.

57. "Proposal for a Grant for a Program of Research in the Field of Chemical and Solid State Physics," May 1959 (SP MIT Proposal for a Grant for Chemical and Solid State Physics).

58. Committee on Materials to C. Soderberg, April 17, 1958 (MIT AC 12 11/Materials Engineering Committee).

59. Committee on Materials Engineering to C. Soderberg, December 10, 1958 (MIT AC 12 11/Materials Engineering Committee).

60. J. H. Holloman to J. Stratton, September 10, 1958 (MIT AC 12 11/Materials Engineering Committee).

61. Morris Cohen to Guyford Stever, April 19, 1950 (MIT AC 12 11/Materials Engineering Committee).

62. J. Slater, "Proposal for a Materials Center at M.I.T.," May 6, 1959 (SP MIT/Proposal for a Materials Center).

63. "Proposal for an Interdisciplinary Laboratory for Basic Research in Materials at M.I.T.," September 1959 (SP MIT/Proposal for Interdisciplinary Laboratory, 1959).

64. Robert L. Sproull, "Materials Research Laboratories: The Early Years," in Peter A. Psaras and H. Dale Langford, eds., *Advancing Materials Research* (Washington, D.C.: National Academy Press, 1987), pp. 25–34.

65. See Richard J. Barber, Associates, *The Advanced Research Projects*

Agency, 1958–1974, (Washington, D.C., ARPA, December 1975), especially chapter III.

66. Ibid., pp. III–62–64.

67. Charles Yost, "Translation of Materials Science to Technology: The Problem and a Possible Solution," April 7, 1964 (MIT AC 31 2/CMSE).

68. Slater to Carl Floe, October 6, 1960 (SP MIT/Department of Physics #45); Slater, "Proposal for a Materials Center at M.I.T.," May 6, 1959.

69. Slater, "Proposal for a Materials Center at M.I.T.," May 6, 1959.

70. V. A. Fulmer, "Proposal for an Institute Conference, Materials Science and Engineering, Spring 1960," October 7, 1959 (SP MIT/Department of Physics #19).

71. V. A. Fulmer, "DOD Support of the Materials Center," September 30, 1960 (MIT AC 31 2/CMSE).

72. J. Stratton to J. Slater, December 29, 1960 (SP Stratton, J. A. #3).

73. James McCormack to J. Slater, January 18, 1961 (SP MIT/Department of Physics #52).

74. Killian to Alfred Sloan, April 11, 1960 (MIT AC 134 10/CMS).

75. J. Stratton to G. Brown, January 31, 1962 (MIT AC 143 10/CMS).

76. Von Hippel to J. Stratton, May 1, 1961 (MIT AC 134 10/CMS).

77. J. Slater, P. Elias, N. Grant to Members of the Faculty, September 20, 1961 (SP MIT/Department of Physics #76).

78. V. A. Fulmer to J. Killian, May 22, 1963 (AC 31 2/CMSE).

79. Nicholas Grant, interview with author, Cambridge, Massachusetts, January 20, 1988.

80. "Proposal for an Interdisciplinary Laboratory for Basic Research in Materials," May 1961 (MIT AC 134 10/CMS).

81. R. A. Smith, "Physics at the Radar Research Establishment, Malvern," *Proceedings of the Royal Society of London* 235 (June 12, 1956): 1–10.

82. Slater to Charles Townes, April 13, 1961 (MIT AC 31 2/CMSE).

83. Slater to R. Smith, April 13, 1961 (MIT AC 31 2/CMSE).

84. R. Smith to J. Slater, April 20, 1961 (MIT AC 31 2/CMSE).

85. R. Smith, "The Mutual Interaction between Pure Physics Research and Technology," January 31, 1962 (MIT AC 31 2/CMSE).

86. Slater to R. Smith, July 5, 1962 (MIT AC 31 2/CMSE).

87. Annual Administrative Report, 1962–63, to the Advanced Research Projects Agency, Contract SD-90, April 5, 1963 (MIT AC 31 2/CMSE.

88. See Robert Smith, "Materials Research in a New Center," *Technology Review* (December 1965): 15ff.

89. Quoted in Paul Forman, "Behind Quantum Electronics: National Security as Basis for Physical Research in the United States, 1940–1960," *Historical Studies in the Physical Sciences* 18, no. 1 (1987): 221.

90. "Renewed Proposal to Advanced Research Projects Agency," March 15, 1963 (MIT AC 31 2/CMSE).

91. W. R. Hindle to J. Slater, May 24, 1962 (SP MIT/Department of Physics #114).

92. Fulmer to J. Killian, May 22, 1963 (MIT AC 31 2/CMSE).

93. Walter Hibbard to G. Brown, July 22, 1962 (MIT AC 31 7/Metallurgy).

94. Wildes and Lindgren, *A Century of Electrical Engineering and Computer Science at MIT*, pp. 175–77.

95. Slater, *Solid-State and Molecular Theory*, p. 275.

96. Fulmer to J. Killian, May 22, 1963 (MIT AC 31 2/CMSE).

97. Wildes and Lindgren, *A Century of Electrical Engineering and Computer Science at MIT*, p. 174.

98. A. von Hippel, "The University in Transition," December 1958 (SP MIT/Department of Physics #4).

8 | Materiel Science

1. Robert Huggins, interview with author, Palo Alto, Calif., July 30, 1987.

2. R. Huggins to W. Massey, October 12, 1976 (Huggins Papers).

3. Stanford University News Service release, June 23, 1978.

4. William Nix to William Miller, June 30, 1970; Huggins to Members, Center for Materials Research, "Some Data on Materials Research at Stanford," January 22, 1971 (Huggins Papers).

5. In 1987 the DOD still provided $31.4 million (32 percent) for academic R&D in metallurgy and materials, the DOE $20.7 million (21 percent), and the NSF $20.5 million (21 percent). *Federal Support to Universities, Colleges and Selected Non-Profit Institutions: Fiscal Year 1987*, NSF Surveys of Science Resources Series, p. 27.

6. William O. Baker, "Advances in Materials Research and Development," in Peter A. Psaras and H. Dale Langford, eds., *Advancing Materials Research* (Washington, D.C.: National Academy Press, 1987), p. 12.

7. Benjamin Lax, "Materials for Microwaves," *Microwave Journal* (September 1959): 9–20.

8. See Thomas J. Misa, "Military Needs, Commercial Realities, and the Development of the Transistor, 1948–1958," in Merritt Roe Smith, ed., *Military Enterprise and Technological Change: Perspectives on the American Experience* (Cambridge: MIT Press, 1985), pp. 253–87.

9. Baker, "Advances in Materials Research and Development," pp. 16–18.

10. Huggins to F. E. Terman, February 5, 1958 (SA SC 160 III 4/12).

11. Robert Huggins, interview with author, Palo Alto, Calif., July 30, 1987.

12. R. Huggins, "Air Force, Industry, Foundations Support Research Programs in Physical Metallurgy," *School of Mineral Sciences Newsletter* (December 1957), gives a detailed account of the project (SA SC 160 III 14/2).

13. See Huggins to Julius Harwood, September 8, 1959 (SA SC 160 III 14/3).

14. Huggins, "Air Force, Industry, Foundations Support Research Programs in Physical Metallurgy," p. 6.

15. O. Cutler Shepard to F. Terman, June 8, 1956 (SA SC 160 III 14/2).

16. Huggins to F. Terman, February 25, 1958 (SA SC 160 III 4/12).

17. Huggins to F. Terman, February 5, 1958 (SA SC 160 III 4/12).

18. Huggins to F. Terman, February 25, 1958 (SA SC 160 III 4/12).

19. F. Terman, "Memorandum and Plans for Proposed ARPA Program in Materials Research at Stanford University [c. 1961]" (SA SC 160 III 38/7).

20. Huggins to Terman, February 5, 1958 (SC SA 160 III 4/12).

21. Annual Report for the Academic Year 1960–61, Department of Materials Science (SC 165 IV 1/5).

22. Robert L. Sproull, "Materials Research Laboratories: The Early Years," in Psaras and Langford, eds., *Advancing Materials Research*, pp. 25–34.

23. PSAC report, quoted in Baker, "Advances in Materials Research and Development," p. 23.

24. *Strengthening American Science: A Report of the President's Science Advisory Committee* (Washington, D.C.: GPO, December 1958), pp. 28ff.; Baker, "Advances in Materials Research and Development," p. 20, details the background of the report.

25. See James R. Killian, Jr., *Sputnik, Scientists, and Eisenhower: A Memoir of the First Special Assistant to the President for Science and Technology* (Cambridge: MIT Press, 1977), pp. 184–85.

26. Richard J. Barber, Associates, *The Advanced Research Projects Agency, 1958–1974* (Washington, D.C.: ARPA, December 1975), pp. IV–21–22.

27. Ibid., p. III–65.

28. Ibid.

29. Charles F. Yost and Earl C. Vicars, "The Interdisciplinary Laboratory Program in Materials Sciences," *Physics Today* (September 1962): 40–46, offers an overview of the program as seen by two of its architects.

30. Sproull, "Materials Research Laboratories: The Early Years," p. 30.

31. Albert Bowker to F. Terman, August 20, 1959 (SA SC 160 III 4/12).

32. Huggins to J. Harwood, September 8, 1959 (SA SC 160 III 14/3).

33. Huggins to J. Harwood, May 20, 1960 (SA SC 160 III 39/2).

34. F. Terman to Cutler Shepard, R. Huggins et al., April 1, 1960 (Huggins Papers).

35. Huggins to A. Bowker, March 18, 1960 (Huggins Papers).

36. Robert Huggins, interview with author, Palo Alto, Calif., July 30, 1987.

37. Lyman Nickel, "ARPA Interdisciplinary Materials Sciences Center (IDL)," July 22, 1960; A. W. Betts to J. E. W. Sterling, Enclosure A—Interdisciplinary Laboratories for Basic Research in Materials Science (Huggins Papers).

38. "Materials Science at Stanford University: A Submission to the Ad-

vanced Research Projects Agency of the Department of Defense," October 1960 (Huggins Papers).

39. F. Terman, Notes on Materials Science at Stanford University (SA SC 160 III 38/7).

40. Sproull, "Materials Research Laboratories: The Early Years," p. 32.

41. "A Proposal Relating to the Interdisciplinary Materials Laboratory Program Submitted to the Advanced Research Projects Agency of the Department of Defense," April 25, 1961 (Huggins Papers).

42. Ibid.

43. Charles Yost to A. Bowker, June 9, 1961 (Huggins Papers); New Stanford Center for Research on Materials (SA SC 218 39D).

44. Huggins to H. Heffner, June 14, 1961 (Huggins Papers).

45. F. Terman, Memo to File, Discussions with Eitel-McCullough Regarding Support for the Physics Building (SA SC 160 III 39/1).

46. "McCullough Gift Assures New Engineering Building," *Stanford Engineering News* 33 (November 1961).

47. Robert Huggins, interview with author, Palo Alto, Calif., July 30, 1987.

48. "A Renewal Proposal Relating to the Interdisciplinary Materials Laboratory Program Submitted to the Advanced Research Projects Agency of the Department of Defense," November 1964 (Huggins Papers).

49. Huggins to Members of the Center for Materials Research, April 26, 1968 (SA SC 160 III 39/1).

50. William Nix to William Miller, June 30, 1970 (Huggins Papers).

51. Huggins, "Some Data on Materials Research at Stanford," CMR, January 22, 1971 (Huggins Papers).

52. Waldemar A. Nielsen, *The Big Foundations* (New York: Columbia University Press, 1972), pp. 89ff.

53. J. E. W. Sterling to Carl Norgman, September 20, 1960 (SA SC 160 III 22/6).

54. J. Pettit to K. Cuthbertson, January 11, 1960 (SA SC 160 III 22/6).

55. Nix to William Miller, June 30, 1970 (Huggins Papers), gives a detailed list of the CMR's contributions to materials-oriented research projects throughout the university.

56. Richard J. Barber, Associates, *The Advanced Research Projects Agency, 1958–1974*, pp. VI–46–48.

57. Charles Yost, Memorandum for the Directors, Materials Sciences Program, IDL Universities, April 23, 1964 (Huggins Papers).

58. Sproull, quoted in Richard J. Barber, Associates, *The Advanced Research Projects Agency, 1958–1974*, p. VI–48.

59. Charles Yost, Memorandum for the Directors, Materials Sciences Program, IDL Universities, April 23, 1964 (Huggins Papers).

60. Wayland Griffith to Robert Sproull, May 19, 1964 (SA SC 132 17/ARPA).

61. Lockheed-Stanford Cooperative Materials Program, August 1964 (SA SC 132 17/ARPA).

62. W. Rambo to J. Pettit, May 8, 1964 (SA SC 132 17/ARPA).

63. Rambo to R. Sproull, May 27, 1964 (SA SC 132 17/ARPA).

64. Lockheed-Stanford Cooperative Materials Program, August 1964.

65. Ibid.

66. Griffith to W. Rambo, December 31, 1964 (SA SC 132 17/ARPA).

67. S. Harris to R. Huggins, June 12, 1973 (Huggins Papers).

68. Ibid.

69. Harris to R. Huggins, June 12, 1973, gives a list of recent graduates in the laser program and their corporate and government positions.

70. See Richard J. Barber, Associates, *The Advanced Research Projects Agency, 1958–1974*, pp. V–111ff., for a discussion of the agency's response to campus unrest and the implications for the materials sciences program.

71. Earl A. Cilley, "Inquiry re University posture with the DOD," May 8, 1969 (SA SC 99 2/22).

72. R. Huggins, Memo for Record, IDL Transfer, November 6, 1970 (Huggins Papers). See also Lyle H. Schwartz, "Materials Research Laboratories: Reviewing the First Twenty-Five Years," in Psaras and Langford, eds., *Advancing Materials Research*, pp. 35–48.

73. Schwartz, "Materials Research Laboratories: The First Twenty-Five Years," pp. 41–42.

74. James Ling and Mary Ann Hand, "Federal Funding in Materials Research," *Science* 209 (September 12, 1980): 1203–1207, offer a performance comparison of the ARPA/NSF laboratories with other materials science programs.

75. Robert A. Huggins, "Accomplishments and Prospects of the Interdisciplinary Laboratories," *Problems and Issues of a National Materials Policy* (Washington, D.C.: GPO, 1970), pp. 232–33; Schwartz, "Materials Research Laboratories: The First Twenty-Five Years," p. 41.

76. MRL Program Policy Statement, February 1973 (Huggins Papers).

77. Huggins to R. J. Wasilewski, November 27, 1972 (Huggins Papers).

78. Robert Huggins, "Basic Research in Materials," *Science* 191 (February 20, 1976): 647–50.

79. Huggins, "Basic Research in Materials," pp. 647–50.

9 | The Days of Reckoning

1. Bryce Nelson, "Scientists Plan Research Strike at M.I.T. on 4 March," *Science* 163 (January 24, 1969): 373.

2. B. Magasanik, J. Ross, V. Weisskopf, "No Research Strike at M.I.T.," *Science* 163 (February 7, 1969): 517.

3. Jonathan Allen, ed., *March 4: Scientists, Students, and Society* (Cambridge: MIT Press, 1970), pp. xxii–xxiii.

4. Ibid.

5. "The Misuse of Science," *The Nation* 208 (February 24, 1969): 228.

6. "March 4 at MIT," *New Republic* 160 (March 15, 1969): 10–11.

7. Richard Todd, "The 'Ins' and 'Outs' at M.I.T.," *New York Times Magazine*, May 18, 1969, p. 67.

8. Allen, ed., *March 4*, includes transcripts of these talks. See also Roger Salloch, "March 4, the Movement, and M.I.T.," *Bulletin of the Atomic Scientists*, vol. 25, no. 5 (May 1969): 32–35.

9. Quoted in Todd, "The 'Ins' and 'Outs' at M.I.T.," p. 35.

10. Noam Chomsky, "Responsibility," in Allen, ed., *March 4*, pp. 13–14.

11. "Day of Reckoning," *The Nation* 209 (November 24, 1969): 556.

12. "Can Defense Work Keep a Home on Campus," *Business Week*, June 7, 1969, p. 70.

13. *New York Times*, April 27, 1966, p. 4.

14. "Dow Day at M.I.T.," *Technology Review* (December 1967): 54–55.

15. The Cox Commission Report, *Crisis at Columbia: Report of the Fact-Finding Commission Appointed to Investigate the Disturbances at Columbia University in April and May 1968* (New York: Random House, 1968), describes the Columbia movement in detail. For the students' point of view, see Jeffrey Avorn, *Up Against the Ivy Wall* (New York: Atheneum, 1969).

16. Adam Ulam, *The Fall of the American University* (New York: Library Press, 1972), wittily recounts the Harvard "bust."

17. Paul Conrad, reproduced in *Technology Review* (December 1969), p. 96A.

18. See Dorothy Nelkin, *The University and Military Research: Moral Politics at M.I.T.* (Ithaca, N.Y.: Cornell University Press, 1972), pp. 58–59, for the stated position of the SACC.

19. C. S. Draper, in Barton Hacker's oral history interview, Cambridge, Mass., January 19, 1976, p. 120 (MIT MC 134 1).

20. "Can Defense Work Keep a Home on Campus?" *Business Week*, June 7, 1969, p. 69; also John Walsh, "M.I.T.: Panel on Special Laboratories Asks More Nondefense Research," *Science* 164 (June 13, 1969): 1264.

21. Nelkin, *The University and Military Research*, pp. 66–85, discusses the origins and deliberations of the Pounds Panel. See also Marti Mueller, "M.I.T. Reviews Its Military Priorities," *Science* 164 (May 9, 1969): 653.

22. Review Panel on Special Laboratories, Final Report, October 1969 (MIT Museum, CSDL HC Activism Reports).

23. Review Panel on Special Laboratories, Final Report, pp. 17–20. See also Nelkin, *The University and Military Research*, p. 80.

24. Review Panel on Special Laboratories, Final Report, pp. 44–45.

25. William Leavitt, "The Dethronement of Dr. Draper," *Air Force/Space Digest* (December 1969): 49 (MIT Museum, CSDL HC Activism Reports, news clipping).

26. Mark R. Jensen, "Future of Air Force Projects at the MIT Instrumentation Laboratory," June 5, 1969 (MIT Museum, CSDL HC Activism Cor.).

27. Nelkin, *The University and Military Research*, pp. 88–93; C. S. Draper and H. Johnson to Members of the Instrumentation Laboratory, September 24, 1969 (MIT Museum, CSDL HC Activism Cor.).

28. John Noble Wilford, "M.I.T.'s Draper Out ('I Got Fired') After 47 Years," *New York Times*, October 17, 1969, p. 45.

29. Leavitt, "The Dethronement of Dr. Draper," p. 50.

30. William Denhard to Jerome Coe, October 31, 1969 (MIT Museum, CSDL HC Activism Cor.).

31. "The First 70 Days—A Chronicle," *Technology Review* (December 1969): 96D.

32. C. S. Draper to All Laboratory Personnel, October 29, 1969 (MIT Museum CSDL HC Activism Cor.).

33. "Treading the Narrow Line: The First Week of November," *Technology Review* (December 1969): 96B; *New York Times*, November 6, 1969, p. 26; " 'Go Back! Go Back!' " *Newsweek*, November 17, 1969, pp. 79–80.

34. *New York Times*, November 9, 1969, p. 61.

35. "The First 70 Days—A Chronicle," *Technology Review*, p. 96D.

36. Joseph Alsop, "M.I.T.'s I-Lab in Danger After New Left Assaults," *Boston Globe*, November 26, 1969 (MIT Museum CSDL HC Activism Reports, news clipping).

37. "New Left v. National Security," *National Review*, January 13, 1970, p. 18.

38. "Day of Reckoning," *The Nation*, p. 556.

39. George Katsiaficas, "A Personal Statement," Review Panel on Special Laboratories, Final Report, p. 91.

40. R. F. Probstein, "Reconversion and Academic Research," in Allen, ed., *March 4*, p. 33.

41. Peter Guynne, "A Physics Lab Goes Relevant," *Science News* 96 (August 16, 1969): 132.

42. Massachusetts Institute of Technology, *Report of the President* (1968), pp. 187–89.

43. Guynne, "A Physics Lab Goes Relevant," p. 132.

44. Ascher H. Shapiro, "A Position Paper on Retention or Divestiture of the

Special Laboratories," February 1970, pp. 11–12 (MIT Museum, CSDL HC, Activism Reports).

45. Denhard to Col. William R. Manlove, March 13, 1970 (MIT Museum CSDL HC Activism Cor.).

46. Nelkin, *The University and Military Research*, p. 99.

47. Nelkin, *The University and Military Research*, pp. 125–45, chronicles the divestment and includes the text of Johnson's May 20, 1970, speech to the faculty (pp. 178–84).

48. Draper, in oral history interview with Hacker, p. 122.

49. Broxmire, quoted in Leavitt, "The Dethronement of Dr. Draper," p. 50.

50. "Divesting Draper Laboratory: Limits of Academic Freedom," *Technology Review* (June 1970): 82.

51. The Charles Stark Draper Laboratory's first annual report actually included a parody of the Declaration of Independence signed, Hancock-style, by Draper and the board of directors.

52. Elinor Langer, "A West Coast Version of the March 4 Protest," *Science* 163 (March 14, 1969): 1176–77.

53. William J. Rorabaugh, *Berkeley at War: The 1960s* (New York: Oxford University Press, 1989), is the best single account of events there.

54. Irving Horowitz, "Michigan State and the CIA: A Dilemma for Social Science," *Bulletin of the Atomic Scientists* 22, (September 1966): 26–29, reviews the controversy and its implications for university researchers.

55. James Reston, "Stanford: 'Liberate the Faculty'" *New York Times*, May 4, 1966, p. 46.

56. F. Terman to J. E. W. Sterling, May 6, 1966 (SA SC 160 III 10/8).

57. W. R. Rambo, "Remarks on Classified Research presented by W. R. Rambo to the Academic Council on May 17, 1966" (SA SC 160 III 10/8).

58. Committee on Research Policy, "University Policy Regarding Classified Research," September 1, 1967 (SA SC 218 4D/Policy, Classified Research).

59. "Research Goes to War," *Resistance* (campus "underground" newspaper), April 4, 1967 (SA SC 216 57/3).

60. This historical sketch of SRI is drawn from Weldon Gibson's official two-volume history, *SRI: The Founding Years* and *SRI: The Takeoff Days* (Los Altos, Calif.: Publishing Services Center, 1980).

61. Report of the Stanford-SRI Study Committee, April 11, 1969, p. 7 (SA SC 218 4D/Policy, Classified Research).

62. Ibid., p. 5.

63. "Can Defense Work Keep a Home on Campus," *Business Week*, June 7, 1969, p. 70.

64. Jay Neugeboren, "Disobedience Now!" *Commonweal* 56 (June 16, 1967): 367–69.

65. Peter Stern, "Stanford's 'Community of Consent,' " *The Nation* (September 7, 1970): 174; Report of the Stanford-SRI Study Committee, p. 51.

66. Report of the Stanford-SRI Study Committee, p. 1.

67. John Walsh, "Stanford Research Institute: Campus Turmoil Spurs Transition," *Science* (May 23, 1969): 933–36.

68. Report of the Stanford-SRI Study Committee, p. 34.

69. Ibid., p. 51; "Sit-in Chronology," May 1, 1969 (SA SC 216 C7/SRI).

70. "Controlling War Research at SRI and Stanford," April 3 Coalition (SA SC 216 C7/SRI).

71. Lawrence Davies, "Students Occupy Stanford Electronics Laboratory," *New York Times*, April 11, 1969, p. 24.

72. W. R. Rambo to Charles Anderson, May 6, 1969 (SA SC 160 III 54/5).

73. John Walsh, "Confrontation at Stanford: Exit Classified Research," *Science* 164 (May 2, 1969): 534–37; and Stern, "Stanford's 'Community of Consent,' " p. 174.

74. "Chronology of Events," p. 25.

75. Joseph Pettit to Kenneth Pitzer, April 21, 1969 (SA SC 218 4D/Policy, Classified Research).

76. Rambo to Charles Anderson, May 6, 1969 (SA SC 160 III 54/5).

77. Stanford University News Service, April 24, 1969 (SA SC 165 I 1/7).

78. Pettit to Stanford Engineering Alumni, May 1969, and file of responses (SA SC 165 I 1/7).

79. "Closing Remarks by Charles A. Anderson" (SA SC 216 C7/SRI).

80. Stanford University News Service, May 13, 1969 (SA SC 218 4D/Policy, Classified Research).

81. "Sit-In Chronology—May 1, 1969" (SA SC 216 C7 SRI Issue 1969; see also Stern, "Stanford's 'Community of Consent,' " p. 175.

82. *New York Times*, May 13, 1969, p. 31.

83. Trustees Statement, "Stanford University and Stanford Research Institute," May 13, 1969 (SA SC 218 4D/Policy, Classified Research).

84. *New York Times*, May 17, 1969, p. 30.

85. "From North to South," *Newsweek*, May 26, 1969, p. 76.

86. *Stanford Daily*, October 10, 1969, p. 11.

87. *New York Times*, January 14, 1970, p. 22.

88. Norm V. Albers et al., *DOD-Sponsored Research at Stanford*, vol. 2, *Its Impact on the University* (Palo Alto: Stanford Workshop on Political and Social Issues, November 1971), p. 1.

89. Deborah Shapley, "Defense Research: The Names Are Changed to Protect the Innocent," *Science* 175 (February 25, 1971): 866–68.

90. Stanton Glantz et al., *DOD-Sponsored Research at Stanford*, vol. 1, *Two Perceptions: The Investigator's and the Sponsor's* (Palo Alto: Stanford Work-

shop on Political and Social Issues, June 1971), pp. 15–17; and Shapley, "Defense Research: The Names Are Changed to Protect the Innocent," p. 867.

91. Stern, "Stanford's 'Community of Consent,'" pp. 174–78, traces the progressive deterioration of the movement and the campus environment. The campaign history of the spring of 1970 can be traced through the *New York Times*: April 3, 1970, p. 3; April 25, 1970, p. 35; April 30, 1970, p. 36; May 1, 1970, p. 38; May 5, 1970, p. 18; and May 9, 1970, p. 9.

92. Rambo to Charles Anderson, May 6, 1969 (SA SC 160 III 54/5).

93. *New York Times*, February 9, 1971, p. 16.

94. Philip M. Boffey, "Stanford: Why Pitzer Resigned as President," *Science* 169 (August 7, 1970): 561–65.

95. Kenneth Lamott, "In the Matter of H. Bruce Franklin," *New York Times Magazine*, January 23, 1972, pp. 12ff.

96. Linus Pauling, Raymond Giraud, Halsted Holman letter to the *New York Times*, January 26, 1972, p. 36.

97. Report of the Ad Hoc Committee on the Military Presence at MIT, May 1986, Appendix C, p. 34.

98. The figures are drawn from the annual reports of the Charles Stark Draper Laboratory, Inc. The 1975 report includes a handy table of the laboratory's continuing educational efforts (p. 25).

99. Report of the Ad Hoc Committee on the Military Presence at MIT, p. 16.

100. Report of the Ad Hoc Committee on the Military Presence at MIT, Appendix C, p. 33.

101. Ibid., p. 15.

102. John Noble Wilford, "Researchers Cut Link to Stanford," *New York Times*, July 4, 1970, p. 19.

103. *Federal Support to Universities, Colleges, and Selected Non-Profit Institutions: Fiscal Year 1988*, NSF Surveys of Science Resources Series, p. 74.

104. *Federal Support to Universities, Colleges, and Selected Non-Profit Institutions: Fiscal Year 1974*, NSF Surveys of Science Resources Series, p. 23.

105. *Federal Support to Universities, Colleges, and Selected Non-Profit Institutions: Fiscal Year 1988*, NSF Surveys of Science Resources Series, p. 72.

106. "Federal Academic Science/Engineering Obligations to Universities and Colleges by the Type of Activity and Agency: Fiscal Years 1963–87," *Federal Support to Universities, Colleges, and Selected Non-Profit Institutions: Fiscal Year 1987*, NSF Surveys of Science Resources Series, p. 10.

107. *Federal Support to Universities, Colleges, and Selected Non-Profit Institutions: Fiscal Year 1983*, NSF Surveys of Science Resources Series, p. 57.

108. "Federal Obligations for Academic Science/Engineering to the Top 100 Universities and Colleges Receiving the Largest Amounts by Agency: Fiscal Year 1987," *Federal Support to Universities, Colleges, and Selected Non-Profit*

Institutions: Fiscal Year 1987, NSF Surveys of Science Resources Series, p. 19. The NSF measures federal obligations for R&D somewhat differently than obligations for science and engineering, accounting for the different rankings.

109. The figures are compiled from various years of *Federal Support to Universities, Colleges, and Selected Non-Profit Institutions*.

110. Report of the Ad Hoc Committee on the Military Presence at MIT, Appendix C, pp. 6–19.

111. Vera Kistiakowsky, "Military Funding of University Research," in David A. Wilson, ed., "Universities and the Military" (Special Issue) *Annals of the American Academy of Political and Social Science* 502 (March 1989): 140–54.

112. J. R. Pierce, "What Are We Doing to Engineering?" *Science* 149 (July 23, 1965): 398.

113. Carroll W. Pursell, Jr., ed., *The Military-Industrial Complex* (New York: Harper and Row, 1972), pp. 322–23.

114. James Fisk, "The New Role of Graduate Education in Industrial Innovation" (November 3, 1965), William O. Baker Papers, Bell Laboratories.

115. See Lenny Siegel and John Markoff, *The High Cost of High Tech* (New York: Harper and Row, 1986), and Bennett Harrison, "Second Thoughts on the Massachusetts Miracle," *Technology Review* (July 1988): 20ff., for an assessment of the downside of high technology regional development.

116. Ann R. Markusen, "Defence Spending: A Successful Industrial Policy?" *International Journal of Urban and Regional Development* 10 (1986): 103–21.

117. Seymour Melman, *Pentagon Capitalism: The Political Economy of War* (New York: McGraw-Hill, 1970) and *The Permanent War Economy: American Capitalism in Decline* (New York: Simon and Schuster, 1974), was an early and influential advocate of this position. See John Tirman, ed., *The Militarization of High Technology* (Cambridge: Ballinger, 1984), for an update.

118. Stanford School of Engineering, Autumn Quarter Faculty Meeting, December 9, 1970 (SA SC 215 1D/26).

119. Sheila Slaughter, *The Higher Learning and High Technology* (Albany: State University of New York Press, 1990), pp. 48–49, 125-31.

120. Robert Krinsky, "Swords into Sheepskins," *Science for the People* 20 (January–February 1988): pp. 2–5, outlines the genesis and programs of the DOD-University Forum and the DOD fellowship programs.

121. David Dickson, *The New Politics of Science* (New York: Pantheon, 1984), pp. 125–26.

122. See Edward Gerjuoy and Elizabeth Baranger, "The Physical Sciences and Mathematics," in Wilson, ed., "Universities and the Military," p. 75.

123. Cited in Paul Forman, "Behind Quantum Electronics: National Security as Basis for Physical Research in the United States, 1940-1960, " *Historical Studies in the Physical and Biological Sciences* 18, no. 1 (1987): 182.

124. Anthony Difilippo, *From Industry to Arms: The Political Economy of High Technology* (New York: Greenwood, 1990), argues for misplaced military priorities as the key factor in American industrial decline. Lynn E. Browne, "Defense Spending and High Technology Development: National and State Issues," *New England Economic Review* (September–October 1988): 3–22 argues against such an easy conclusion.

List of Abbreviations

AEC	Atomic Energy Commission
AEL	Applied Electronics Laboratory (Stanford)
ARPA	Advanced Research Projects Agency
CMSE	Center for Materials Science and Engineering (MIT)
DEW Line	Distant Early Warning Line
LNSE	Laboratory for Nuclear Science and Engineering (MIT)
NDRC	National Defense Research Committee
NSF	National Science Foundation
ONR	Office of Naval Research
OSRD	Office of Scientific Research and Development
RLE	Research Laboratory of Electronics (MIT)
RRL	Radio Research Laboratory (Havard)
SEL	Stanford Electronics Laboratories
SLAC	Stanford Linear Accelerator Center
SSMTG	Solid State and Molecular Theory Group (MIT)

Index